AF223478

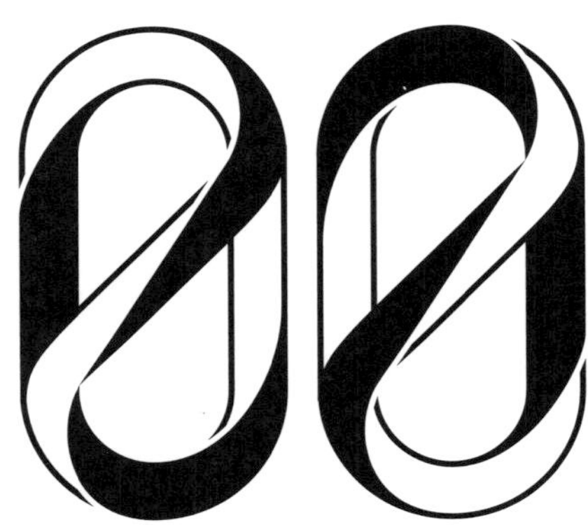

00 Volume 01 Black Material
First published in USA in 2010
by The Vgroupworld USA Inc.
29 E. 19th street
3rd Floor New York
NY 10003
Company No. 27-0231155

Robert Knoke, Casey Spooner, Tim Goosens, Julia Meier, 3 Deep
00 Volume 01 Black Material
1st ed.
ISBN 978-0-615-37614-1
1. Robert Knoke
2. Art - German

757

Creative Direction & Management: The Collective V
Design & Art Direction: 3 Deep Design
Text: Julia Meier, Tim Goosens, Casey Spooner
Photography of Artworks: Roland Schmidt
Photography of Details & Installations: Robert Knoke
Production: Imago
Printed in China

VOLUME 01
BLACK MATERIAL
ROBERT KNOKE
WITH 3 DEEP

SPECIAL THANKS

The Collective V acknowledge Mr. DS Kim, Chairman of Clifford for extending support and resources in order to bring the 00 initiative to life. His life long passion and commitment to fashion have inspired us continually and like every successful partnership, his contribution can be found in every corner of this publication.

ACKNOWLEDGMENT
DS Kim, the chairman of Clifford
Min-Suk Hong, CEO
Hyunoh Kim, Creative director

INTRODUCTION

In the same way that the 00 visual identity symbolises the duality of collaboration and the act of binding collaborators, ideas, processes and philosophies together, The Collective V are very proud to bring you 00 Volume 01, Black Material Robert Knoke with 3 Deep.

This inaugural issue captures the spirit of our vision for 00, while changing the way we collectively engage, perceive and experience creativity. We are excited that Volume 01 records the moving work of Robert Knoke while capturing those at the vanguard of contemporary creative practice such as Rick Owens, Bernhard Willhelm and Patti Smith. The Collective V extend our special thanks to Robert for allowing our team to explore and record those special moments, to follow the path of contact where art meets the public and to witness its organic movement towards a complete and compelling place.

KAI KYUNGAH MIN
CREATIVE DIRECTOR OF THE COLLECTIVE V

FOREWORD
BY CASEY SPOONER

Robert and I share a similar love affair with a certain kind of glamour.
A cultish world inhabited by auteurs living lives that defy definition.
His portraits are an education into the who's who of the most unique
people working in culture today. People you may or may not know...
but you should... or you soon will. The history of portrait painting is
closely tied to the history of aristocracy, royalty and the church. Only
those with the greatest wealth, power and influence would merit or
could commission a portrait. But Robert's drawings represent a very
different hierarchy, a hierarchy that is built from only his most personal
desires and interests. True, some of the subjects portrayed are wealthy
or influential or both. But these drawings are not commissions and thus
we have a window into an aesthetic world that is not only stylistic but
conceptual. Collectively these drawings become more a portrait of
Robert than of the individuals that people them. It is this curation and
the fantasy role that he casts for each subject that defines his uber
world of super cool.

ROBERT KNOKE:
THE HAND OF THE MASTER
BY TIM GOOSENS

The first time I met Robert was at a crowded party during fashion week in New York in 2008. We didn't have any contact until a year later, but I did however look up his artwork upon arrival at home, and have ever since been amazed by them, and drawn to them. The minimal black lines, the rock & roll selection of people of his portraits. A great number of the people in the portraits are personalities whose creative energy I also admire, and who are part of the artistic scene we both spend time in. As a modern day Rubens or Raffael he portrays the people that make the world move and shake: musicians, designers, the creative night owls. I was amazed by the fact of how he was able to capture the energy and significant details of each of his models in such a minimal way by adding an edgy element in the execution to the very traditional technique of drawing. Something that has earned him the nickname of being a punk Schiele.

Even while minimal and abstract, fragmented images feel surprisingly whole. Working on that thin line between realism, Gothic and expressionism, his drawing style mirrors the abstract elements also seen in the aesthetic language of fellow contemporary artists like Banks Violette and Terence Koh.

Always pure and simple, with the occasional use of a red detail or glitter but never over the top. Learning more about him and his work I needed to change a few of my assumptions however....

I met Robert again more than a year later to pose for a portrait on a windy Sunday evening in his downtown basement studio in SoHo—a space he uses during his frequent visits to the Big Apple. One goes to this studio—whether that be in the Soho basement, or in Germany, and he takes your picture, 'don't smile'; 'turn towards me, now turn right, left stop—pose'. Snap snap... all is done in merely 15 minutes.

Experiencing this, and chatting with him afterwards I understood what I did not before: For Robert it's about the materiality, once the photos are printed out he uses them to create the actual portrait, by himself. The person in the image is no longer of any importance. The x-factor of a certain person will definitely not assure the portrait turning out as a great success—Robert seems to have learned early on that one should stay true to himself, his technique, and that this makes for the best results. When drawing from the photographs Robert needs to erase the person and the ego in these pictures and create the image on the paper he is looking for. Using fat markers, grease pencils and ball pens directly applied onto the paper he starts with a few simple black lines, treating the surface in a very fast and intuitive way. Carefully balancing large black zones with empty space. Being familiarized with the materials from early on in his life, he never looses control over them, and works at a very fast speed.

It's during this process that the shift happens… not any longer is it about that initial person with a story, but it become about lines and colour on the paper. The materiality takes over, and the persona is kept aside.

But maybe because of the array of people in his portraits, it is perhaps his biggest challenge to make the spectator see what for him the main focus is: the material on the paper.

As a child of the 1980's it is not surprising to see the mix of creative people in his list of portraits. One can't help as to try to recognize who's who before our eyes get fixed on the lines and materials on the surface. Even when he makes a point for the work being about the drawing and the lines of the paper, it is still very seducing for the viewer to focus more on the selection of the group of people in the work. Working on portrait after portrait he is single-handedly creating a document of our time in these unique works of art, always showing the hand of the master.

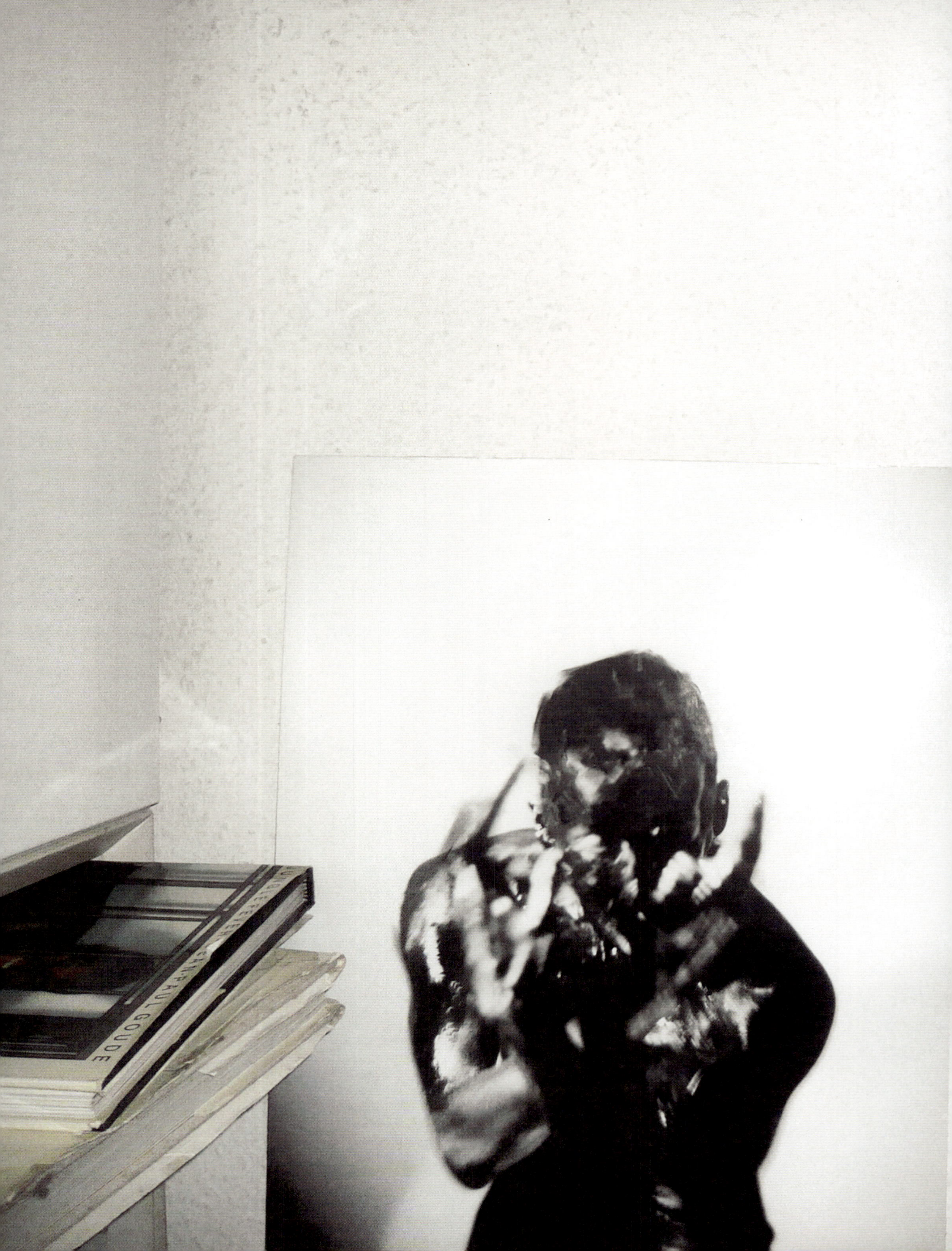
JEAN-PAUL GOUDE

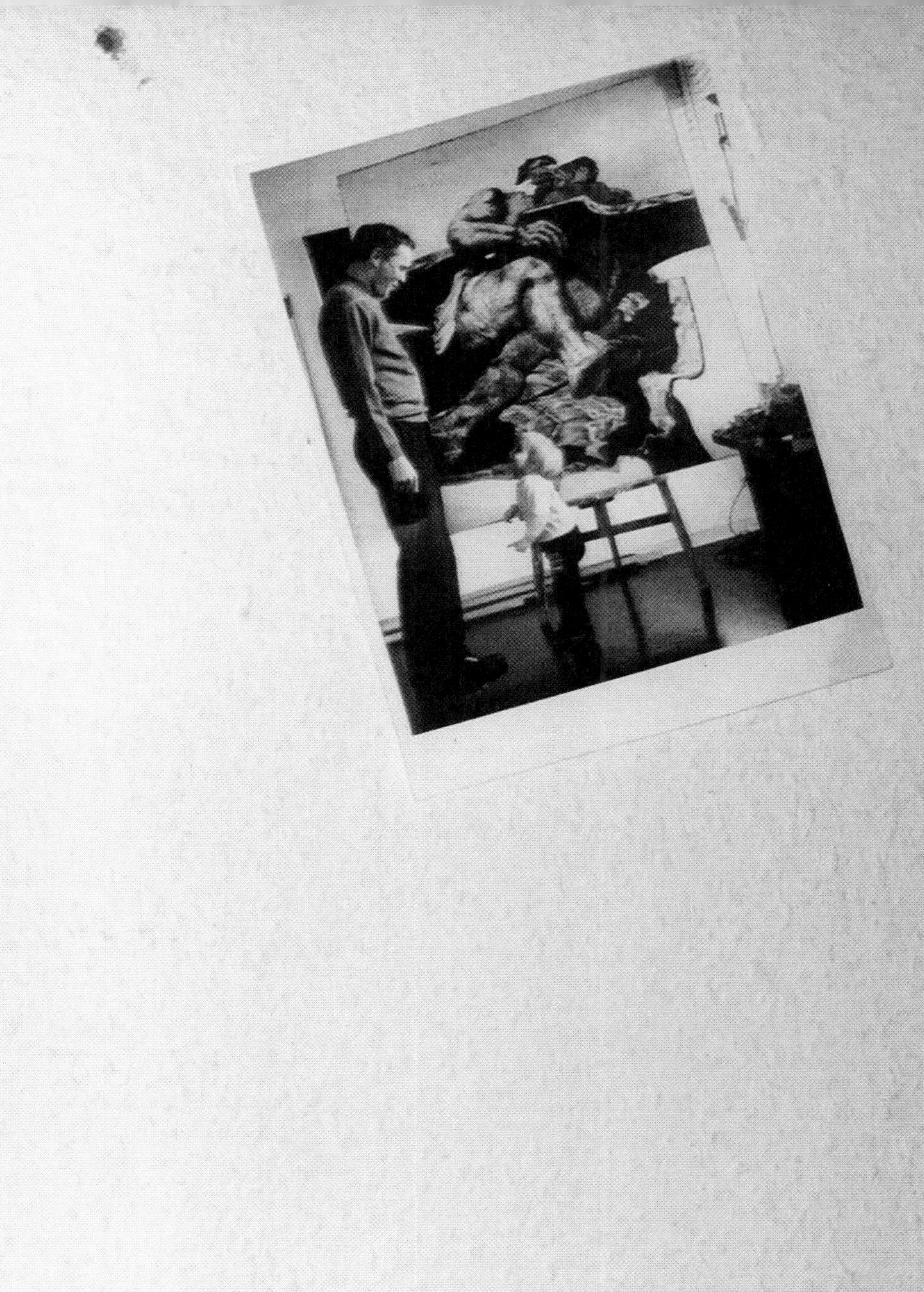

LESS HUMAN
AN INTERVIEW WITH ROBERT KNOKE
BY JULIA MEIER

JULIA MEIER The title of this catalogue – *Black Material* – sounds rather pragmatic to me. It seems that it neglects the aspect of the sitter's individuality. Are the subjects of your portraits *raw* material?

ROBERT KNOKE My last catalogue was just simply called *The Portrait Series*, and somehow the description for my work – portrait – sounds so limited to a certain genre. I don't feel that way when I'm doing this work. After I meet up with the people, take their picture and start to draw, I'm not really thinking about a portrait anymore. I mean, of course I'm concerned about the fact that the portrait should still look like the subject but I'm more concerned about what kind of lines and strokes or structures my markers and pencils produce. So yes, for me the subjects are *raw* material that I transform with black paint into a "black" material. My focus goes more into abstractions than into figurative work.

JULIA MEIER So you mean it's about the *Figure* as the French philosopher Gilles Deleuze describes it when he makes the distinction between the figurative, which is representing the object and therefore is illustrative, and the *Figure*, which is presenting a sensation that attacks your nervous system directly?

ROBERT KNOKE Exactly.

JULIA MEIER You said in an interview for the *New York Times*, that all you are interested in is the surface of a person. Does that mean that the character, psyche or personality of your subjects does not really matter to you?

ROBERT KNOKE That's right. I'm not interested in their personal emotions, and I don't want to represent them. I don't think I can even capture that. If the drawing turns out to be weak, the portrait is weak, and it really doesn't matter what kind of person I had in front of me. If I'm able to produce a strong drawing, the *inside* of the person will show up anyway. That either happens or it doesn't. I can't do anything about that. Of course there are people that tickle my lust to draw them, but at the very end it really doesn't matter whom I'm drawing. It is not *whom* I draw but *how* I draw them.

JULIA MEIER But, if it doesn't matter, why do certain people *tickle* you more than others?

ROBERT KNOKE Well, first of all it's a very personal choice of people that I have. All these people are personalities that I feel somehow related to one way or the other. It's not a voyeuristic gaze at the persons I'm interested in. It is rather that I find something in them, and especially in their work, that feels familiar to me. Although they sometimes live a completely different life there are still certain aspects and, let's say, a certain energy that I feel touched by. But, what I have found out over the years by doing this kind of work is that, even if I feel very close to the personality of my subject, I sometimes fail in doing their portraits. I might get introduced to someone who would not be my first choice but, all of a sudden, the portrait of that person becomes a very good one. I know that a lot of artists who do portraits need to have a very close relationship to their subjects to be able to capture their personality or whatever. In my case I don't feel at all this way. That's the reason why I also take photos first and then work alone on the drawing. After I meet the person I need the distance again. The better I know the person the less I see her or him.

JULIA MEIER Or are they less interesting because they are less foreign, less to discover, to conquer, to work on?

ROBERT KNOKE Maybe. Of course I'm always very excited to meet new people and you need a certain excitement to be able to produce an exciting work. But, of course, that doesn't mean that I'm not interested in people that I'm very close to. It just becomes a different level of interest. But that might also change in the future…

JULIA MEIER Coming back to the title of the book, what does *black* mean to you?

ROBERT KNOKE It's a very strong and elegant color and it's so basic – it's a very, very basic color. And also black to me is not dark. To me the black paint is more a material than a color. When I was working with Diamanda Galás on a photo series, I started to cover her face and body with black paint. Her body became a sculpture that way and I could focus more on the reflection of the wet paint than showing her naked skin. She became less human, even genderless. Later on I used that technique on myself. Covering my whole body in black, shiny paint. Photographing my body parts and putting them back together in collages. I also covered my face with a monkey mask that I made out of rubber and was sticking a high heel on one of my naked feet. Although I was working with a human body, I wasn't interested in showing gender or realism but in working with form itself. So, this is something that is also very important to me when I'm doing my portraits. I'm really interested in the shape of the body as an abstract form, using glossy paints and working with the reflections that they produce. That is also the reason why I lately use glitter in my work. Last year I worked with Spencer Product on my first video clip. Again, I covered him in black paint and lots of black glitter to leave structures on his face and body and to make him less human. Less himself.

JULIA MEIER Why do you prefer to use markers?

ROBERT KNOKE I guess because they are not classical art material like oil colors or pastels. Markers have a cheap image, and I like that. That's probably the reason why I stayed with this technique since my childhood. I'm used to it. I mean, I used to paint in oil, and it's a wonderful technique, but it's also quite heavy and markers are quick and easy to use. I don't enjoy mixing paints and bothering with brushes and all the preparation before you can finally start working. I also like to be in control of the material that I'm using, and charcoal or pastels don't do that to me – in fact, I really hate charcoal or pastels because they are so messy and make a terrible sound on the paper that I can't stand. They are also very academic art supply, which kind of bores me in the first place.

JULIA MEIER That's interesting that you speak of control – and that one sees so many smears and fingerprints in your portraits…

ROBERT KNOKE Yes, I like to be in control of the technique I'm using, but I want to lose control when it comes to the process of making art. The best moment is when I forget that I'm drawing while I'm doing it. With the fingerprints – that's funny that you mention this because I was thinking about these fingerprints a lot, in which way I could use them, because they happened by accident. When I draw, I also use my fingers a lot and especially when I use a grease pencil. So, of course I have dirty fingers after a while and, all of the sudden, I have fingerprints on the paper next to the drawing. So I started to use the fingerprints intentionally in the composition of the drawing. But this is something that is kind of difficult to do because, if you use that too much, it can easily become a mannerism that could destroy the whole drawing.

JULIA MEIER Bruce LaBruce's portrait is an explosion of dirty fingerprints.
ROBERT KNOKE After I started to use fingerprints as a style element, I liked the idea of having a portrait completely overpowered by them. I had this idea for a long time in my head, but I did not know on which subject I could use it the best. After I met Bruce LaBruce, I knew that he would be the one where I would use these fingerprints to almost destroy his face.

JULIA MEIER Sounds very aggressive – or if I were to put meaning into it, I could assume that this heavy printing and, therefore, *burring* of his face and body is related to LaBruce's own work being a director of hardcore zombie/porn movies…
ROBERT KNOKE But, for me, my drawings don't have any meaning except for pooling energy. And yes, maybe it's the aggressiveness that I see in the work of someone like Bruce, which might be the reason why I was interested in meeting him to do his portrait. This energy is not about hardcore sex movies or zombie splatter. It's basically just the raw energy that I'm interested in. And I also like the moment when it comes to raw energy while I'm drawing. To move the fingers so fast over the paper is a sensual moment – the act of capturing energy. It is also about speed that I try to capture by moving my blackened fingers very fast over the paper. It's like hitting the keyboard of a piano very hard and fast, and each touch leaves a fingerprint. So, in LaBruce's portrait I did a lot of touching [laughs].

JULIA MEIER I can imagine that because of the life-sized scale of the drawing, you must have been almost dancing in front of it?
ROBERT KNOKE Literally! Yes! [Laughs]

JULIA MEIER Do you listen to music while you are doing that?
ROBERT KNOKE Sometimes I do and sometimes I don't – it really depends.

JULIA MEIER On what?
ROBERT KNOKE If I need stimulation or if I'm already stimulated enough.

JULIA MEIER Sounds kind of sexual.
ROBERT KNOKE I'm telling you, if I have a good moment when I'm drawing, it's much better than that.

[Both laugh]

JULIA MEIER Your father was an artist as well. Your grandfather, too. Both painters. There is this photograph of you and your father standing in front of a huge painting by him. I love this image: how you both look at each other with so much respect, as if there was no age difference between you. Do you think his influence was big on you?
ROBERT KNOKE I guess so. I always appreciated his ability to be totally unsentimental when it came to my work. He never treated me as his little son who also wants to be an artist, and he never taught me. He let me draw in his studio, and when I showed him a new drawing that I did he either said that it is fantastic or just shit. It was wonderful how he talked about art, literature and politics. He was very radical in his judgments, but he also was very hard on himself. Almost self-destructive. But my Mother, with her sense of style and taste in fashion, furniture and architecture, had also a big influence. There was always the *Vogue* laying around. I guess that's where my interest in fashion started and why I'm very interested in style.

JULIA MEIER Besides your upbringing, are there other important influences that formed your own work?
ROBERT KNOKE I think music and stage performance had also a certain impact. I grew up in the 1980's, and I was fascinated by Punk and New Wave. I was fascinated by Grace Jones and Nina Hagen. I could stare at their record covers for hours. I think all of these influences converge in my work now, and I try to combine this in each person that I'm drawing.

JULIA MEIER Is that why you showed projections of your portraits in night clubs like the Ruff Club in New York or Club Rio in Berlin?
ROBERT KNOKE Yes. I liked the idea of having my work, with all the musicians and fashion people that I drew, presented in a space where they usually hang out anyway. So, after Conny Opper invited me to show at Rio in Berlin, I showed a projection with changing images of my drawings. That's when I started to take photos of the details of the portraits. The presentation looked very good on the dirty walls of the club, and I continued to do the same thing in New York, and later Nathan [a.k.a. Brace Paine from The Gossip] took the show to a club in Portland. So, most of the people that were shown in my projections were hanging out at the clubs on those nights, and meanwhile The Kills or Nathan would be DJing. Perfect!

JULIA MEIER I saw the shows at Ruff Club and Rio and I really loved seeing your images merge with the music, and also with the people – the experience of how art can merge with the atmosphere of a night club – the whole thing just became a real *Gesamtkunstwerk!* That's new. Is this special atmosphere the same reason why you showed drawings in a fashion store?
ROBERT KNOKE Yes. I showed portraits of fashion designers in a space where they also show their clothes. But I'm not interested in showing in a fashion store per se. A store like Seven in New York is more than just a commercial store. They have clothes that are art pieces in themselves. It's the same with the clubs. It depends on the space and what kind of person is running that space. I like to link my work with a certain space to produce a unified installation with multiple layers.

JULIA MEIER Would you like to say how you contact the people and how you win them for your project?
ROBERT KNOKE Well, over the last few years, I have been introduced to more people by people that I did portraits of. I like the fact that they are all kind of related to each other. The internet is also great to get in touch with people.

JULIA MEIER Yes, that's right! You met Marc Jacobs through MySpace!
ROBERT KNOKE Well, yes! One night I saw the online sign blinking on his MySpace page and I just wrote him a short massage. But I wasn't sure if it was really Marc Jacobs himself, and so I was asking him: "I would love to do your portrait. Hope this is really you!" You never know with these pages. But, I got a message right back saying that he would be interested in the project, and he assured me that it's really him. He greeted me at the door of his apartment two days later with the words: "See – it's me!"

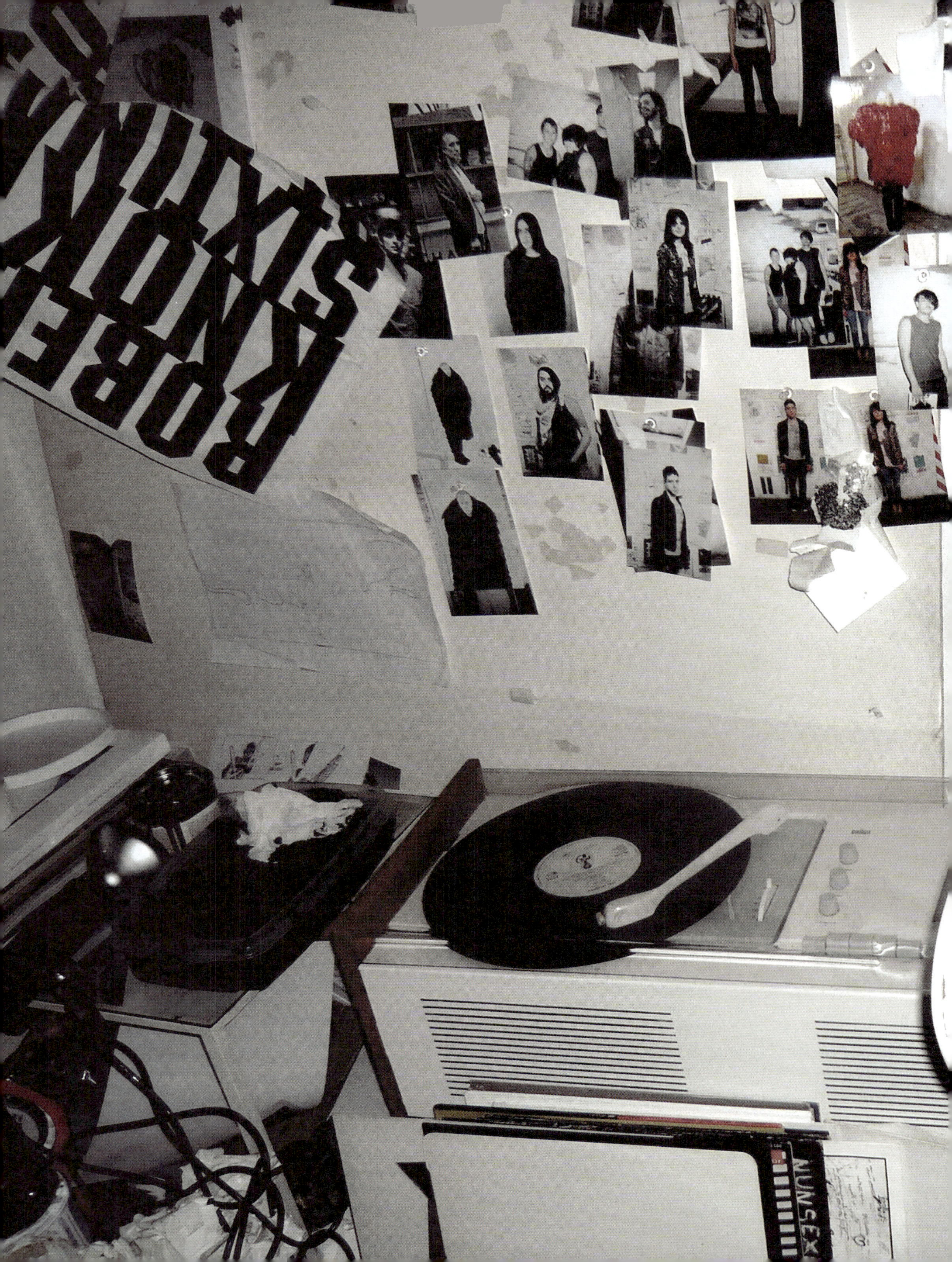

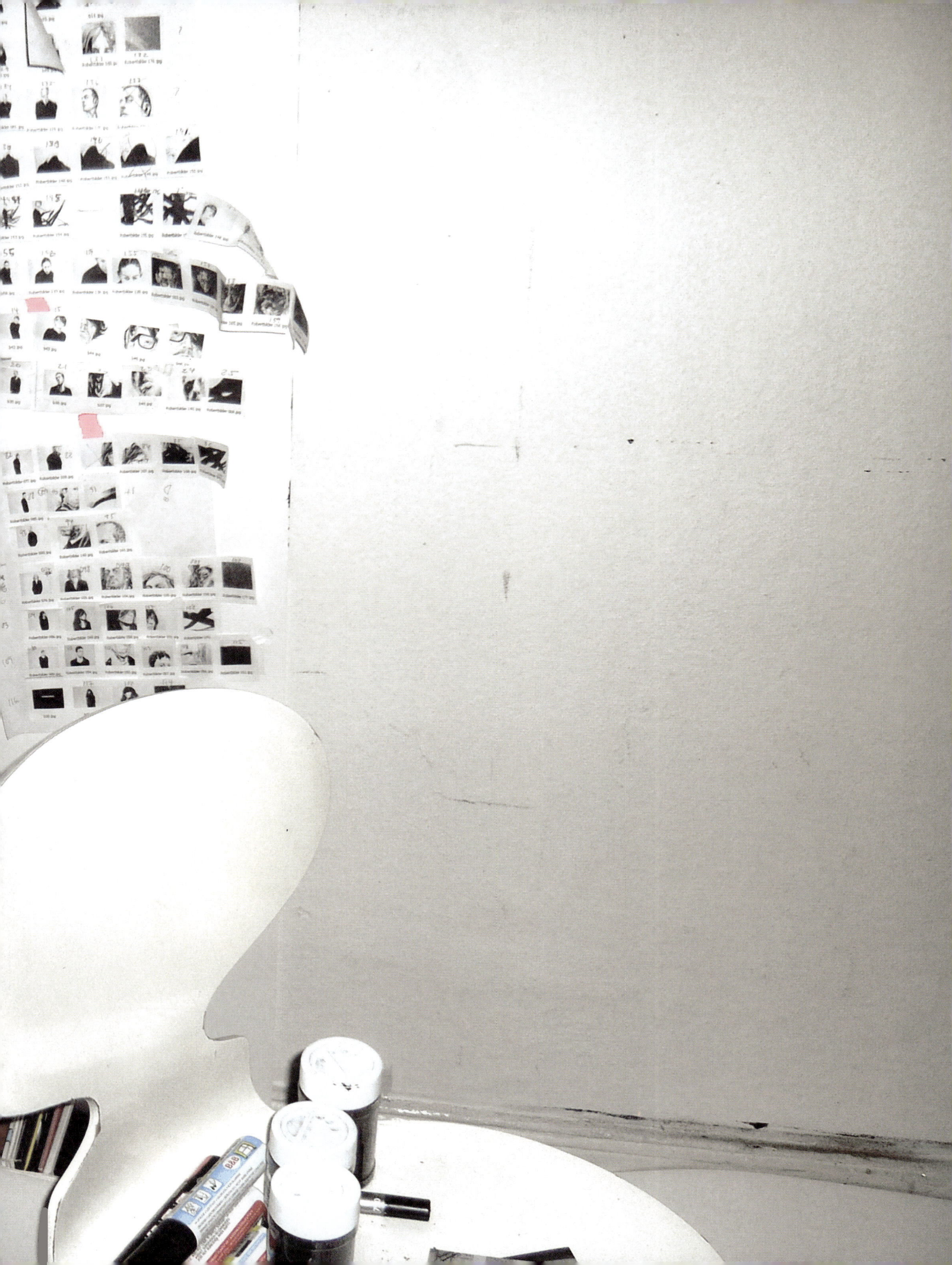

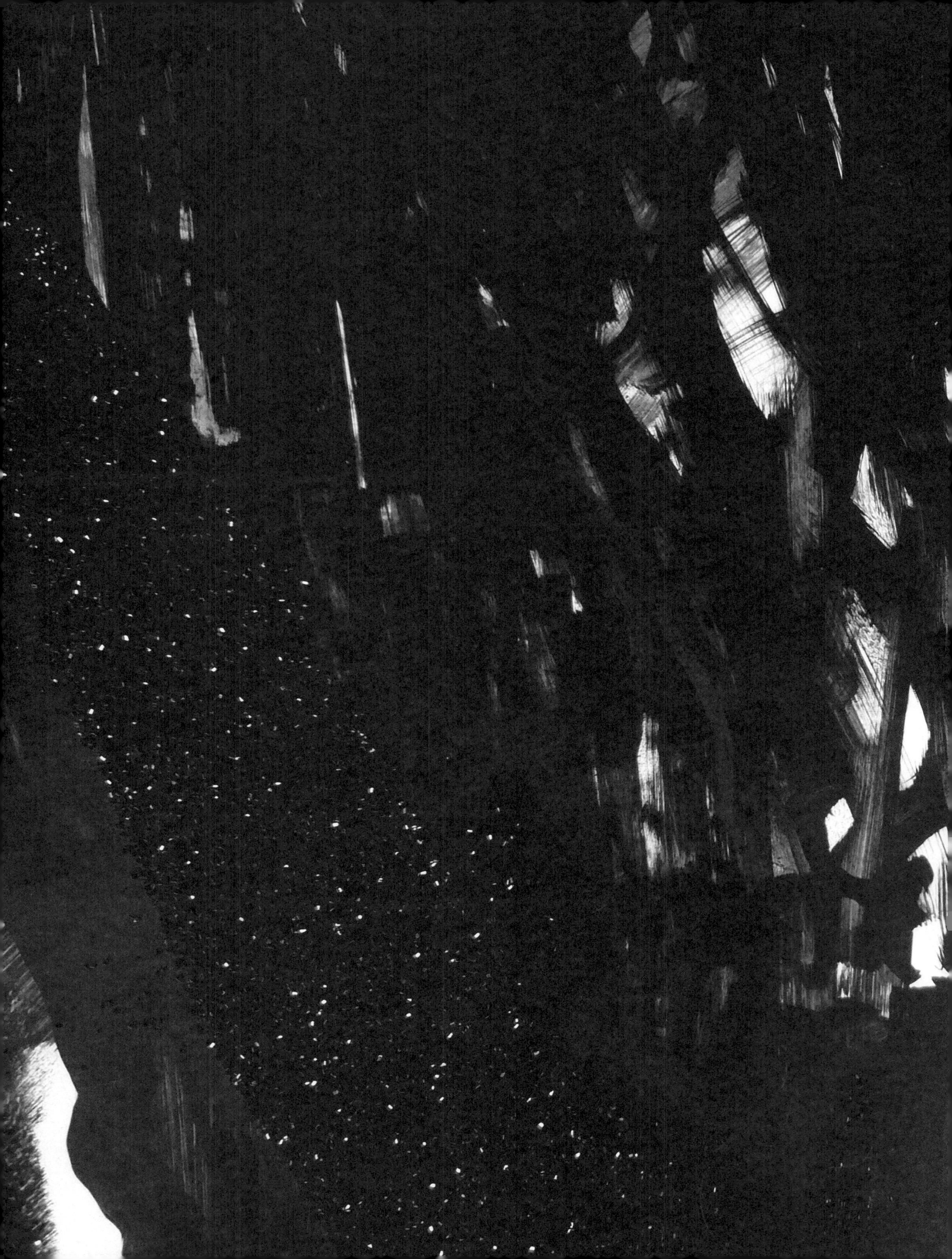

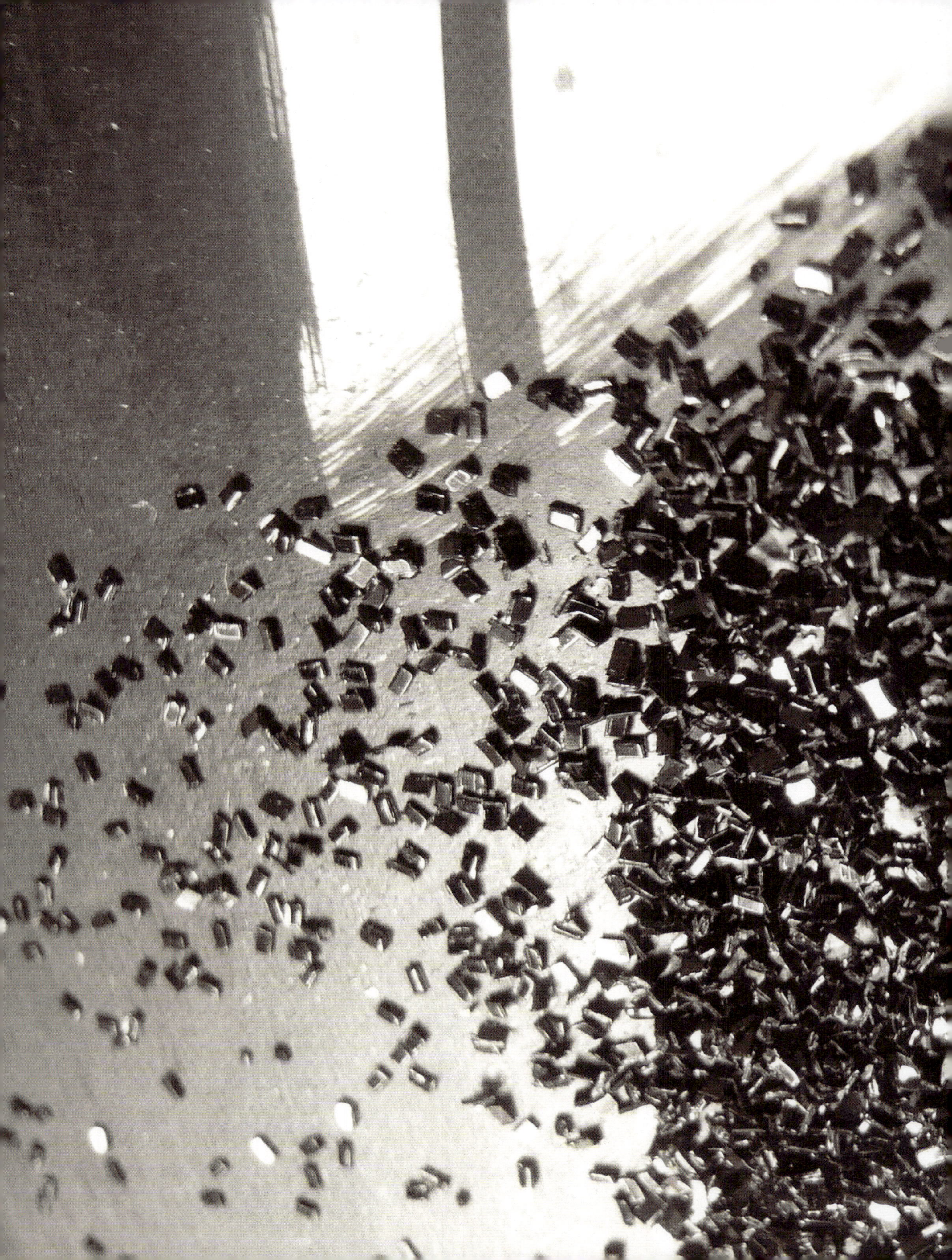

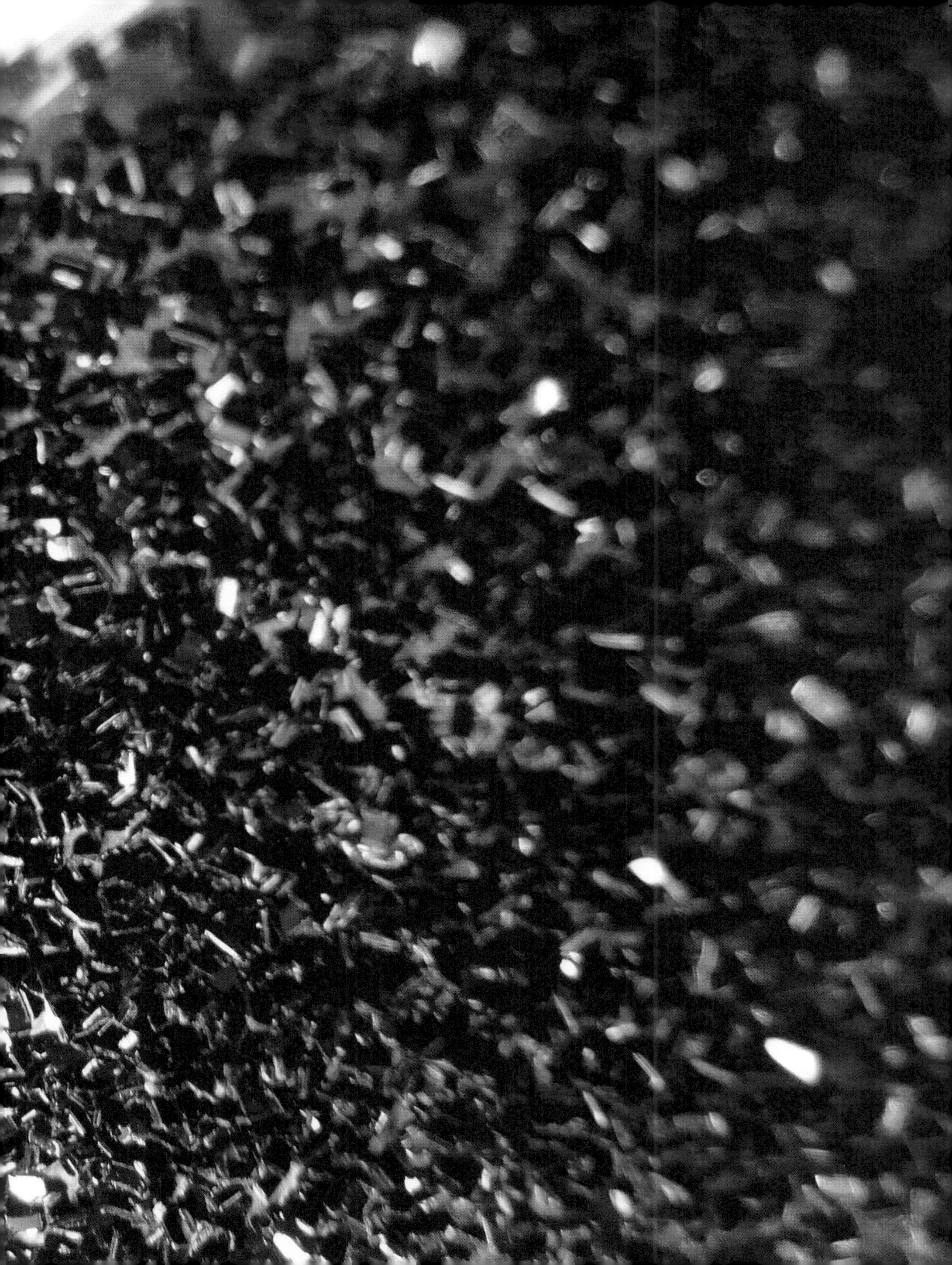

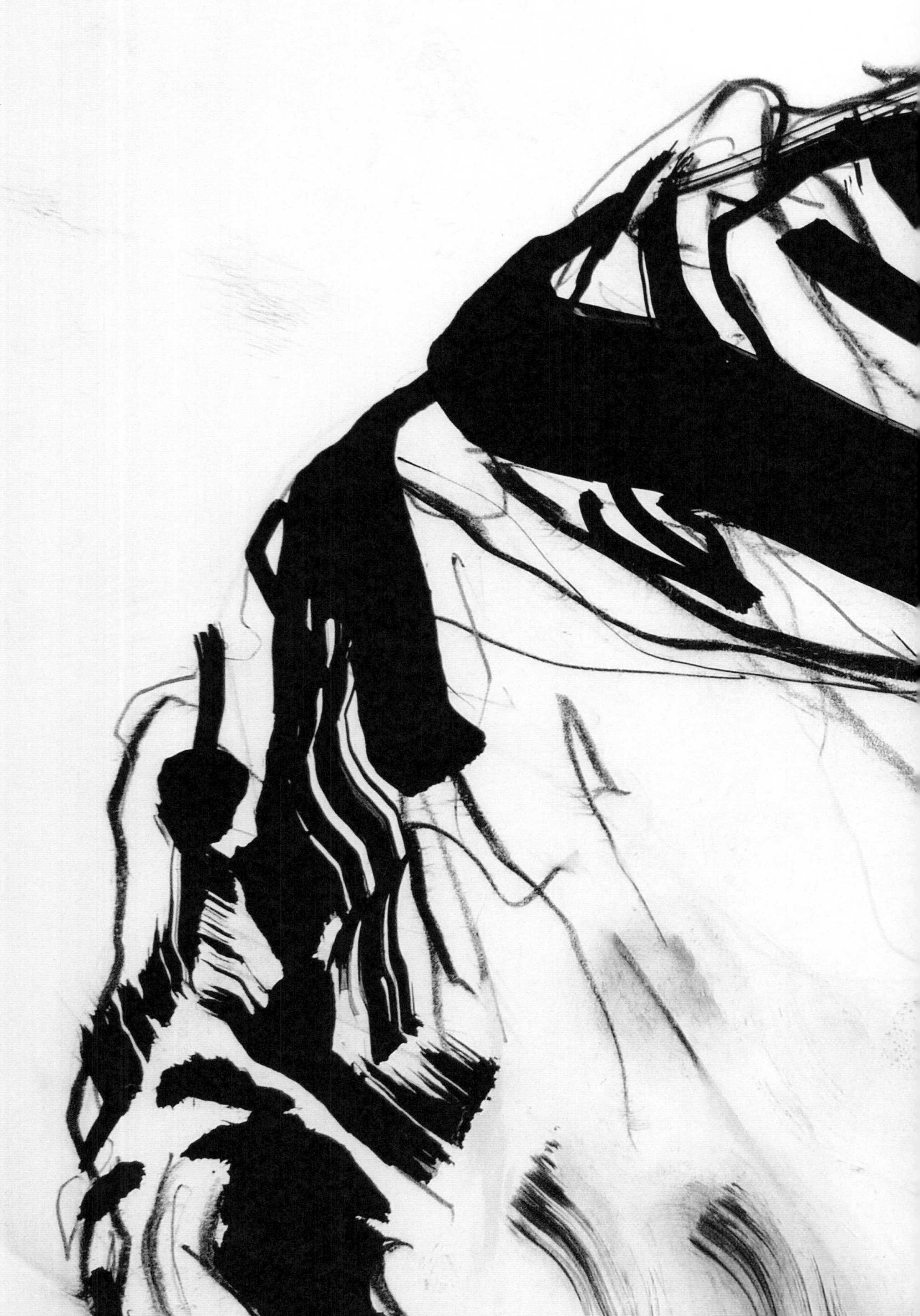

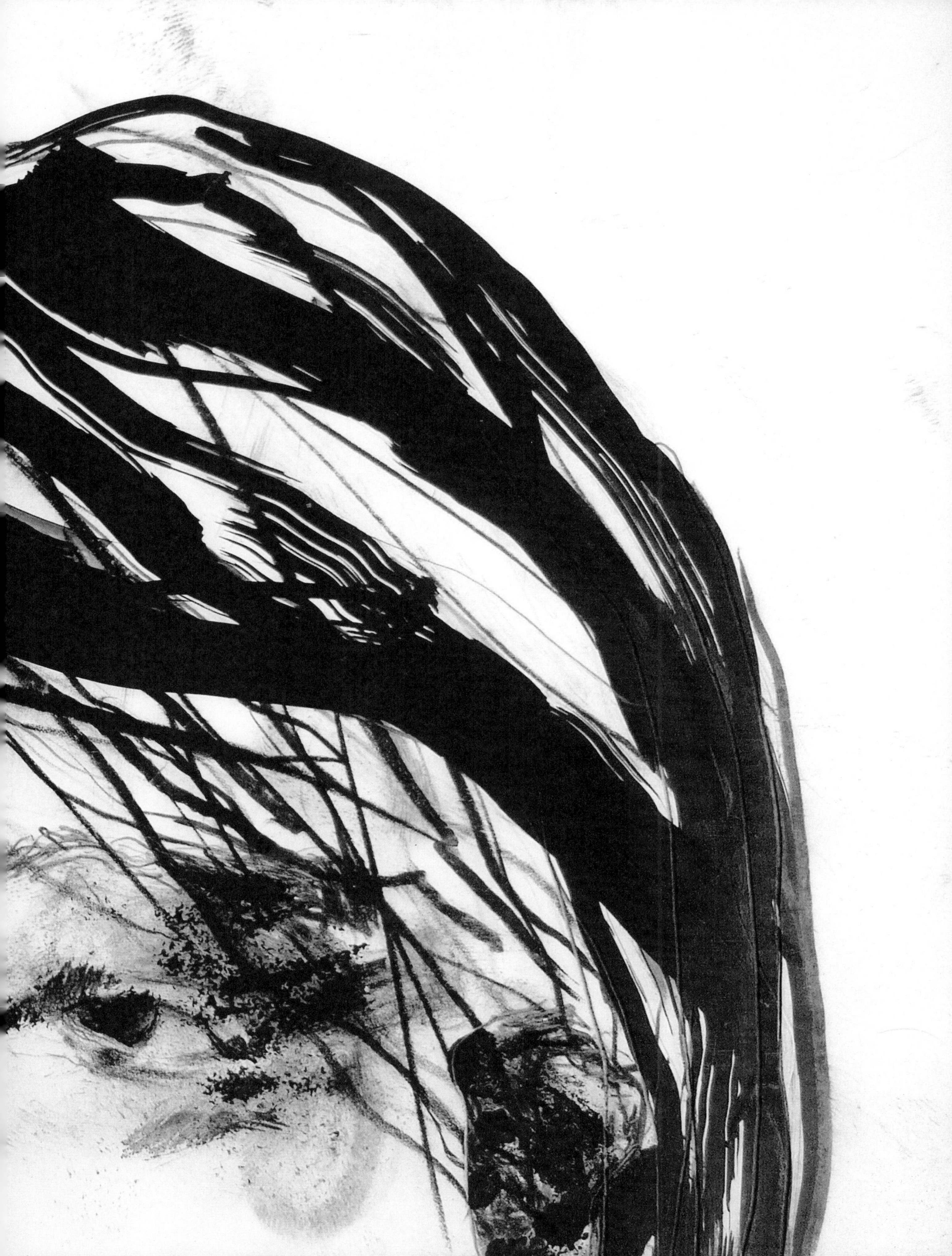

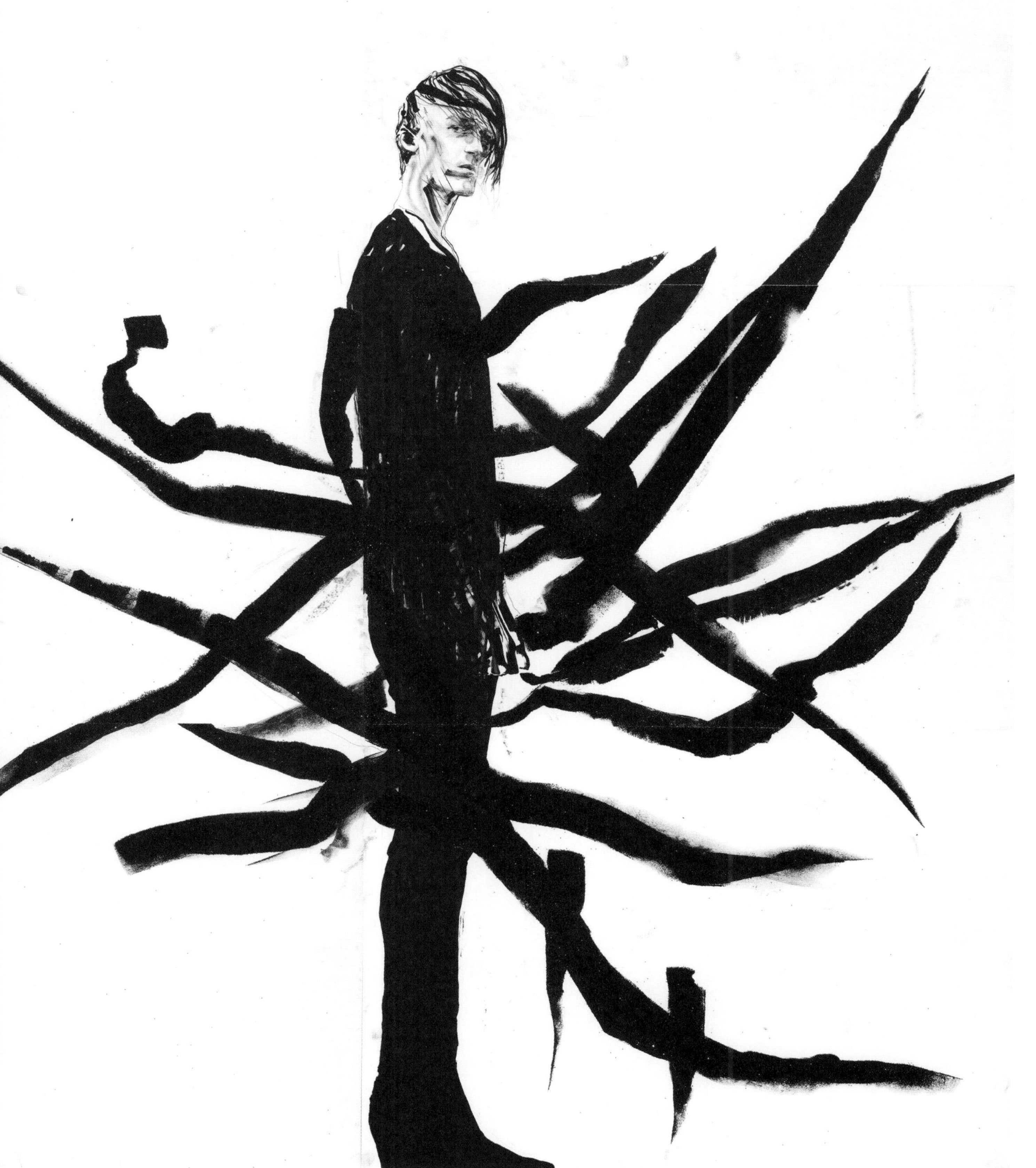

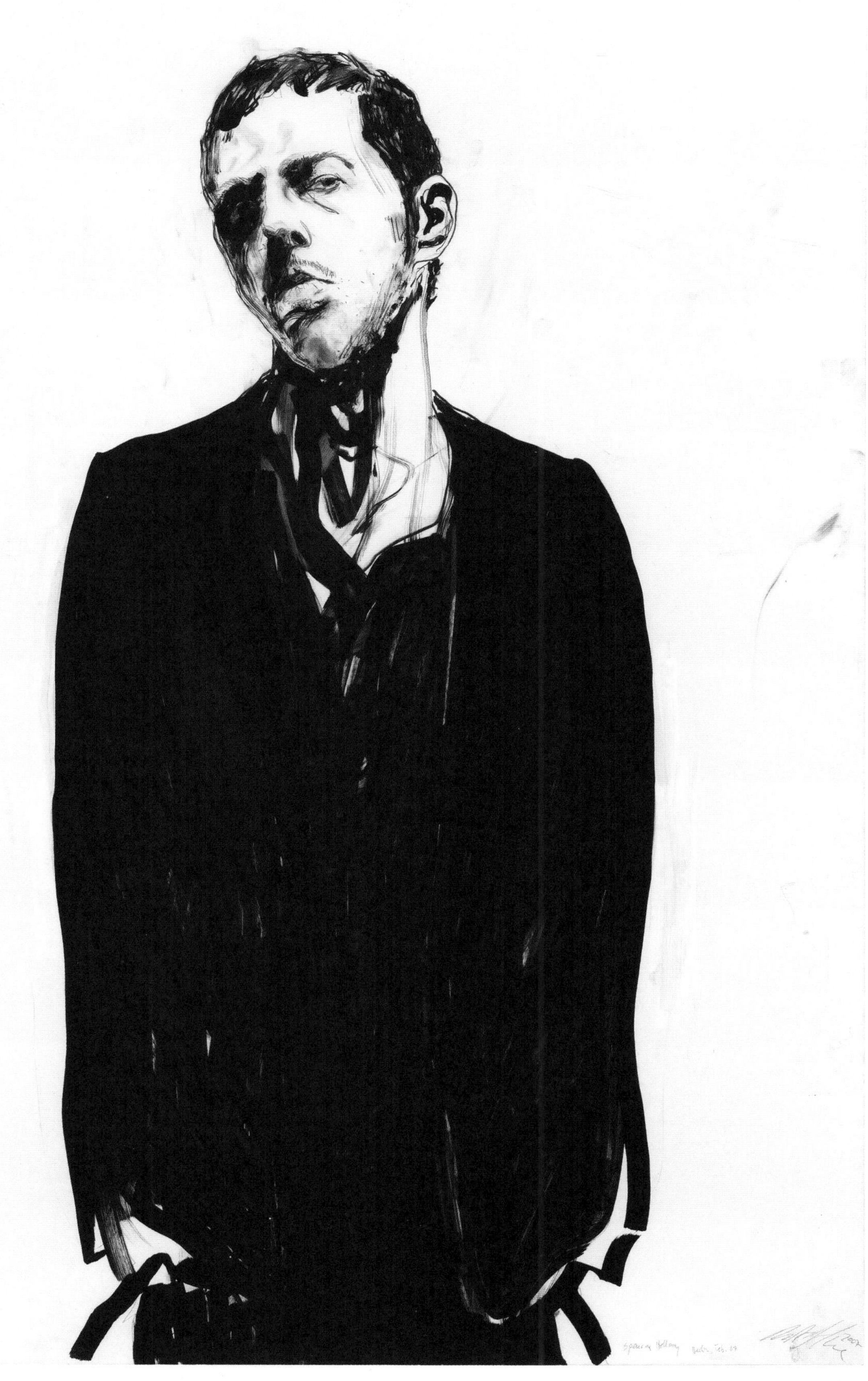

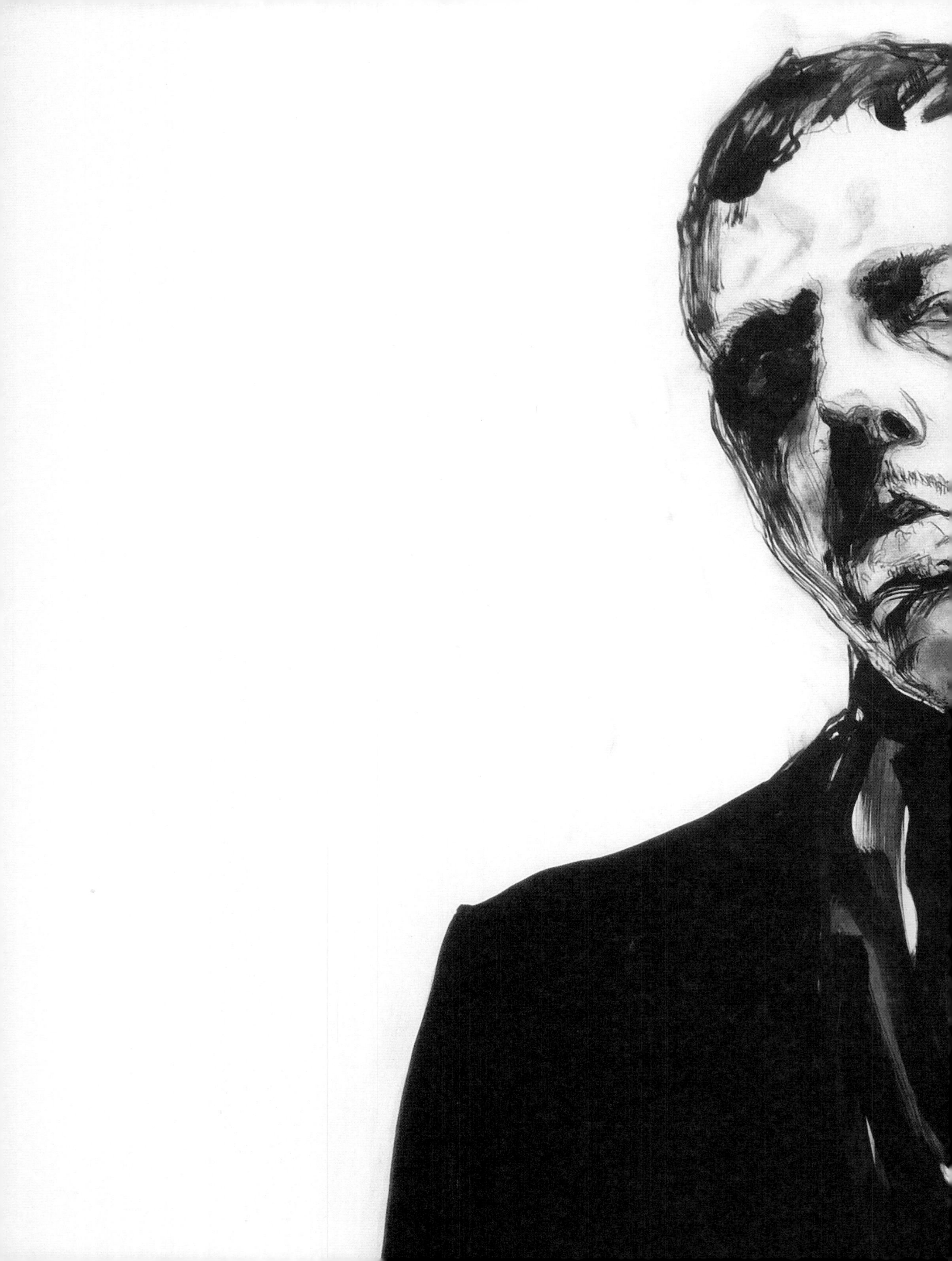

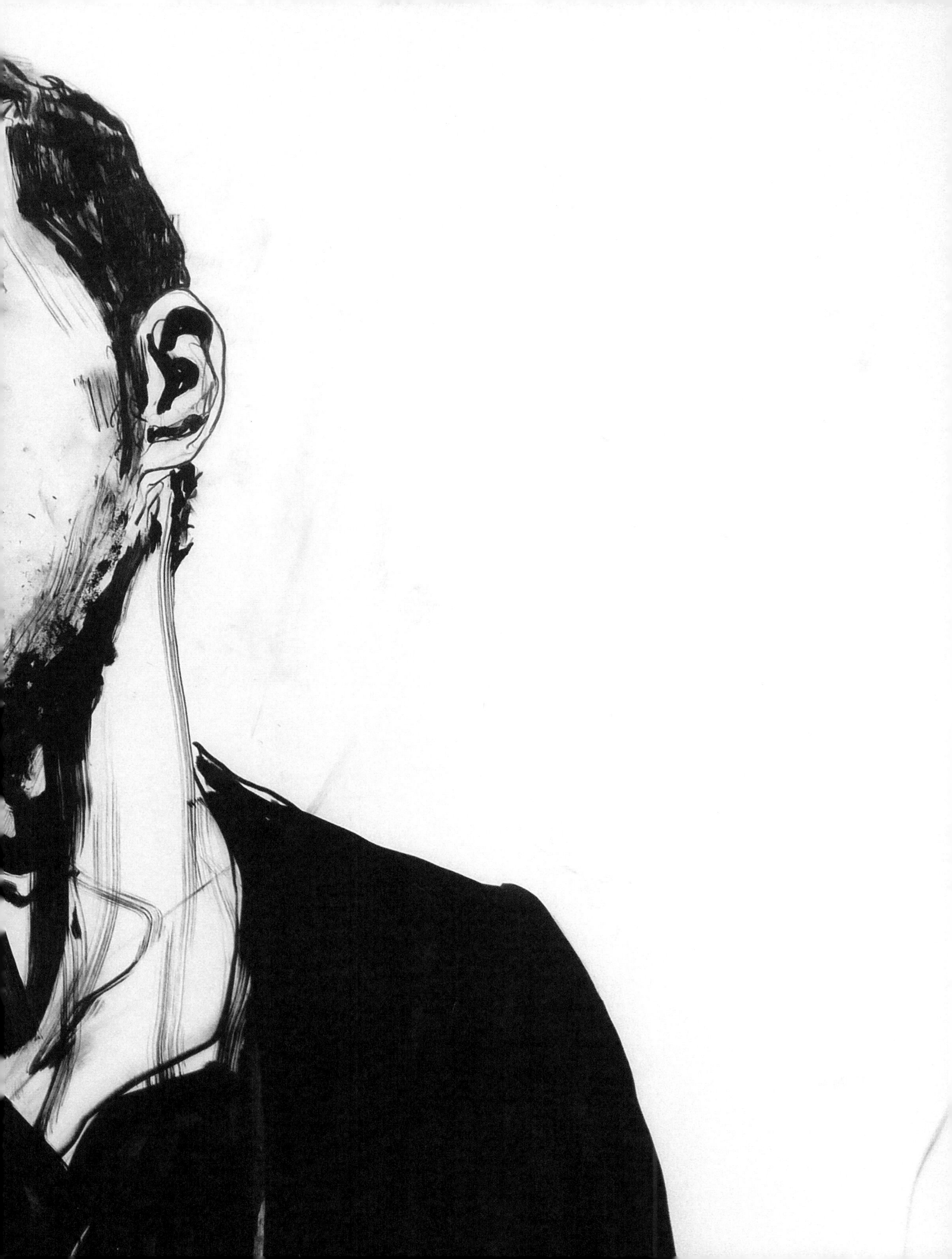

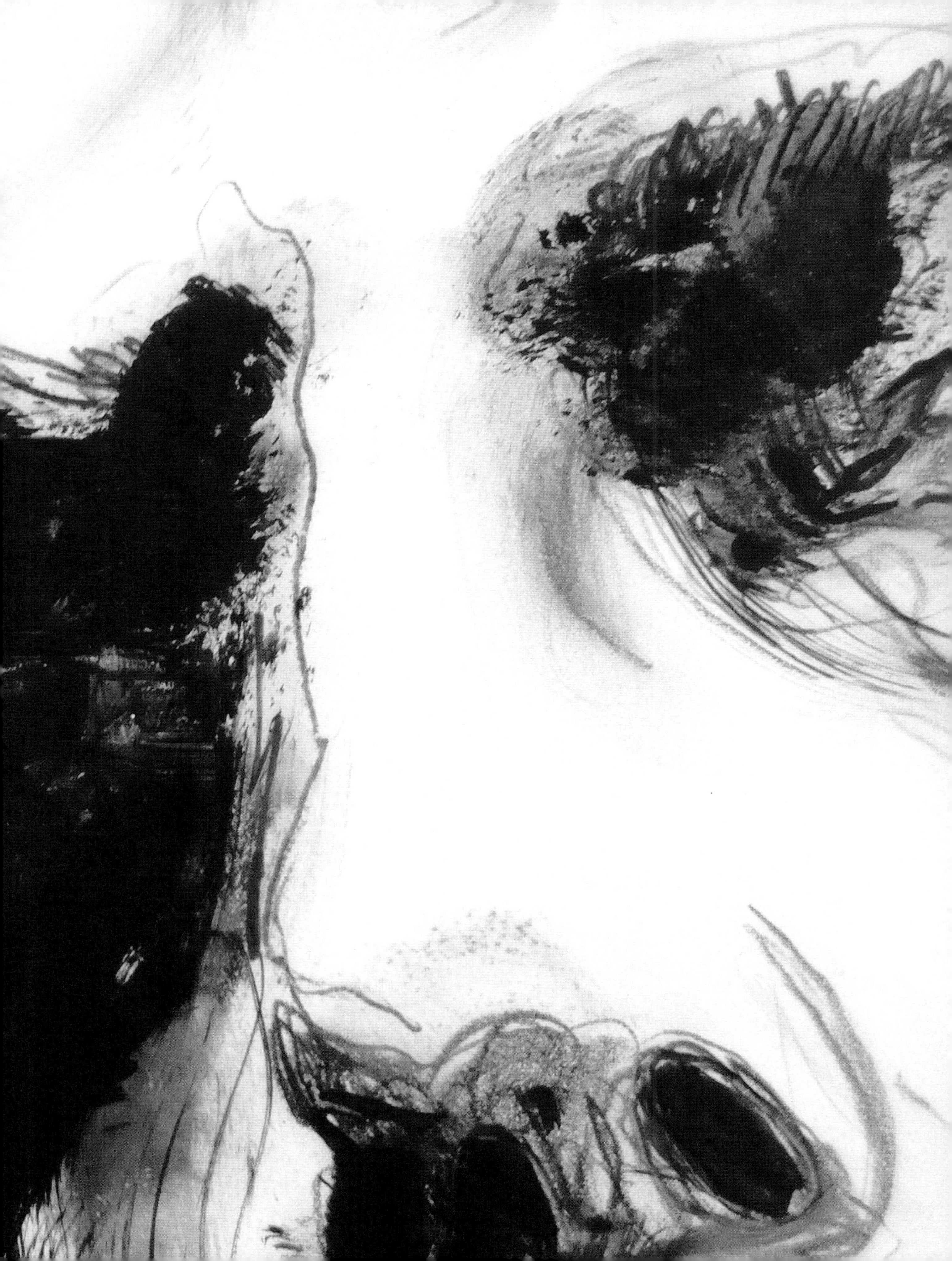

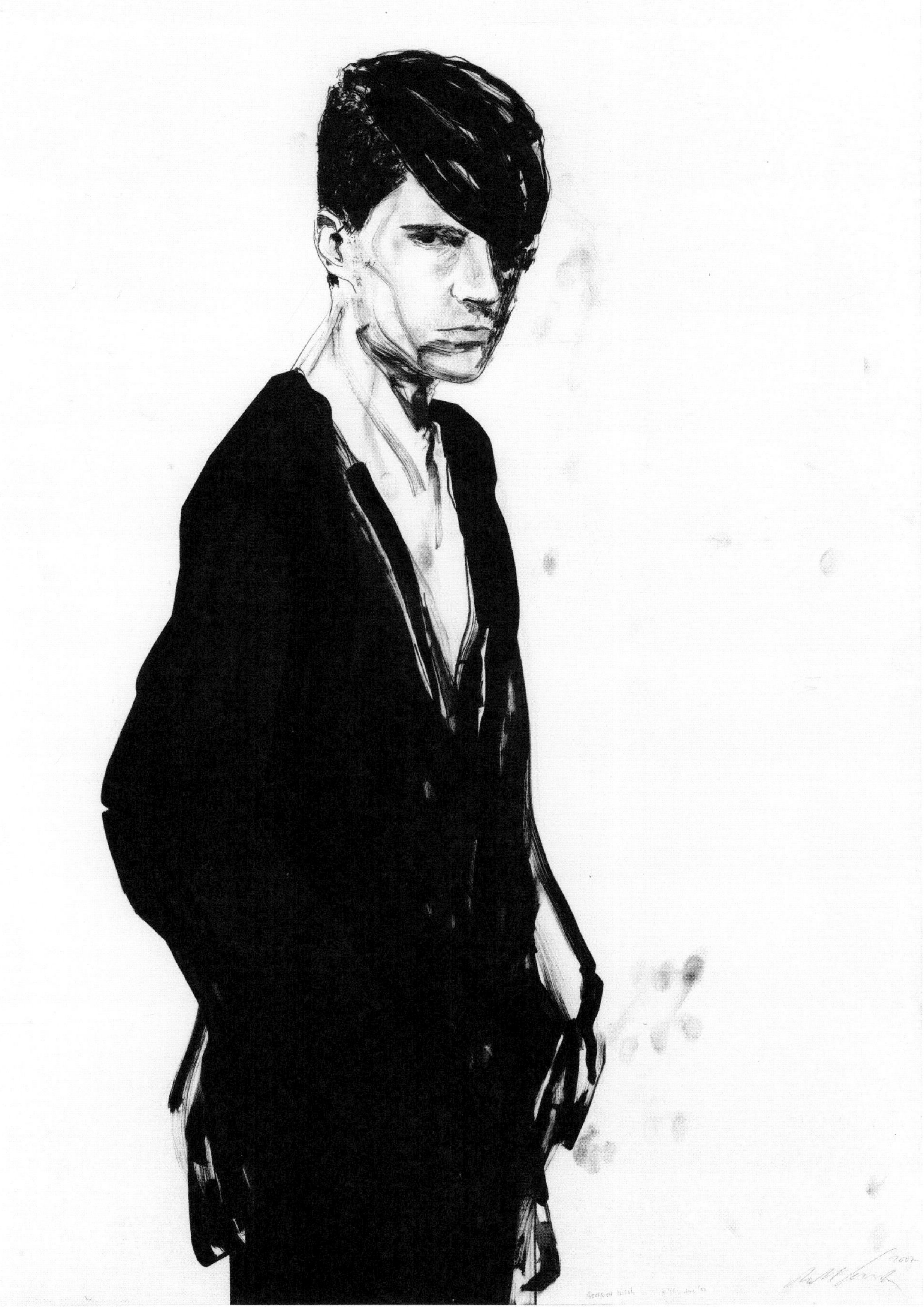

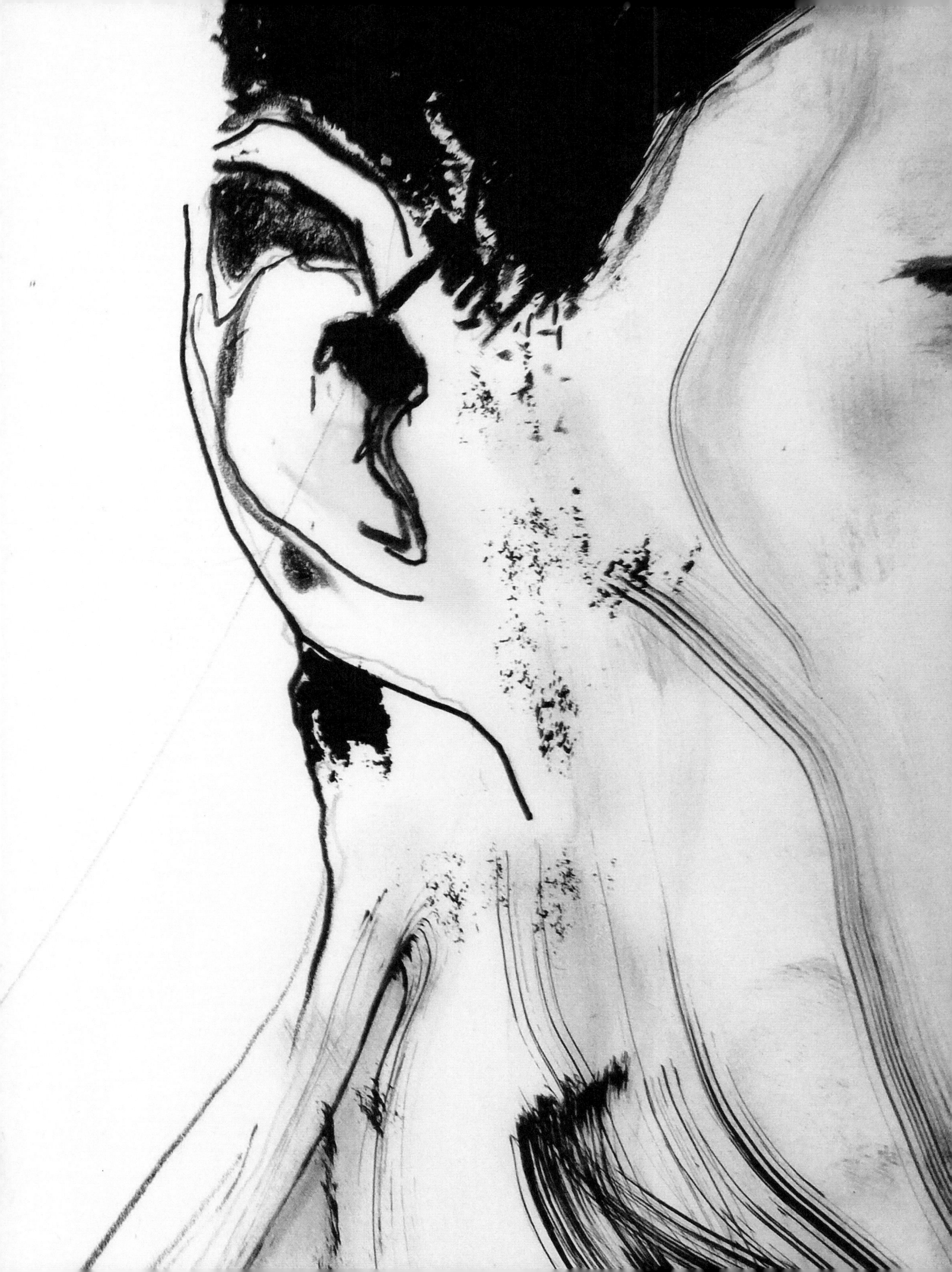

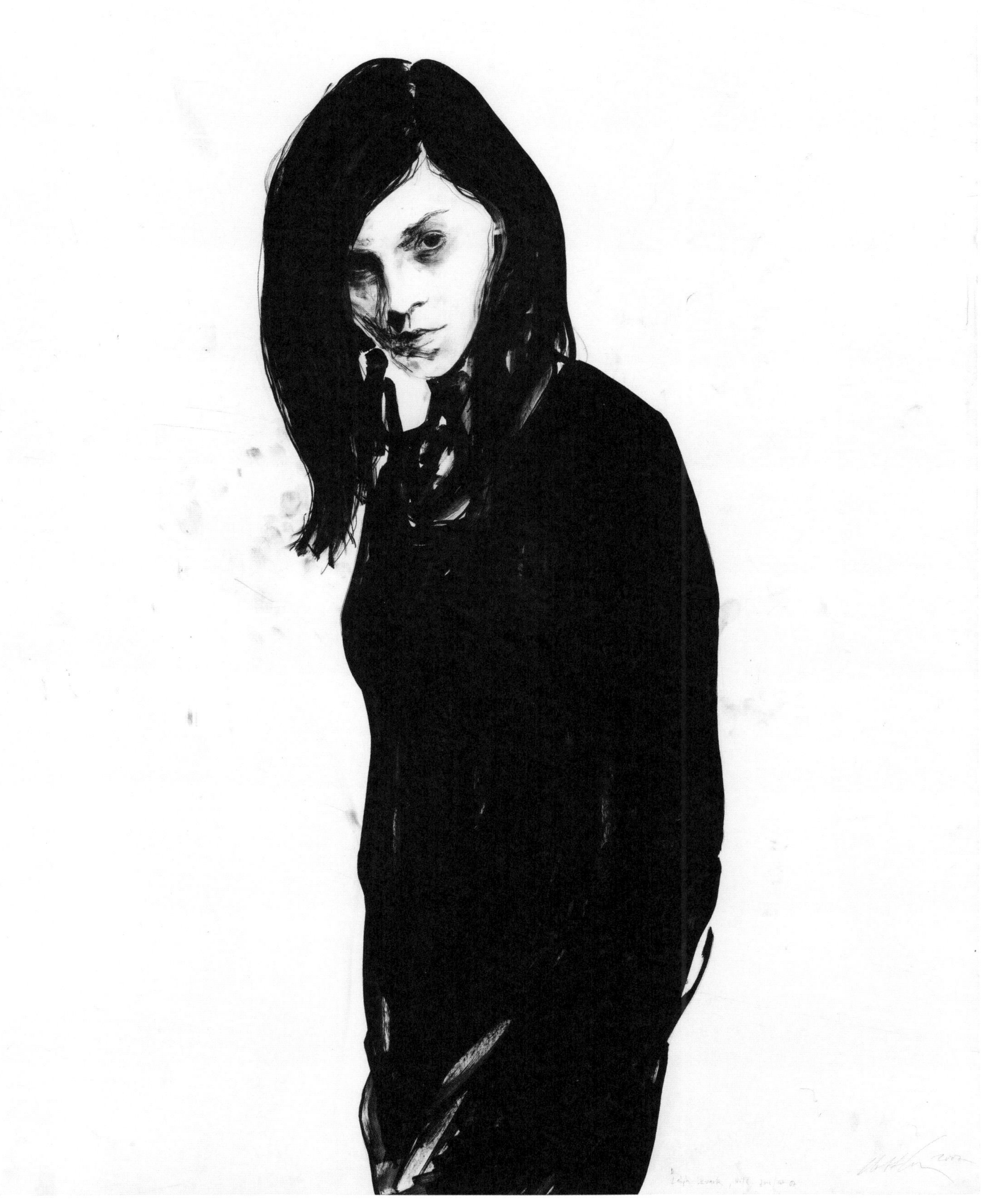

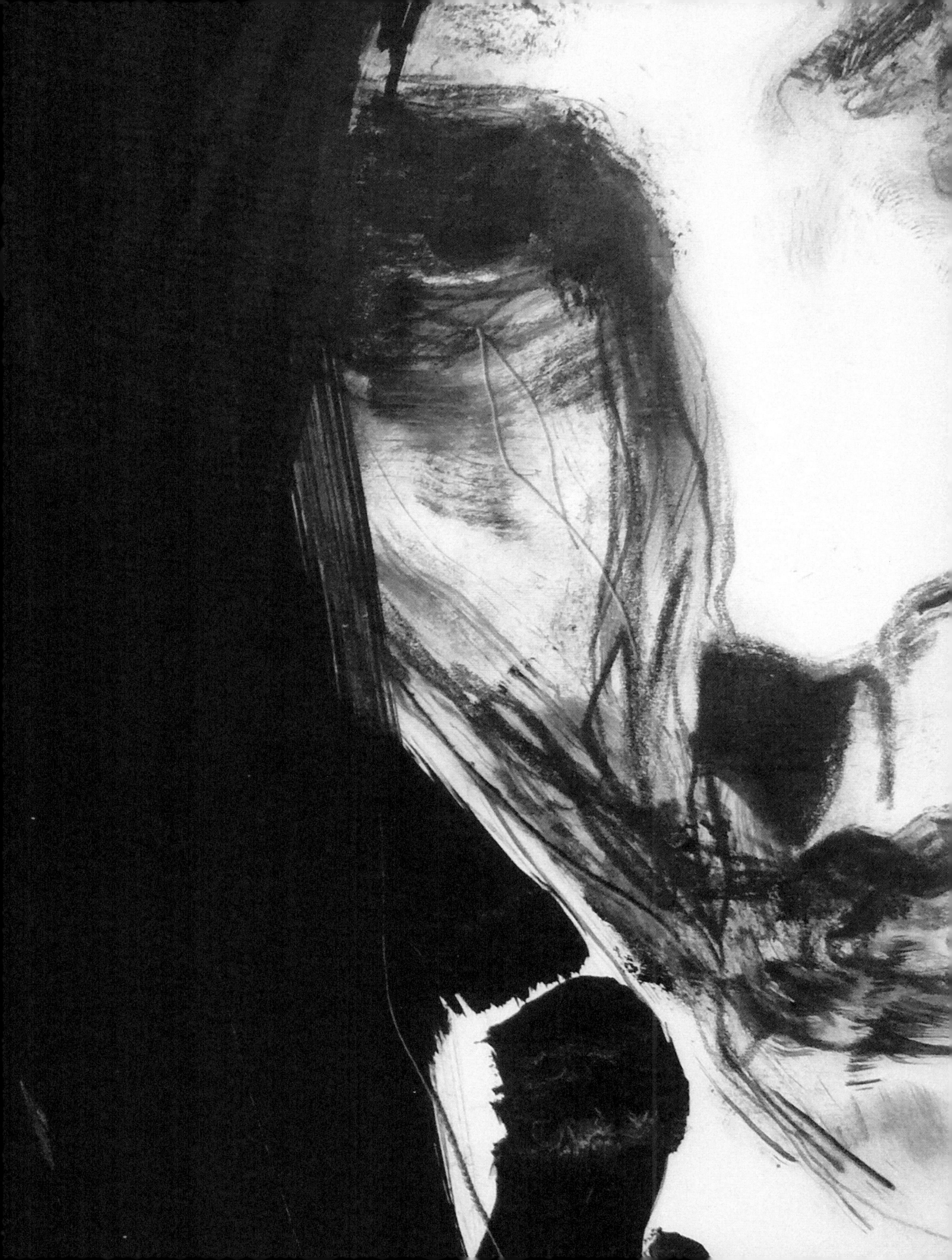

GARRICK GOTT
NEW YORK, 2009

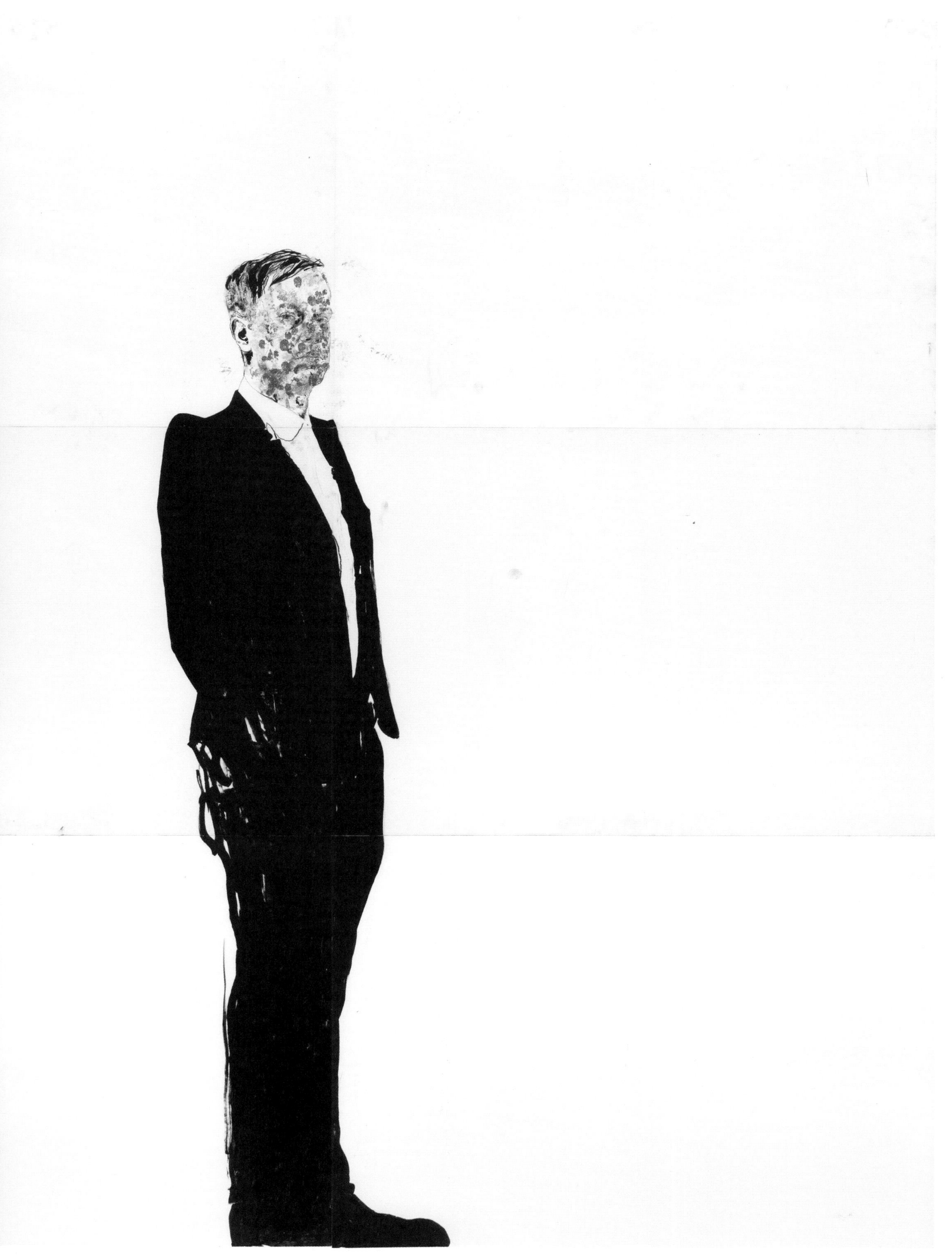

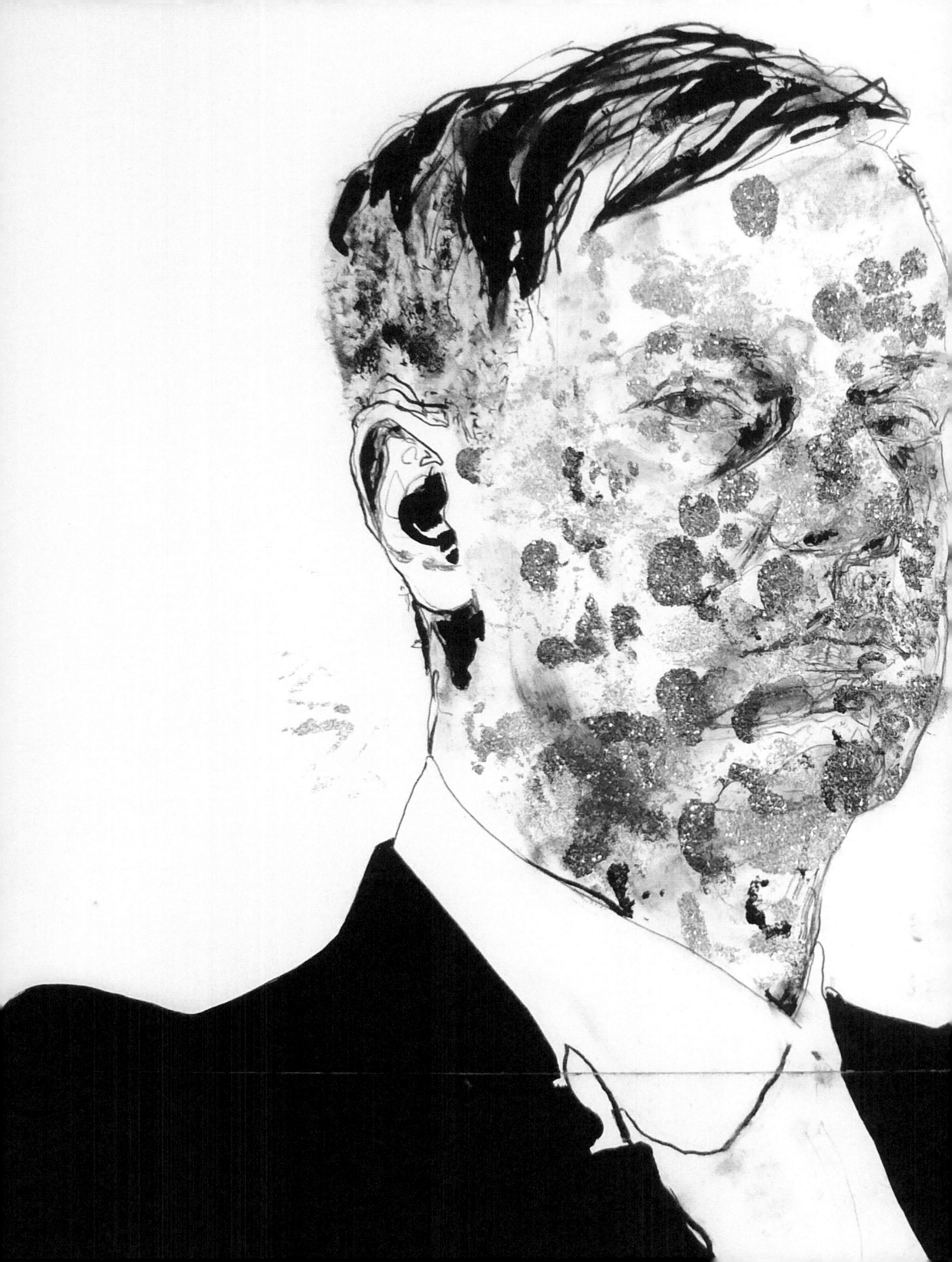

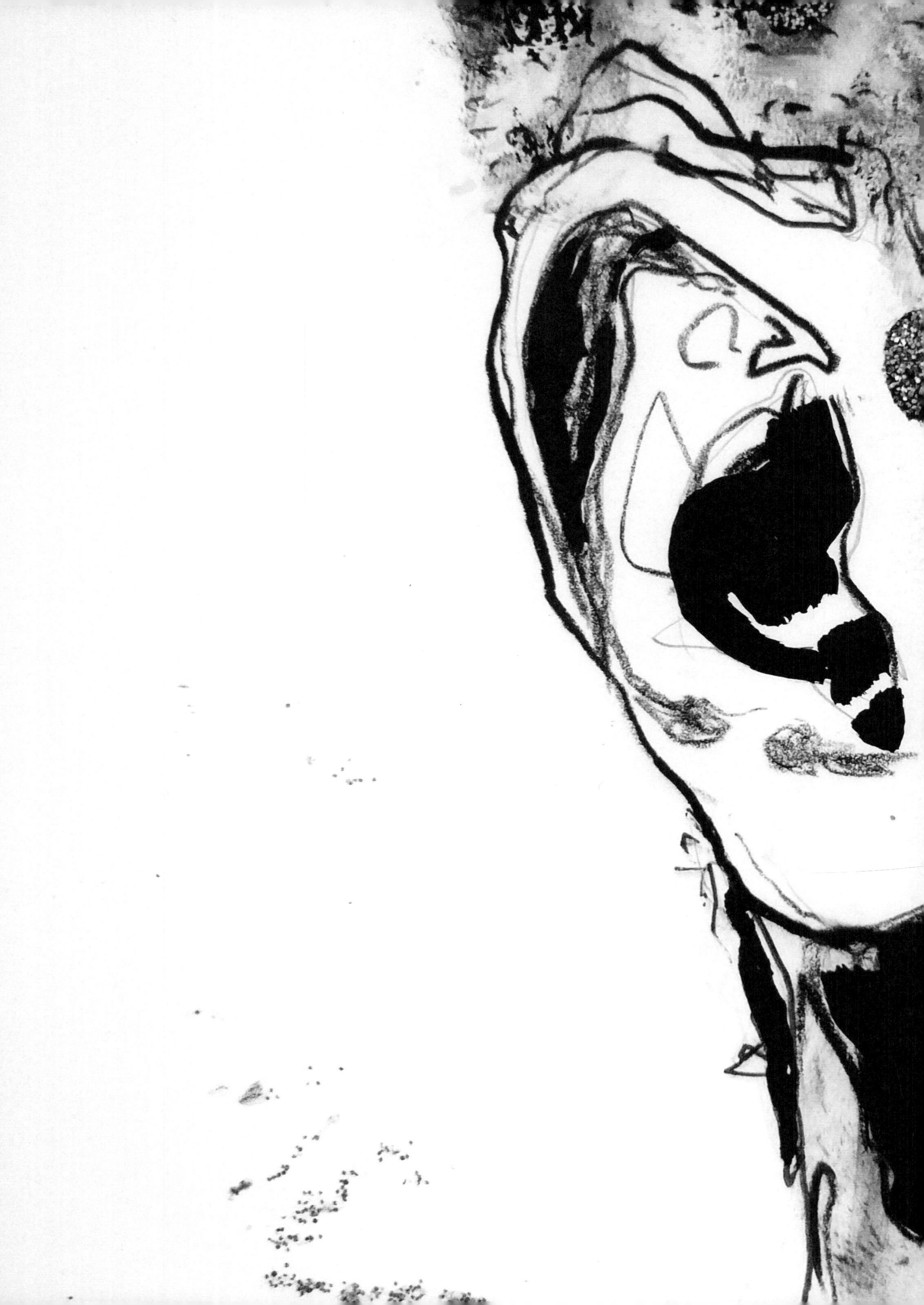

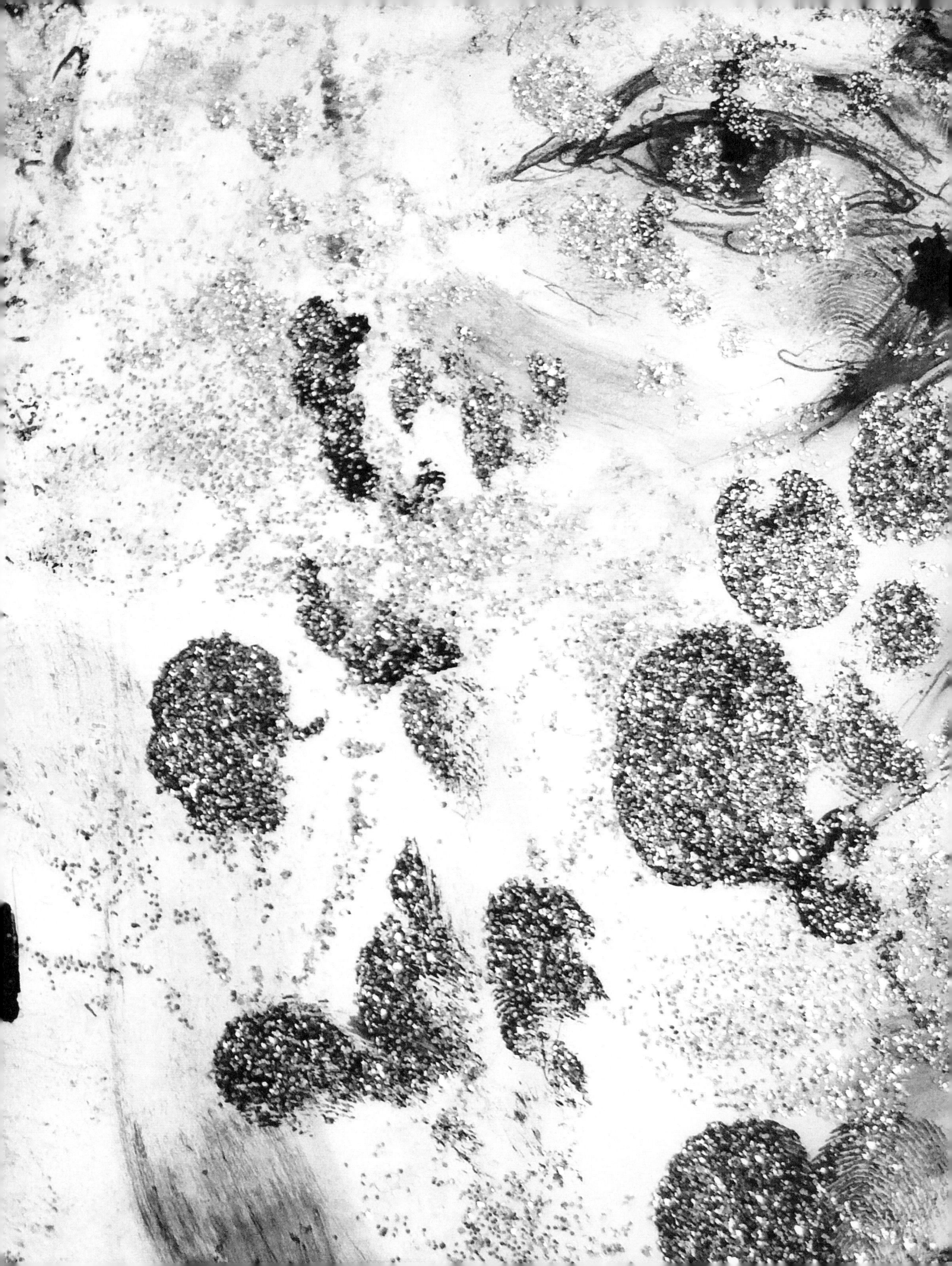

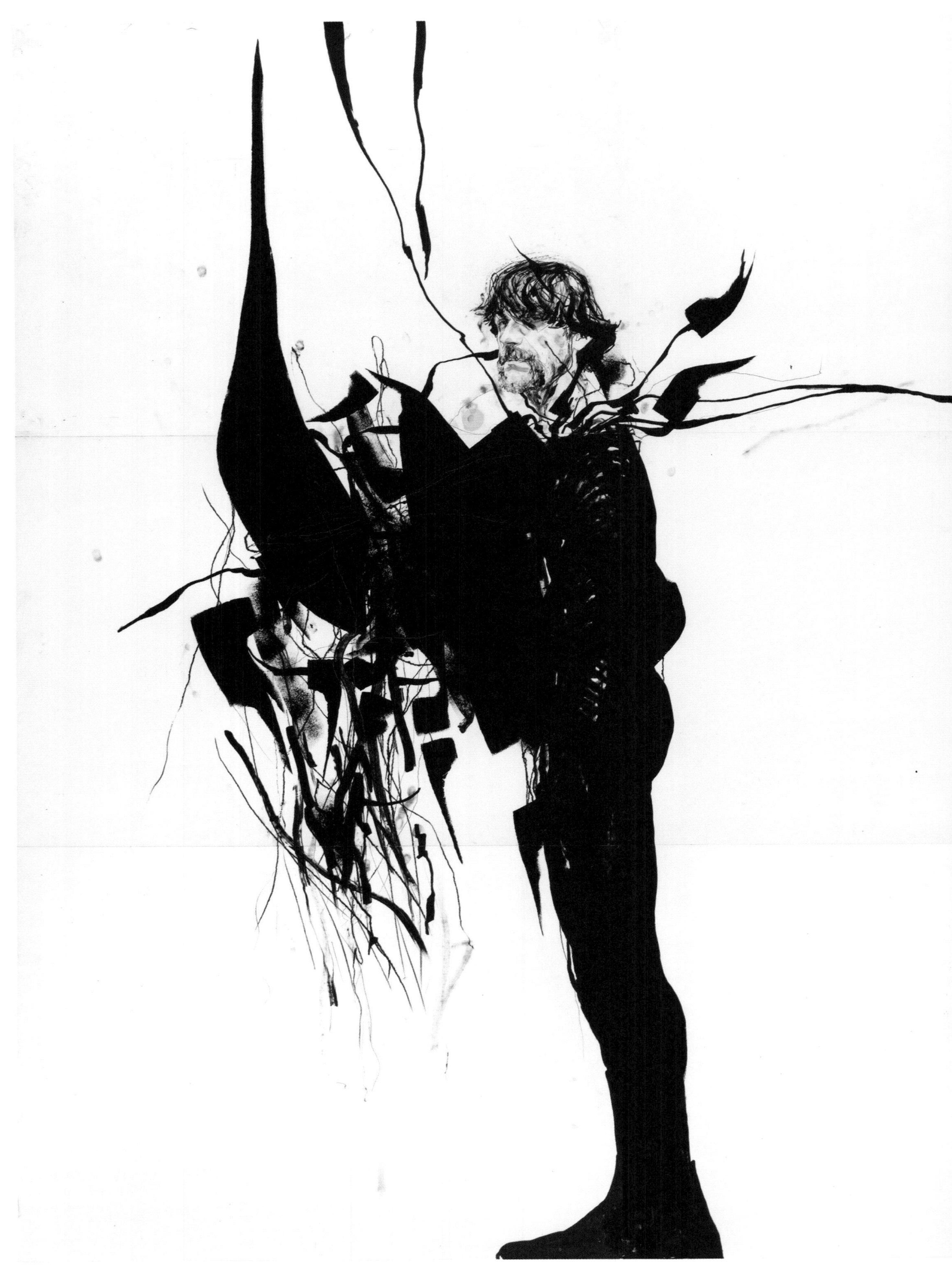

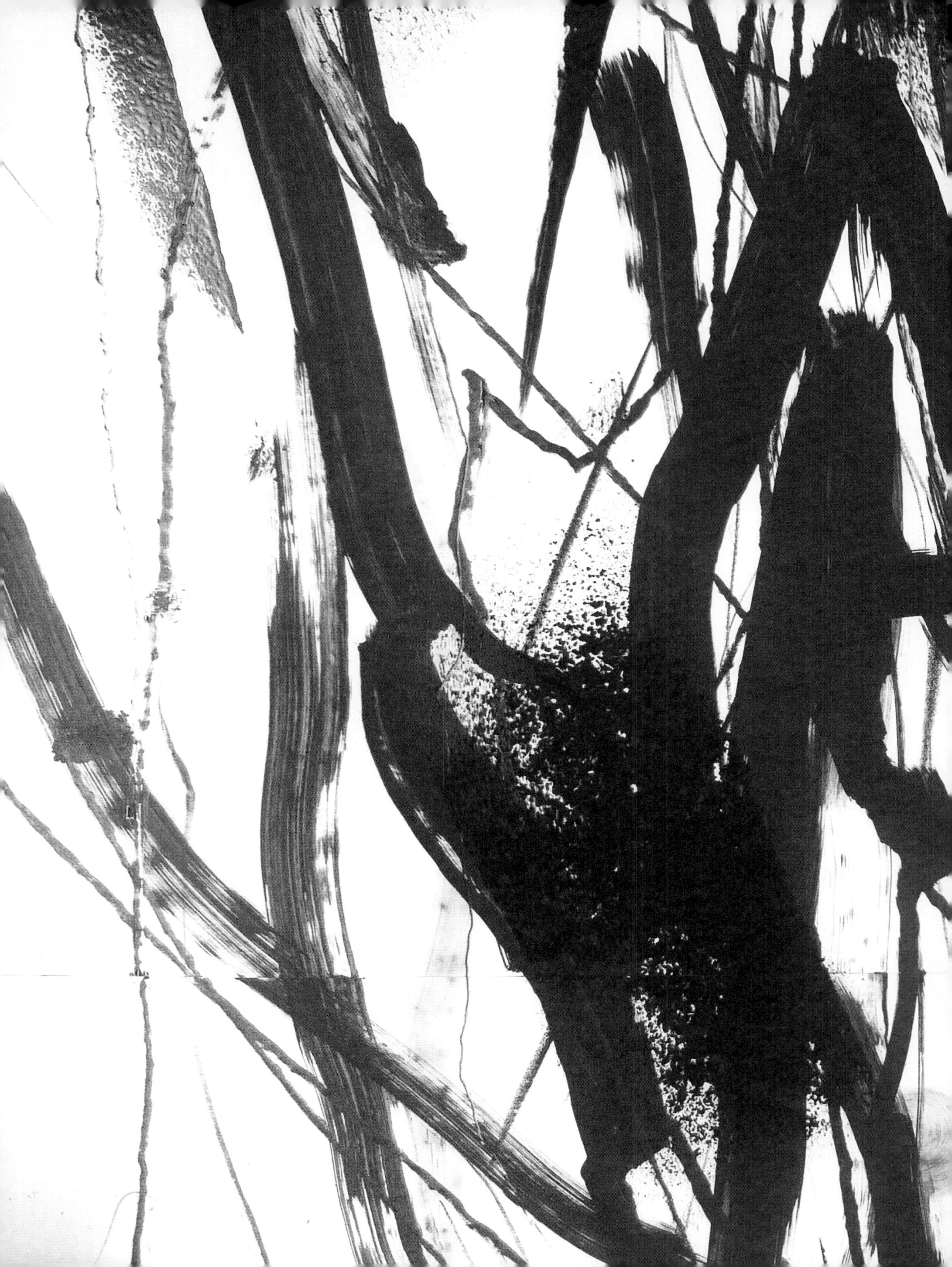

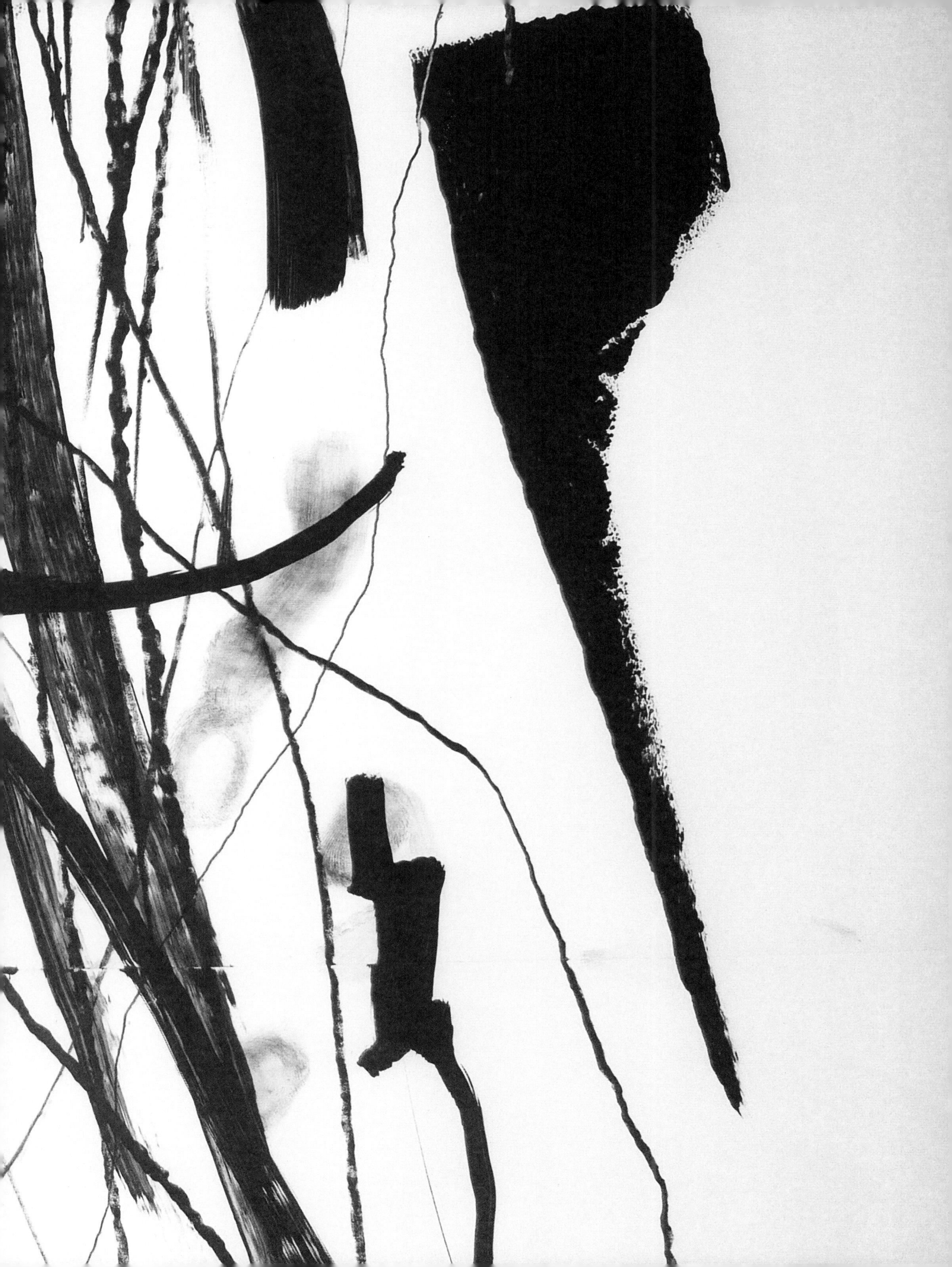

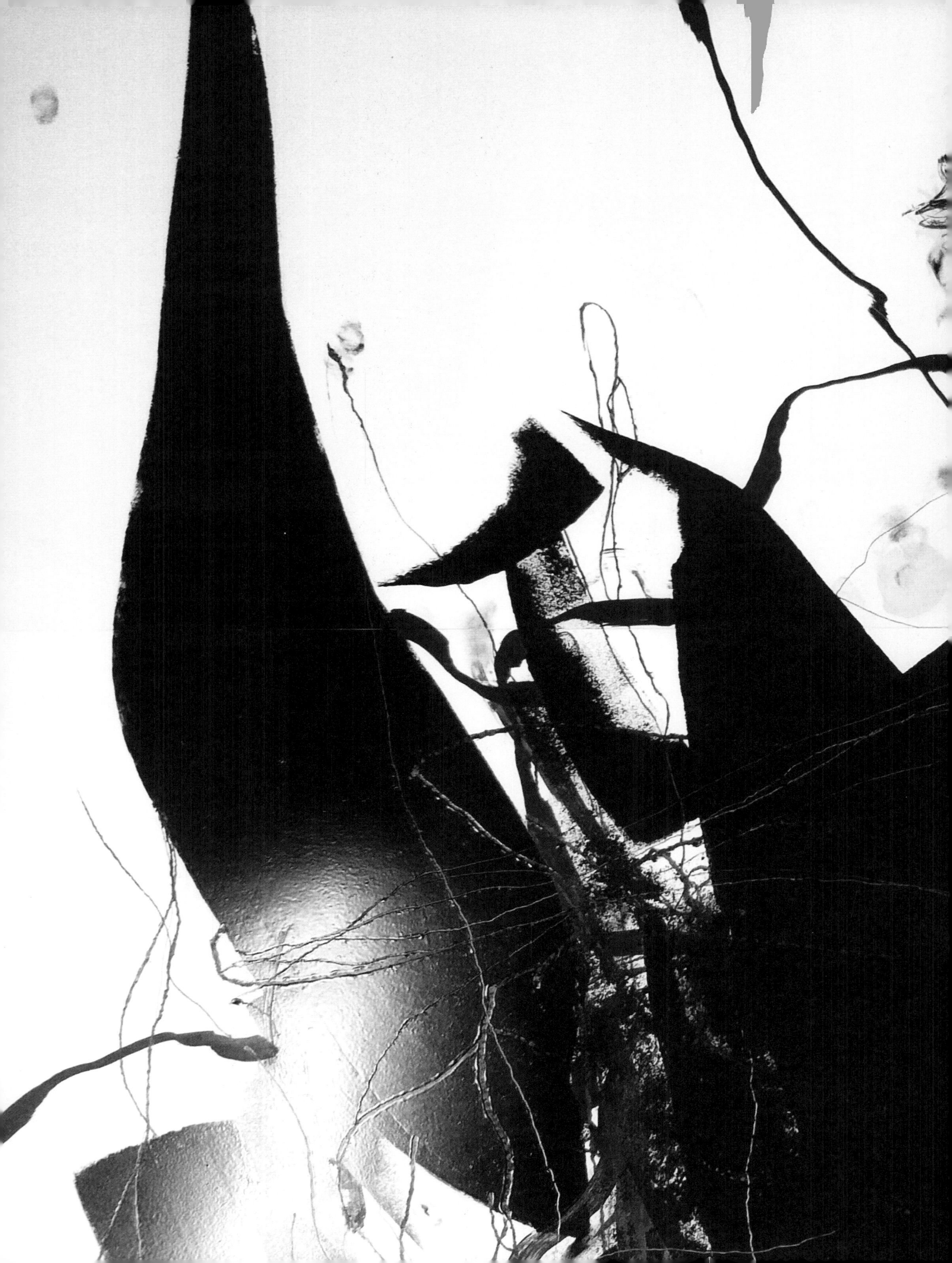

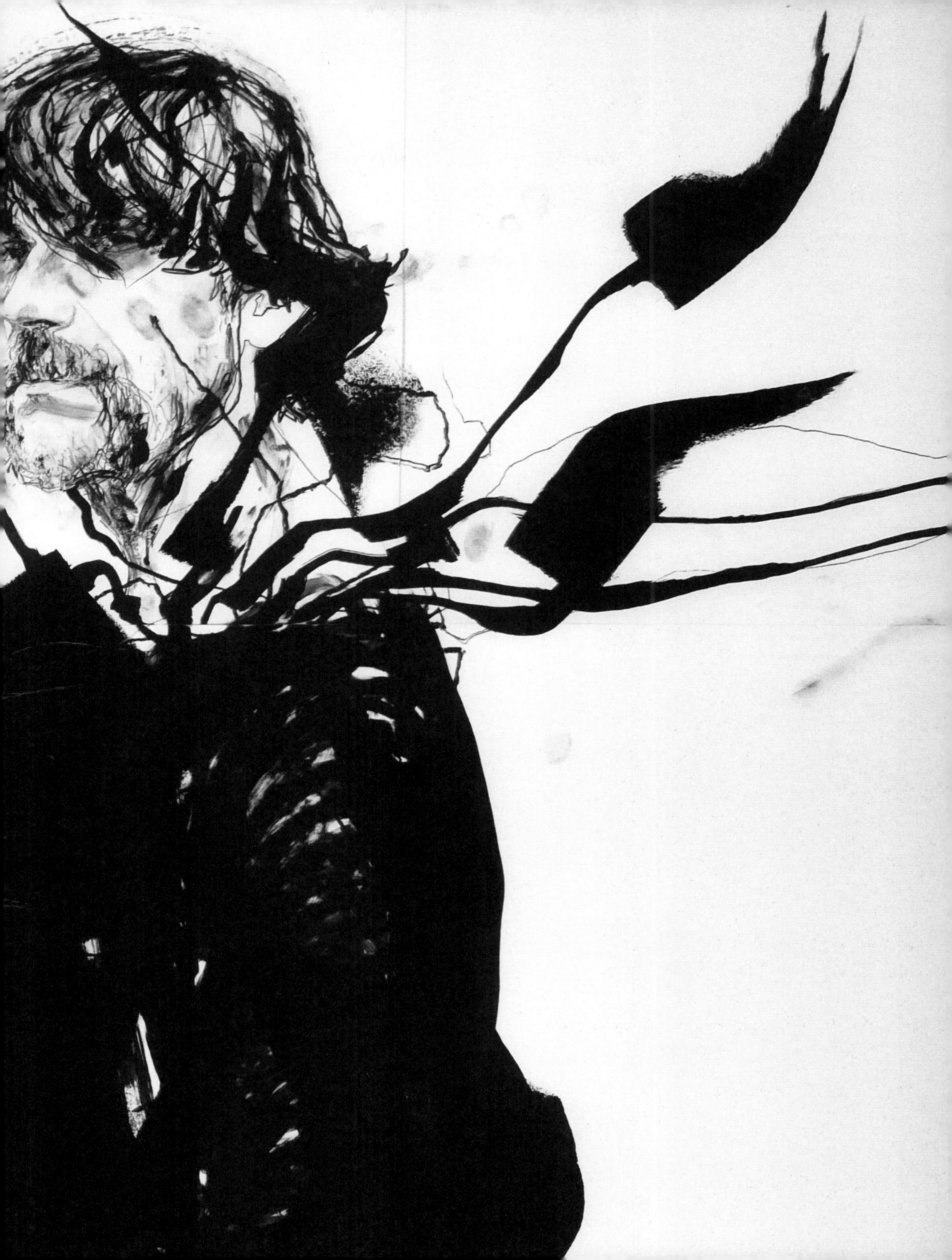

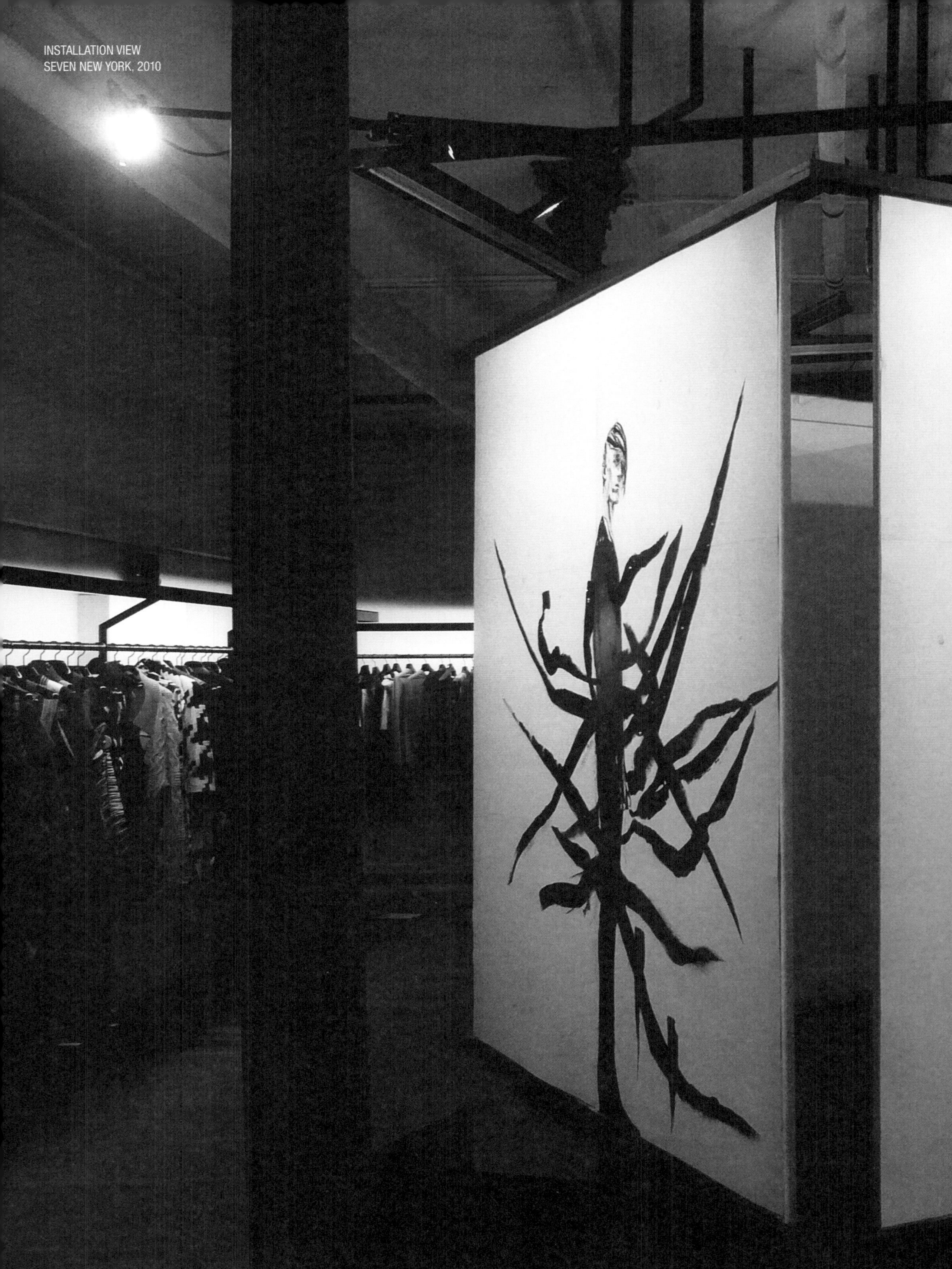

INSTALLATION VIEW
SEVEN NEW YORK, 2010

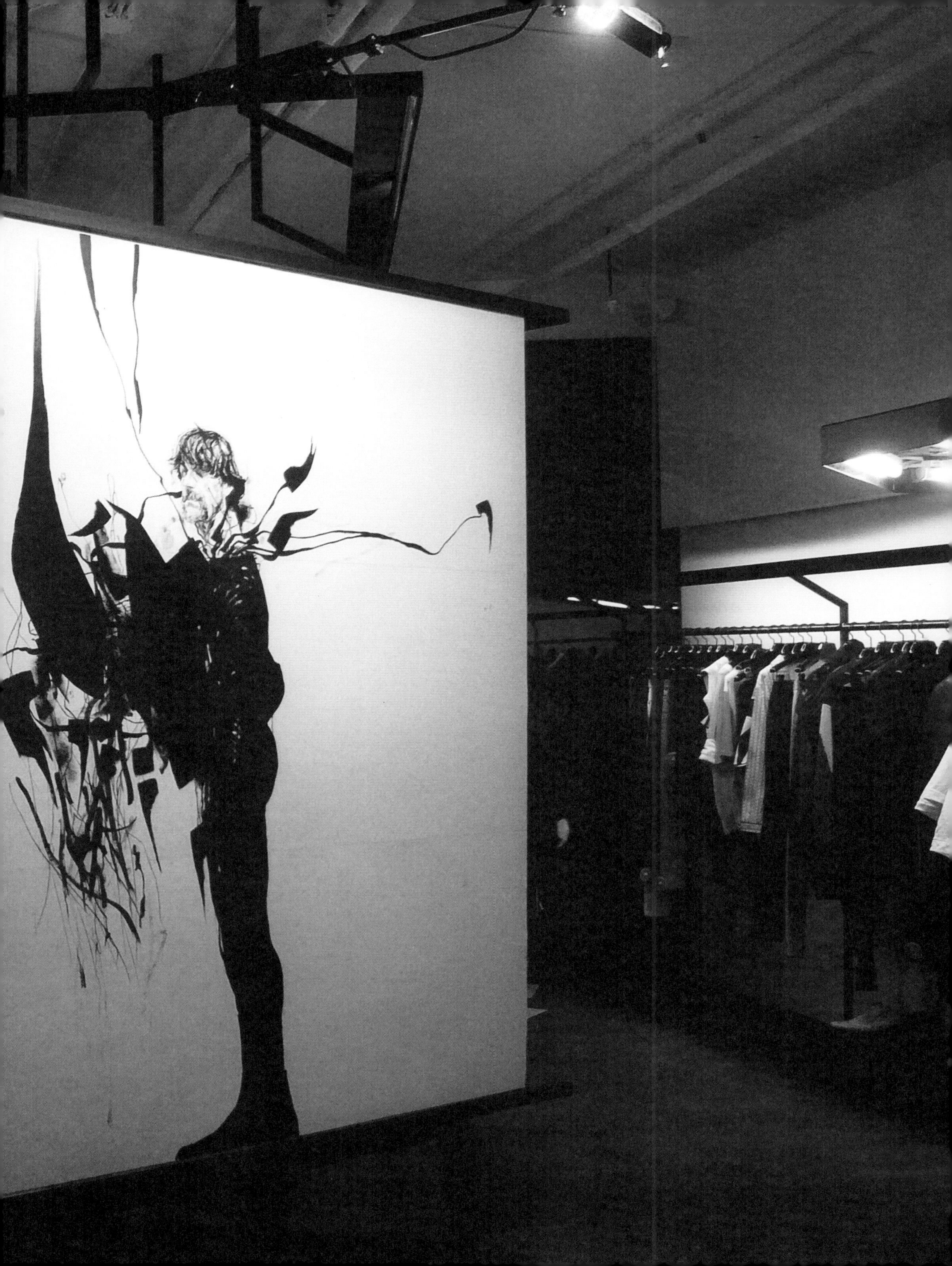

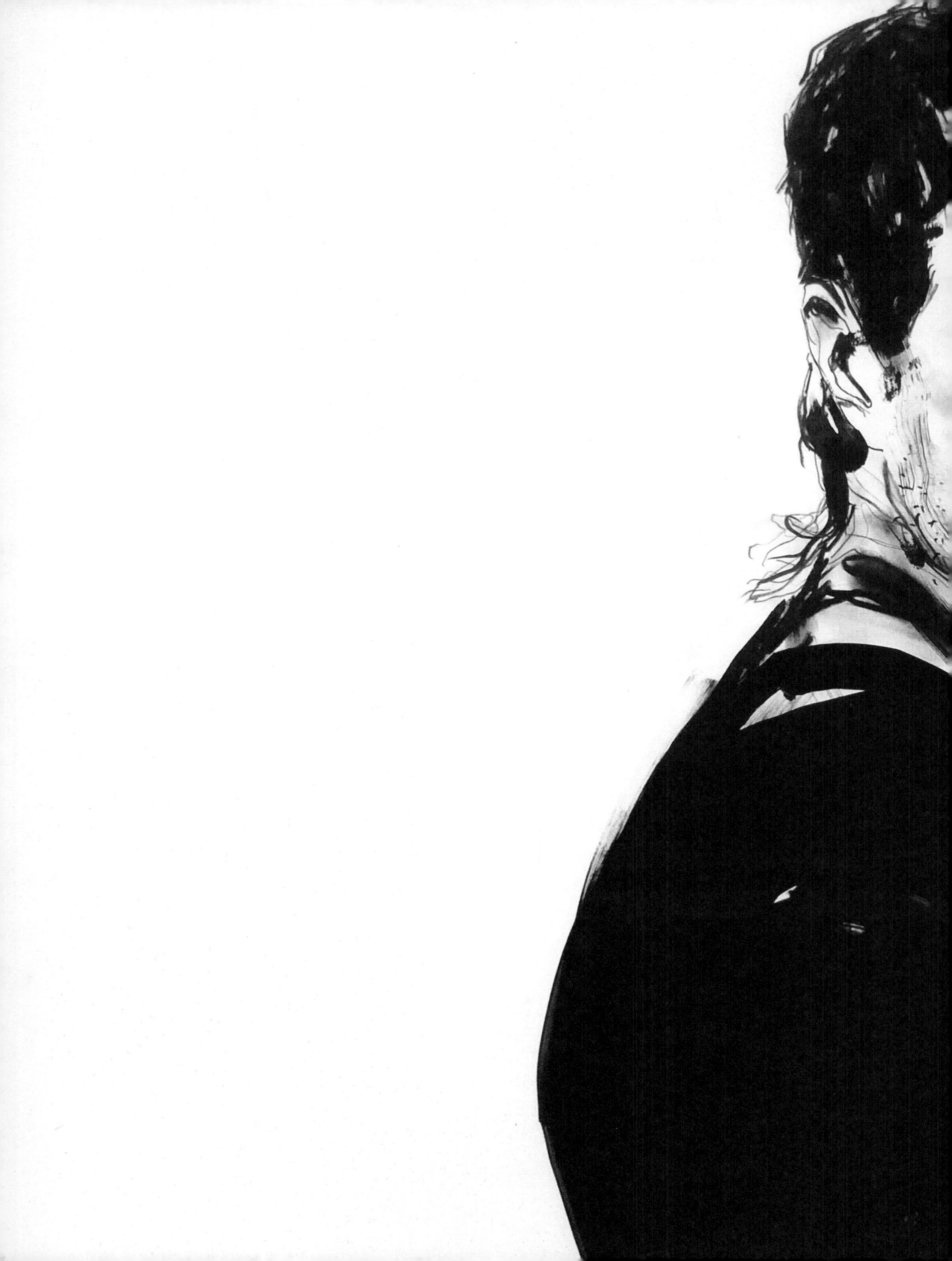

JOSEPH QUARTANA
NEW YORK, 2007

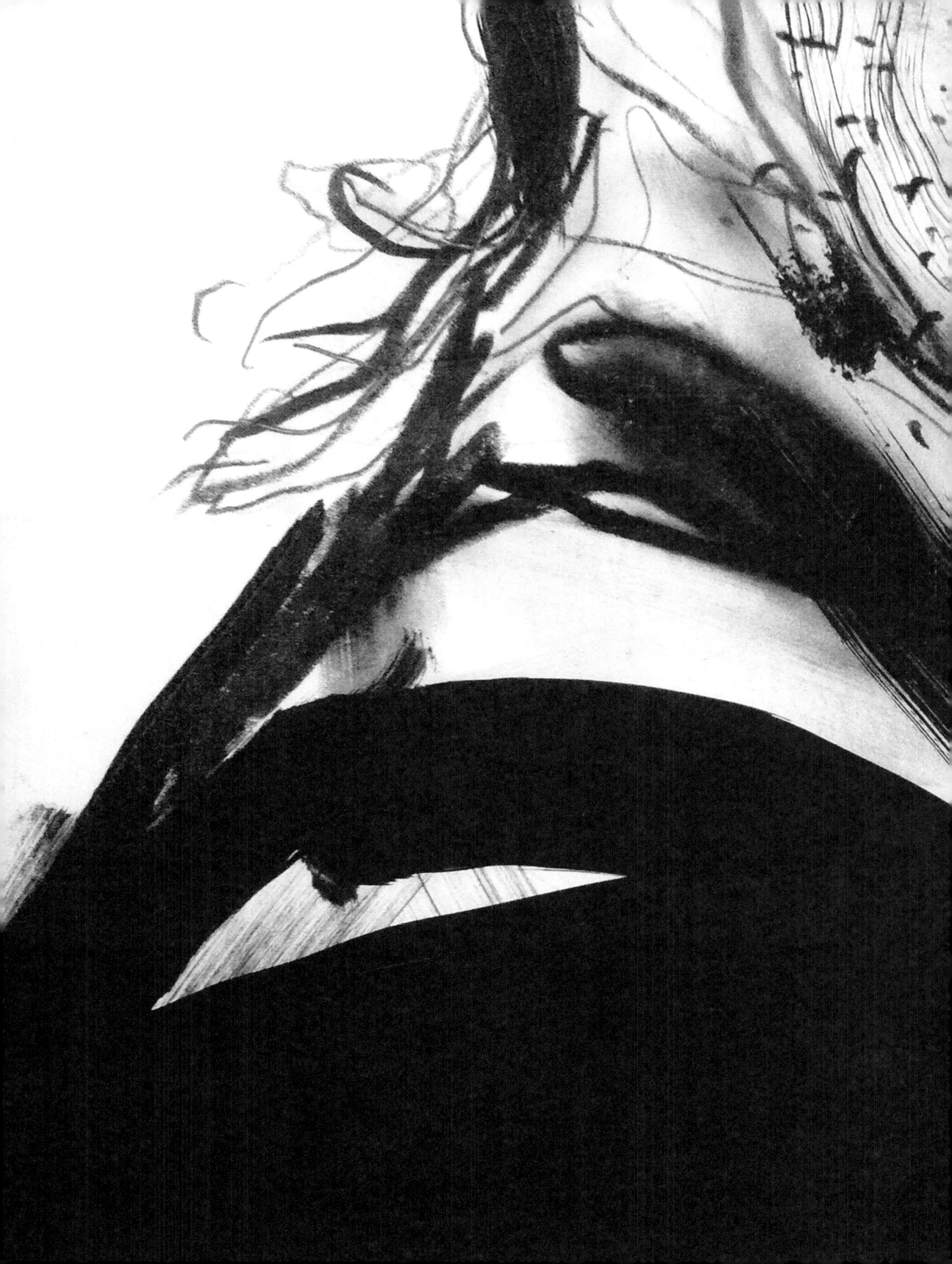

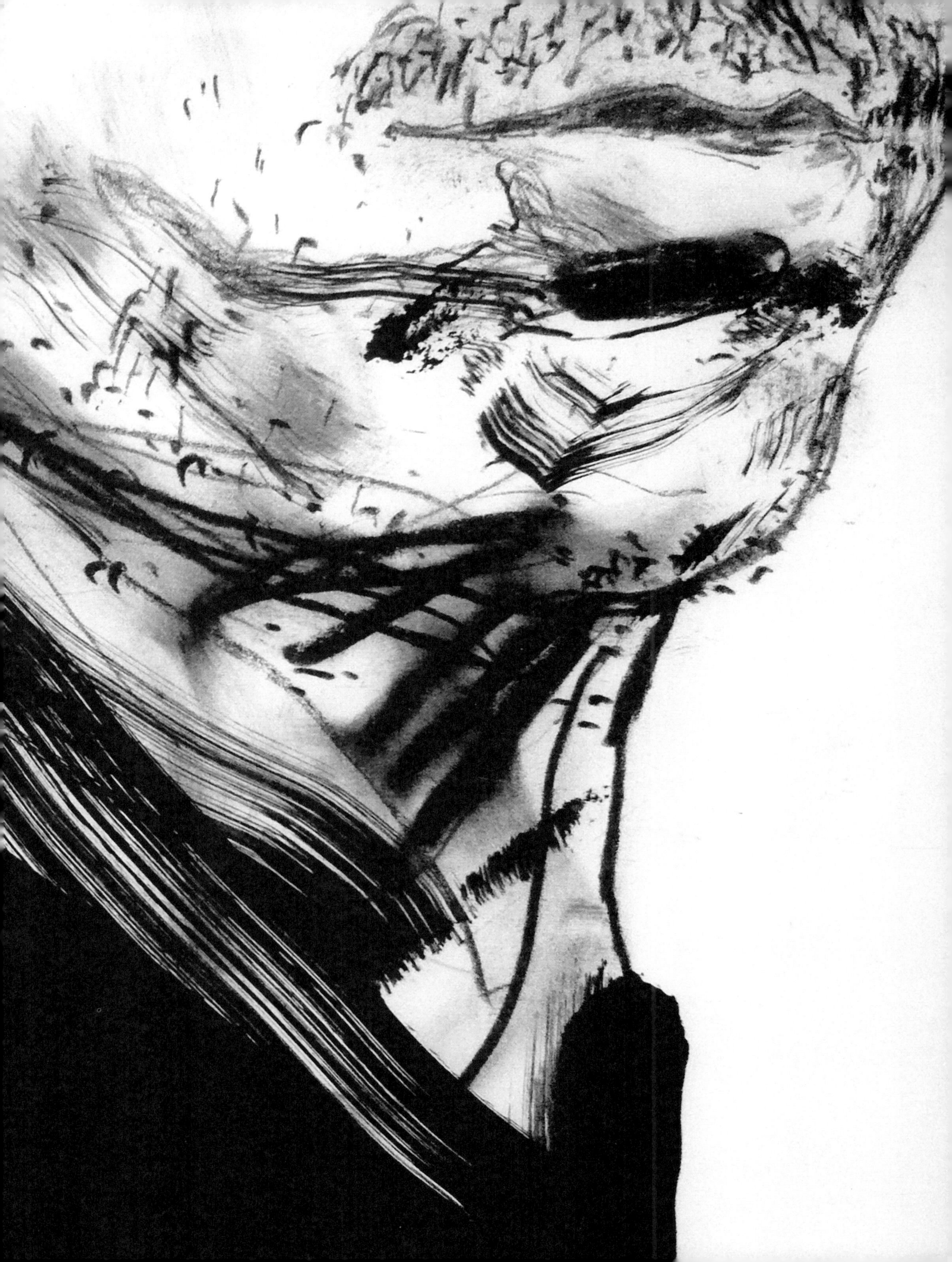

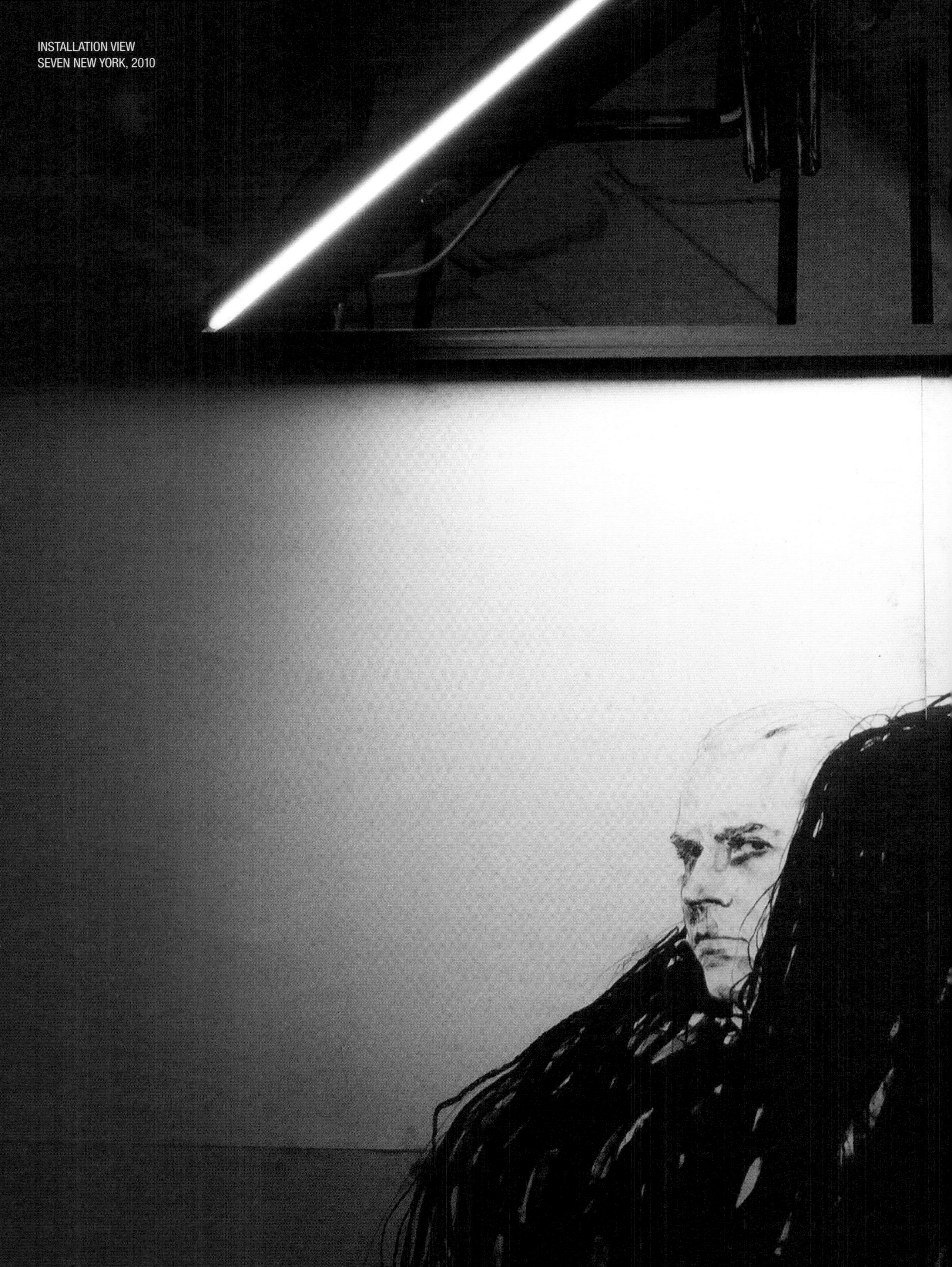

INSTALLATION VIEW
SEVEN NEW YORK, 2010

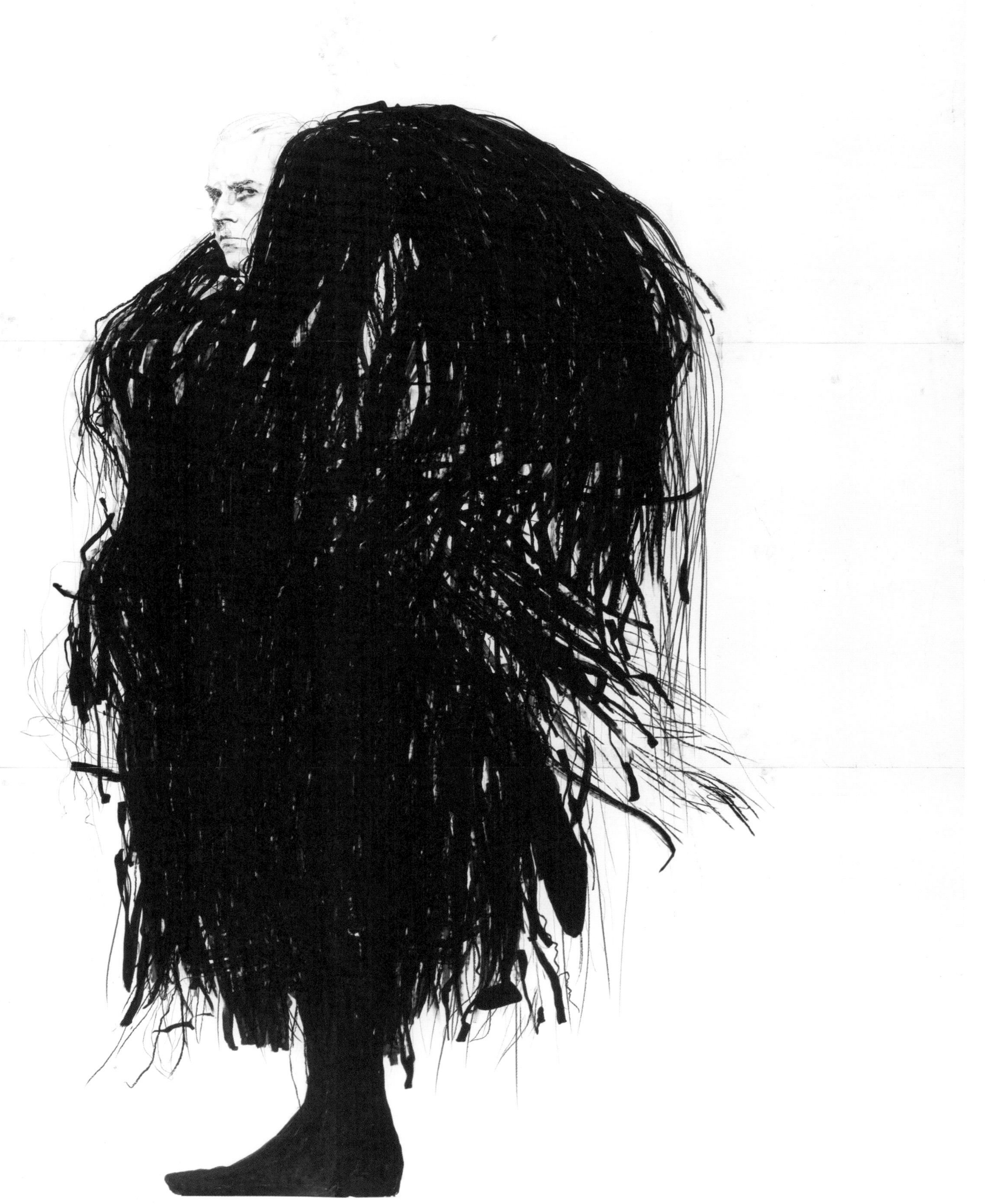

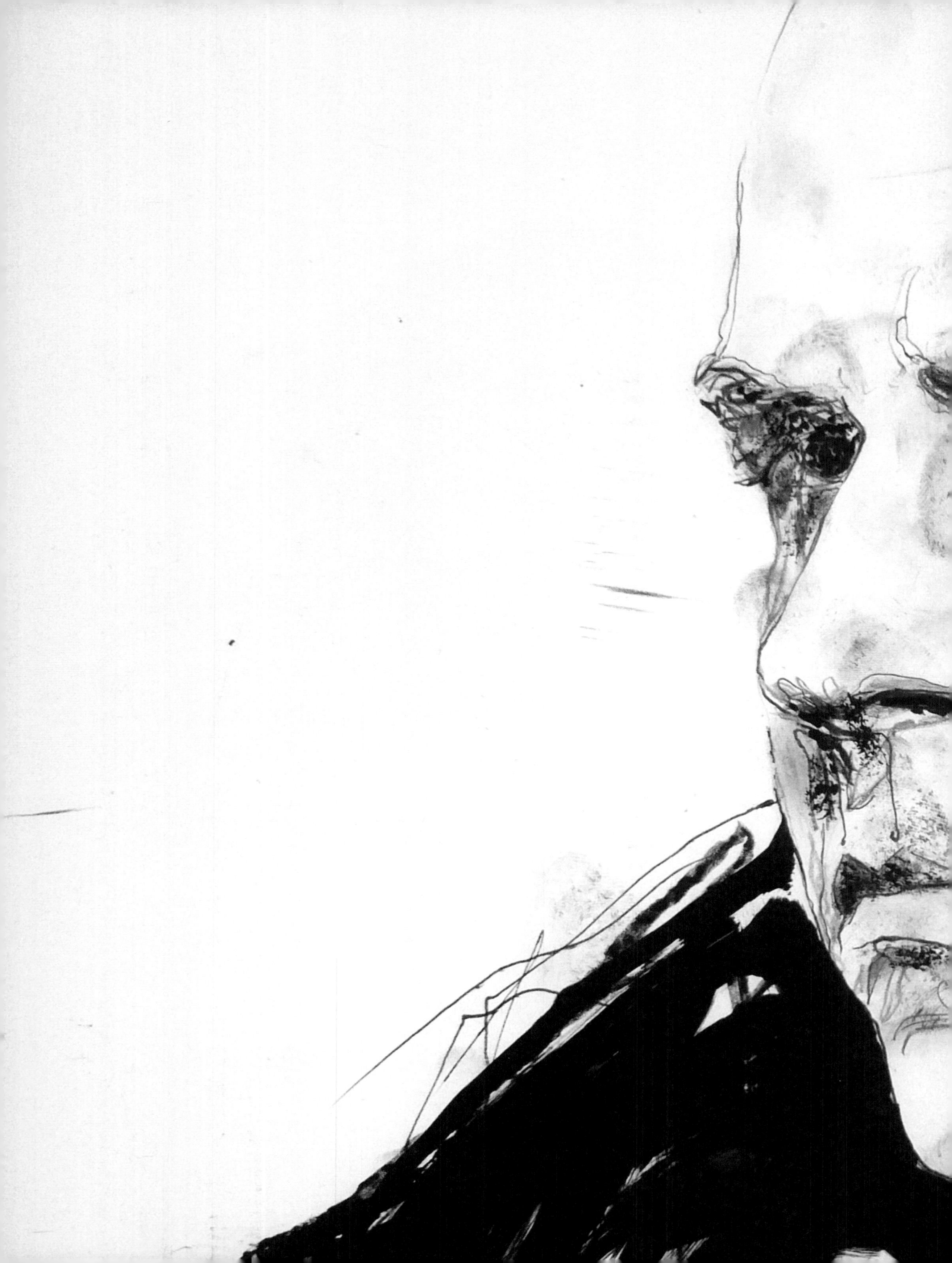

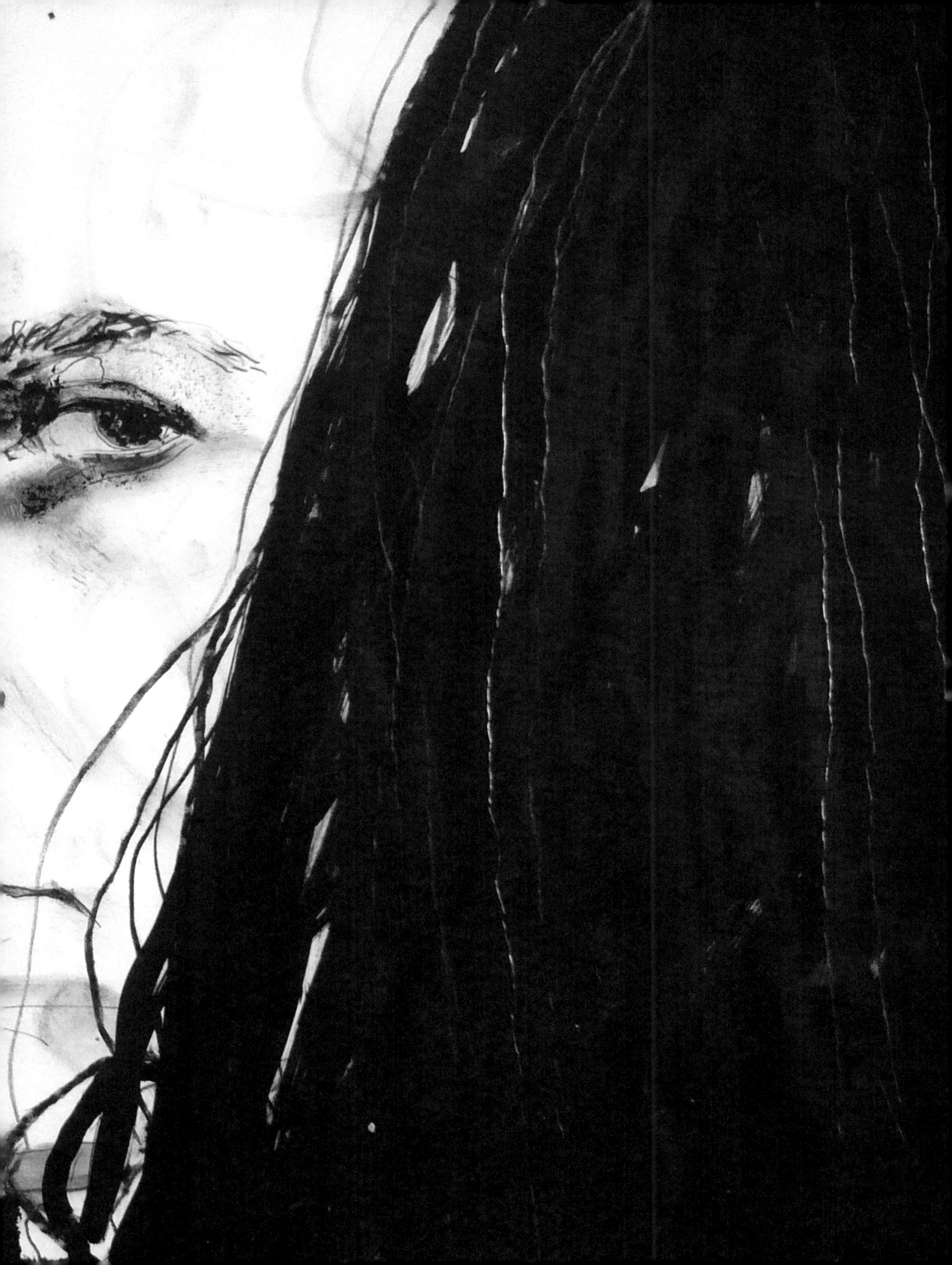

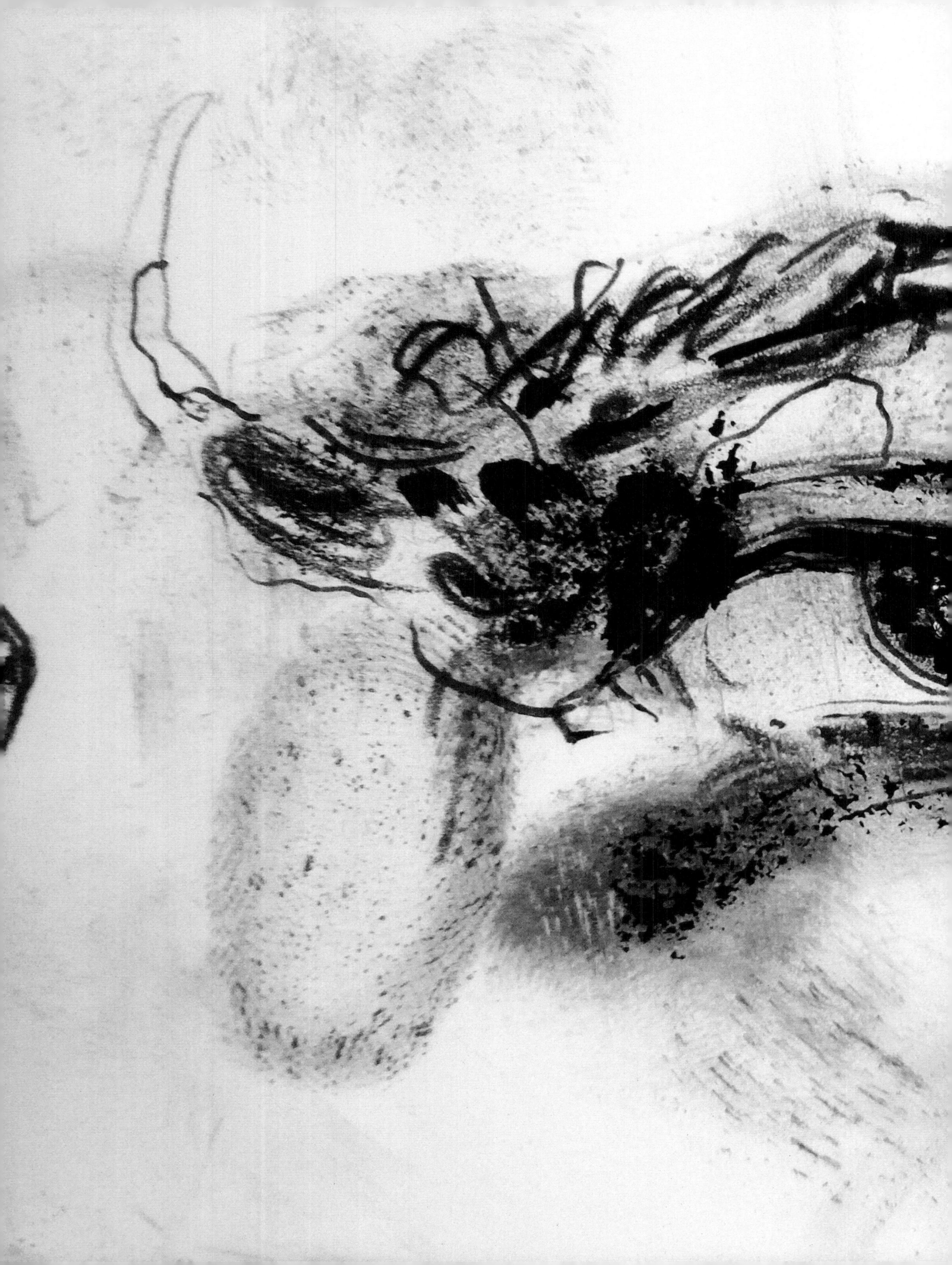

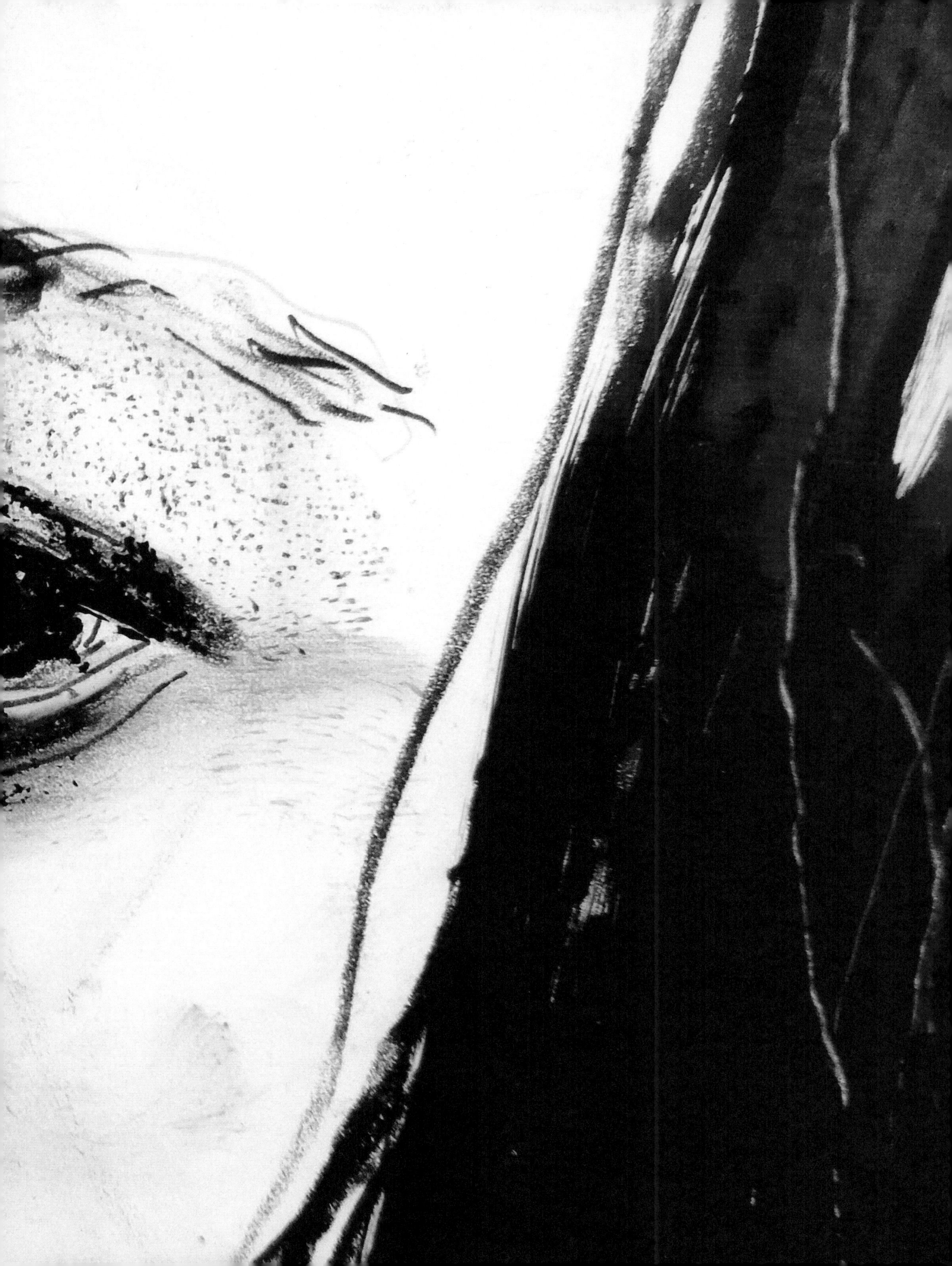

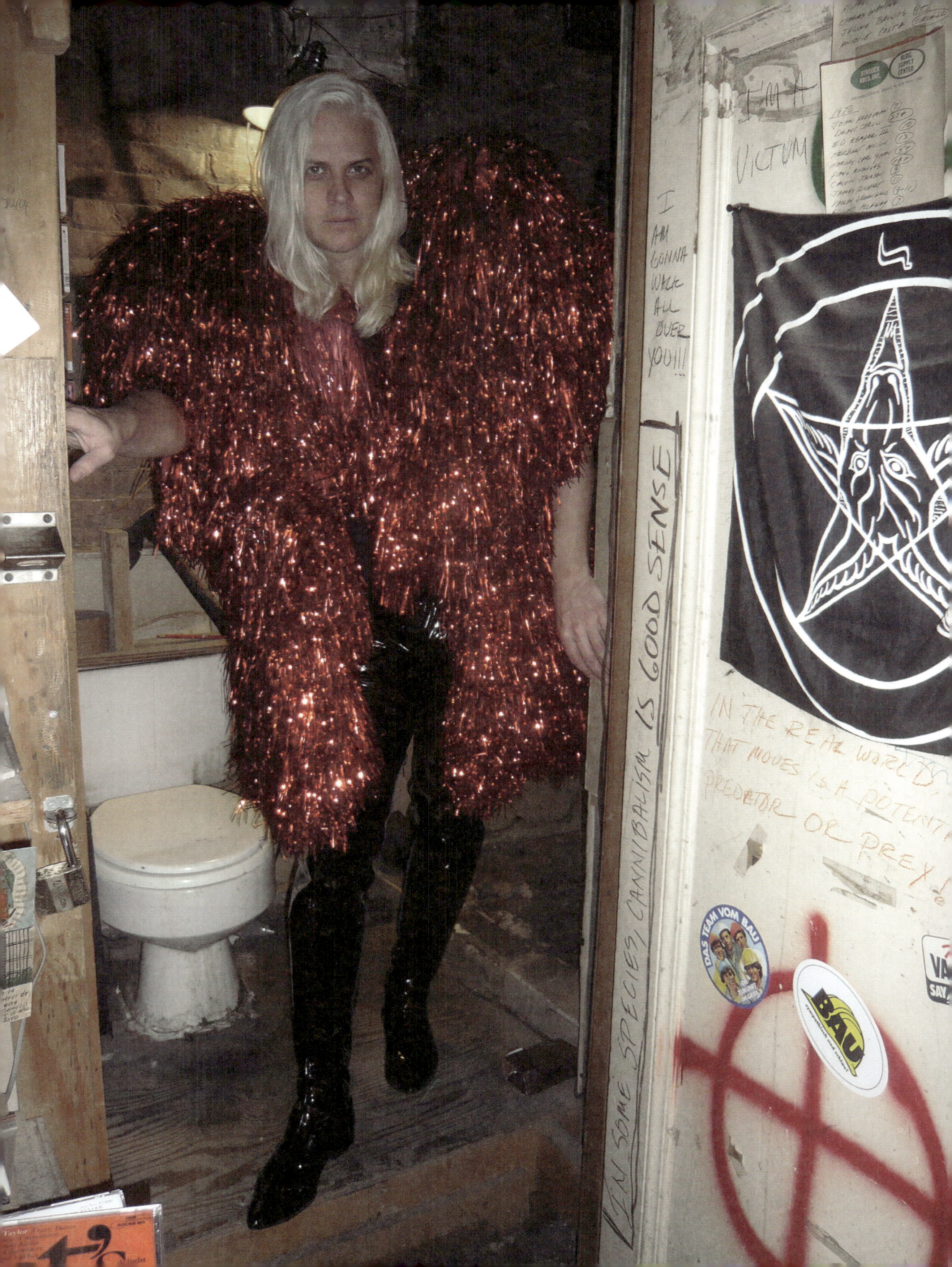
I'M A
VICTIM
I AM GONNA WALK ALL OVER YOU!!!
IN SOME SPECIES, CANNIBALISM IS GOOD SENSE
IN THE REAL WORLD, THAT MOVES IS A POTENTIAL PREDATOR OR PREY!
DAS TEAM VOM BAU

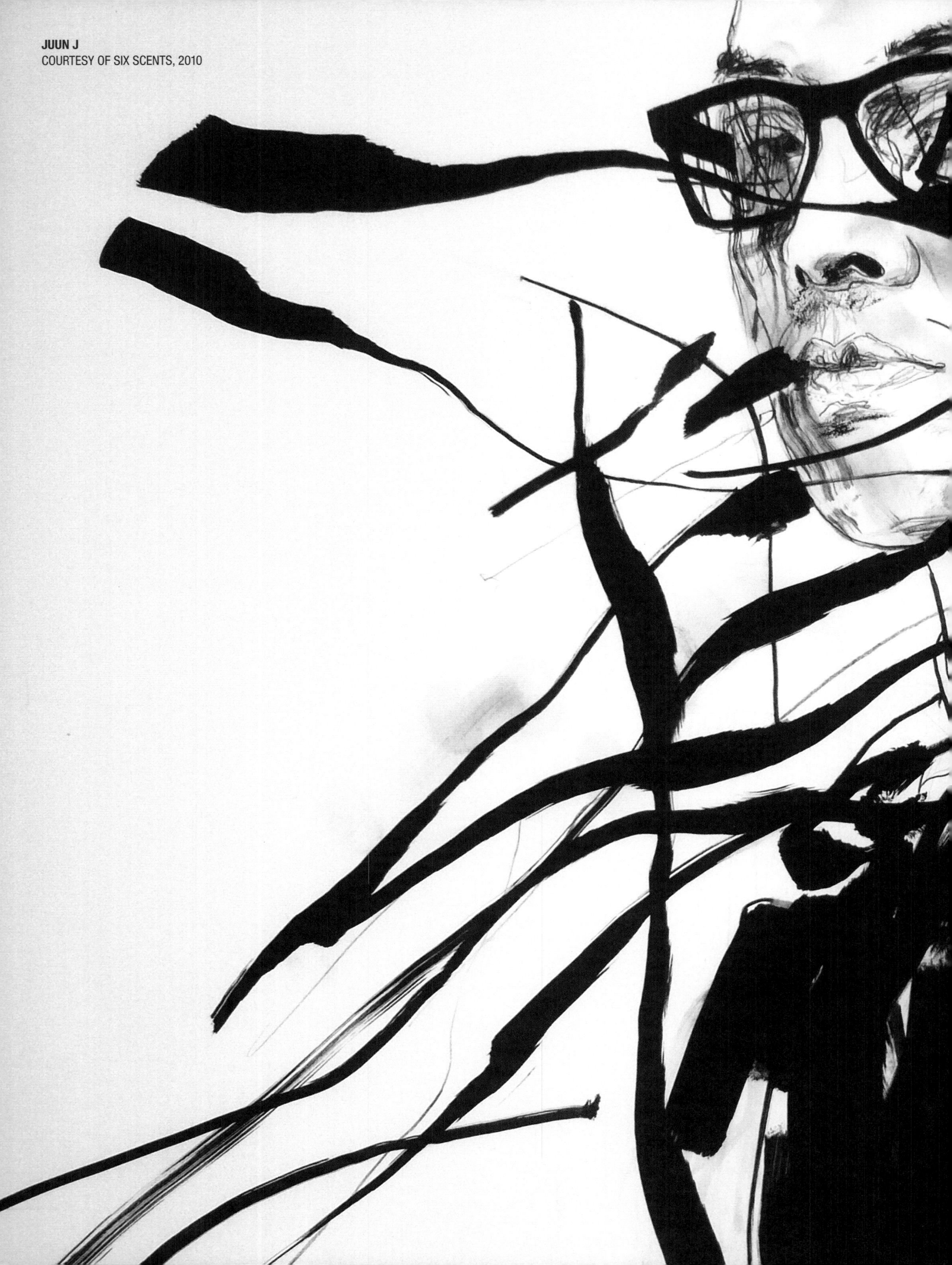

JUUN J
COURTESY OF SIX SCENTS, 2010

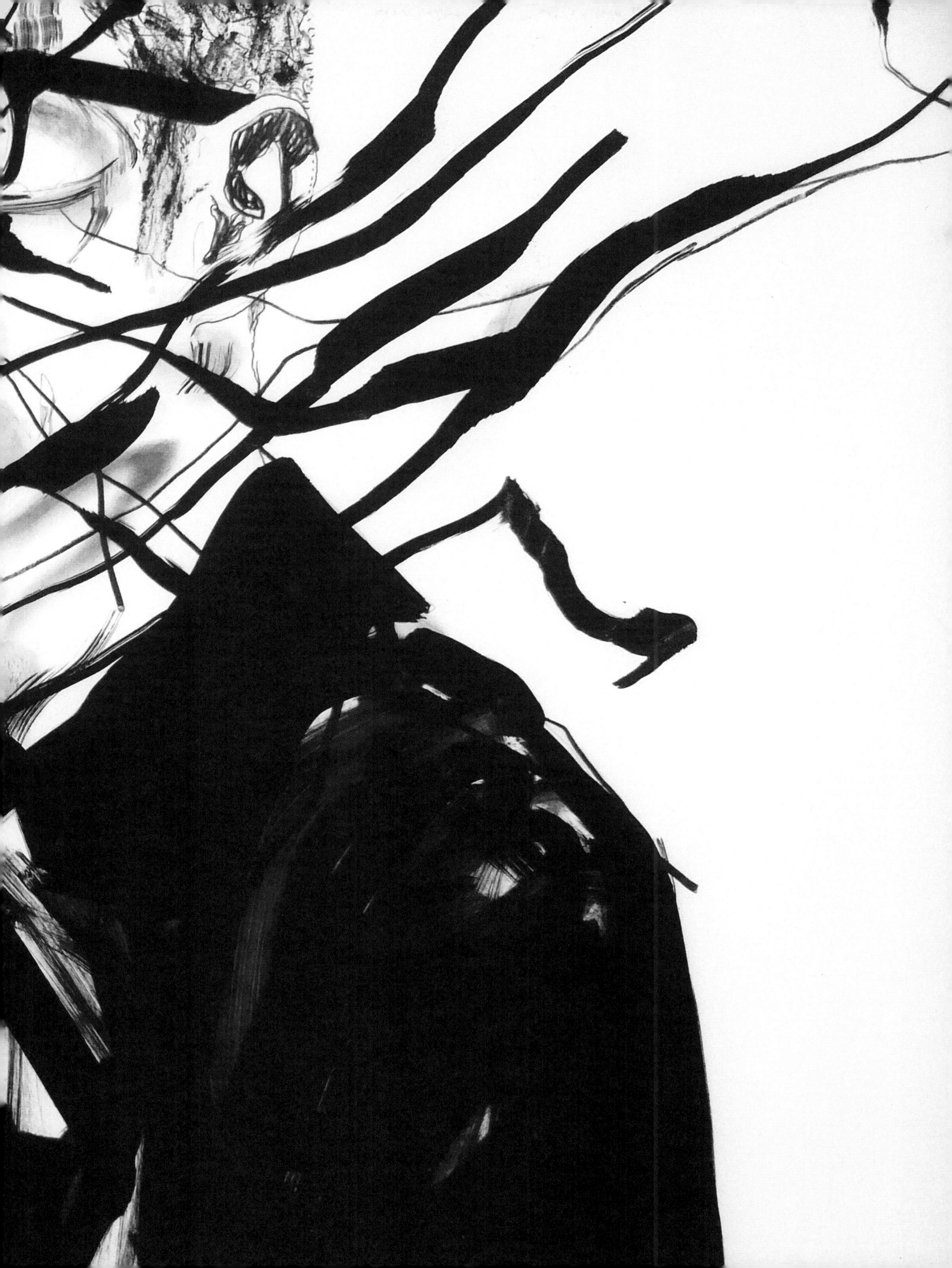

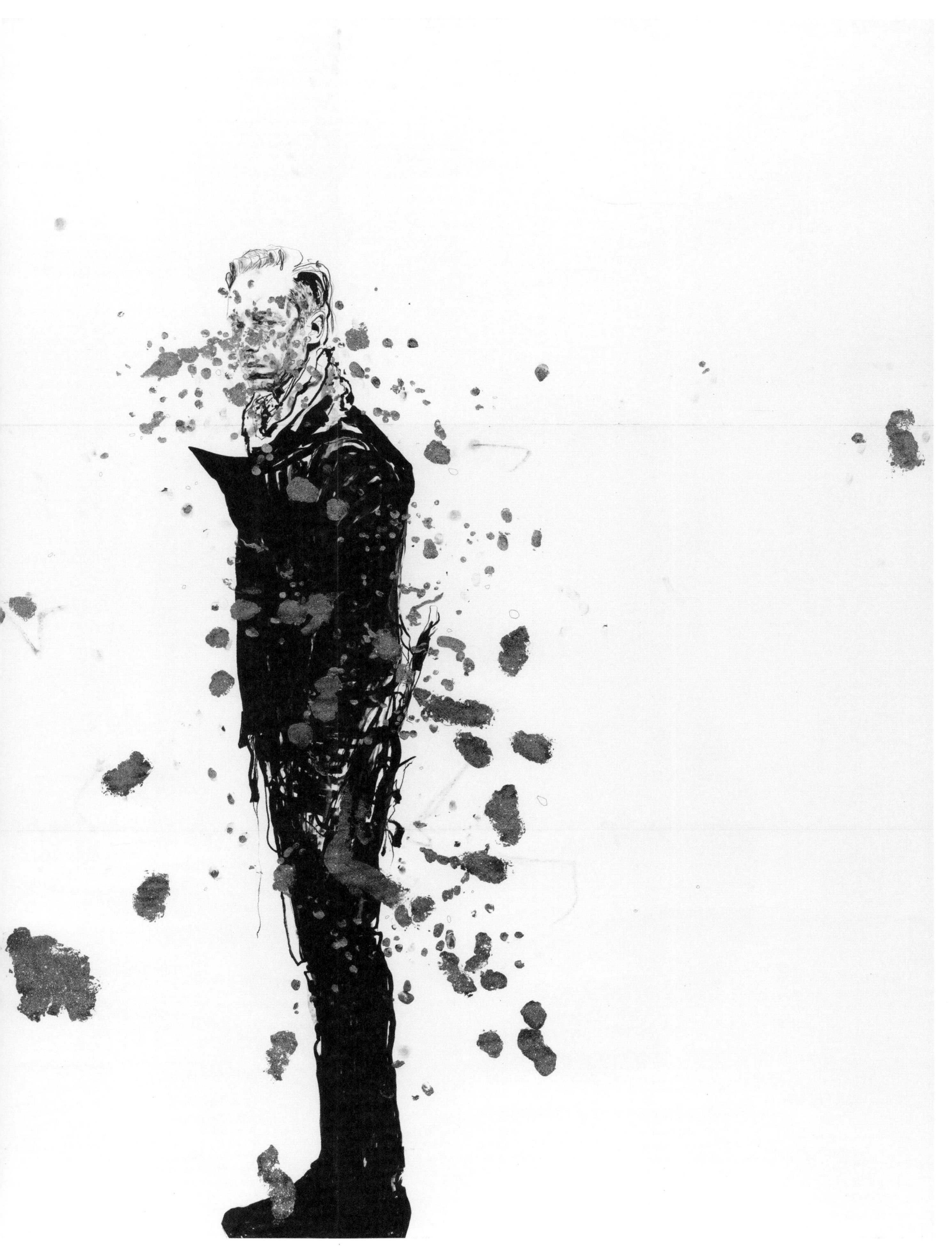

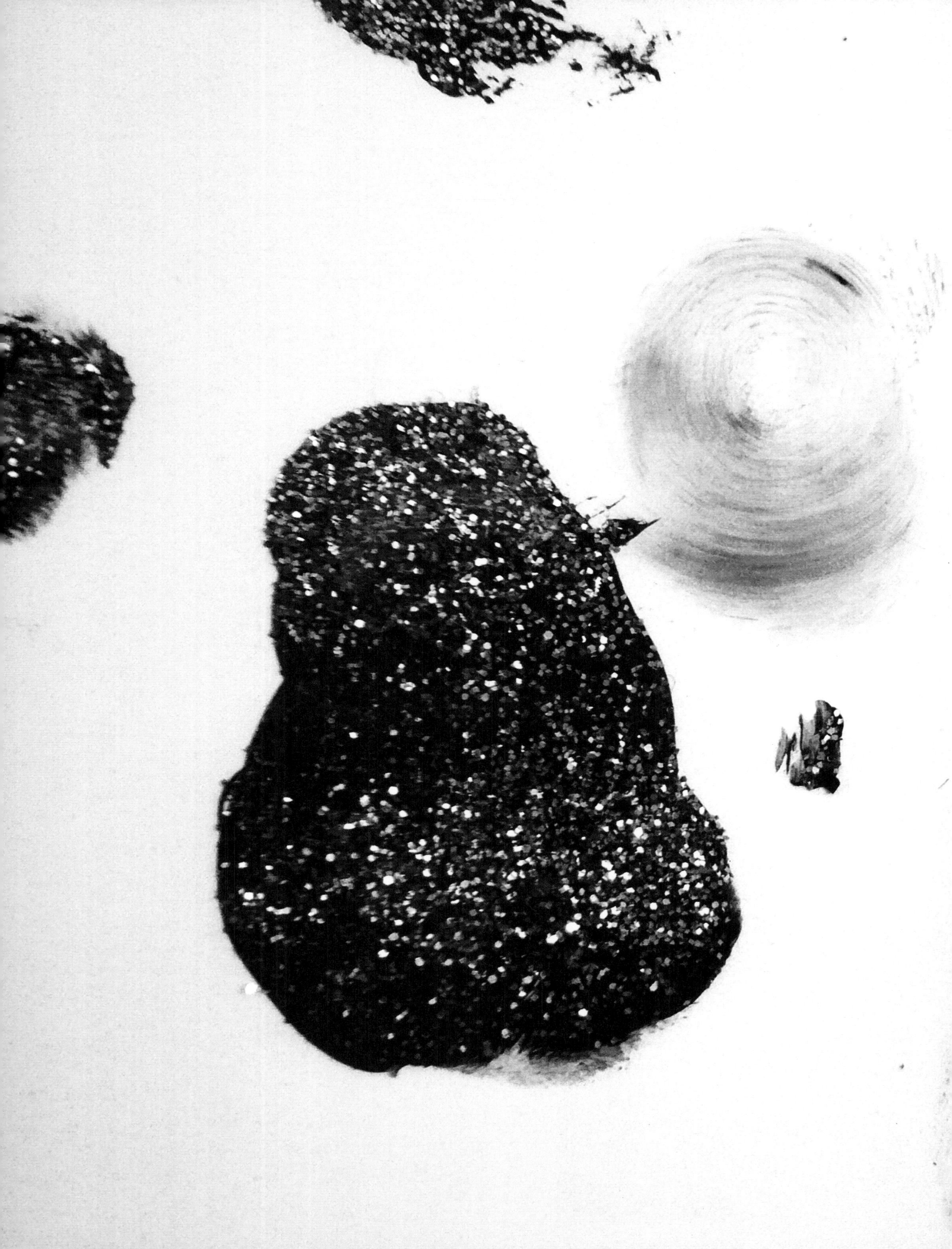

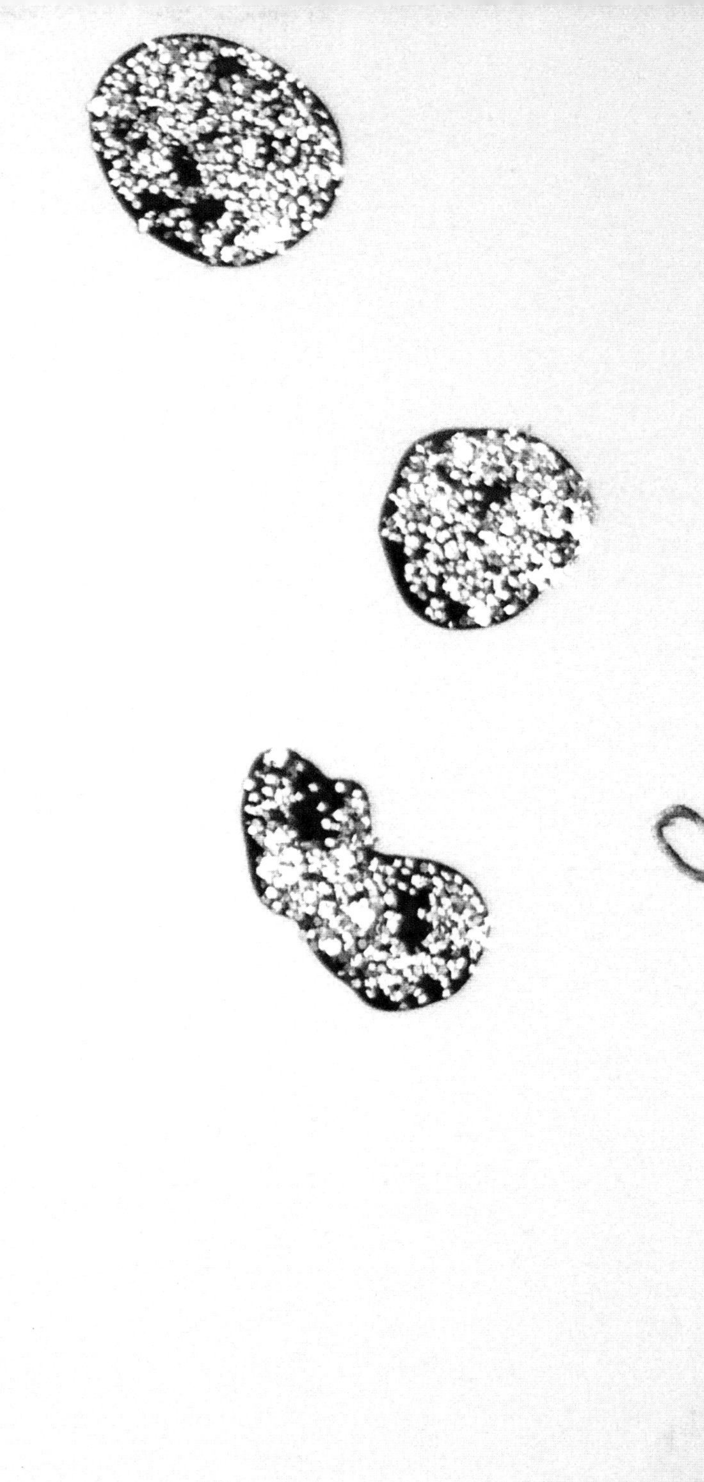
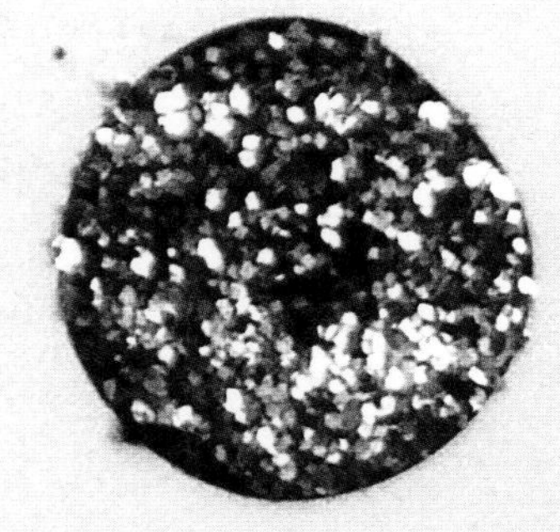

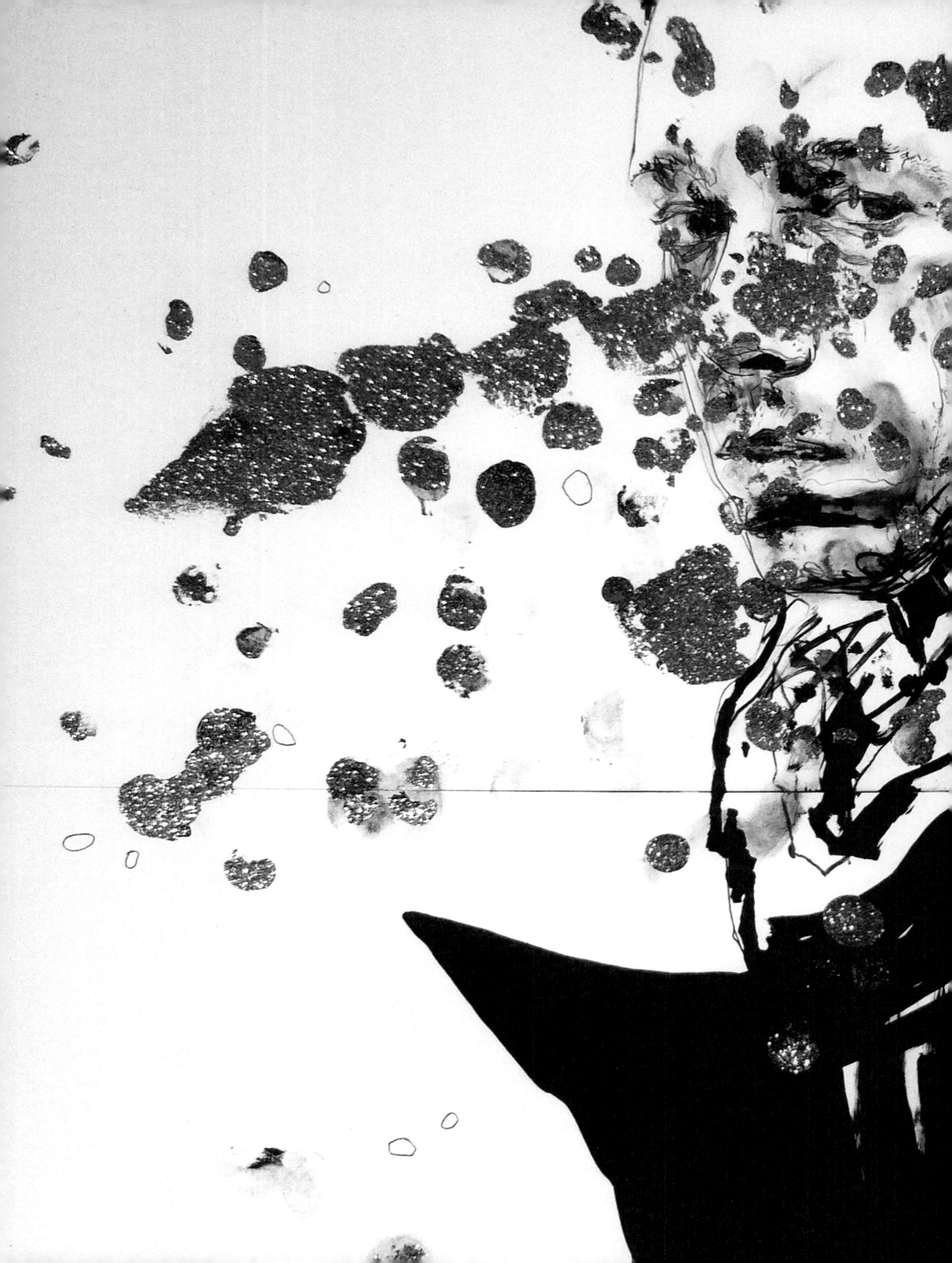

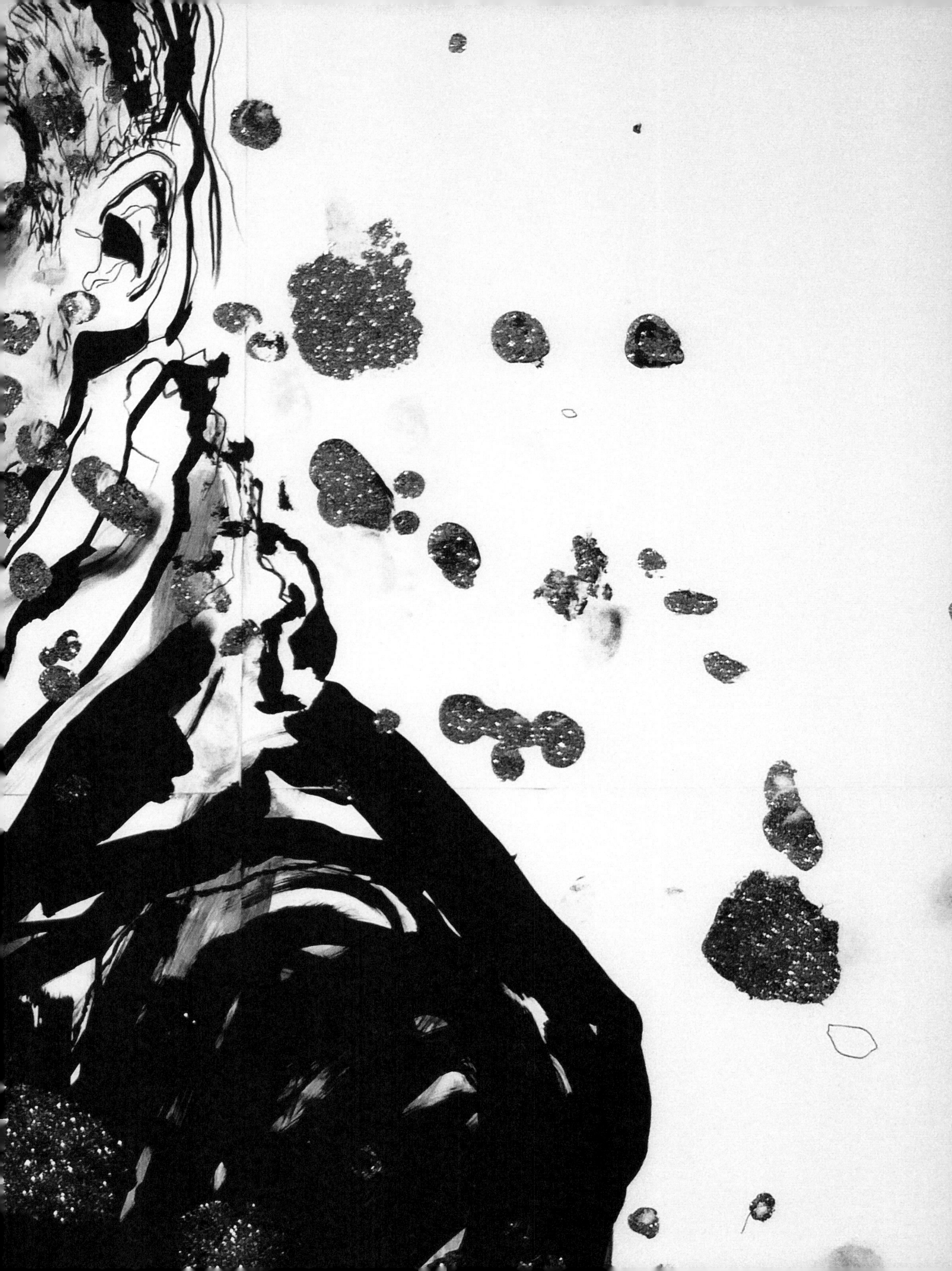

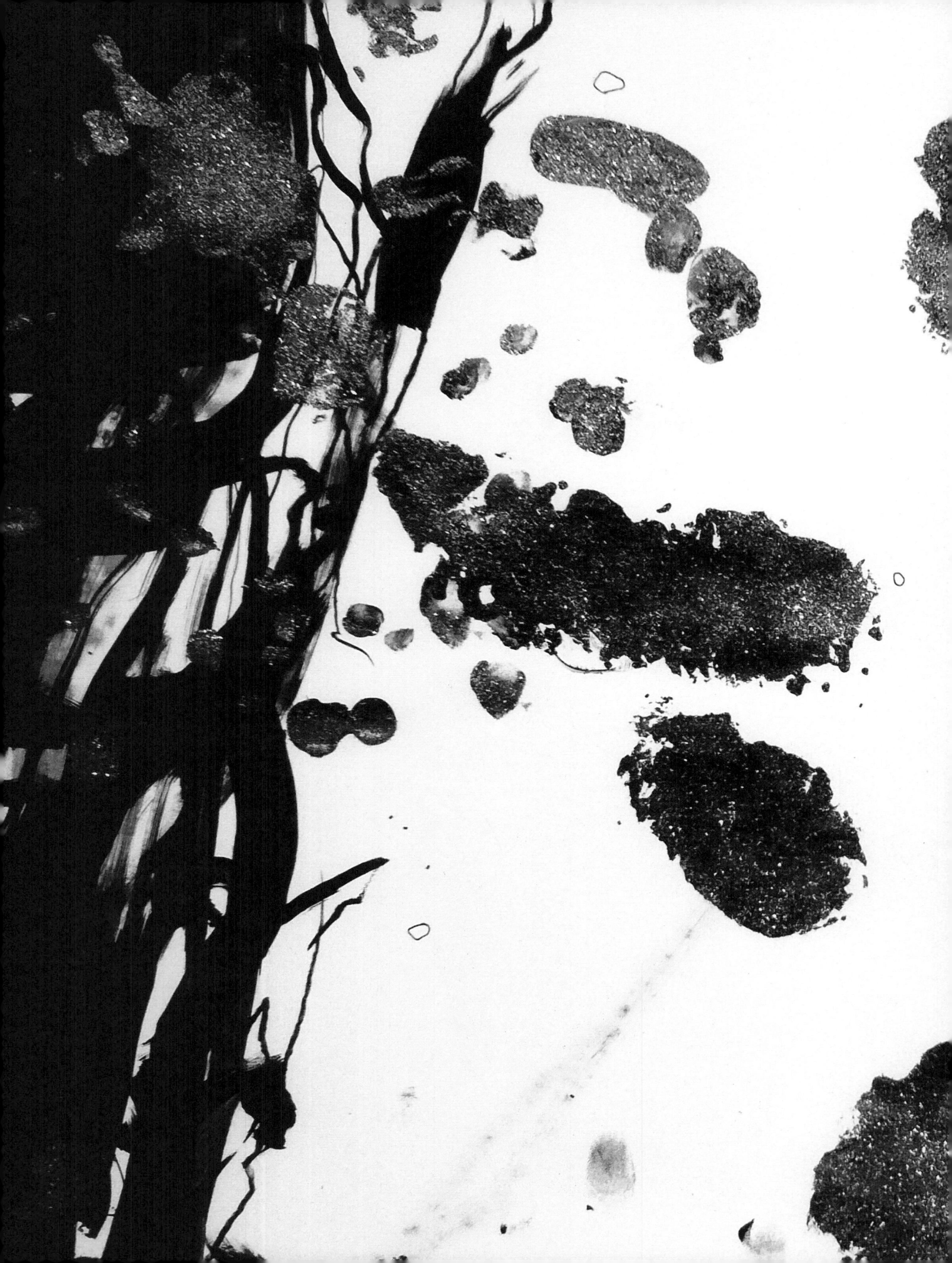

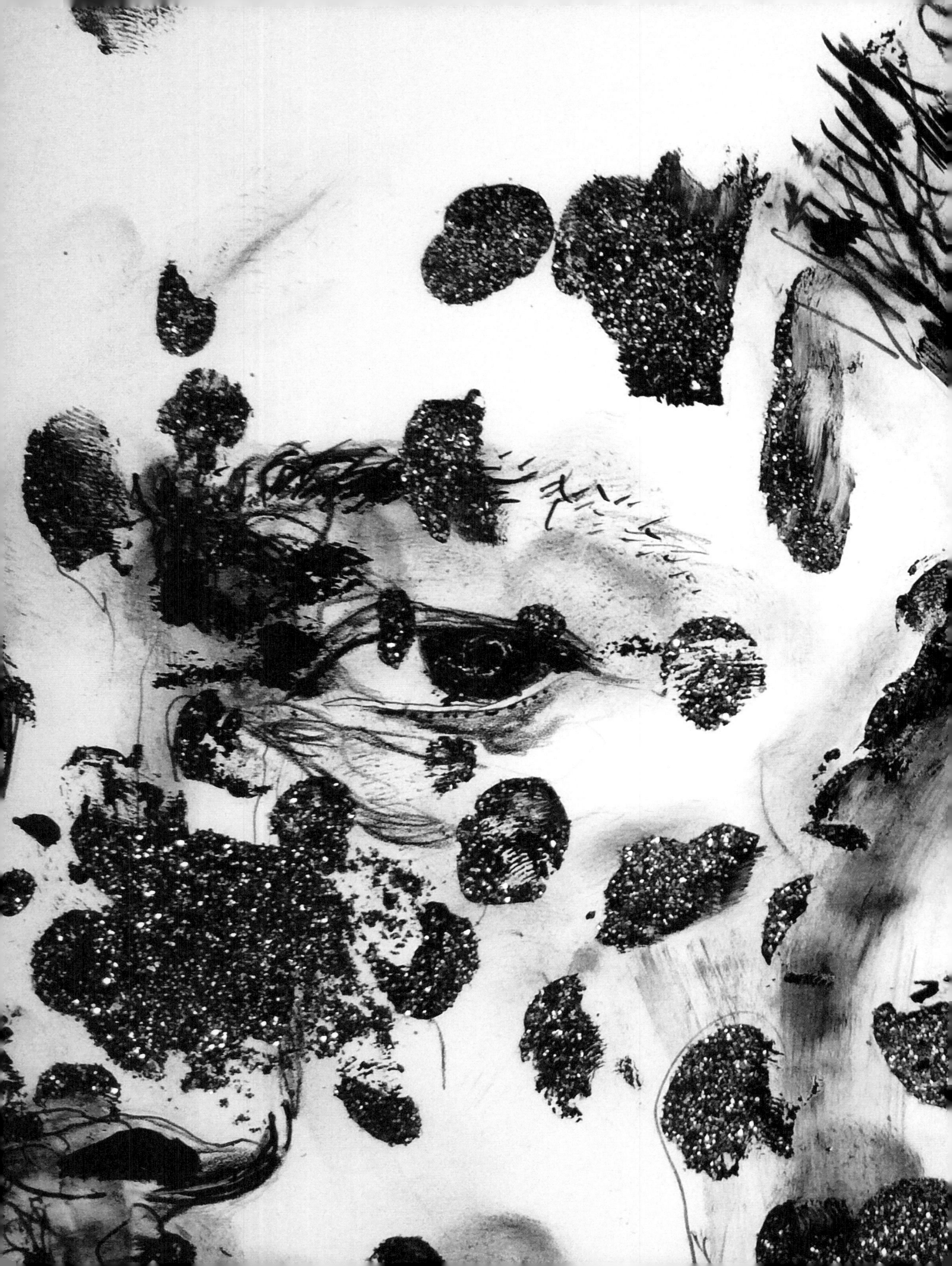

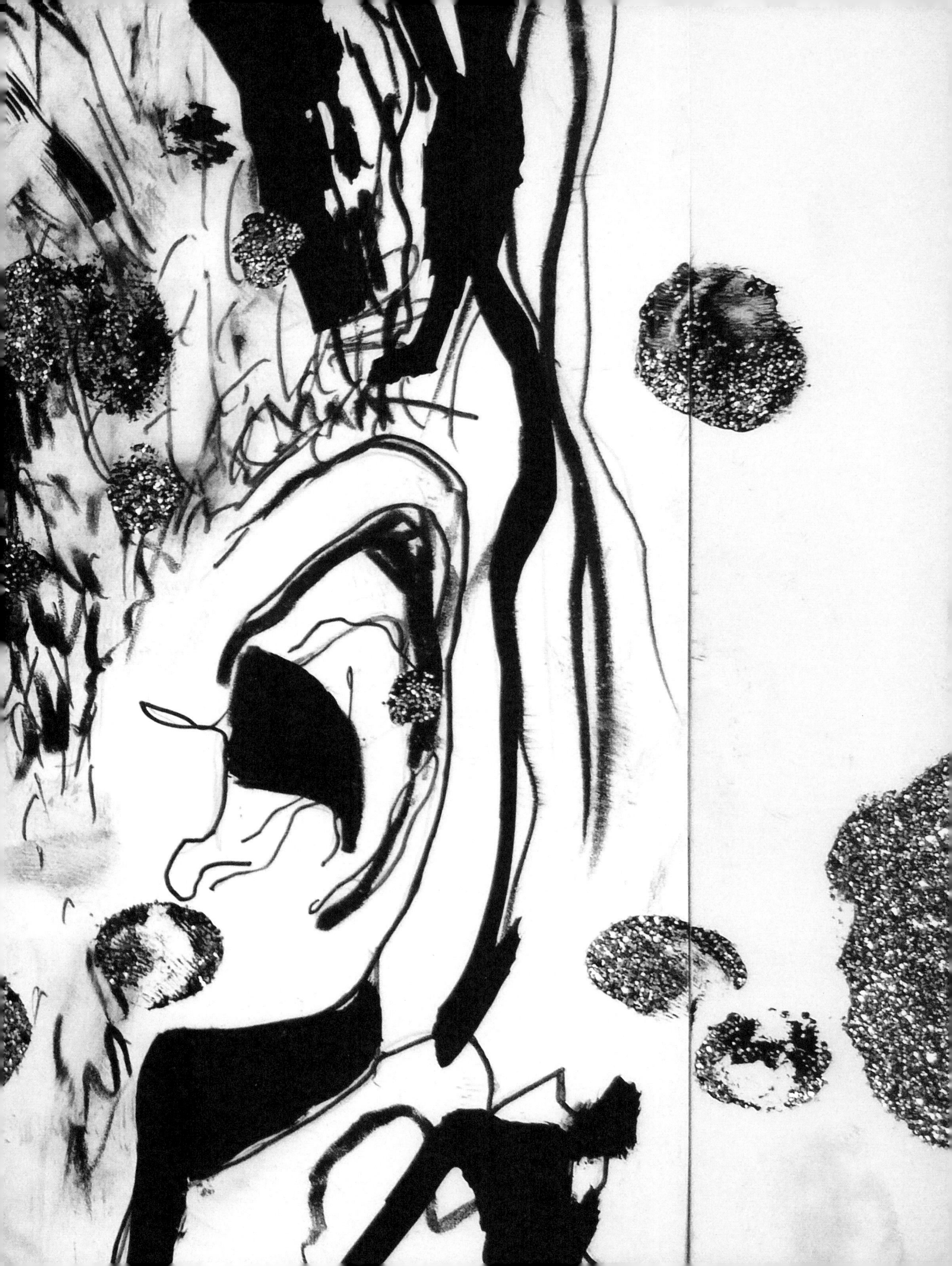

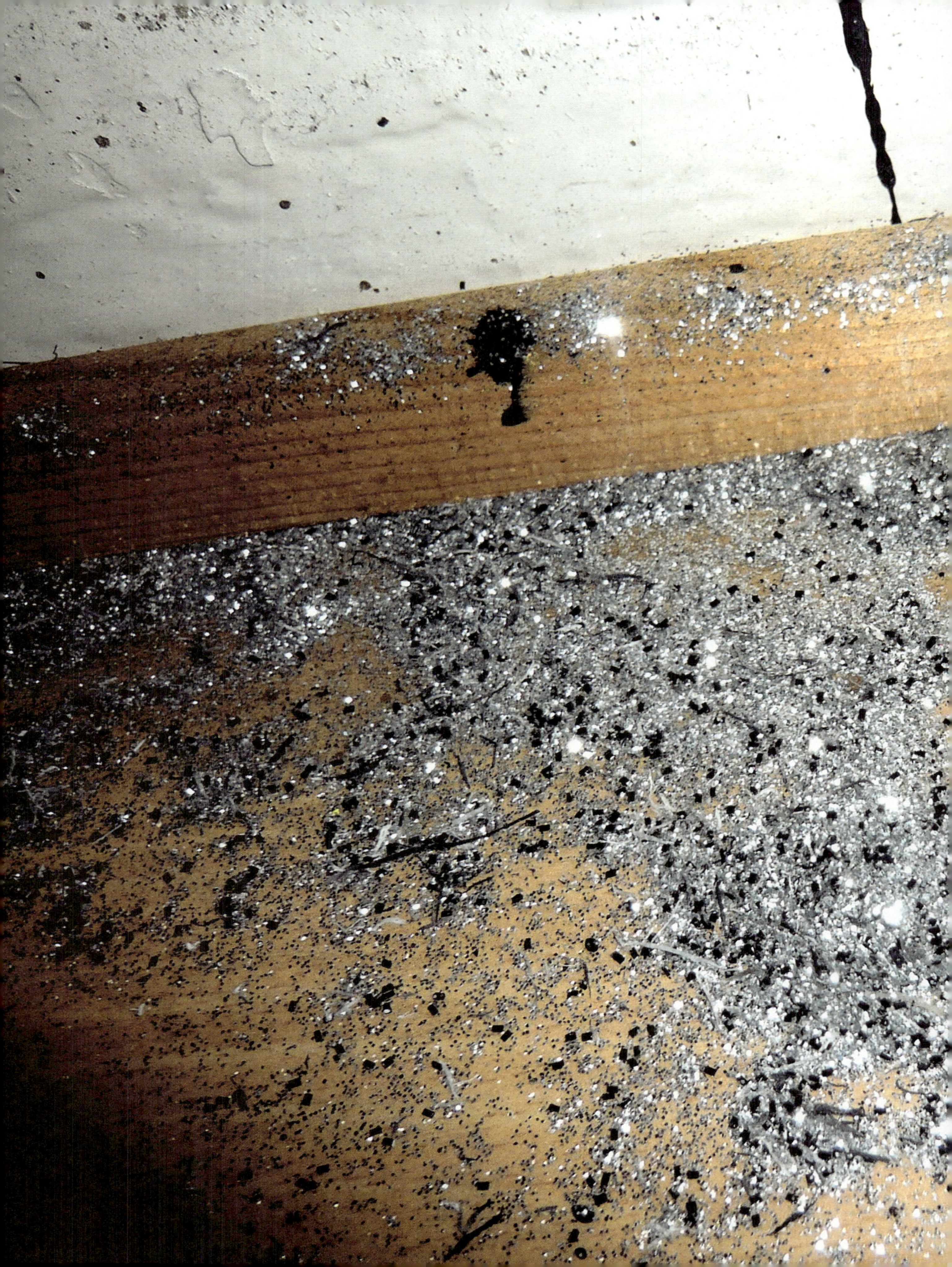

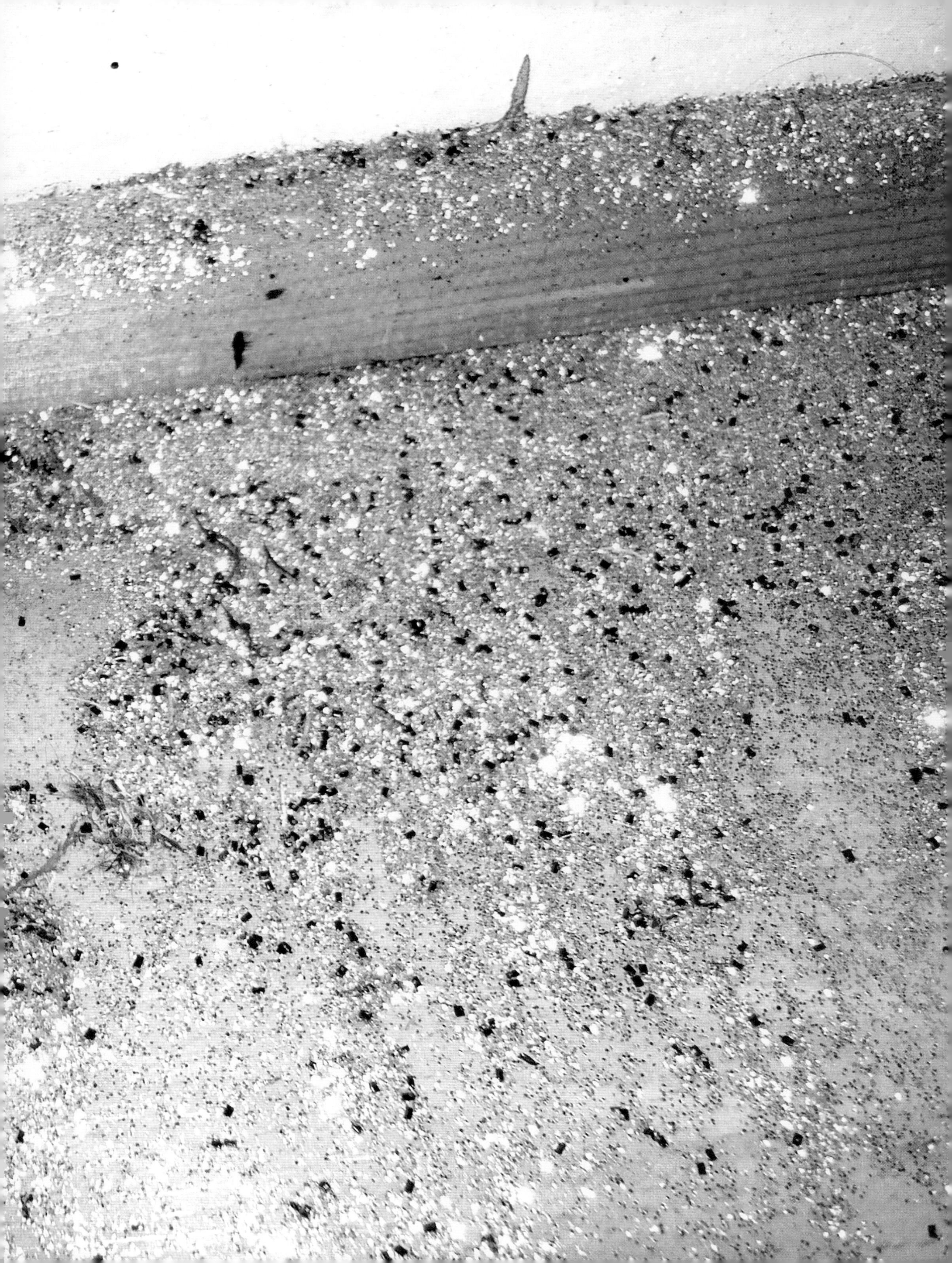

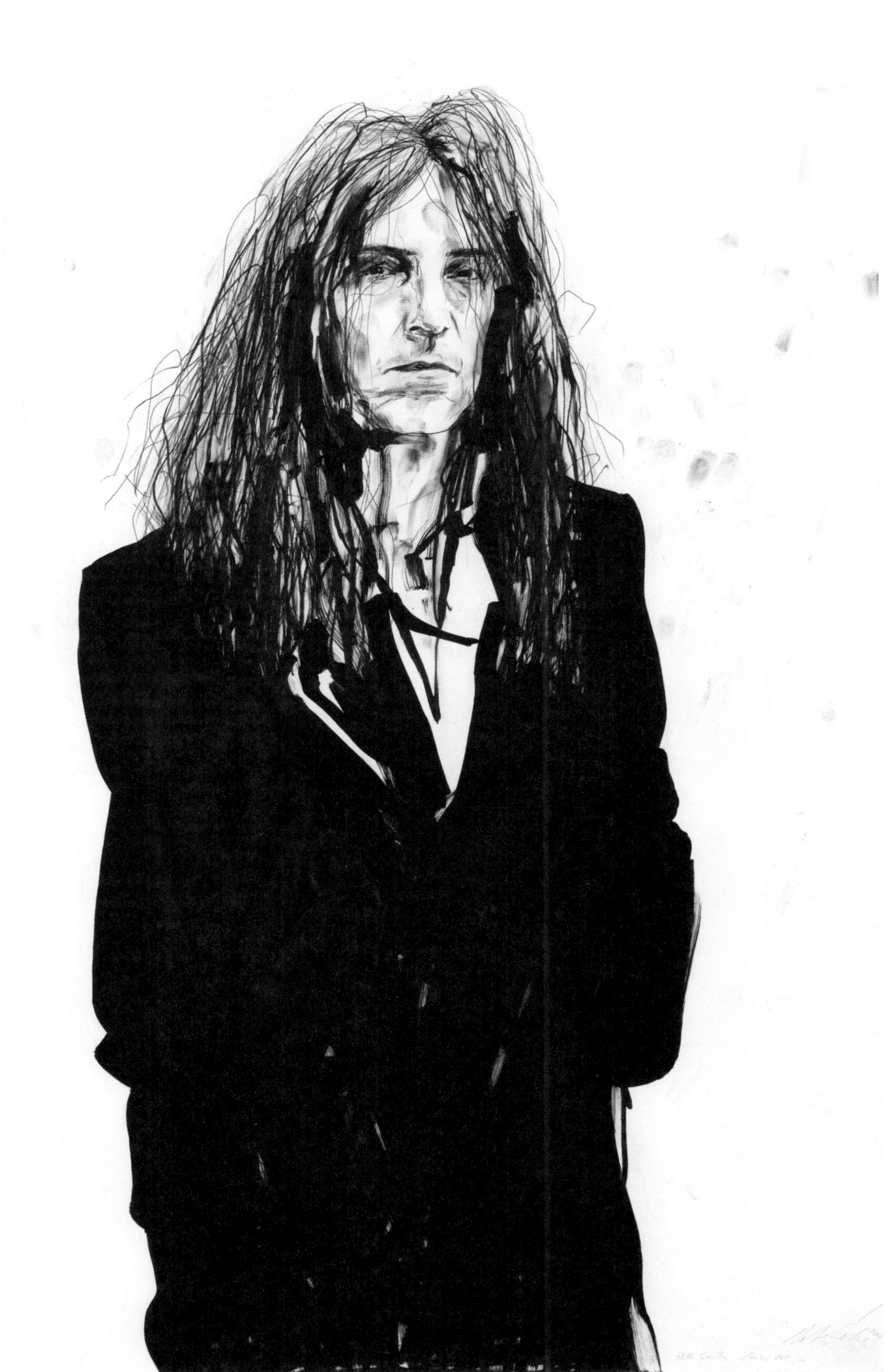

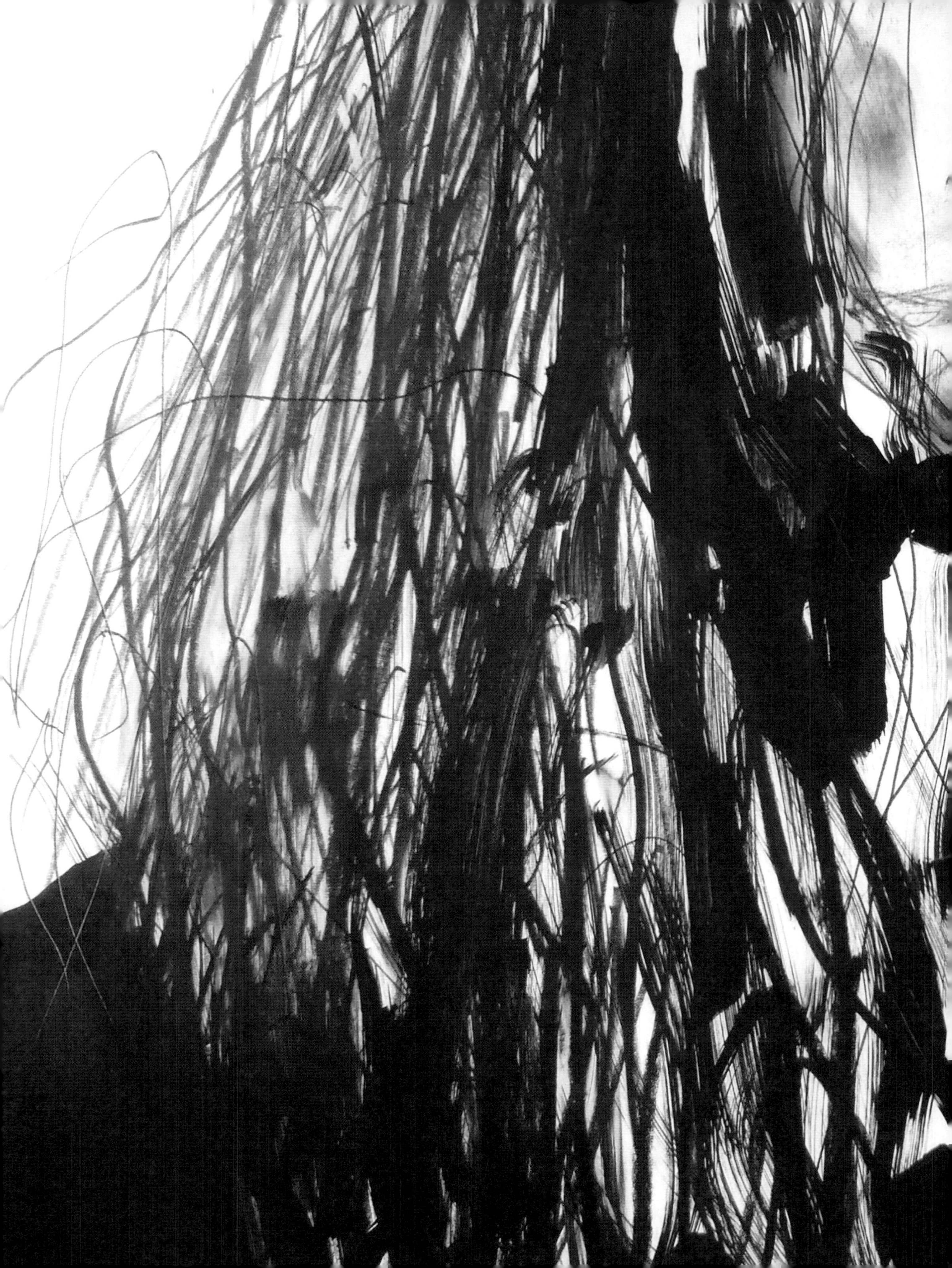

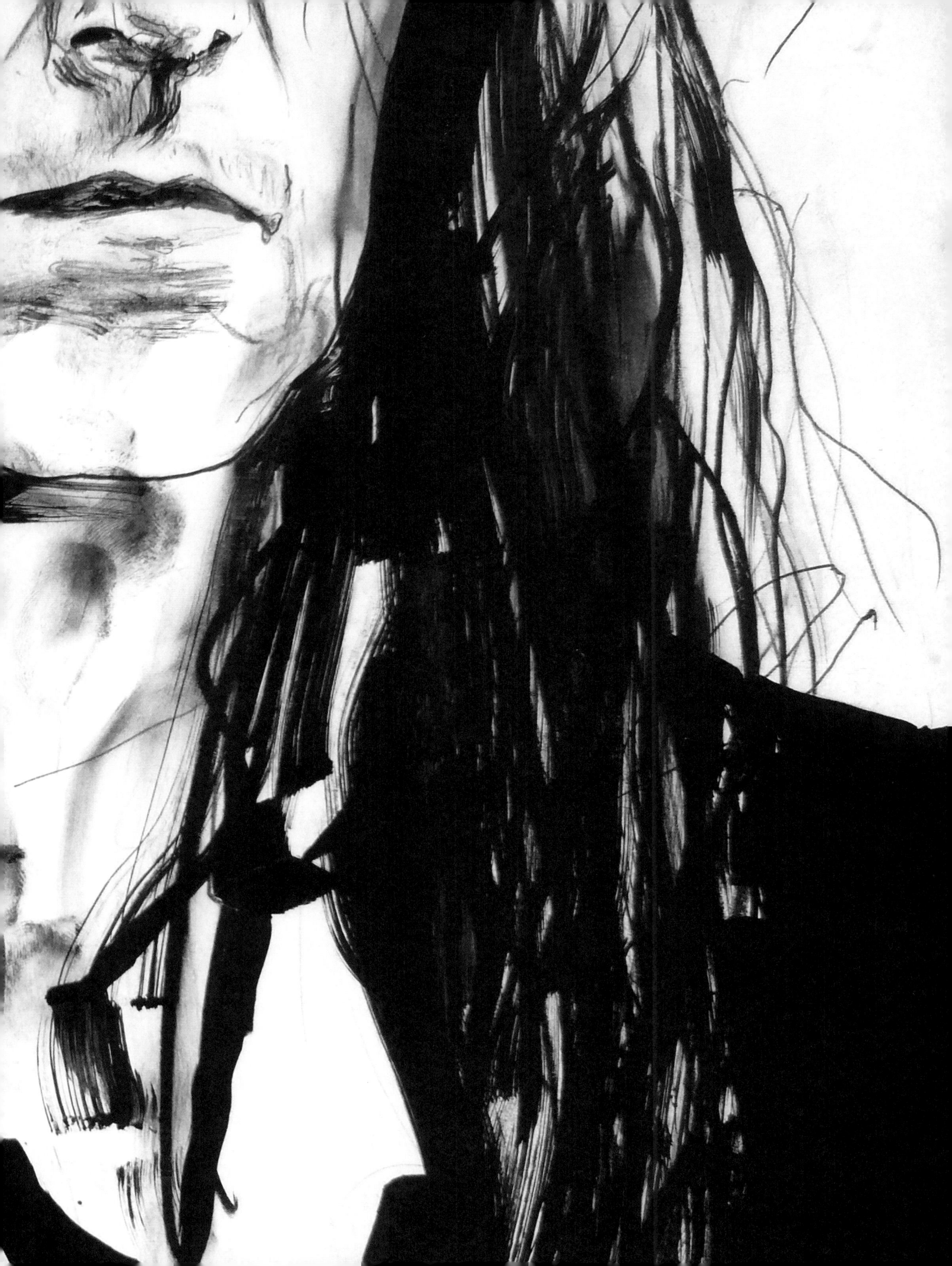

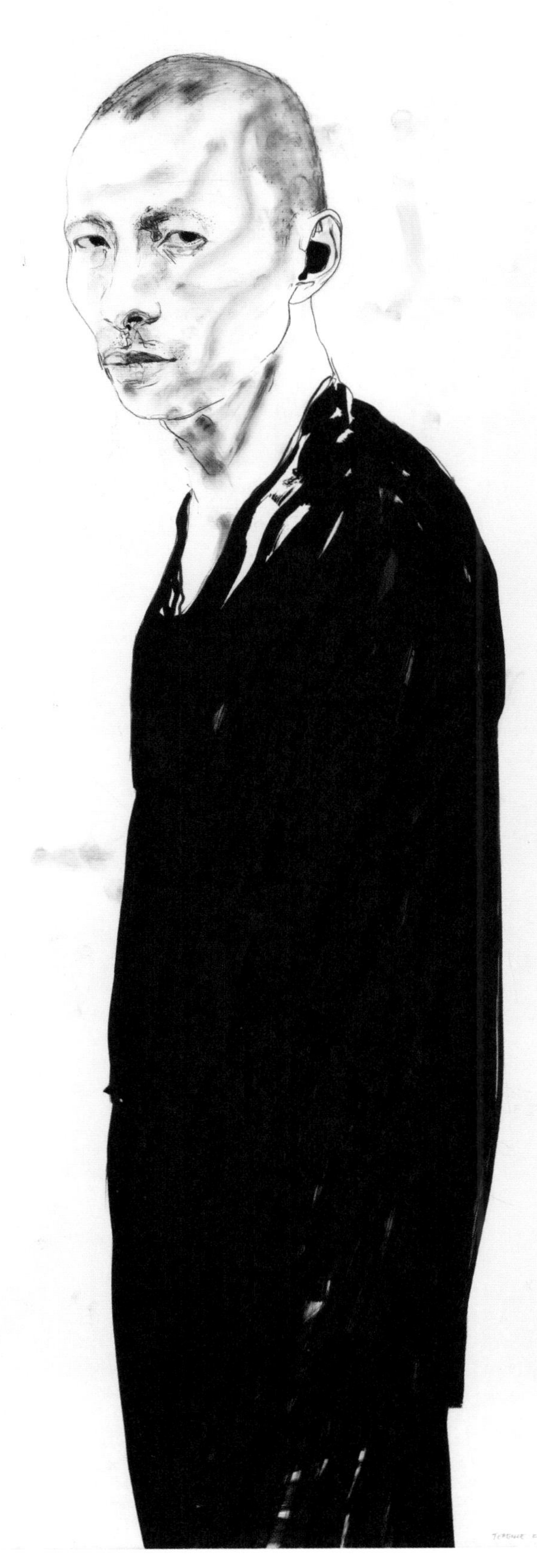

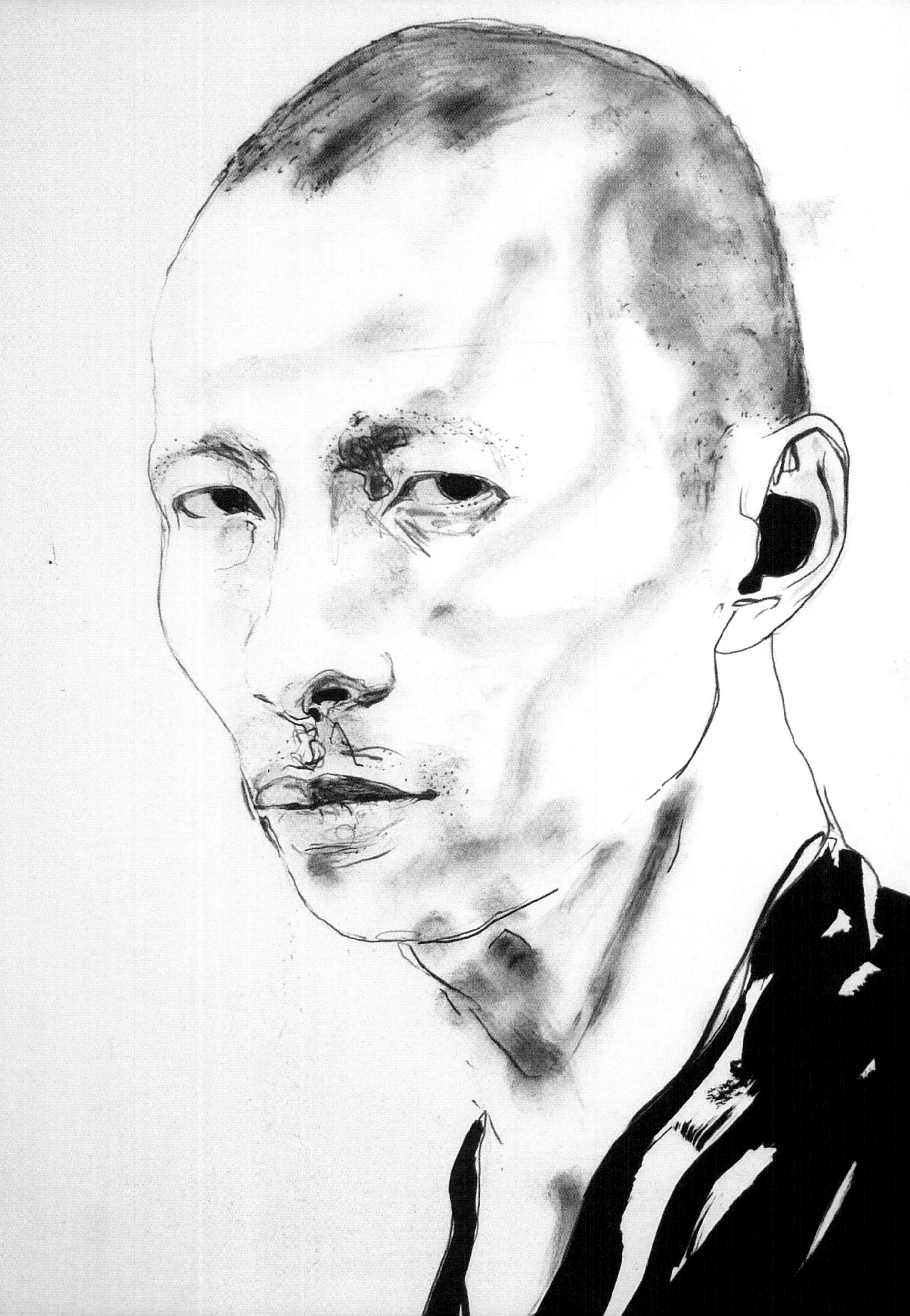

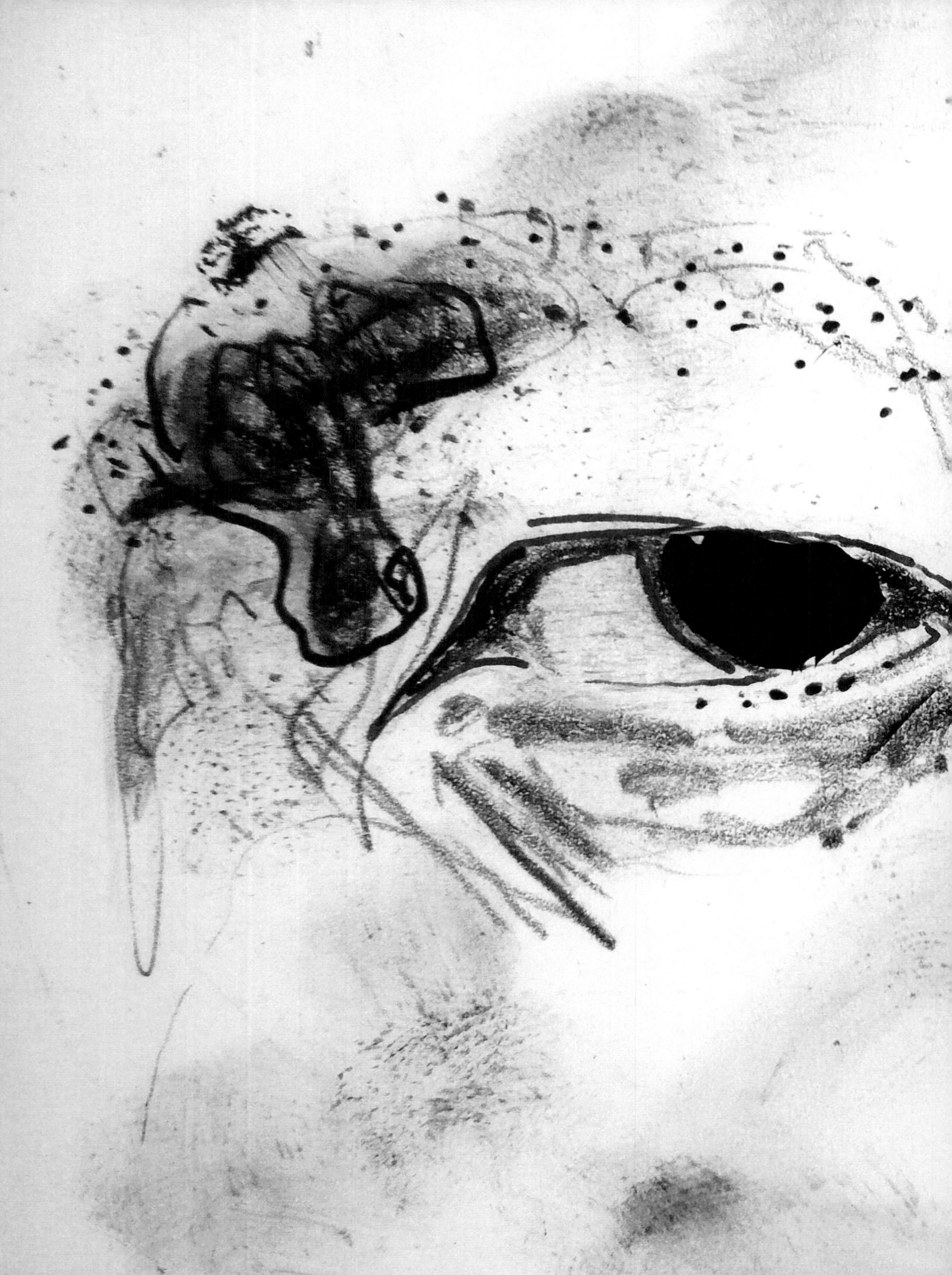

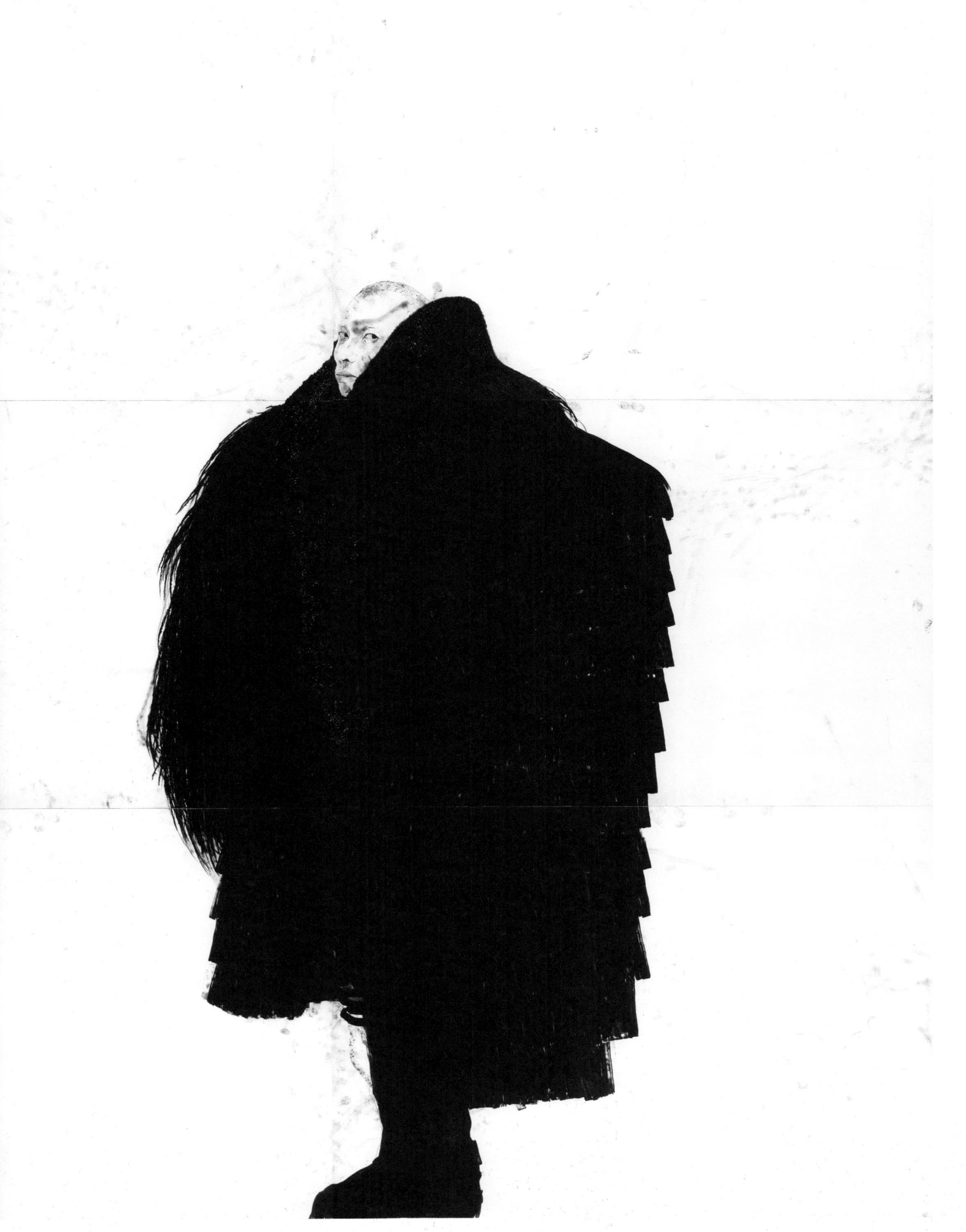

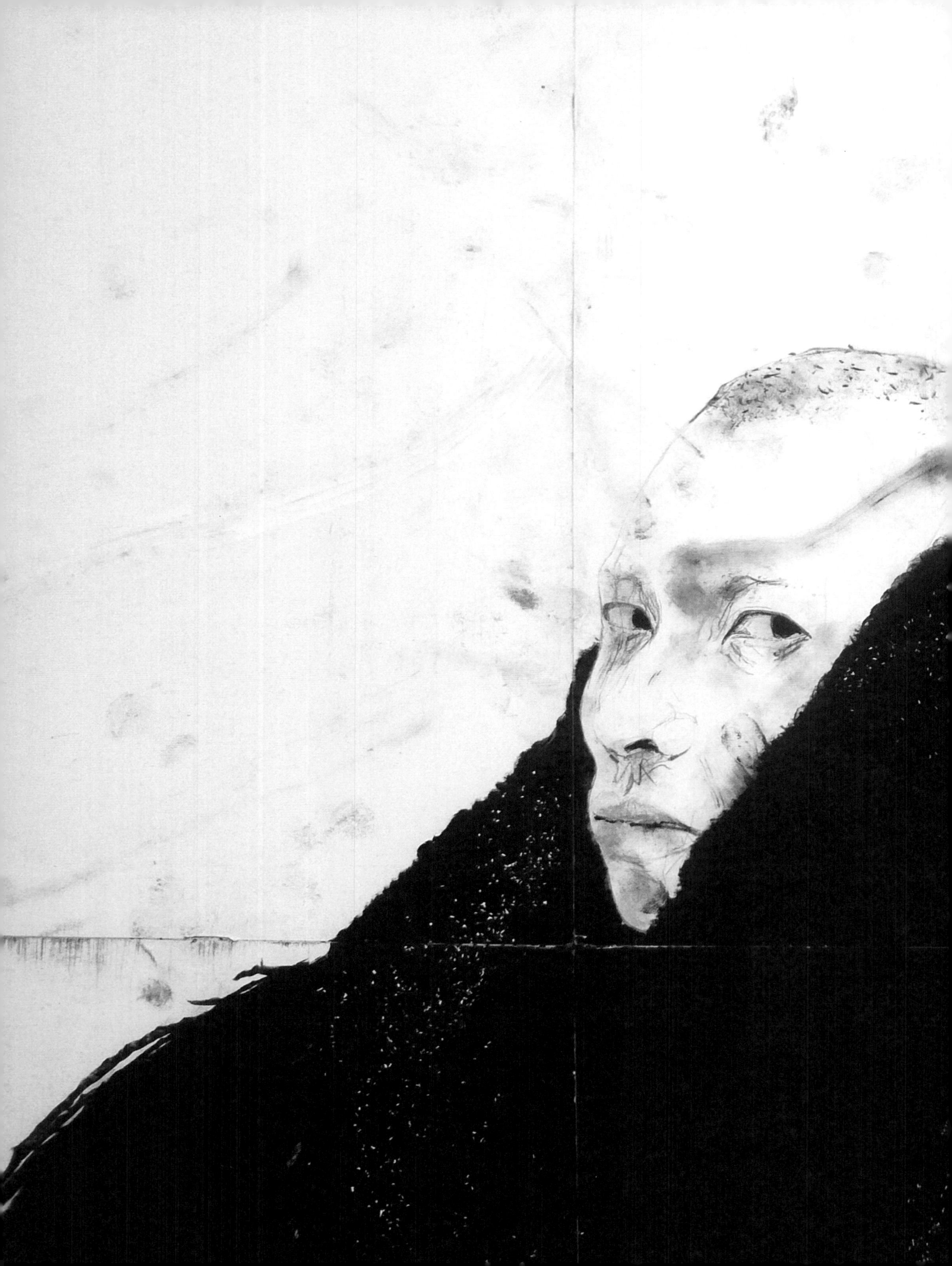

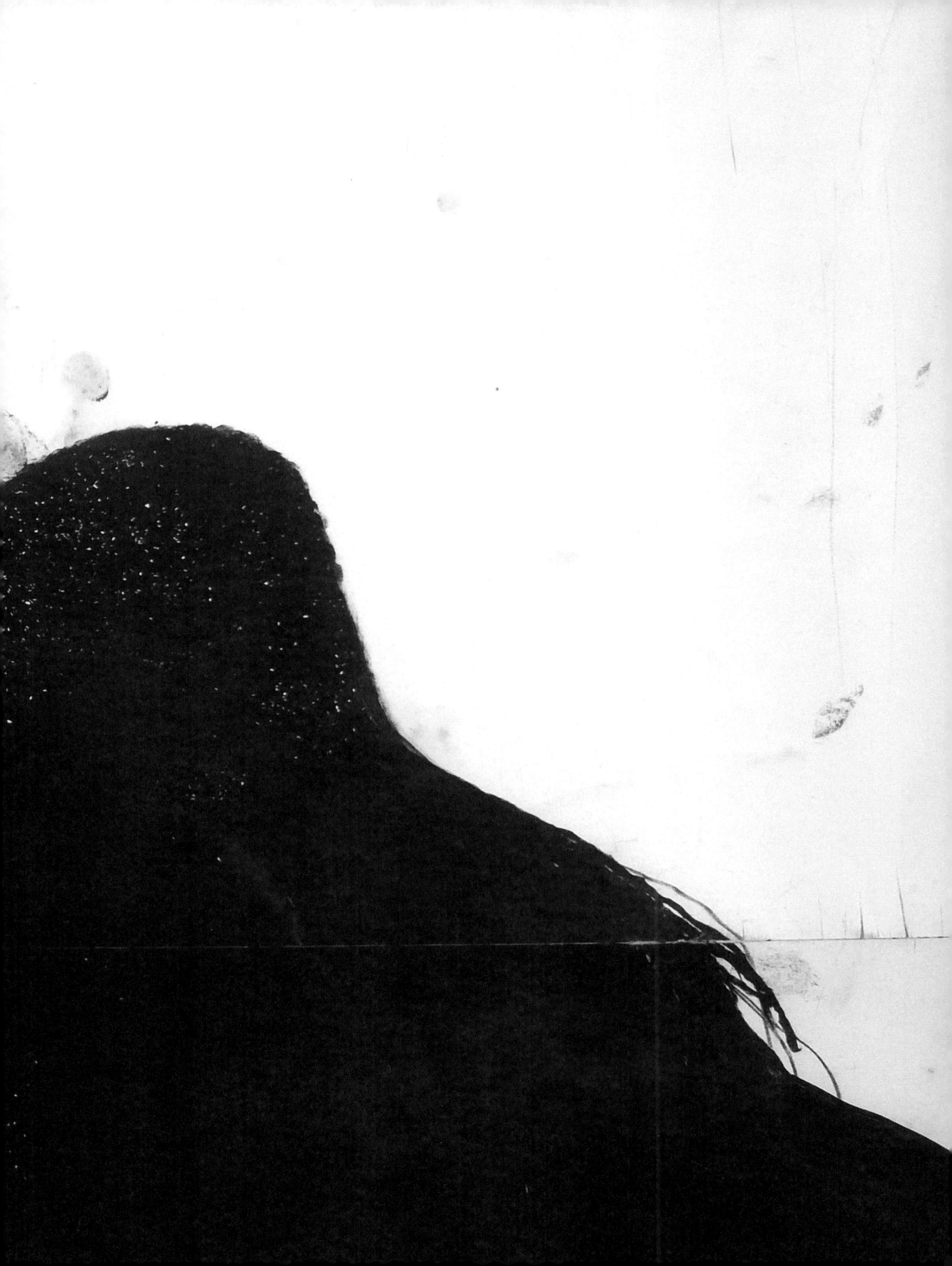

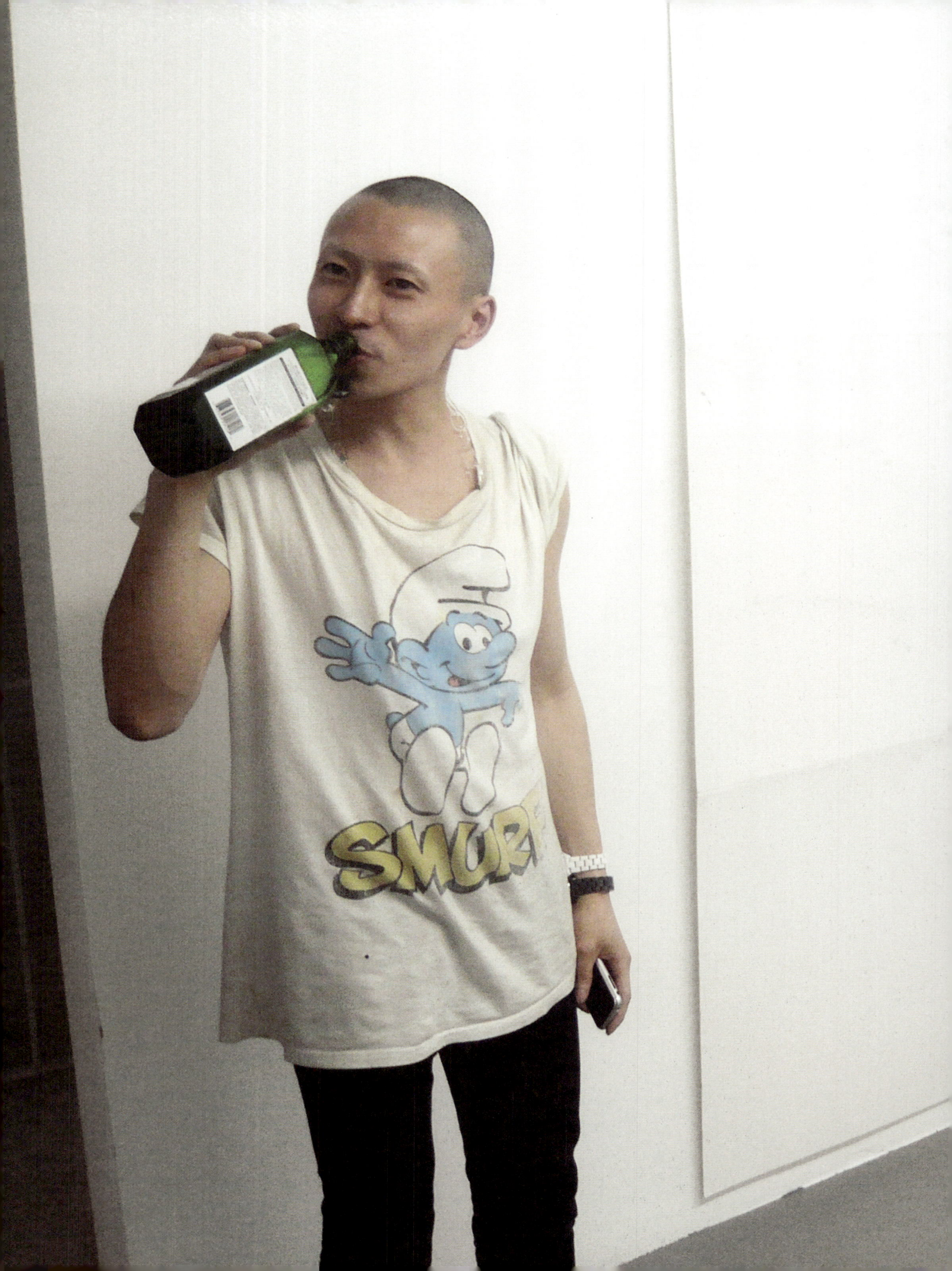

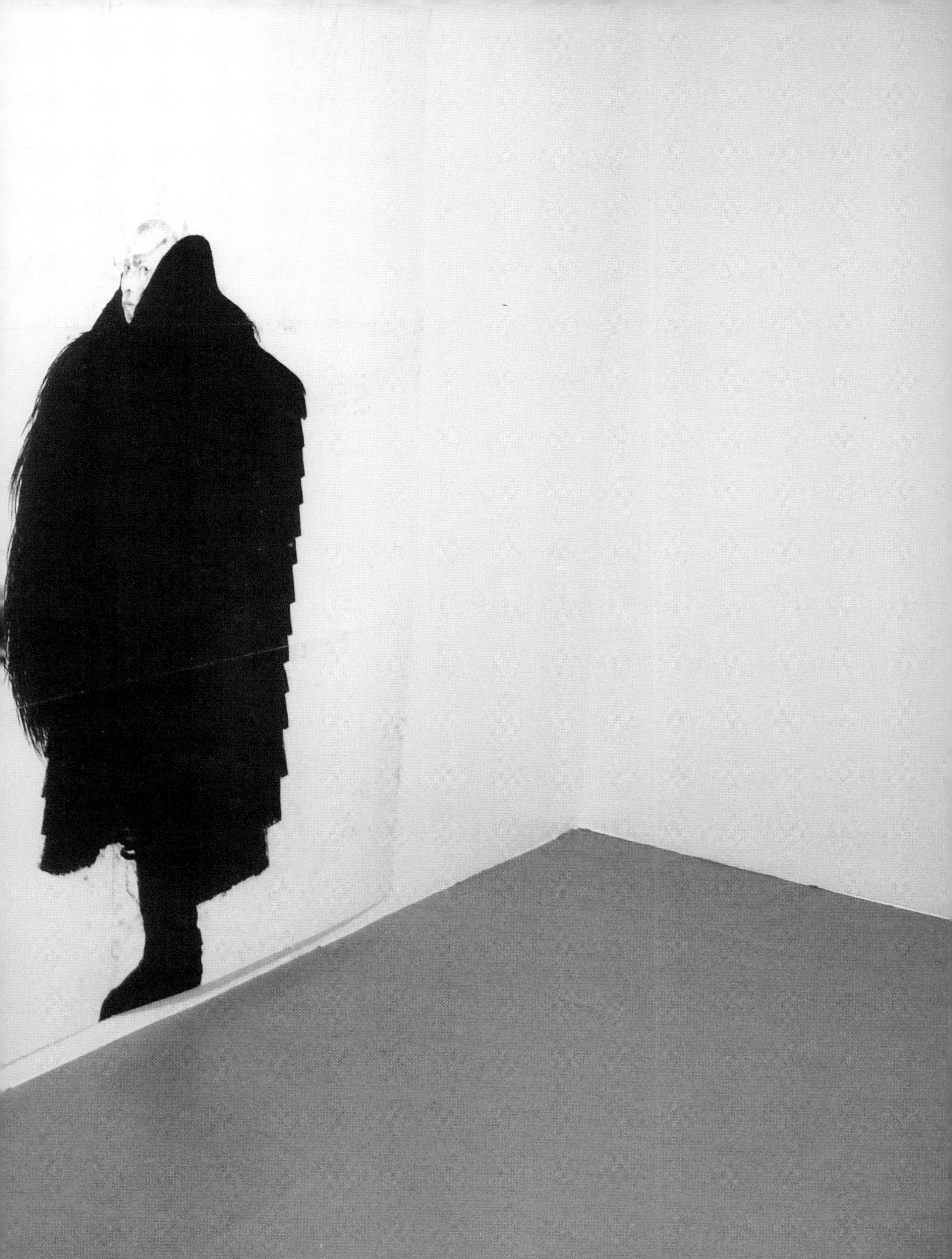

AA BRONSON (VERSION II)
NEW YORK, 2008

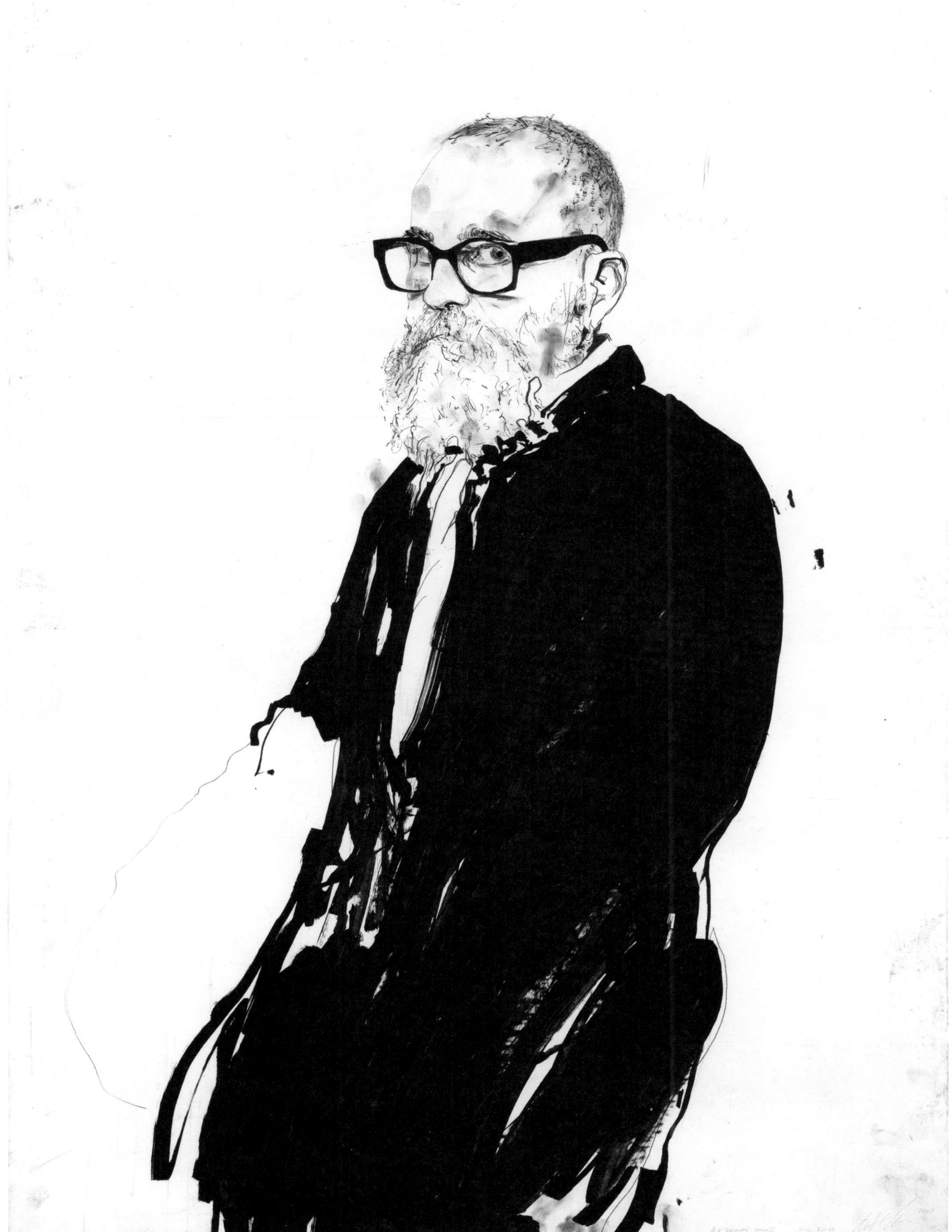

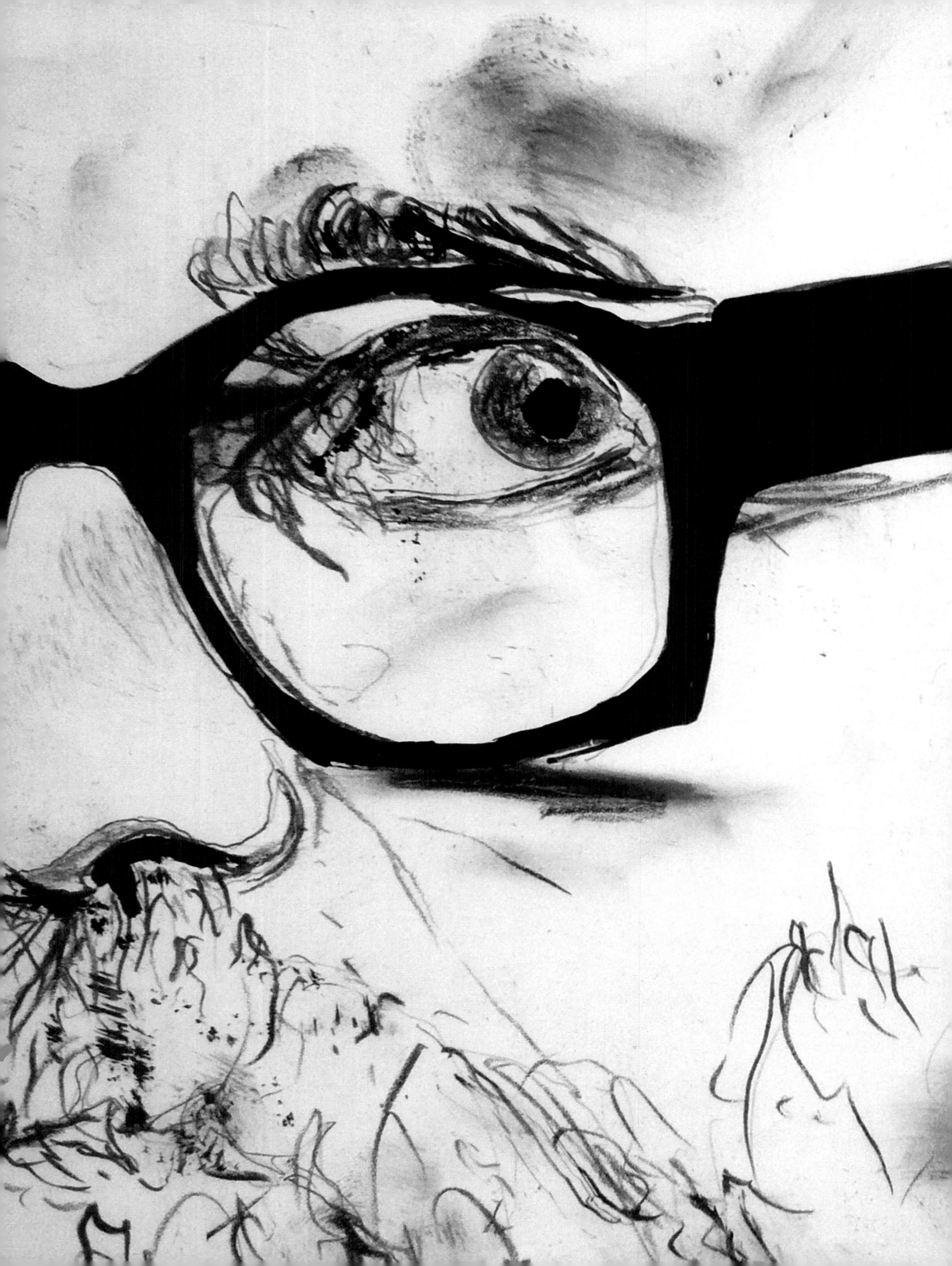

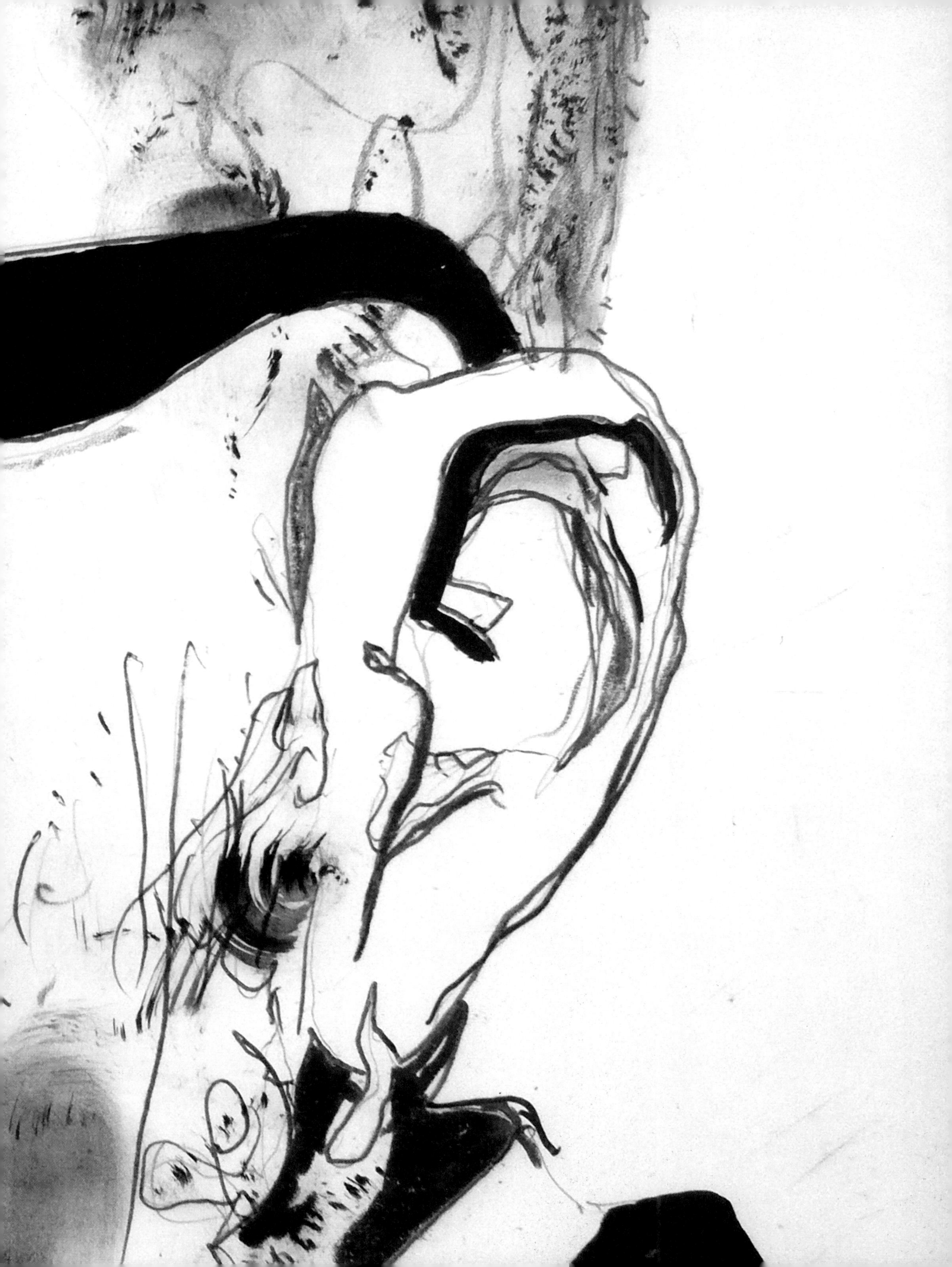

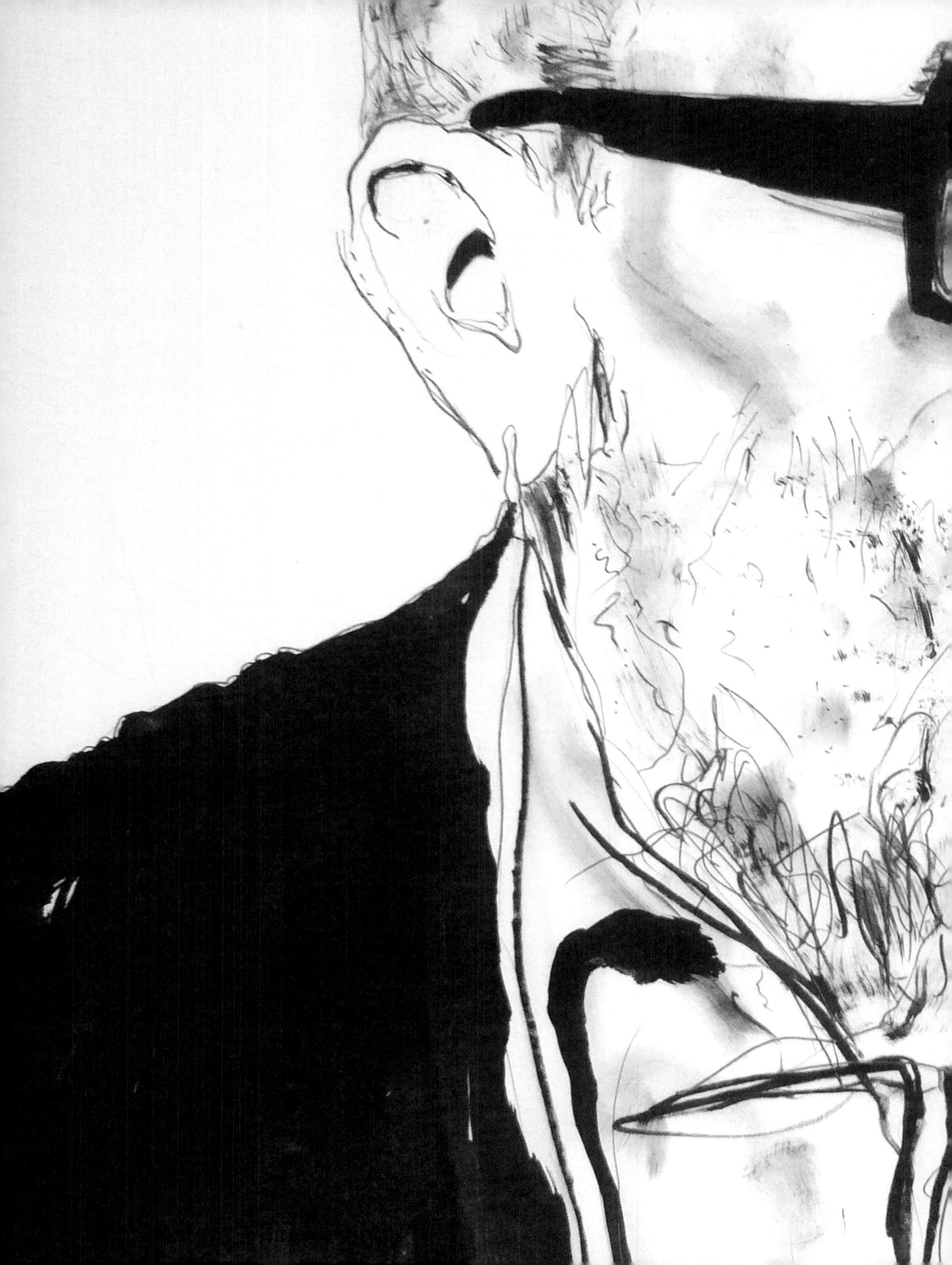

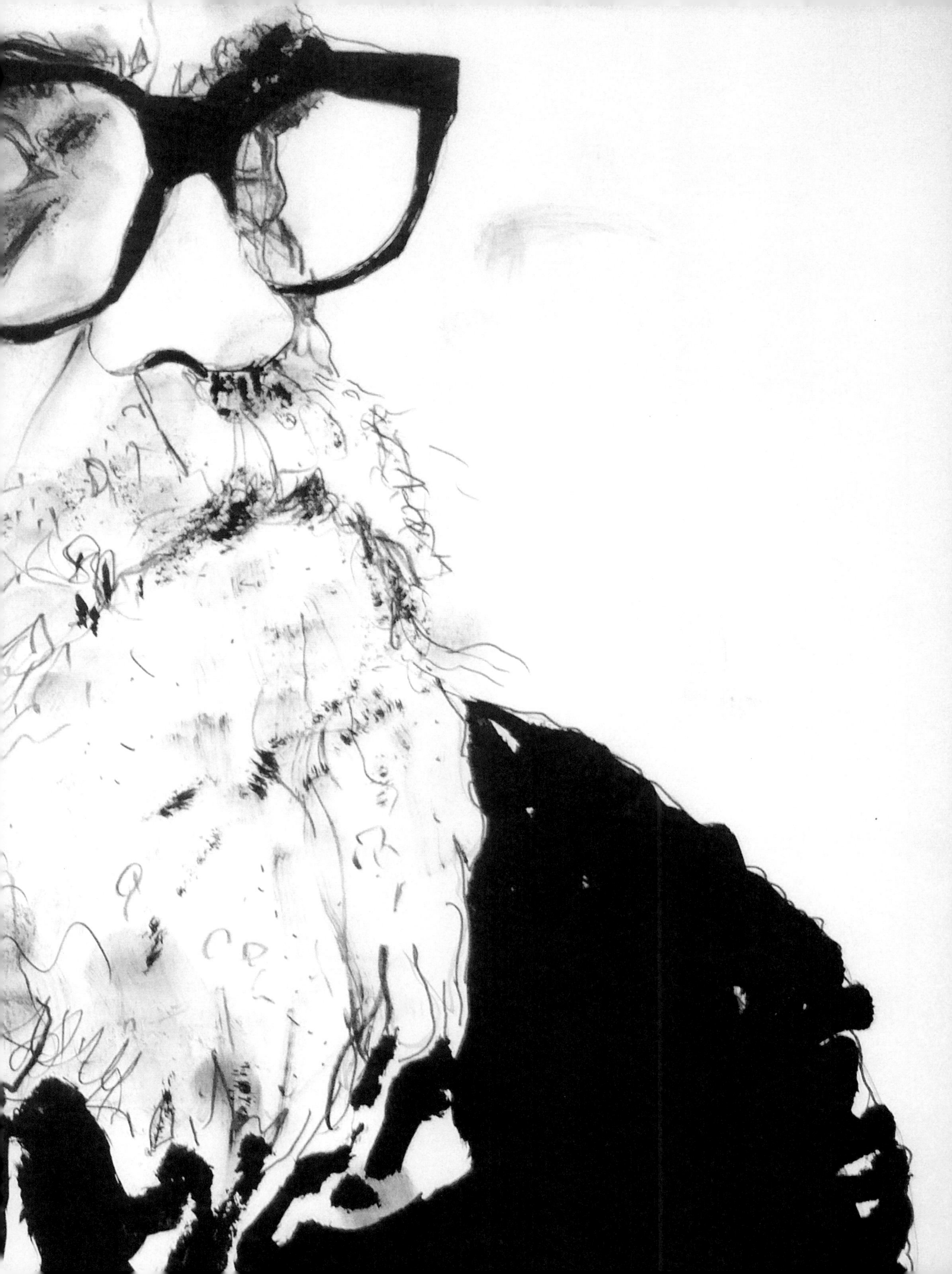

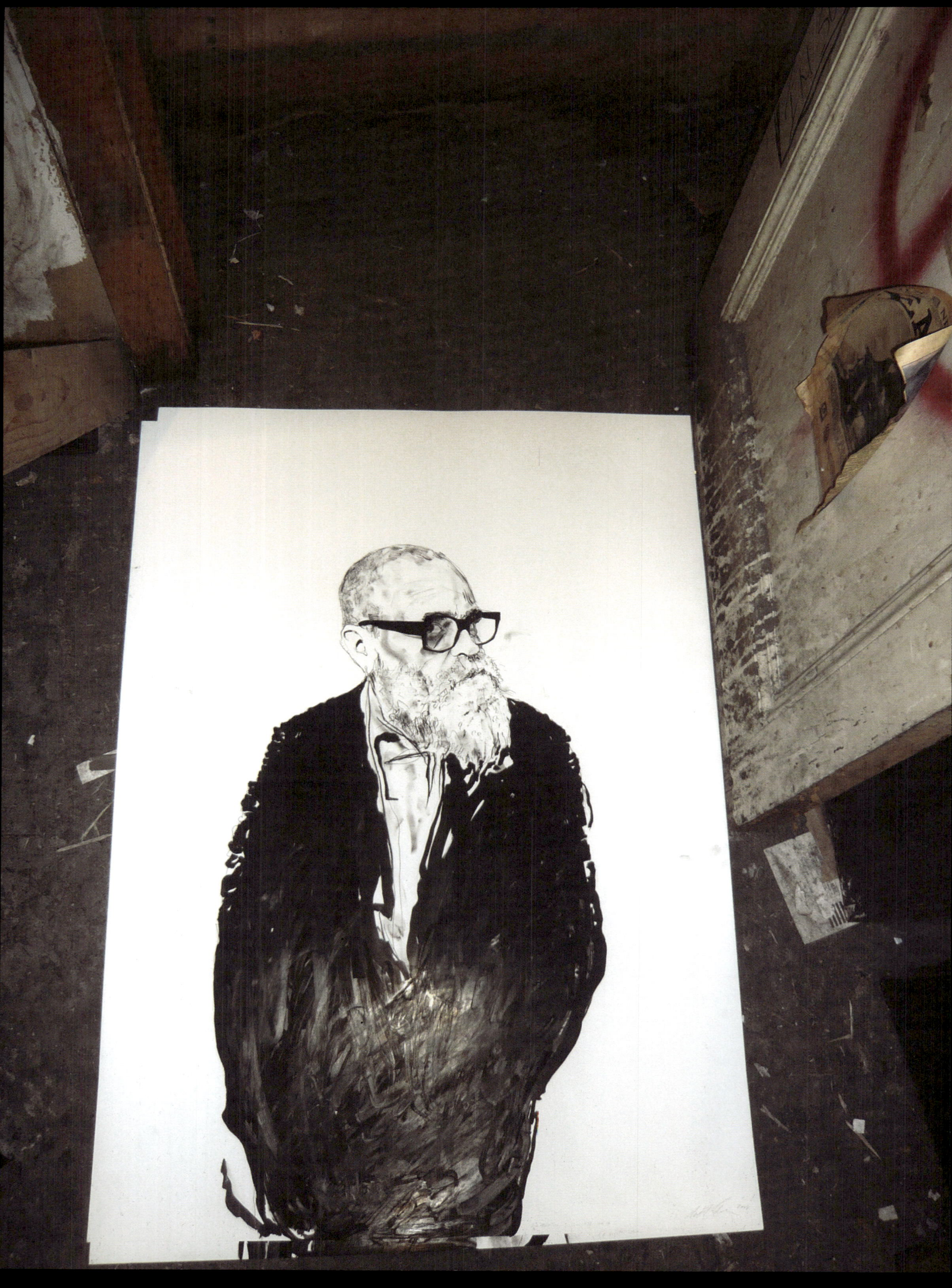

ALISON MOSSHART
NEW YORK, 2007

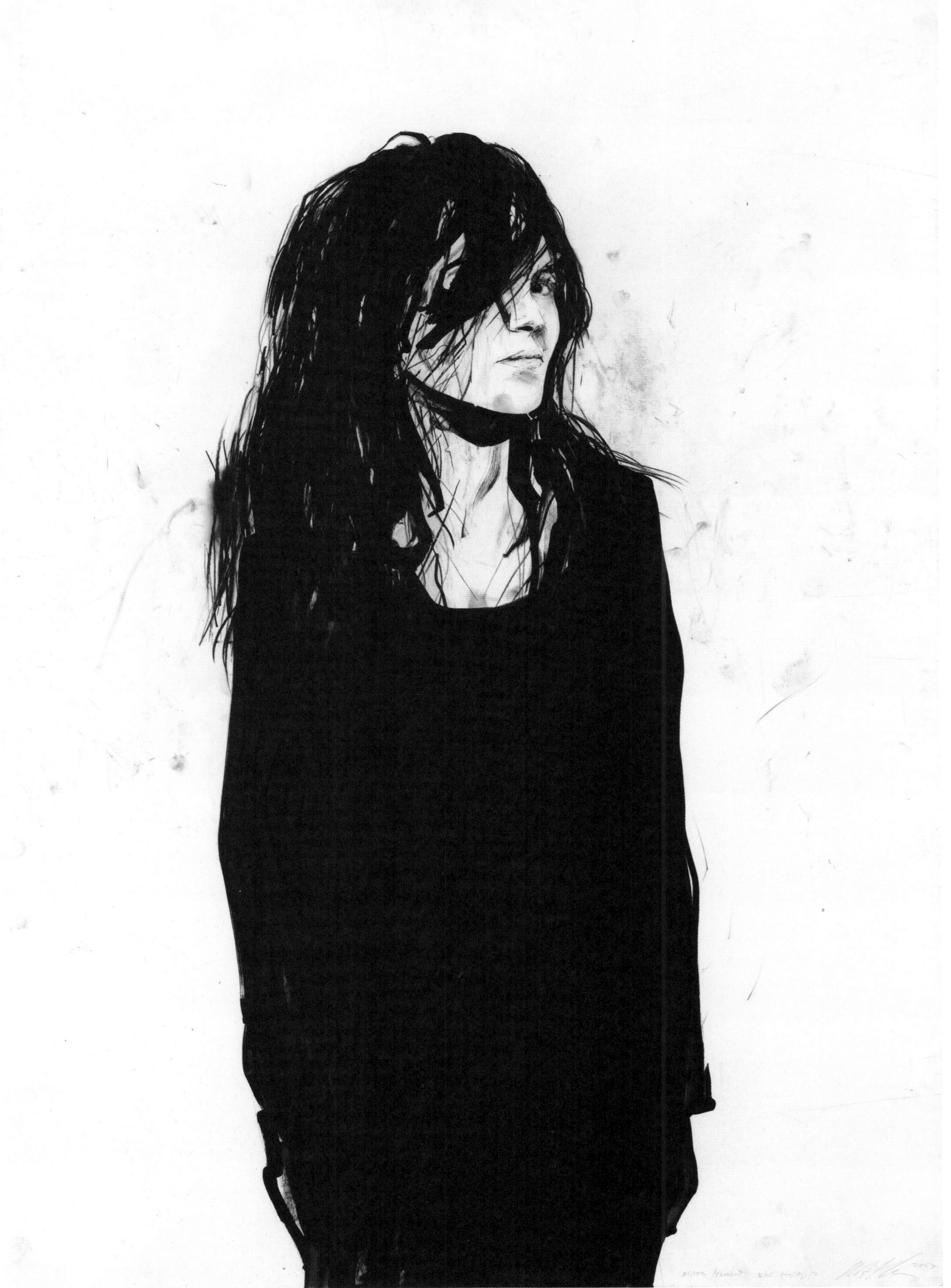

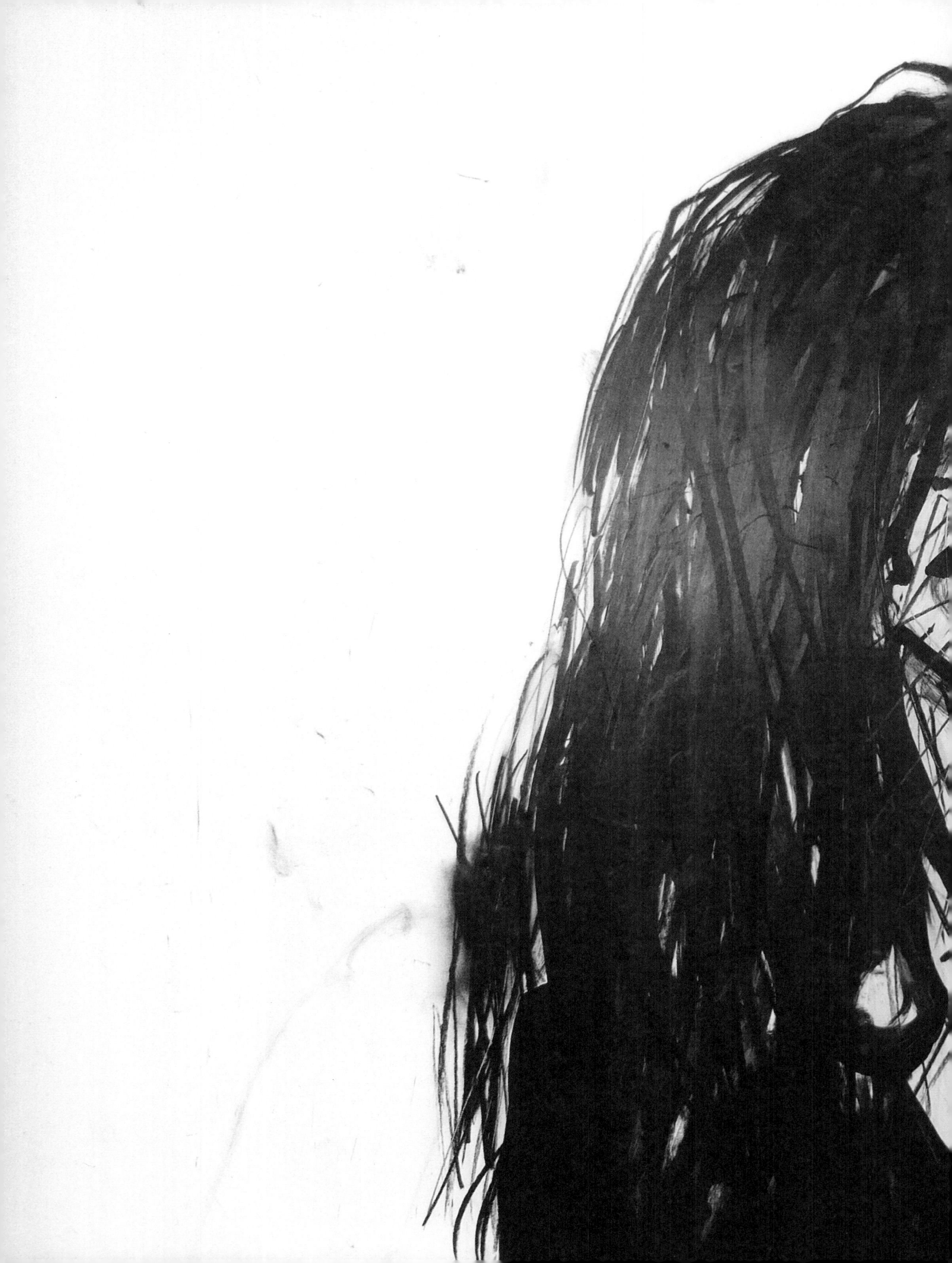

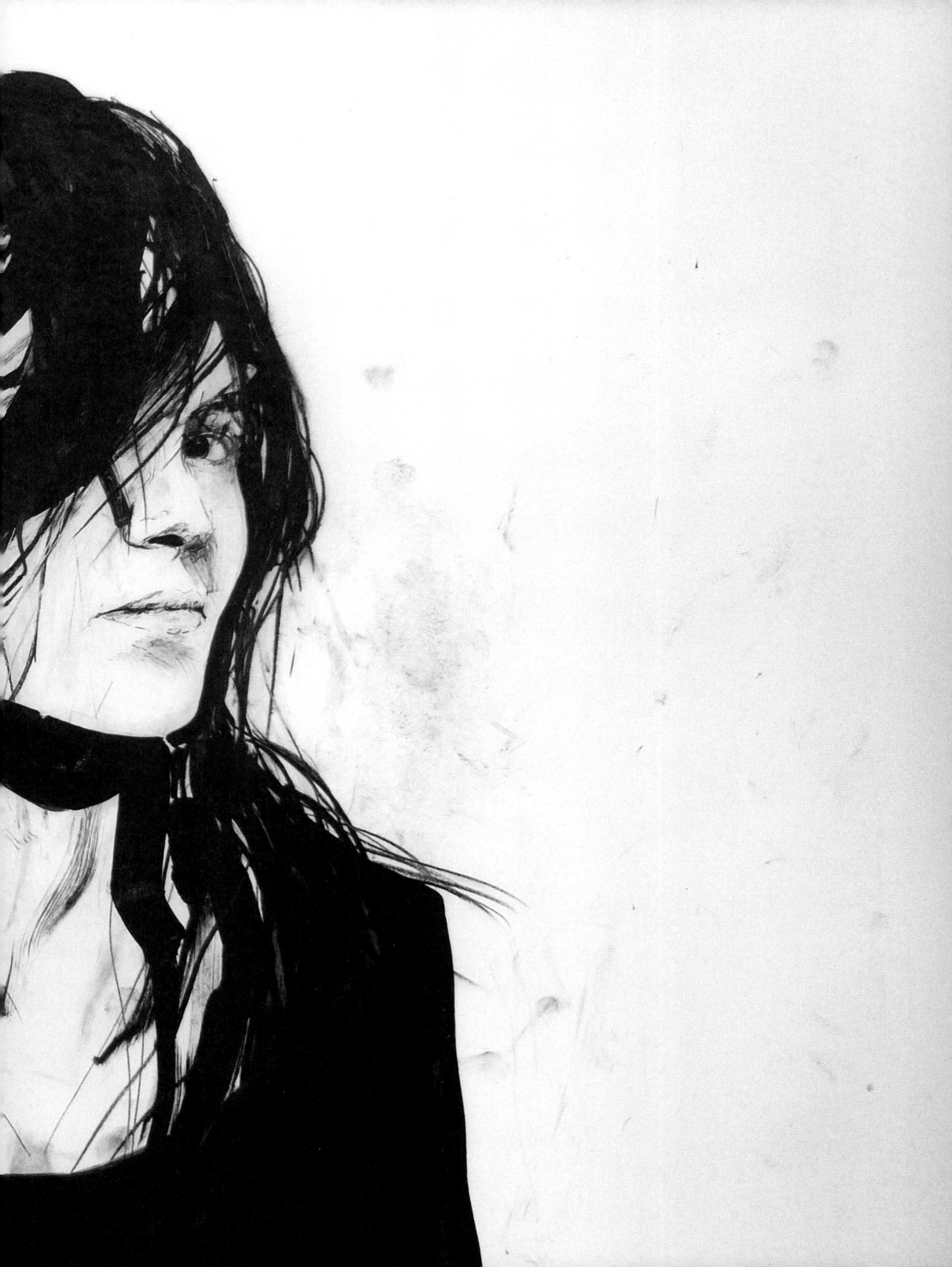

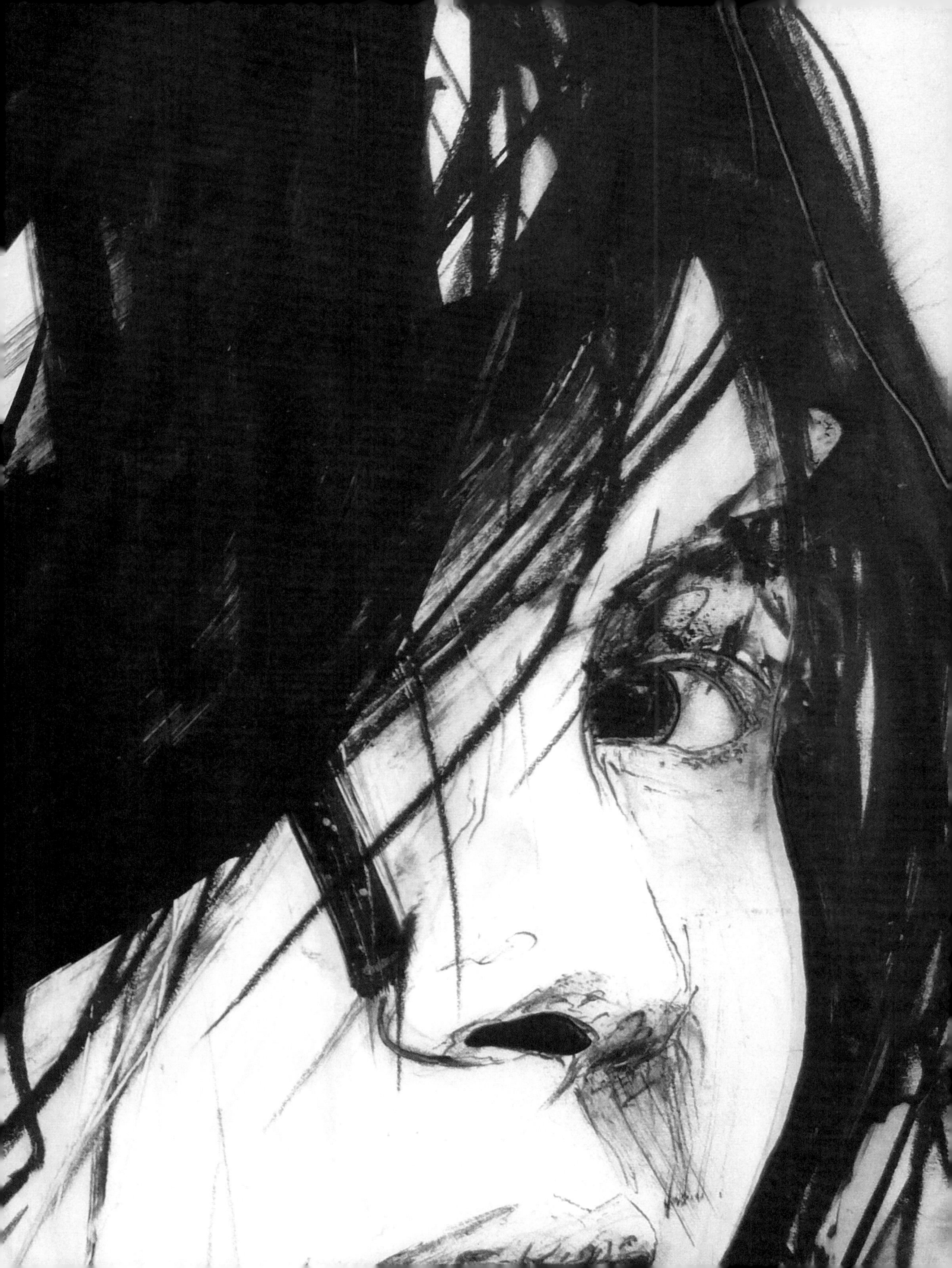

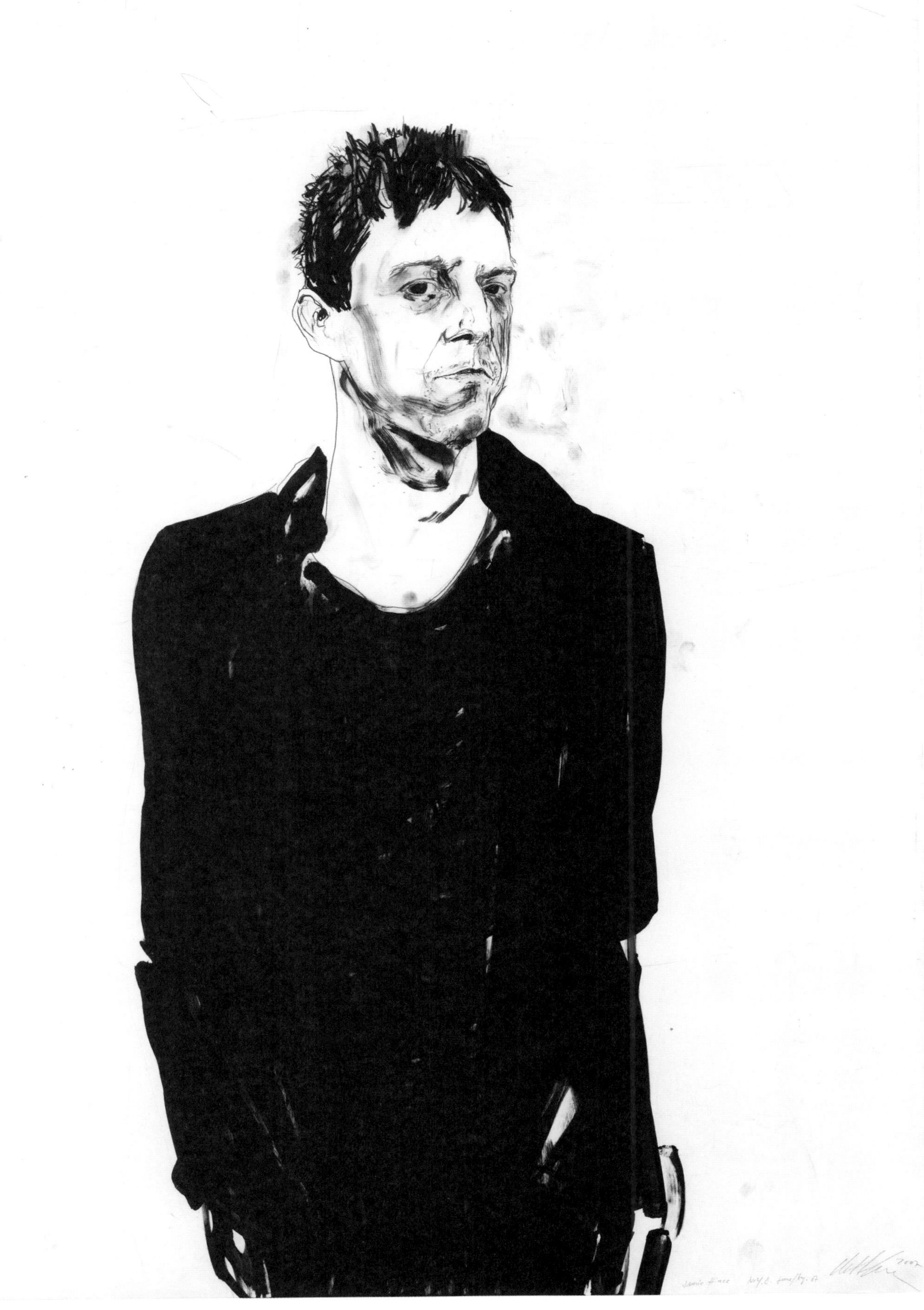

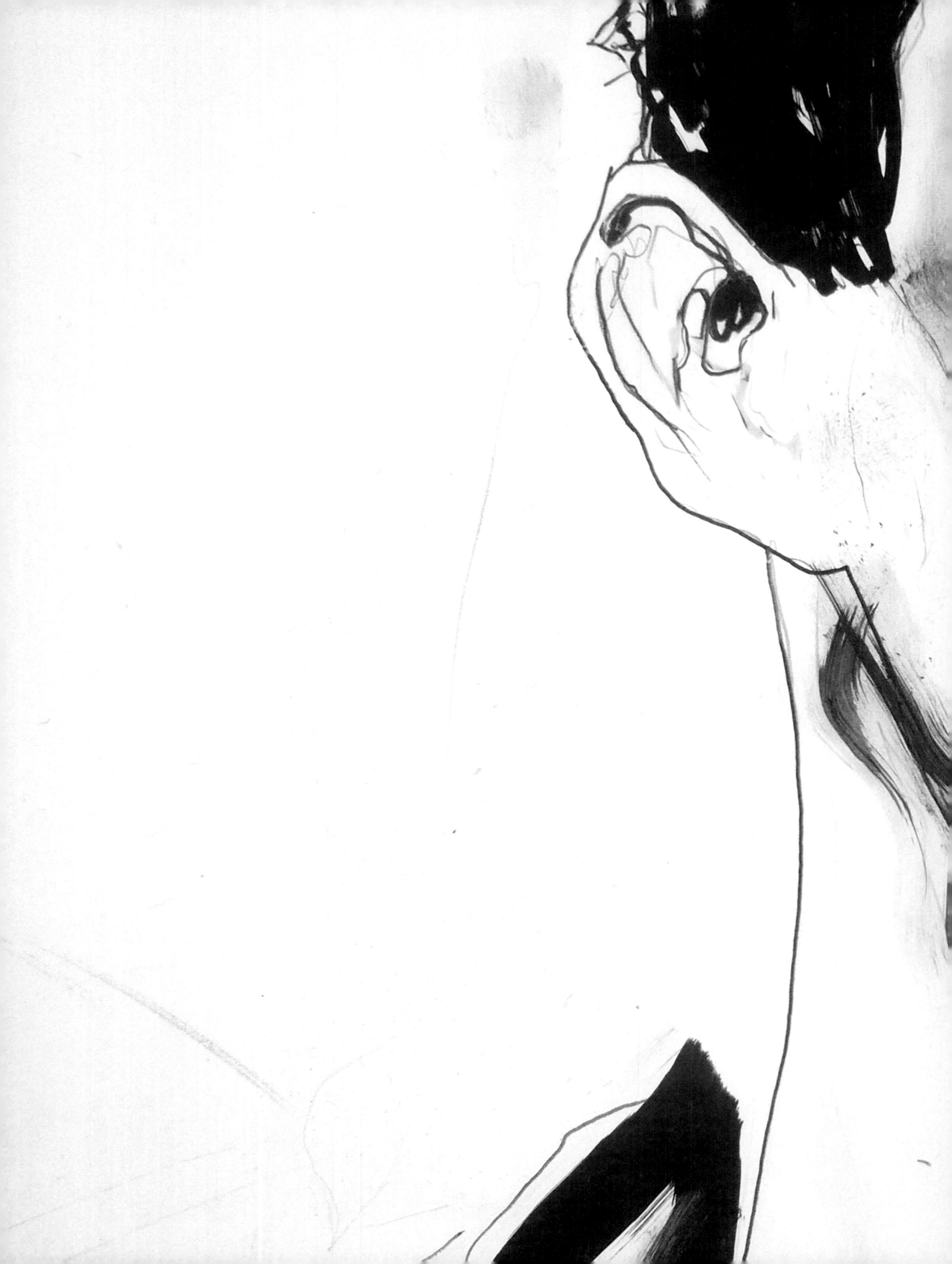

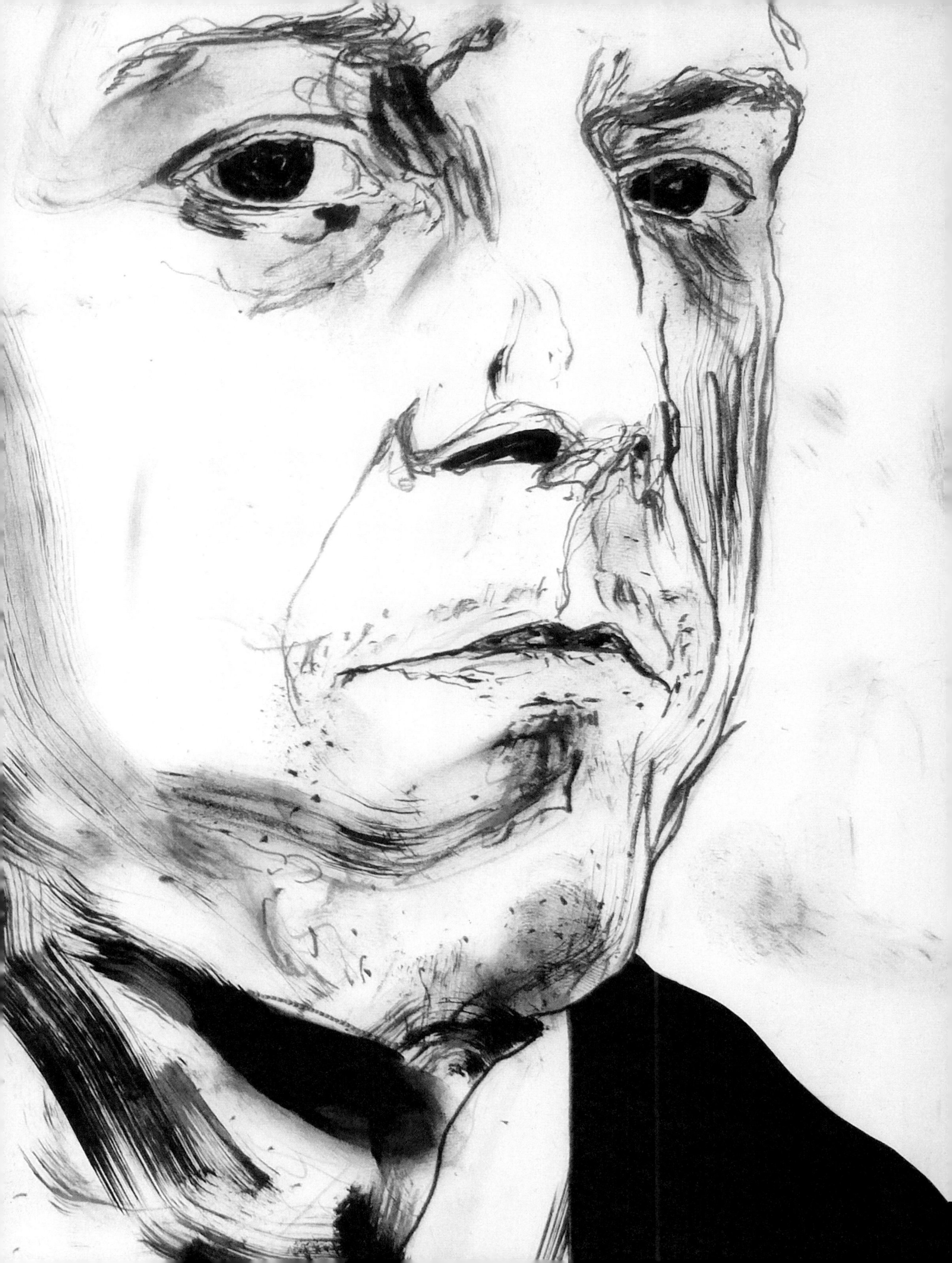

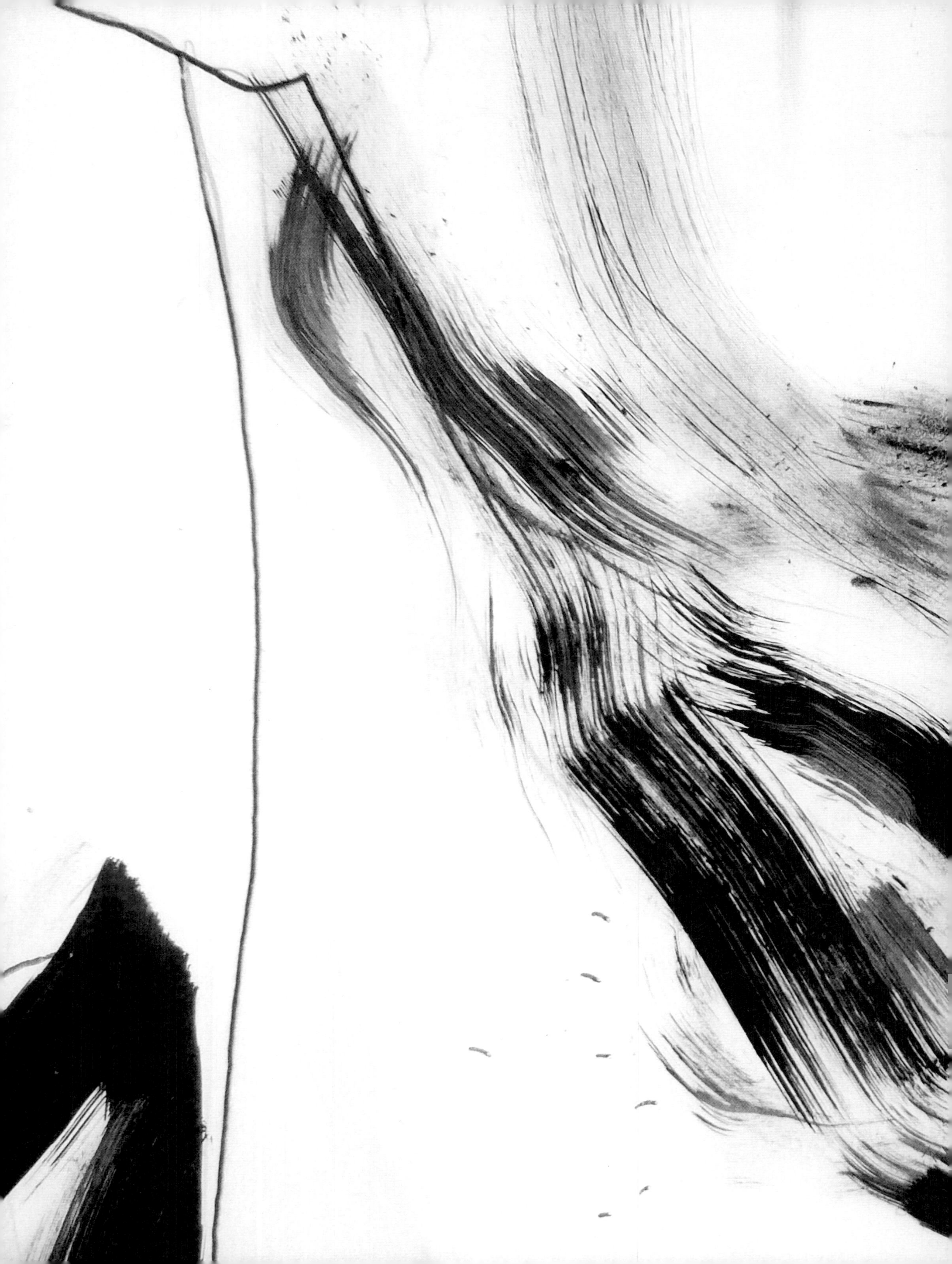

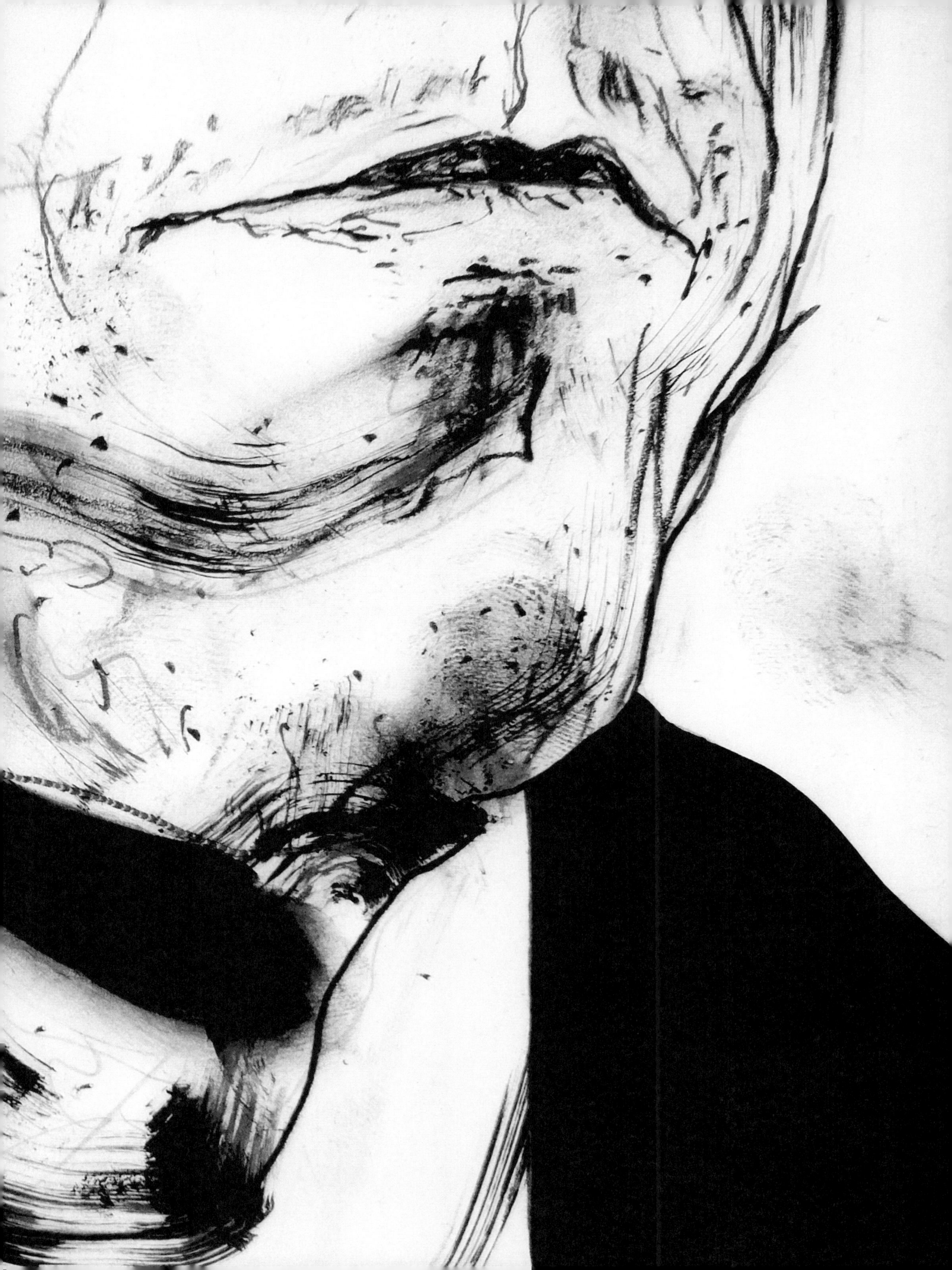

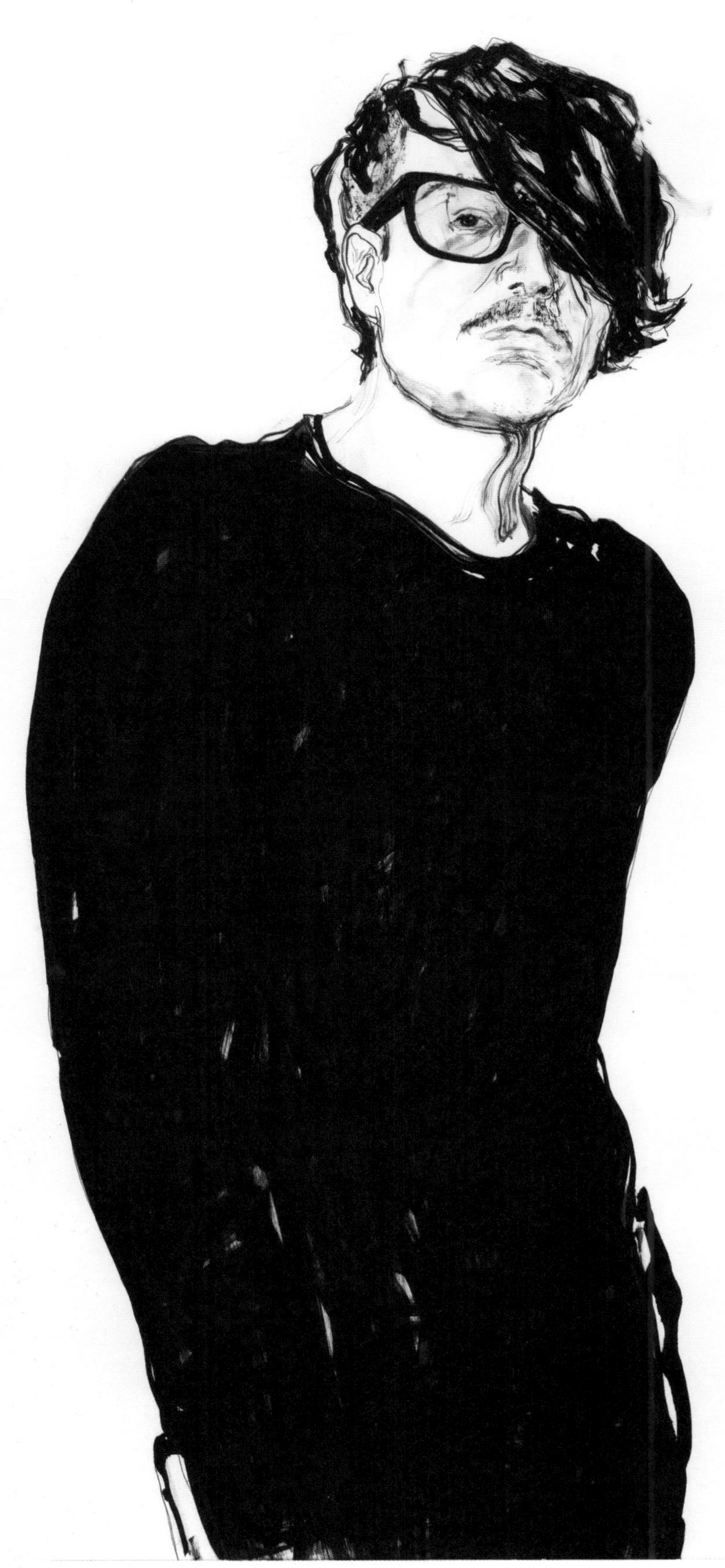

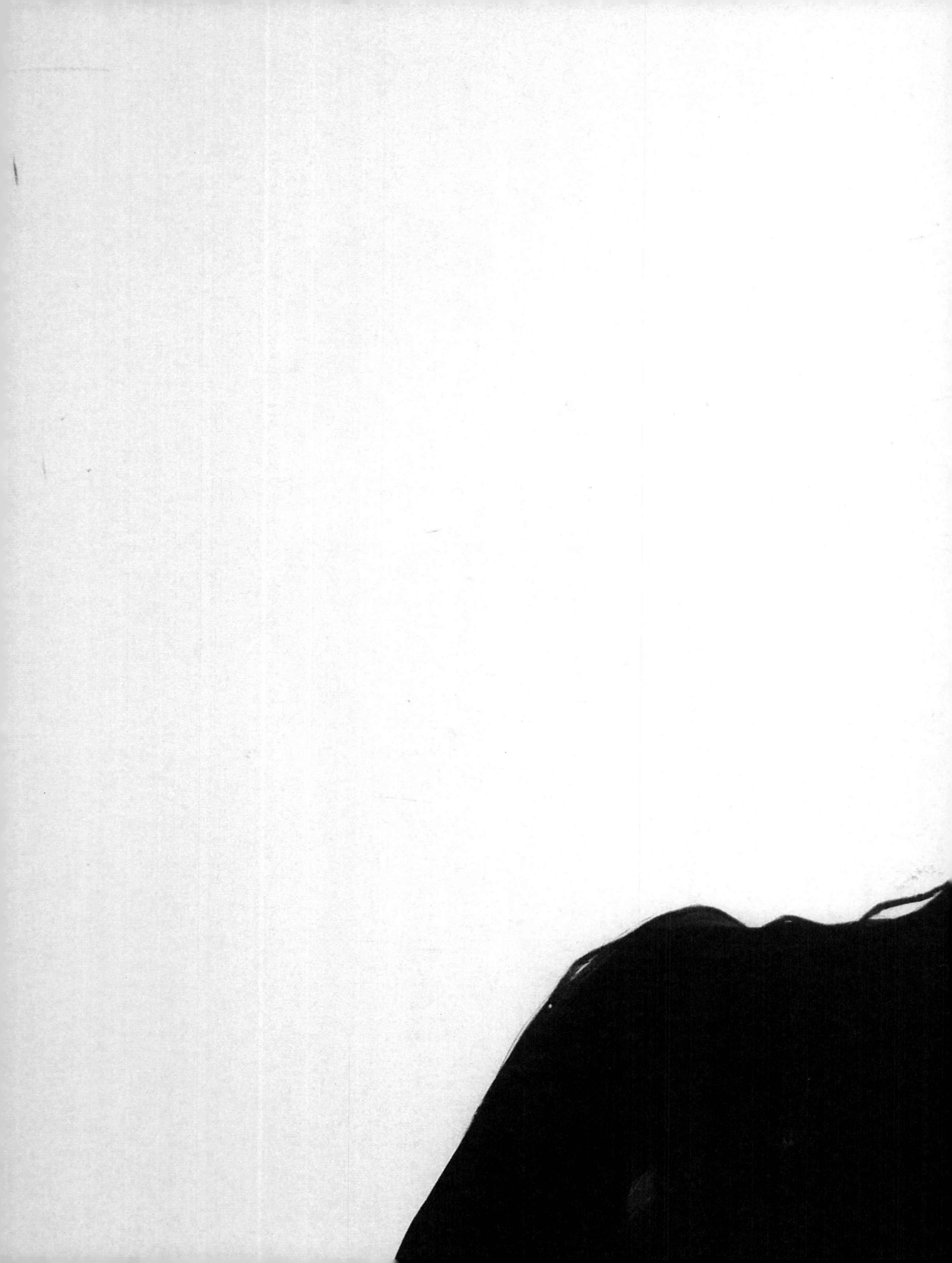

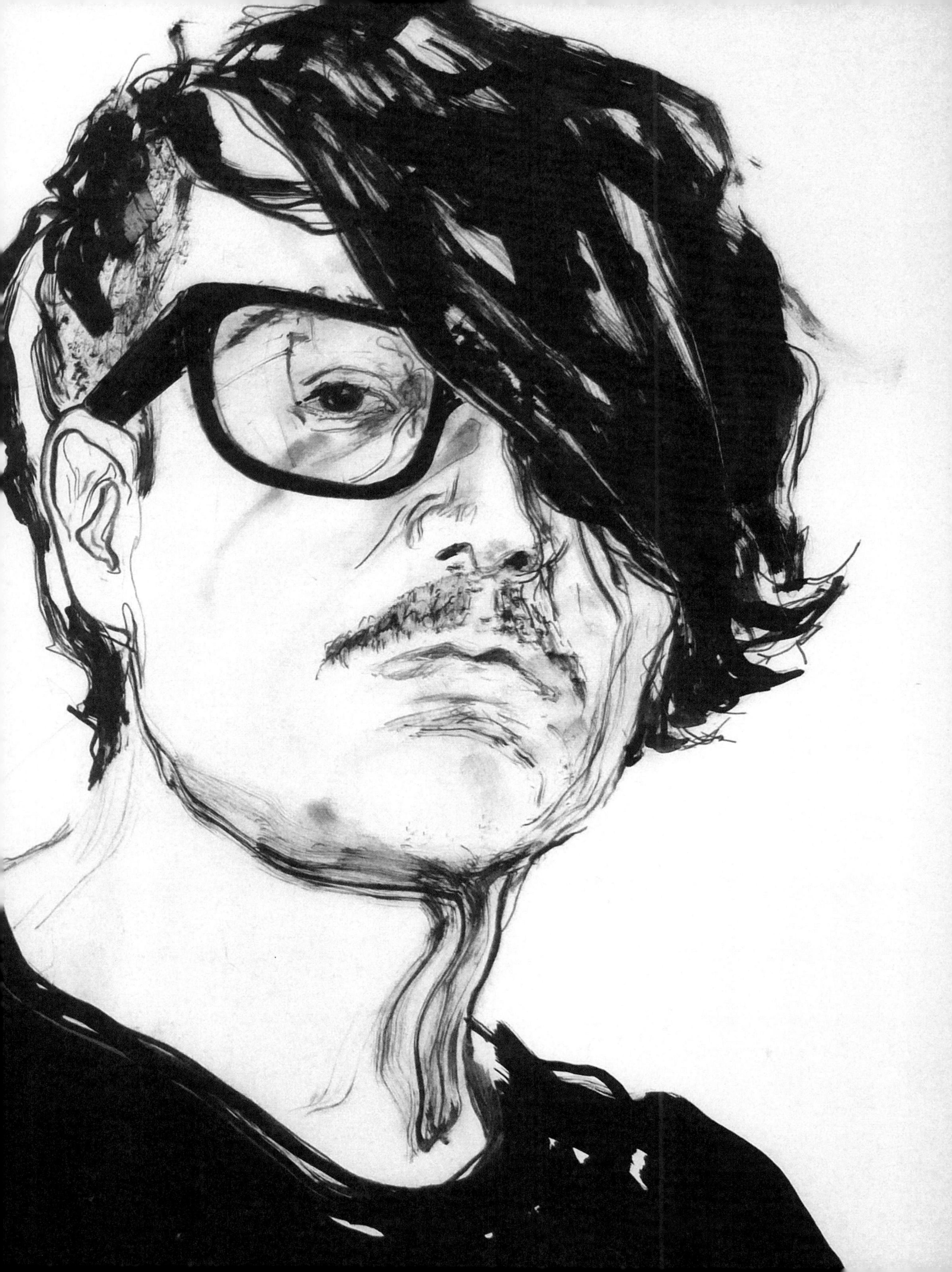

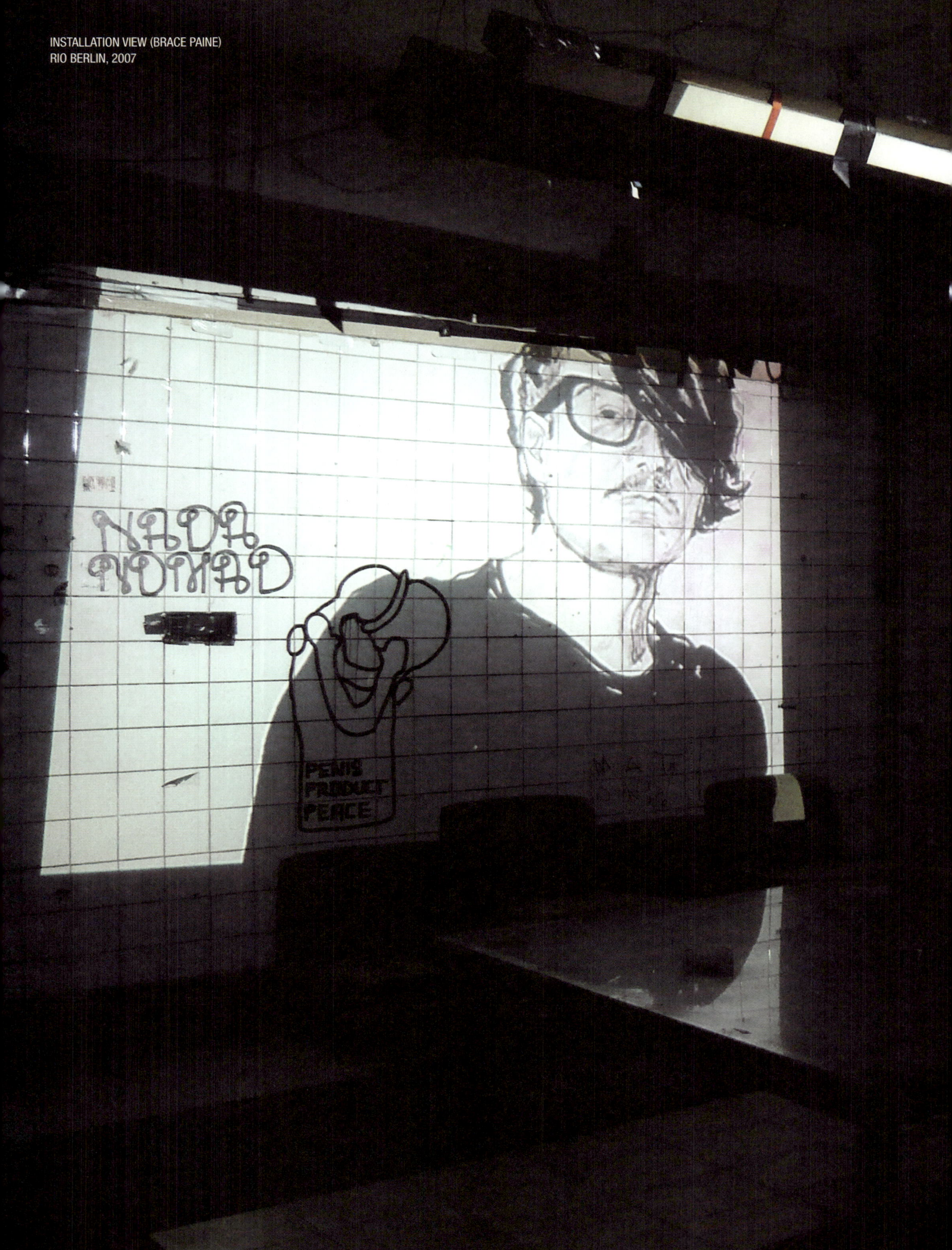

INSTALLATION VIEW (BRACE PAINE)
RIO BERLIN, 2007

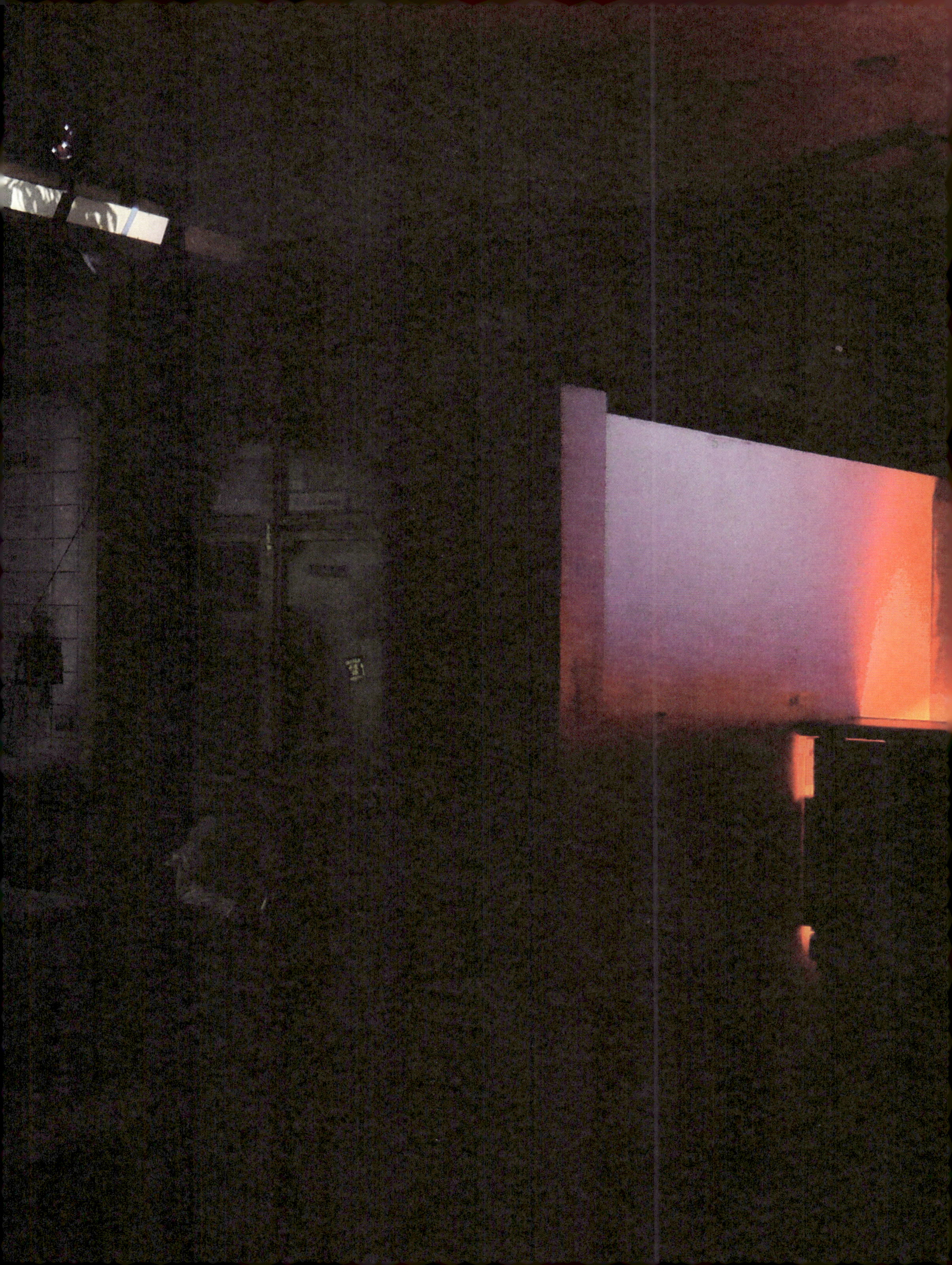

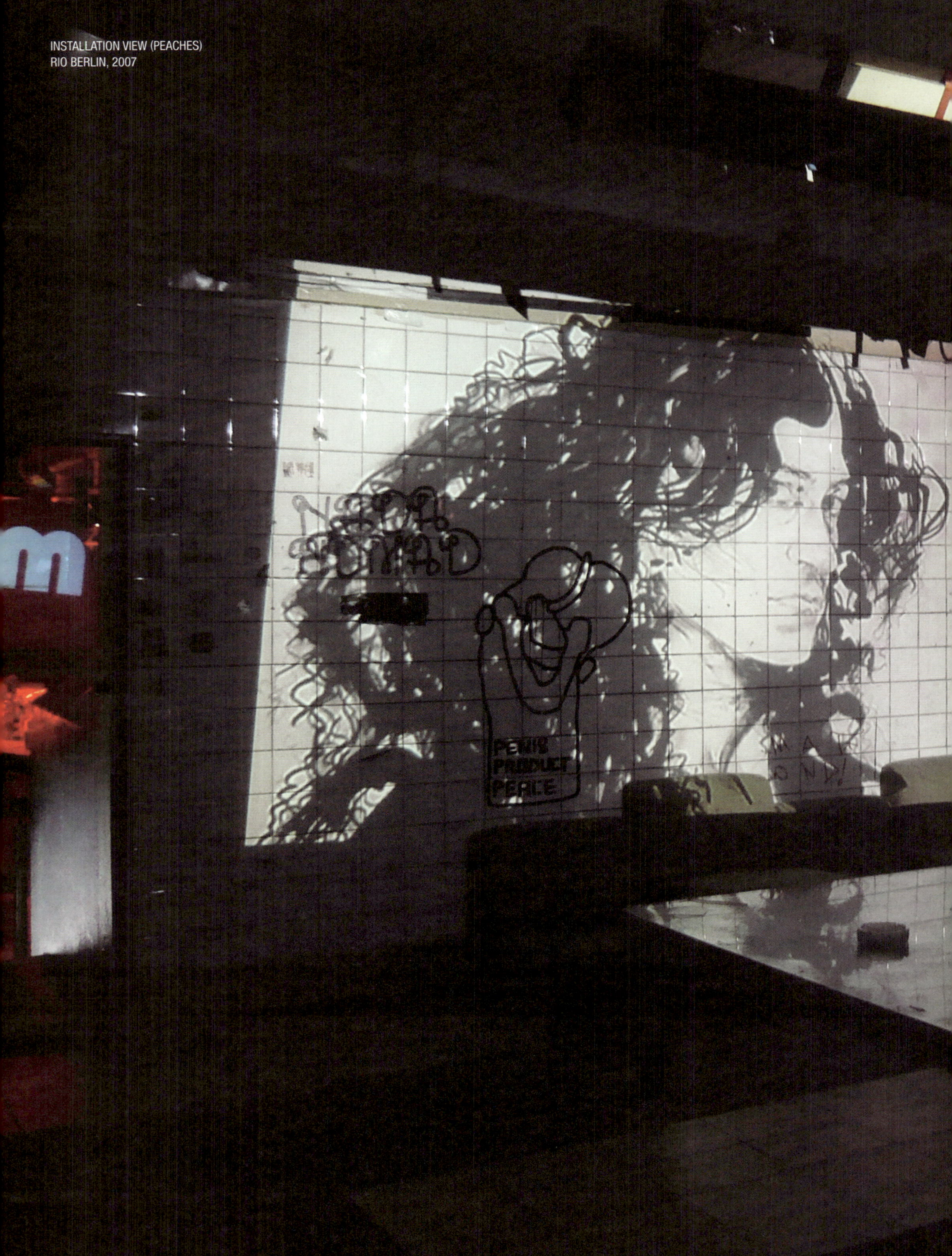

INSTALLATION VIEW (PEACHES)
RIO BERLIN, 2007

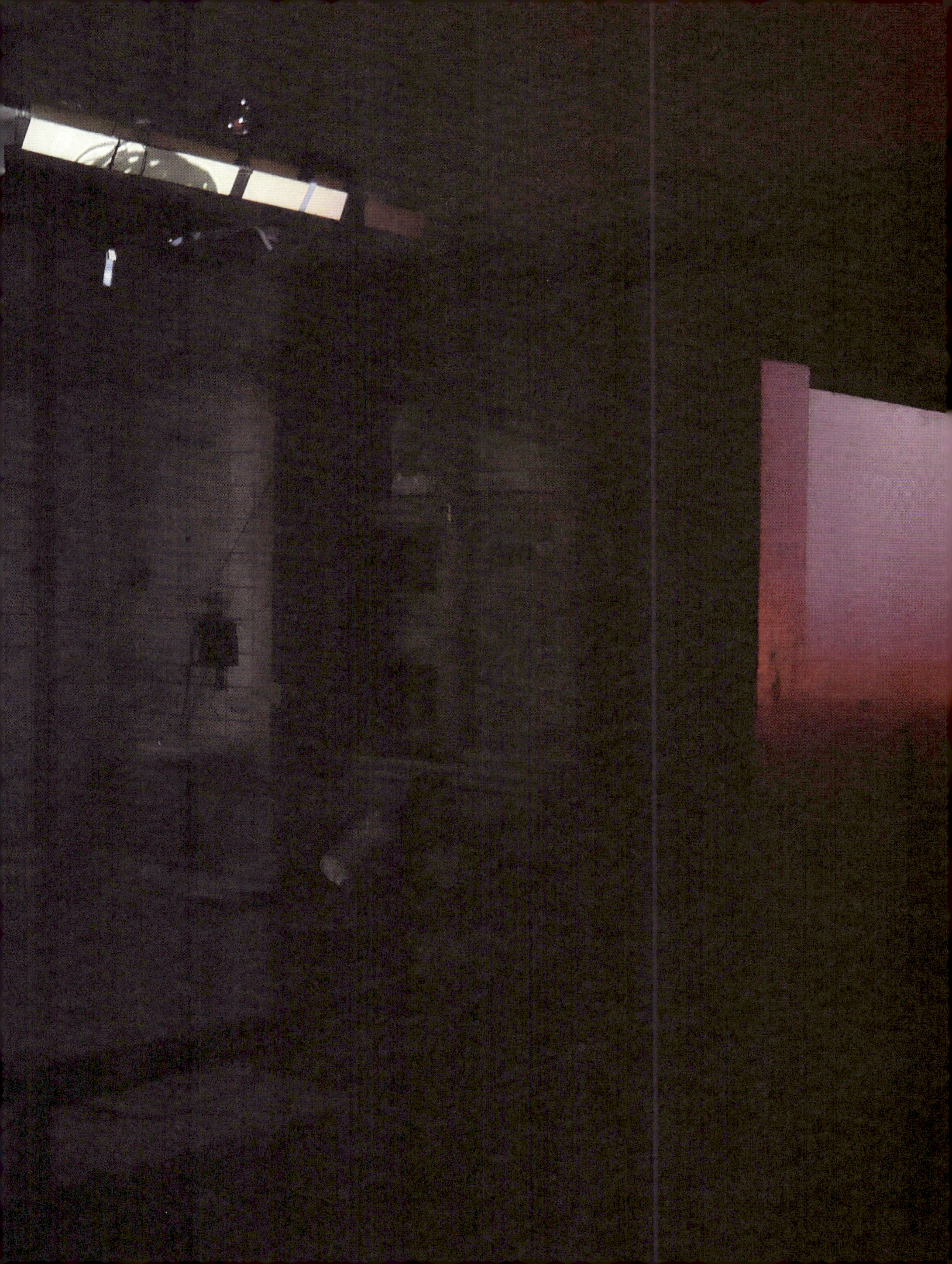

INSTALLATION VIEW (FEIST)
RIO BERLIN, 2007
NADA
NOMAD
PENIS
PRODUCT
PEACE

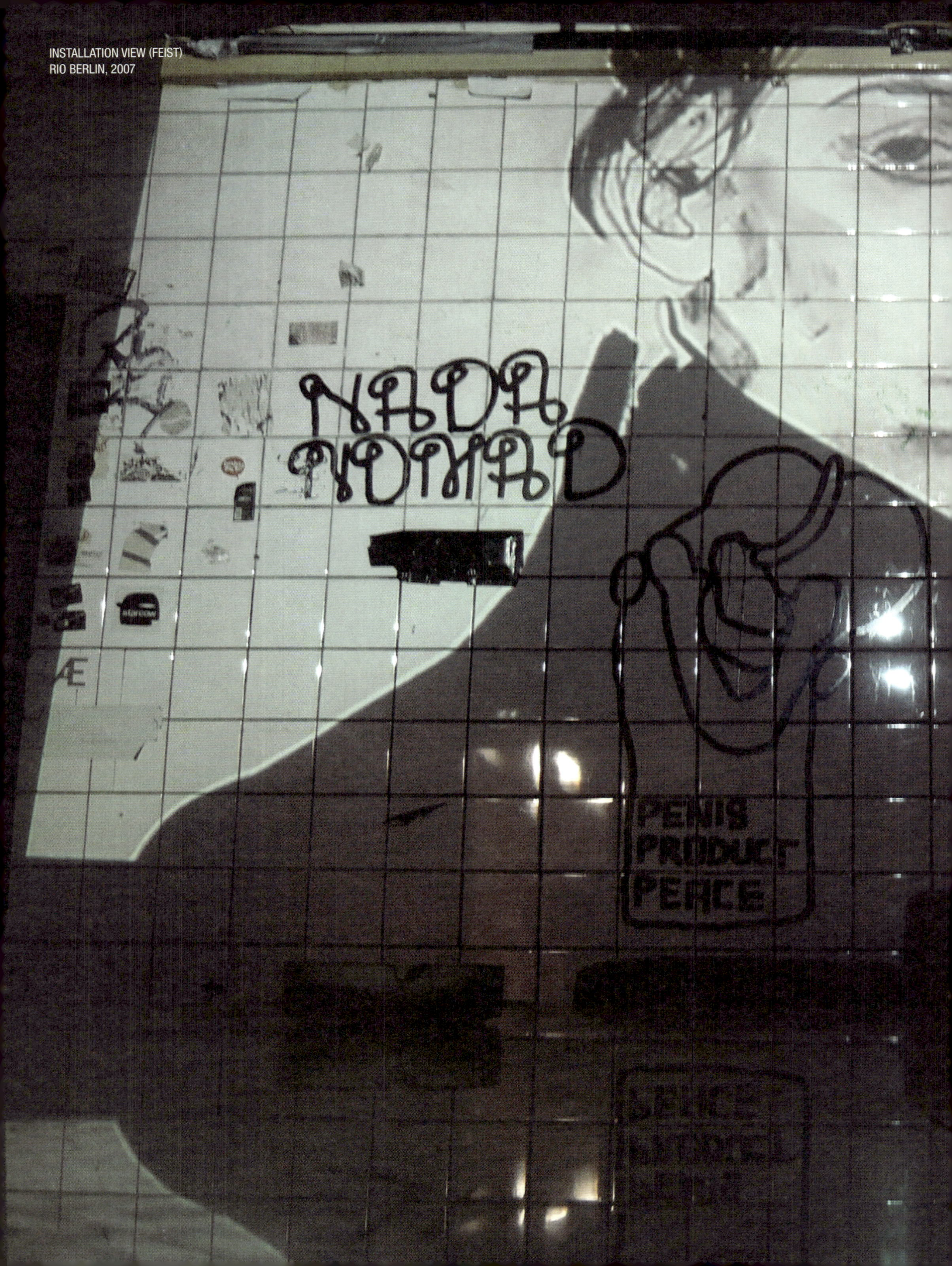

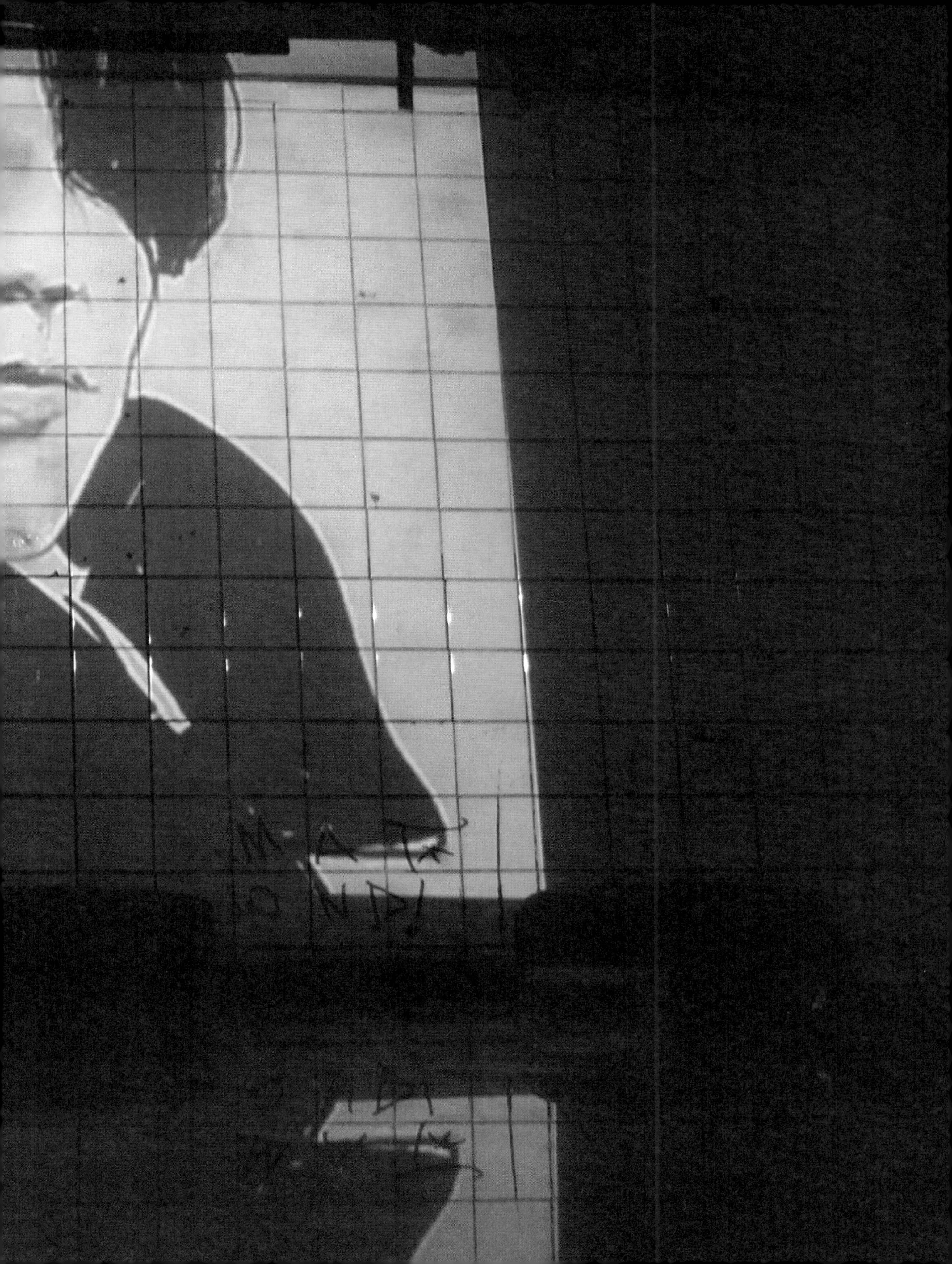
MAT
OND

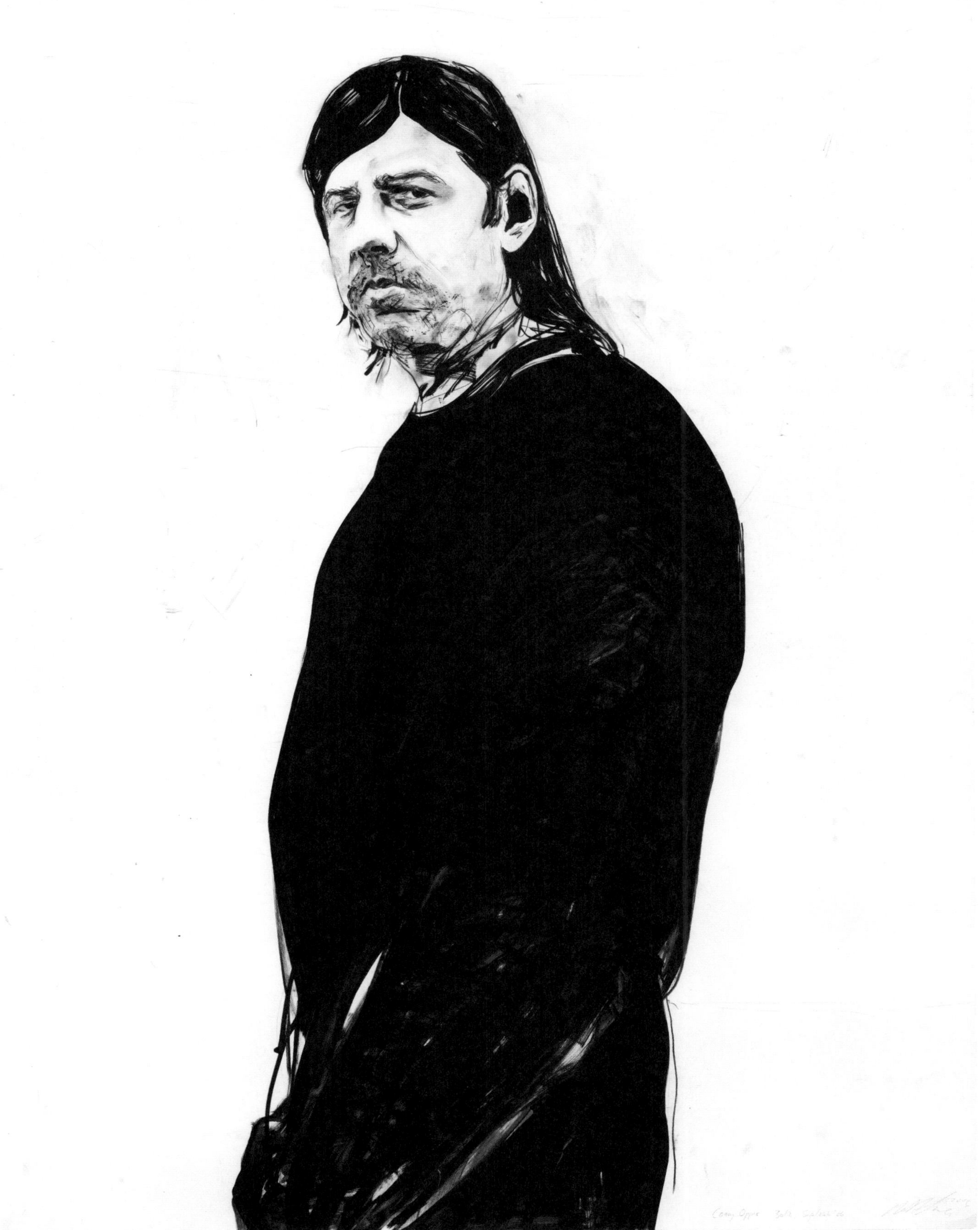

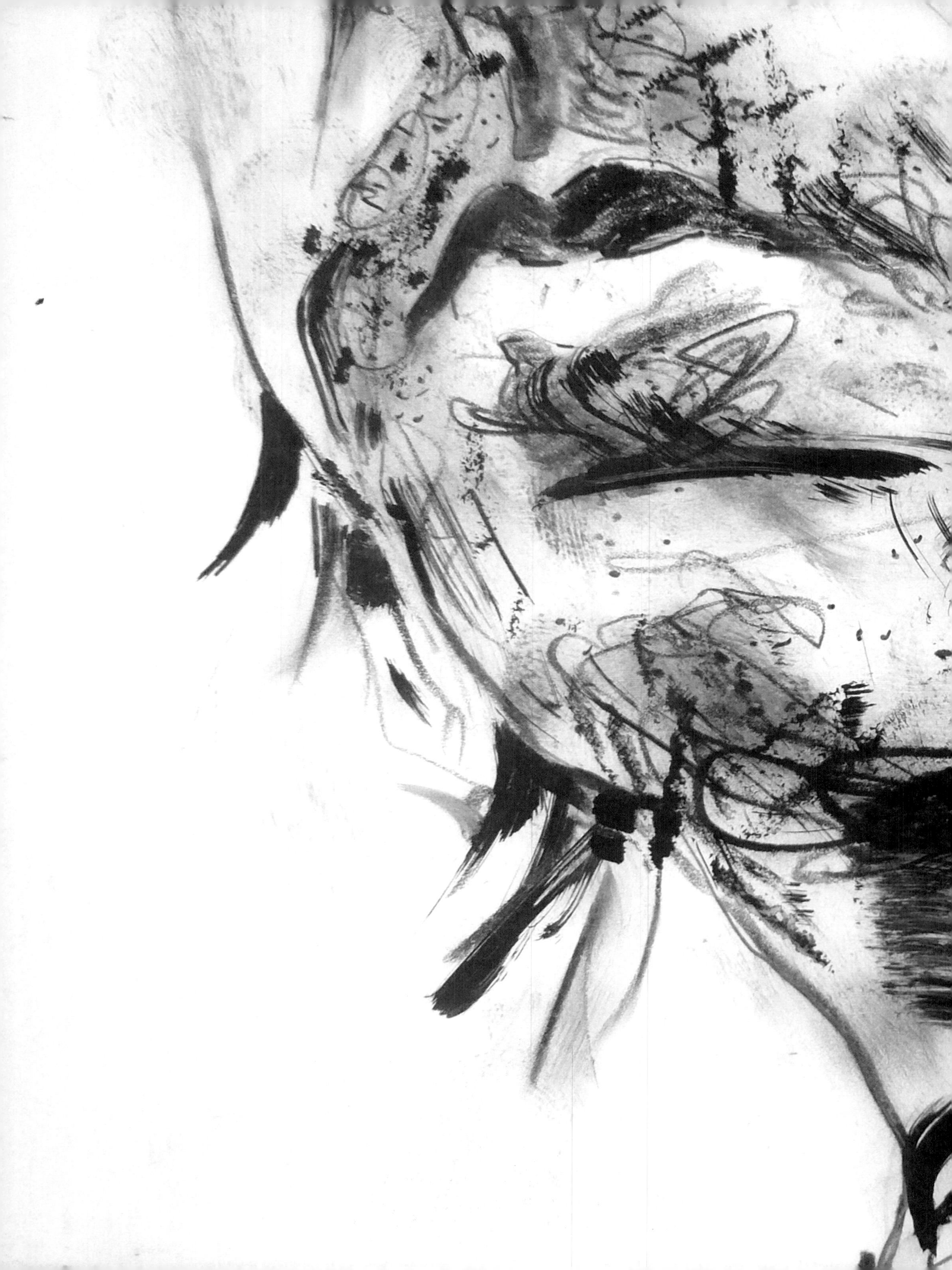

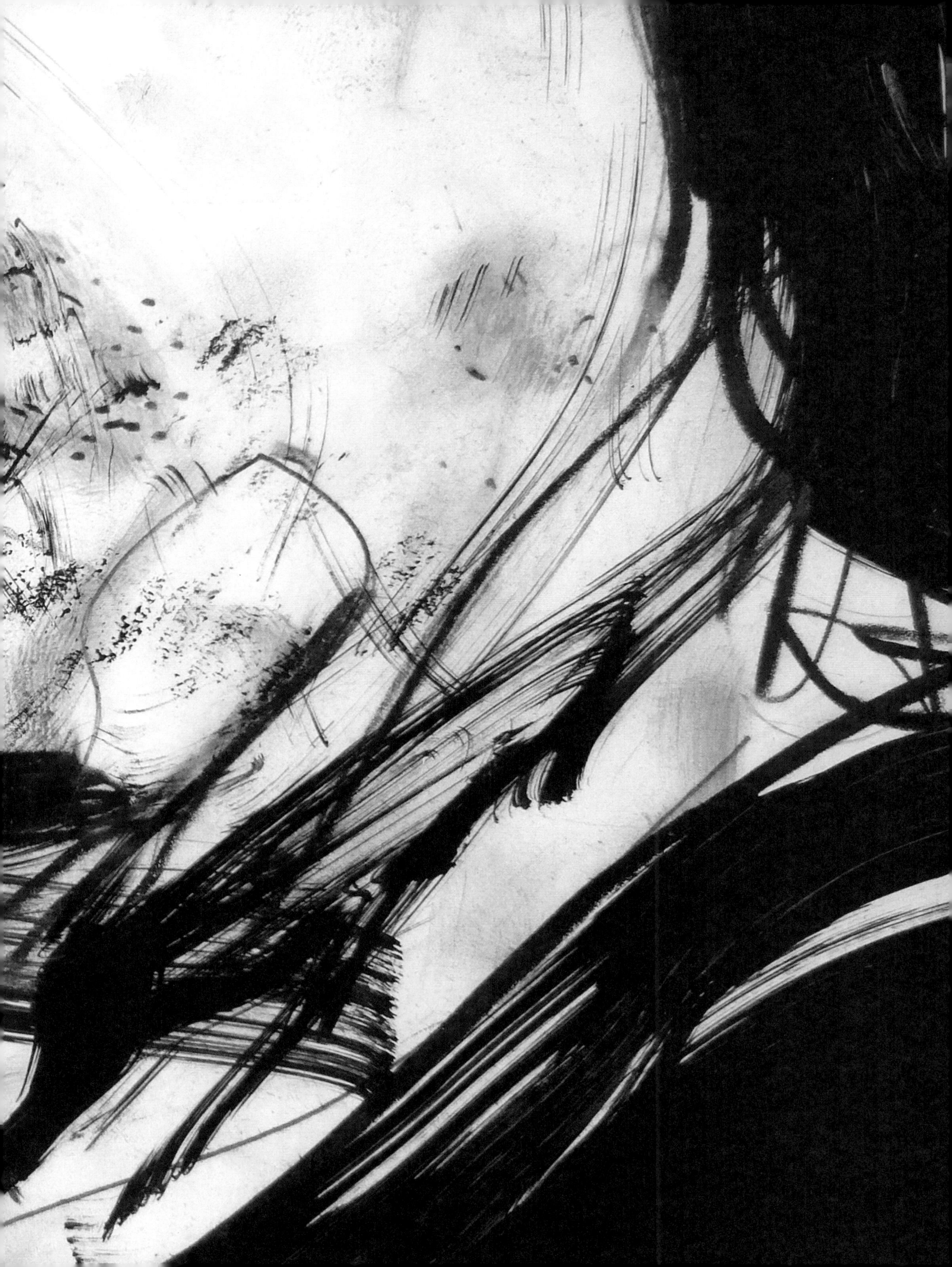

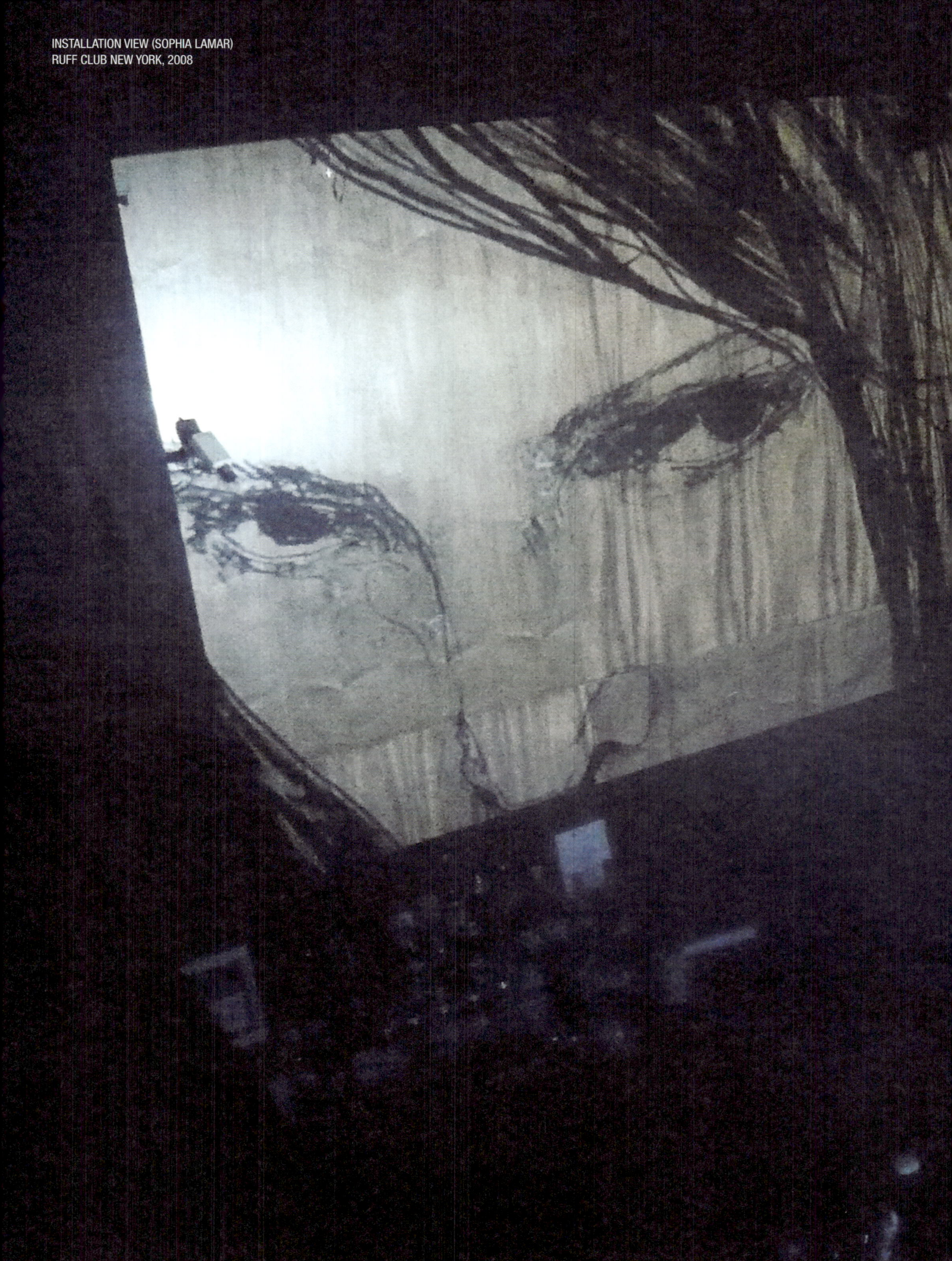

INSTALLATION VIEW (SOPHIA LAMAR)
RUFF CLUB NEW YORK, 2008

EXIT

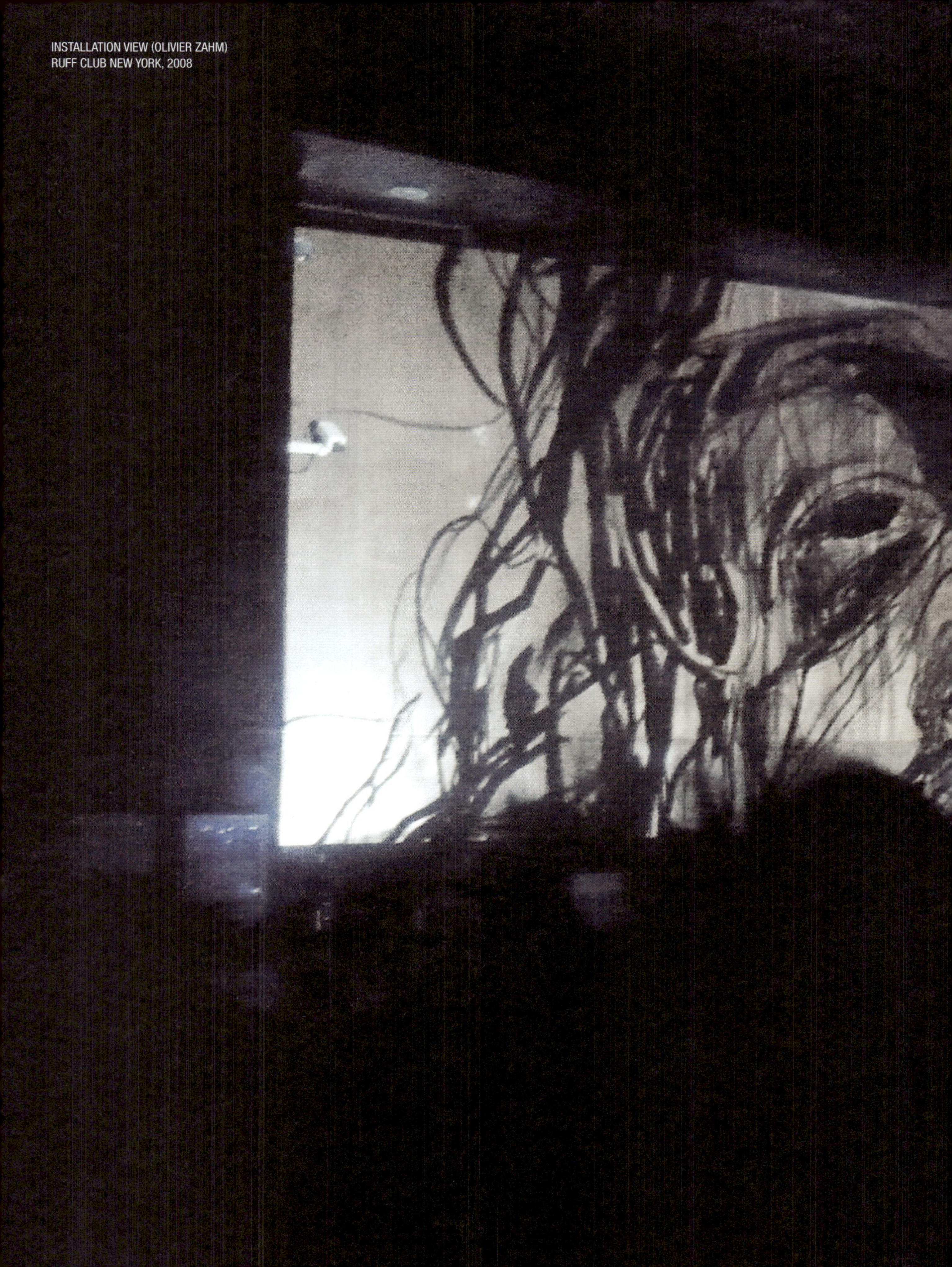
INSTALLATION VIEW (OLIVIER ZAHM)
RUFF CLUB NEW YORK, 2008

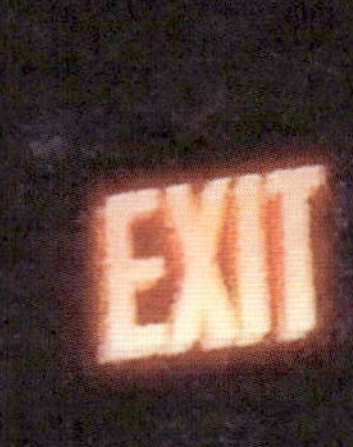
EXIT

OLIVIER ZAHM
PARIS, 2008

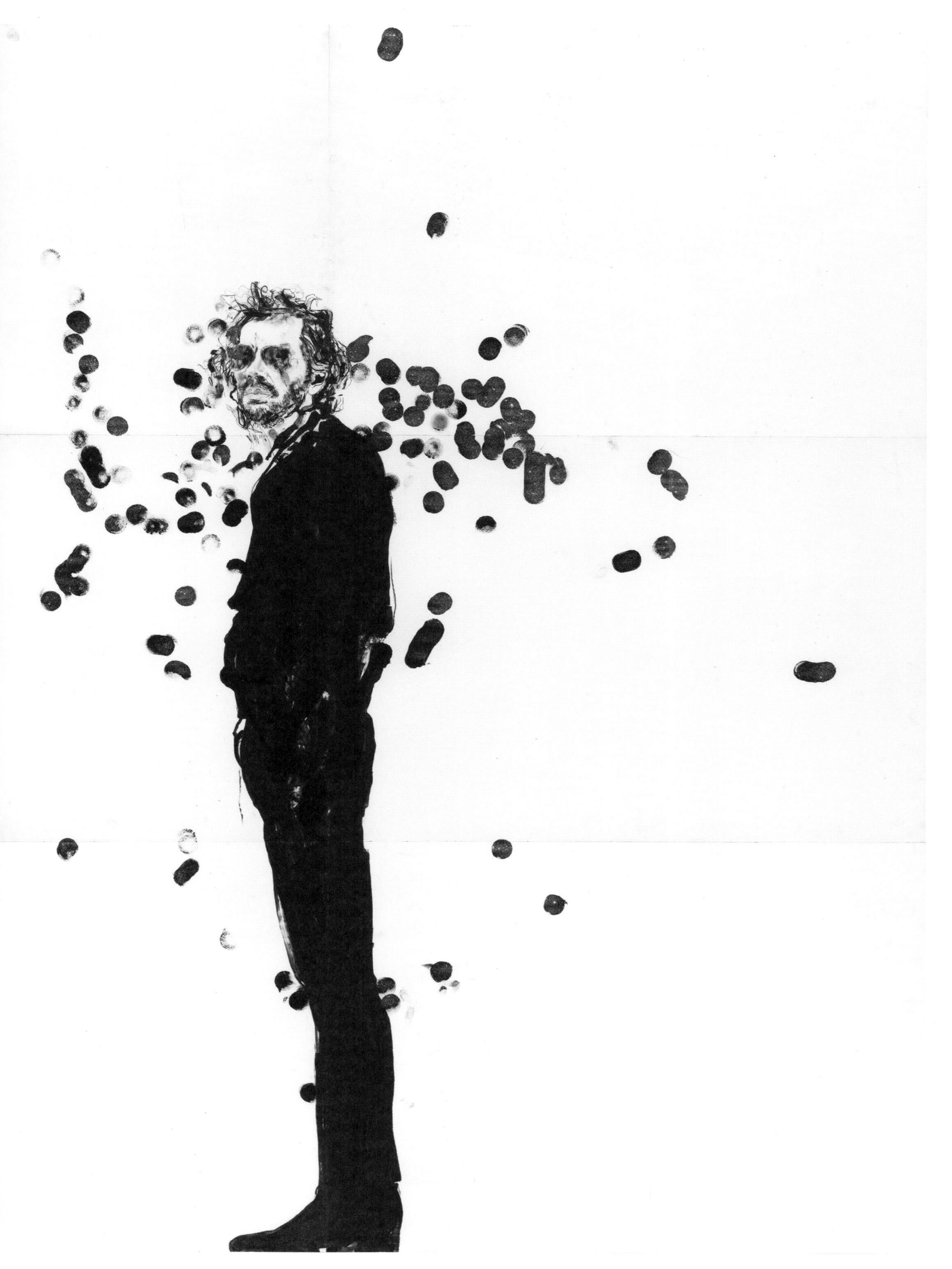

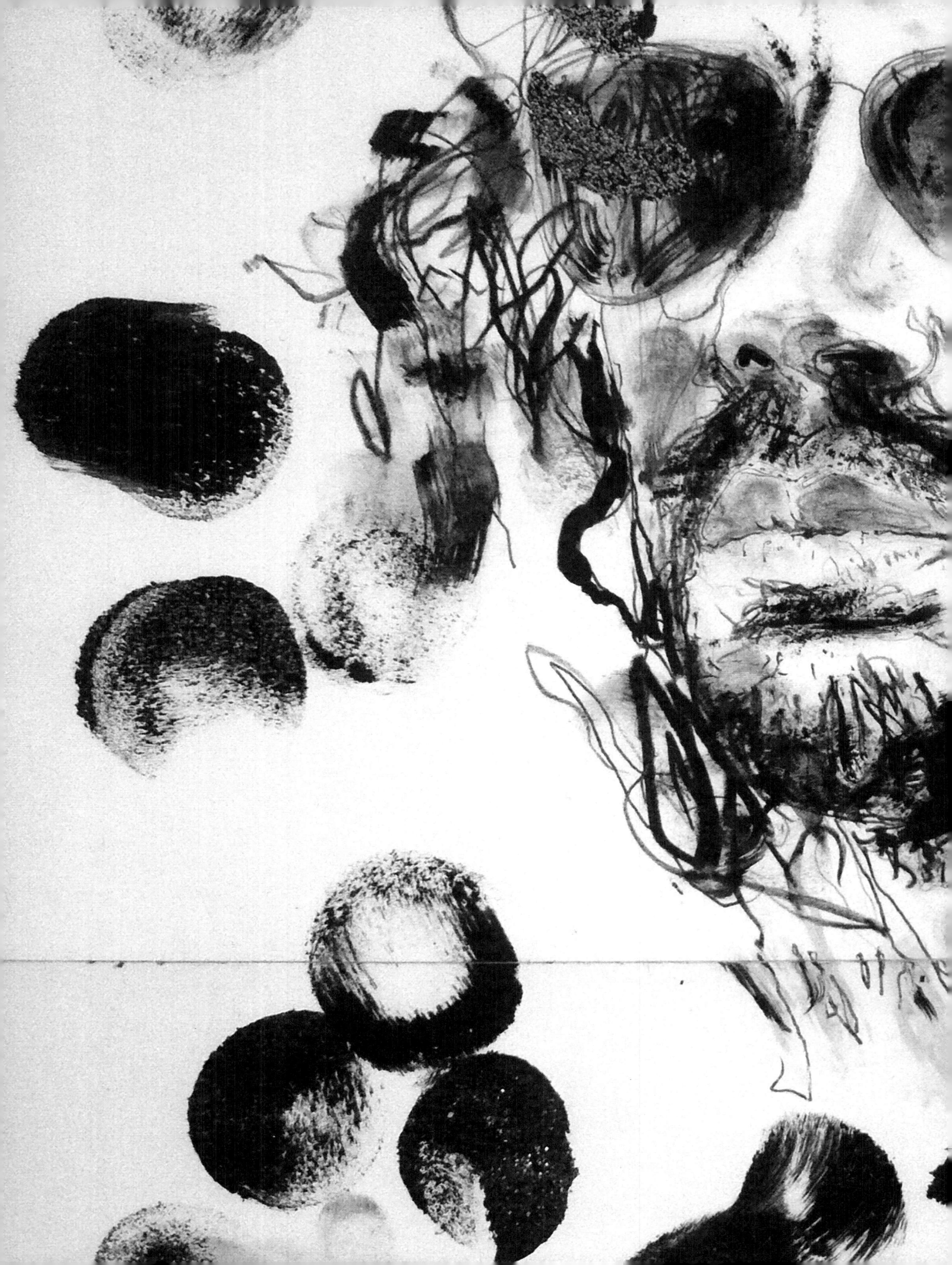

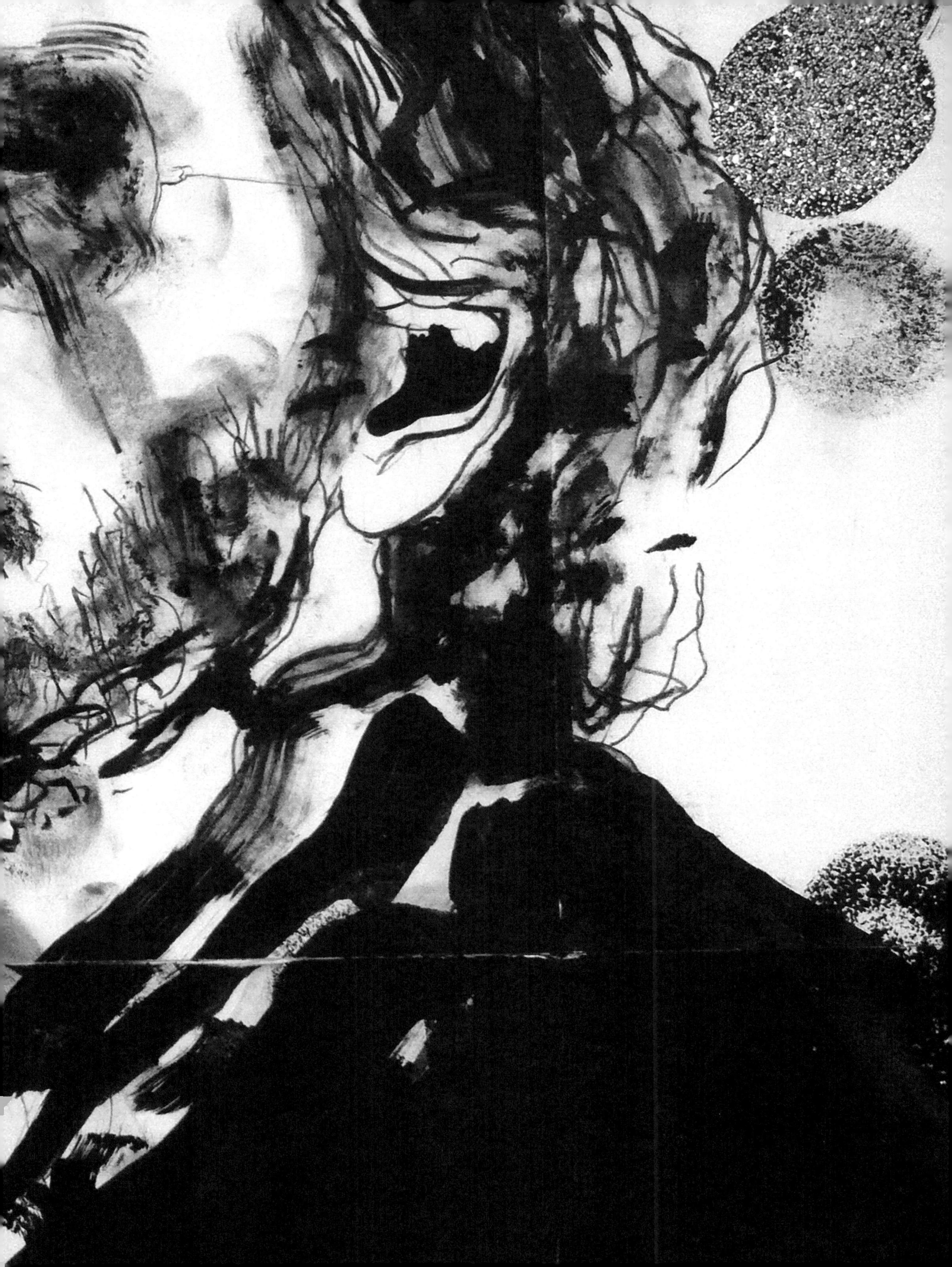

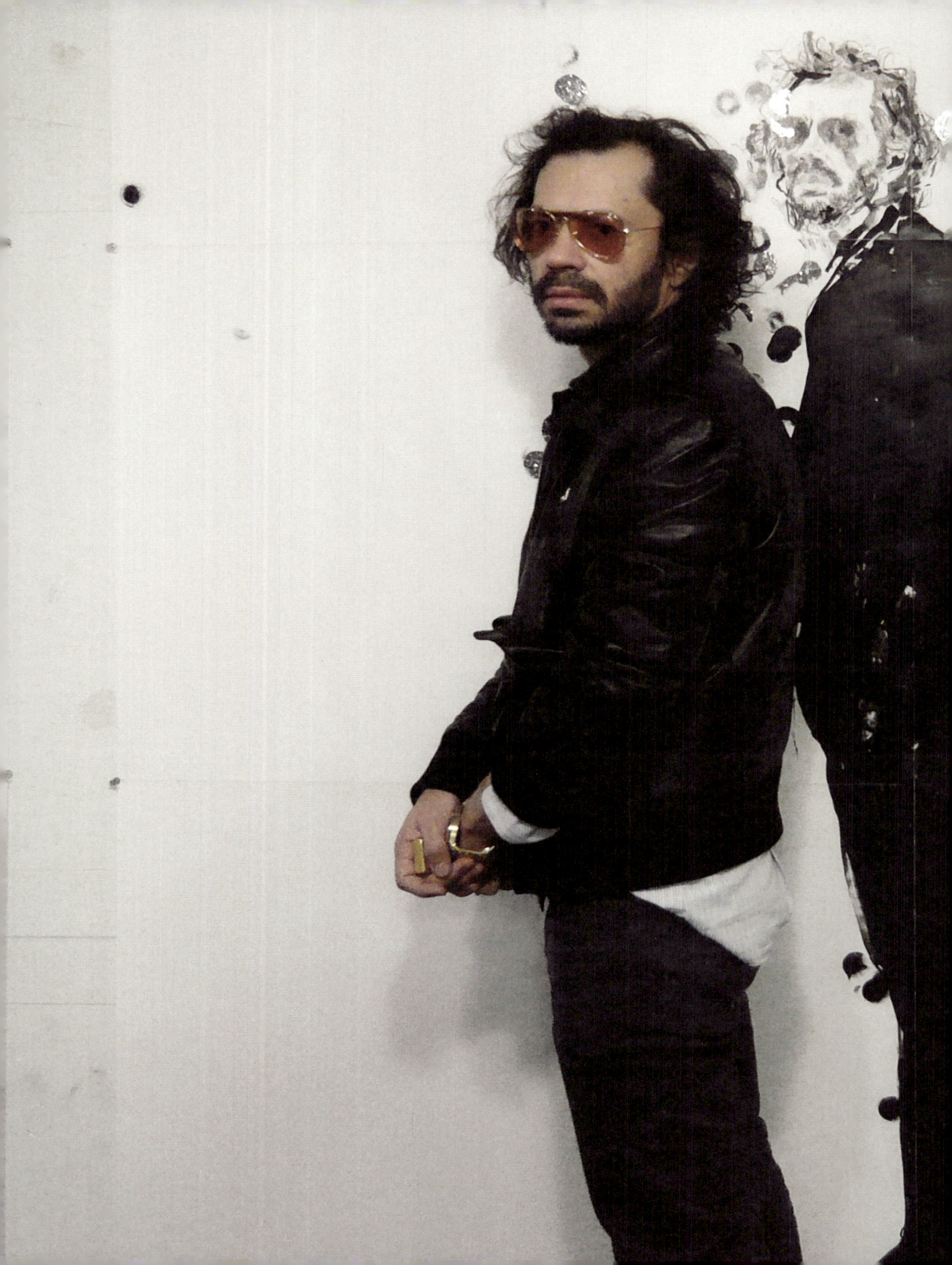

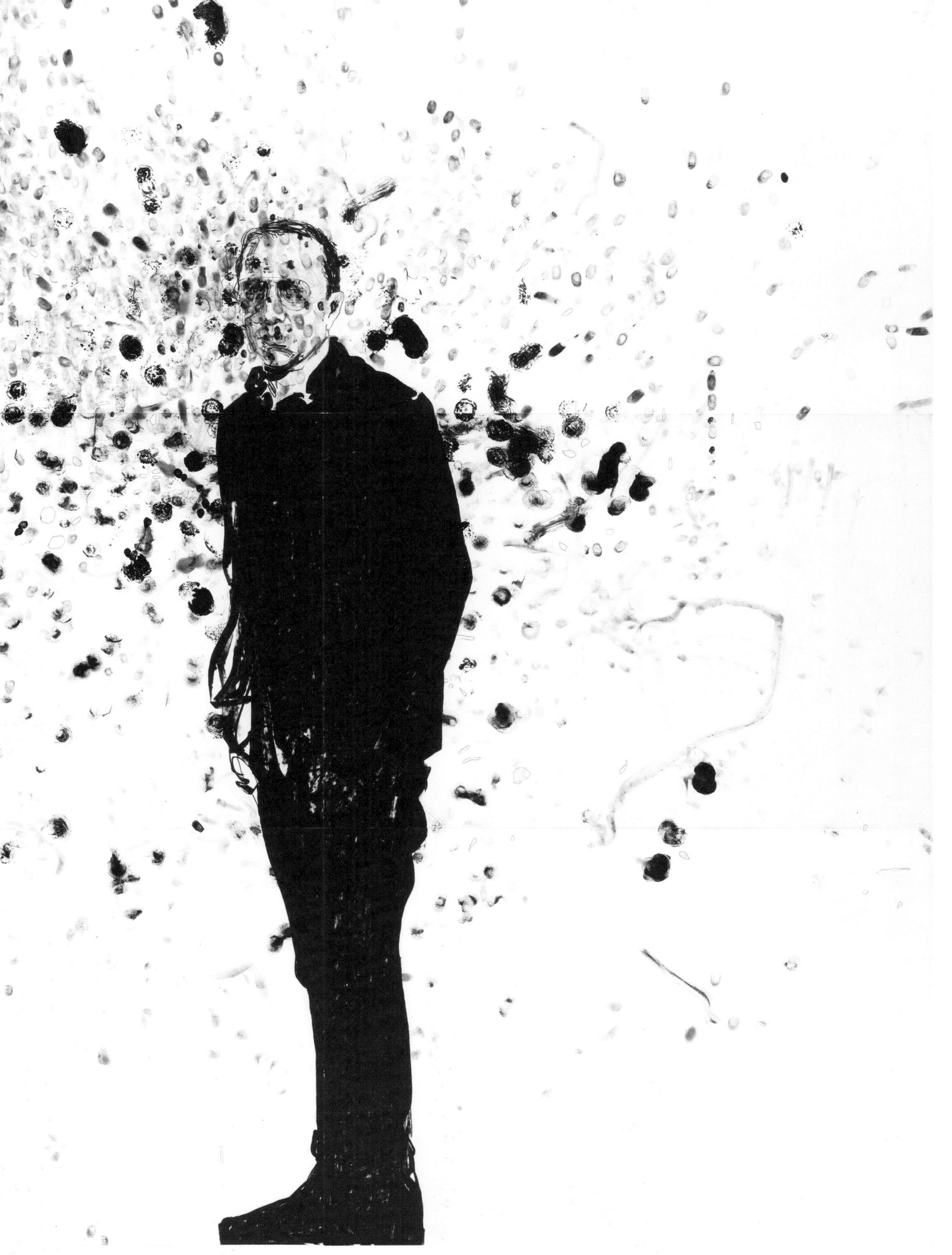

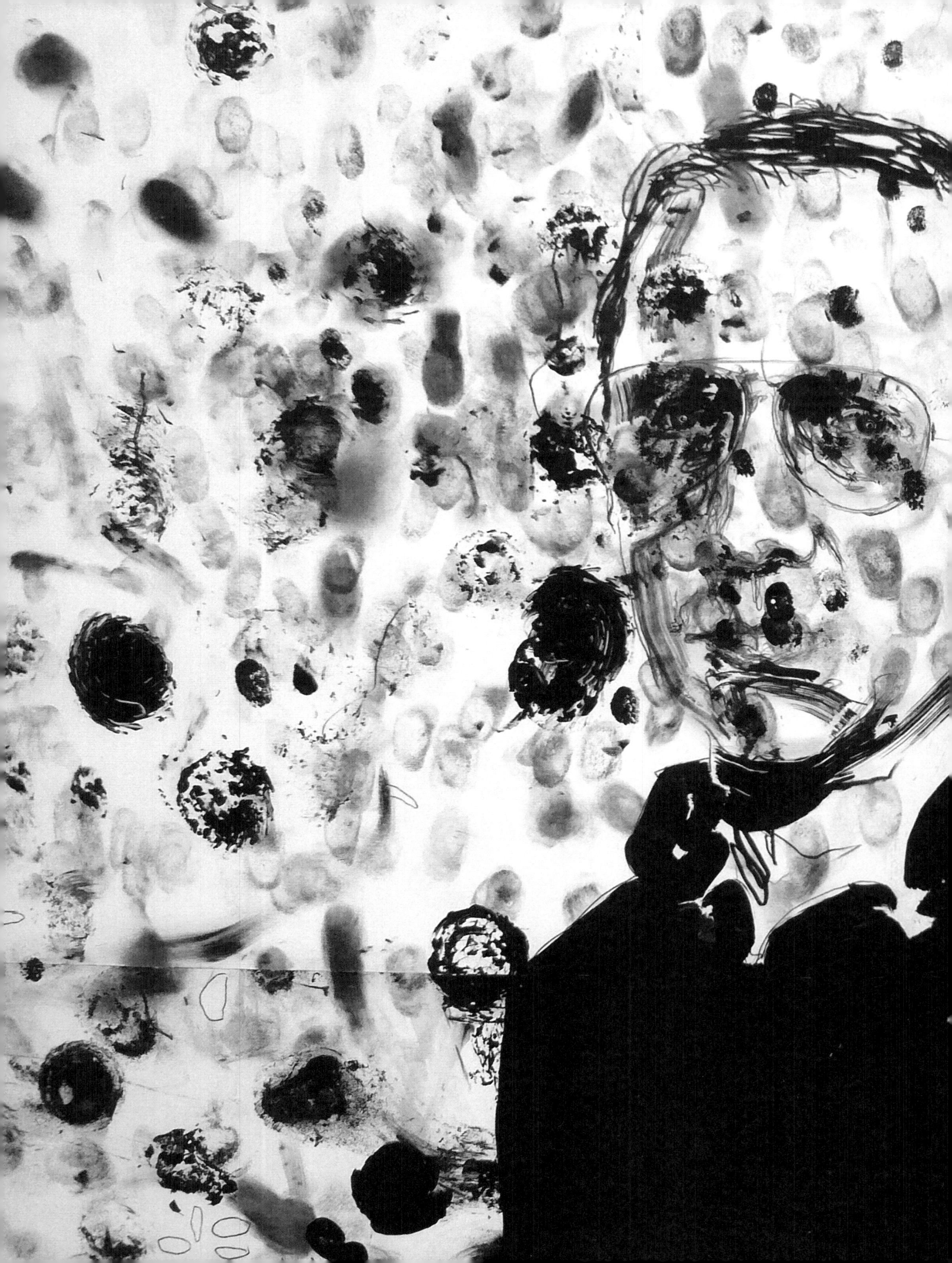

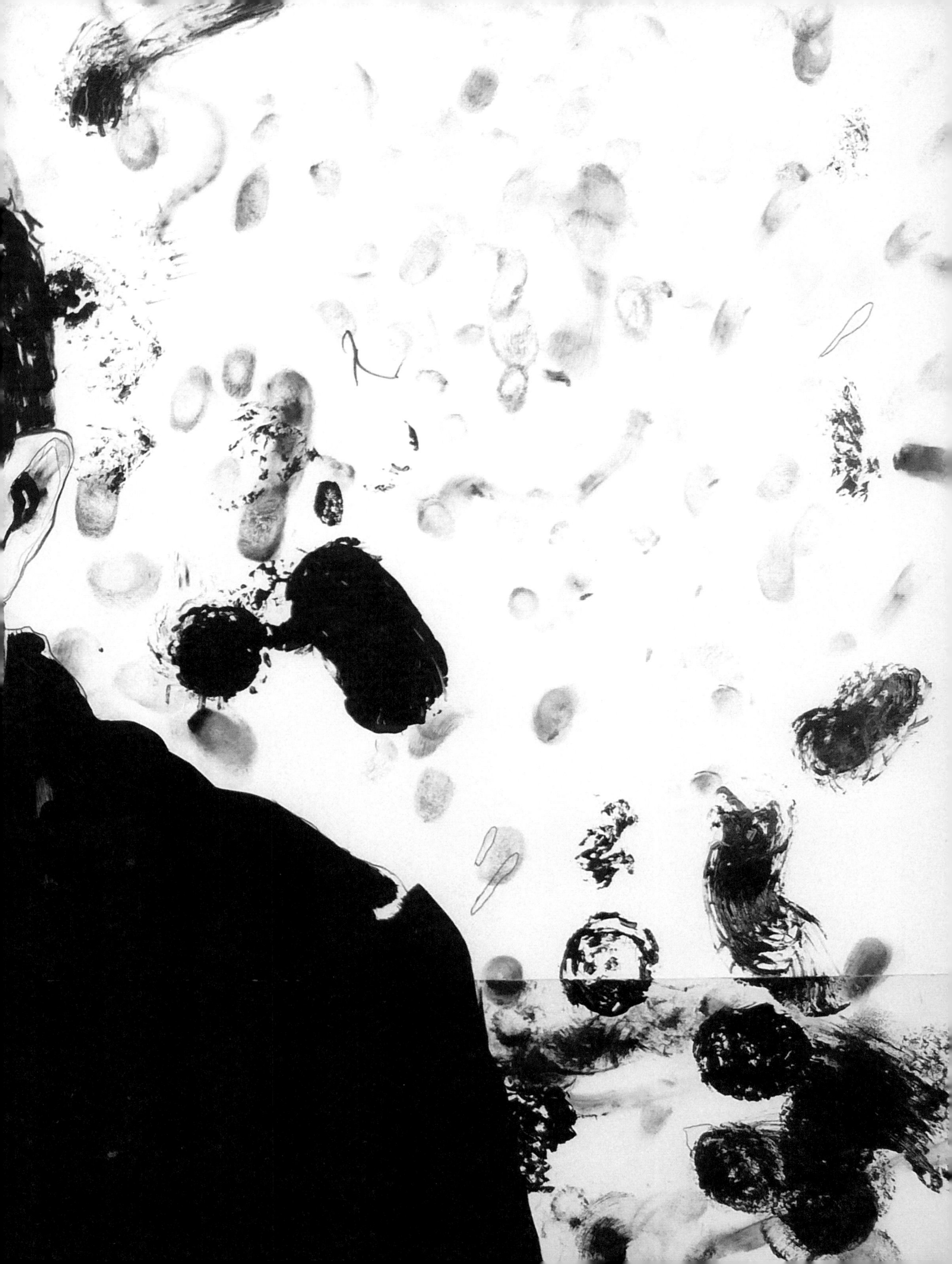

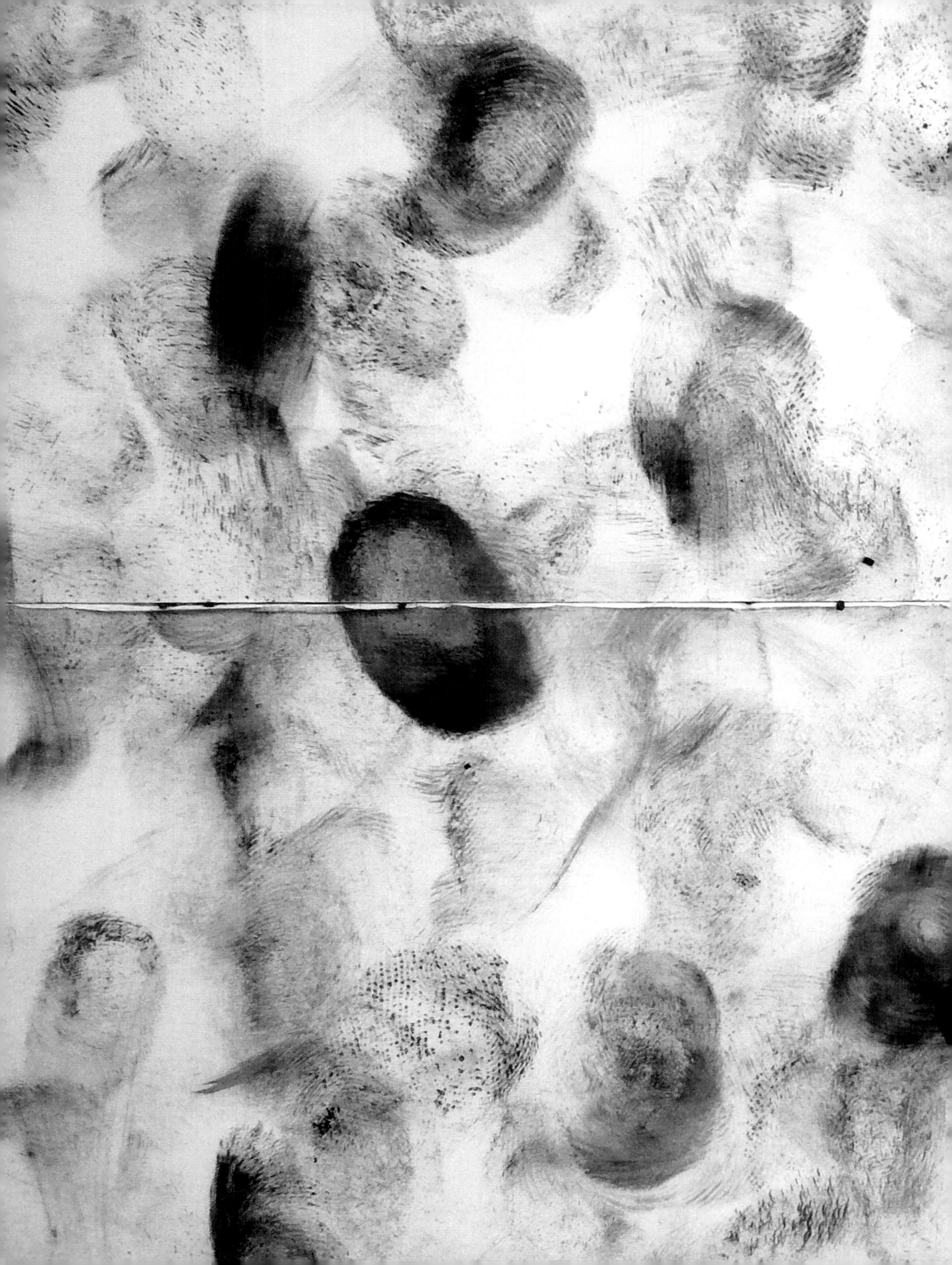

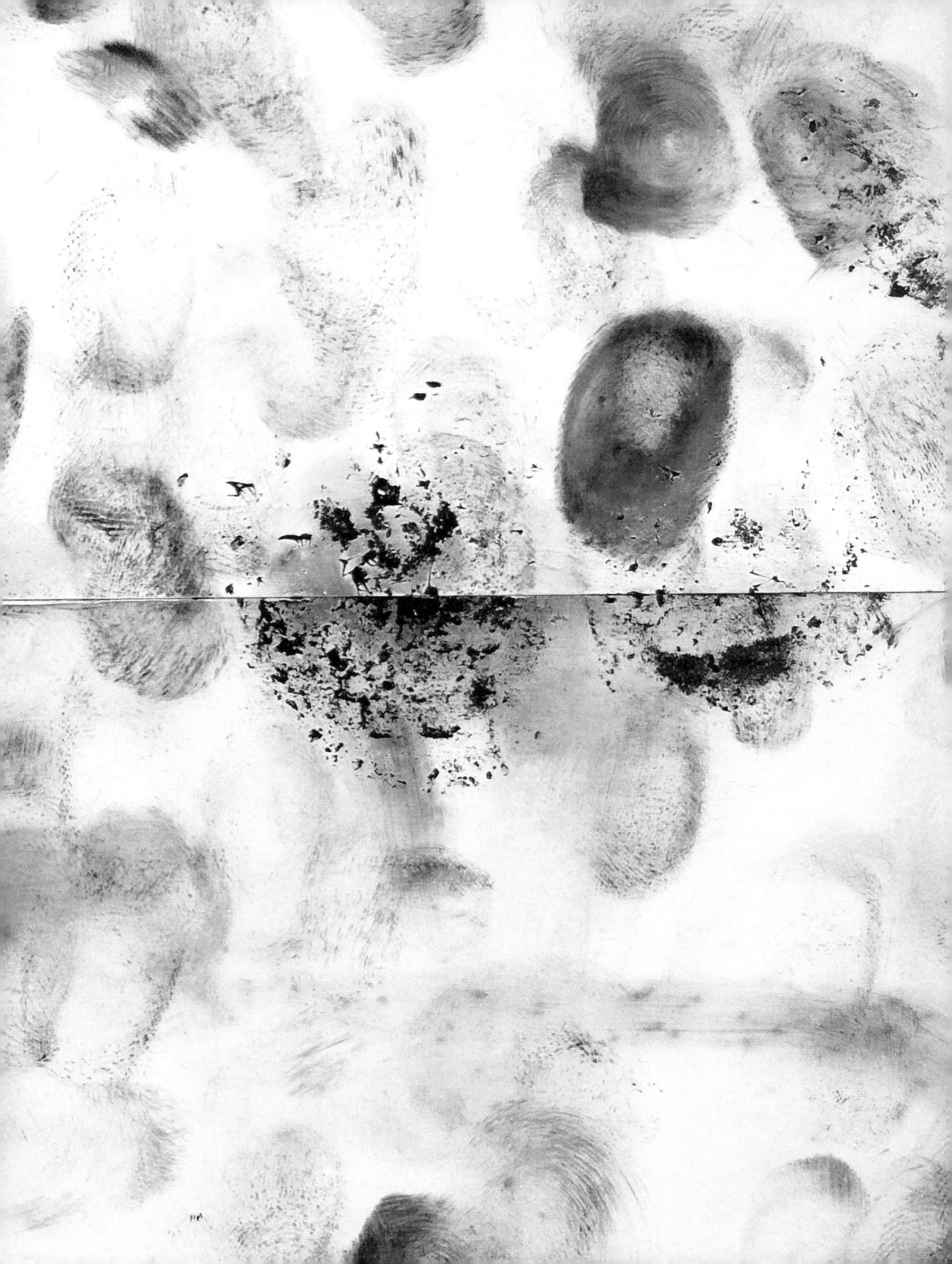

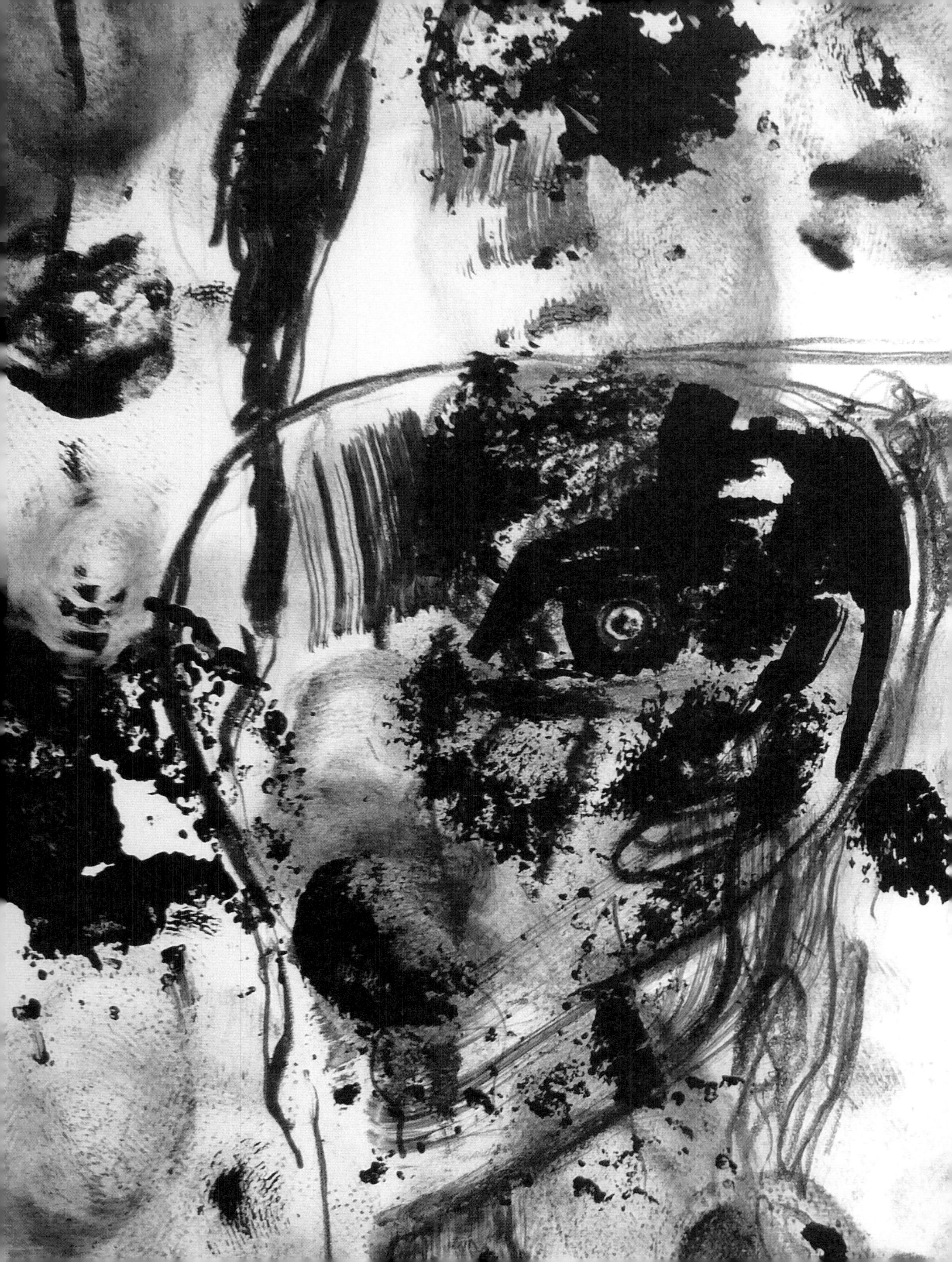

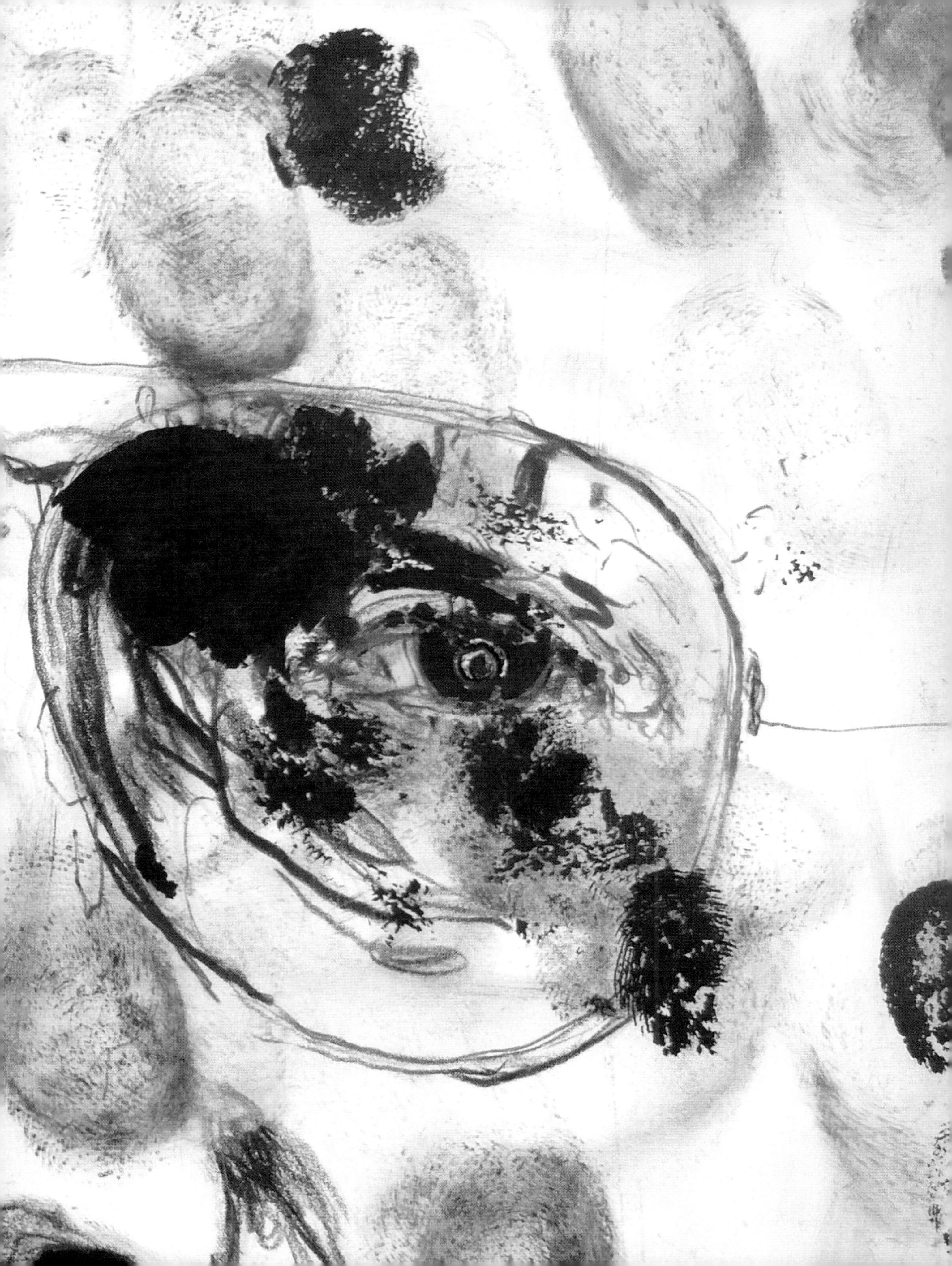

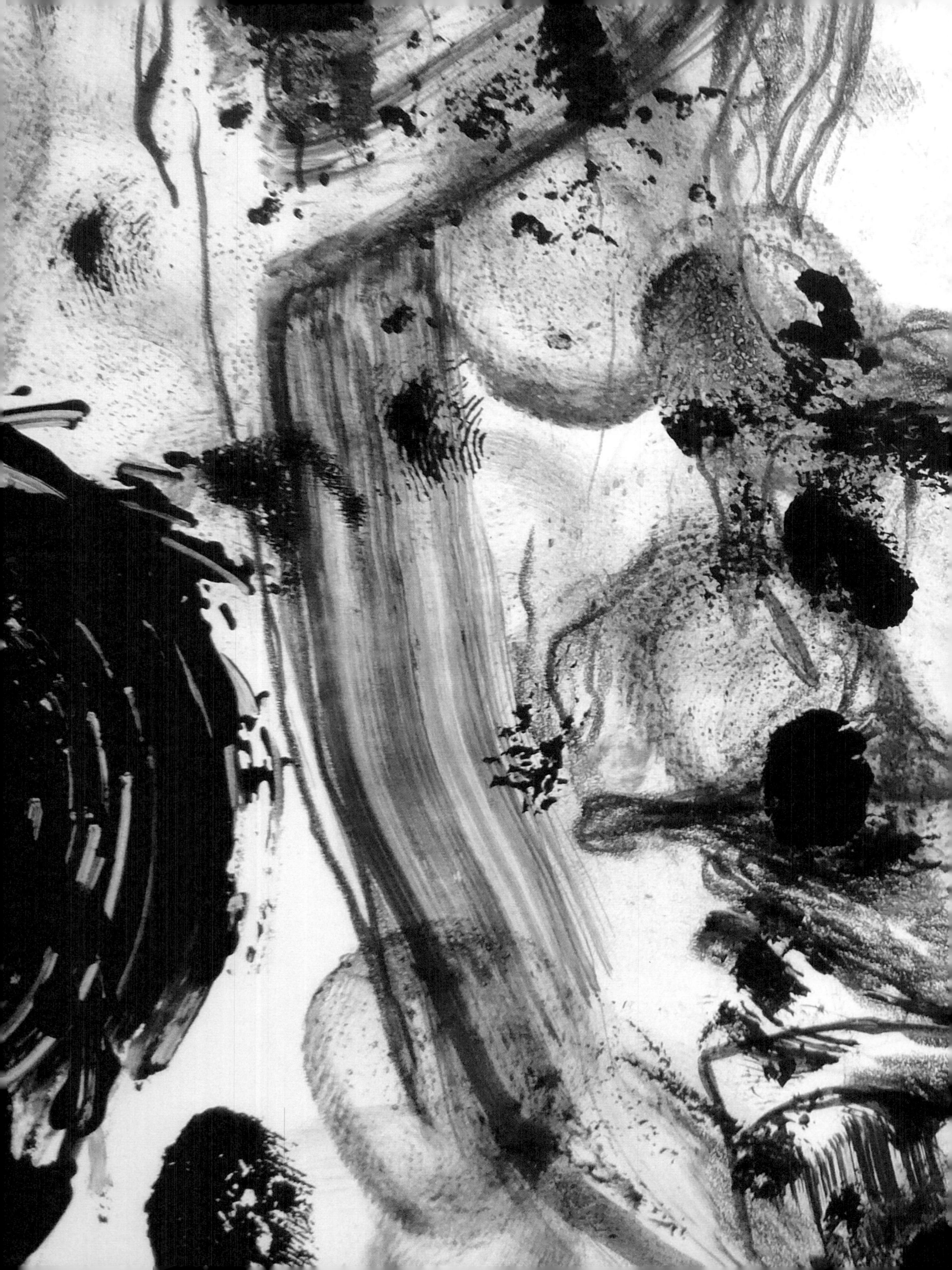

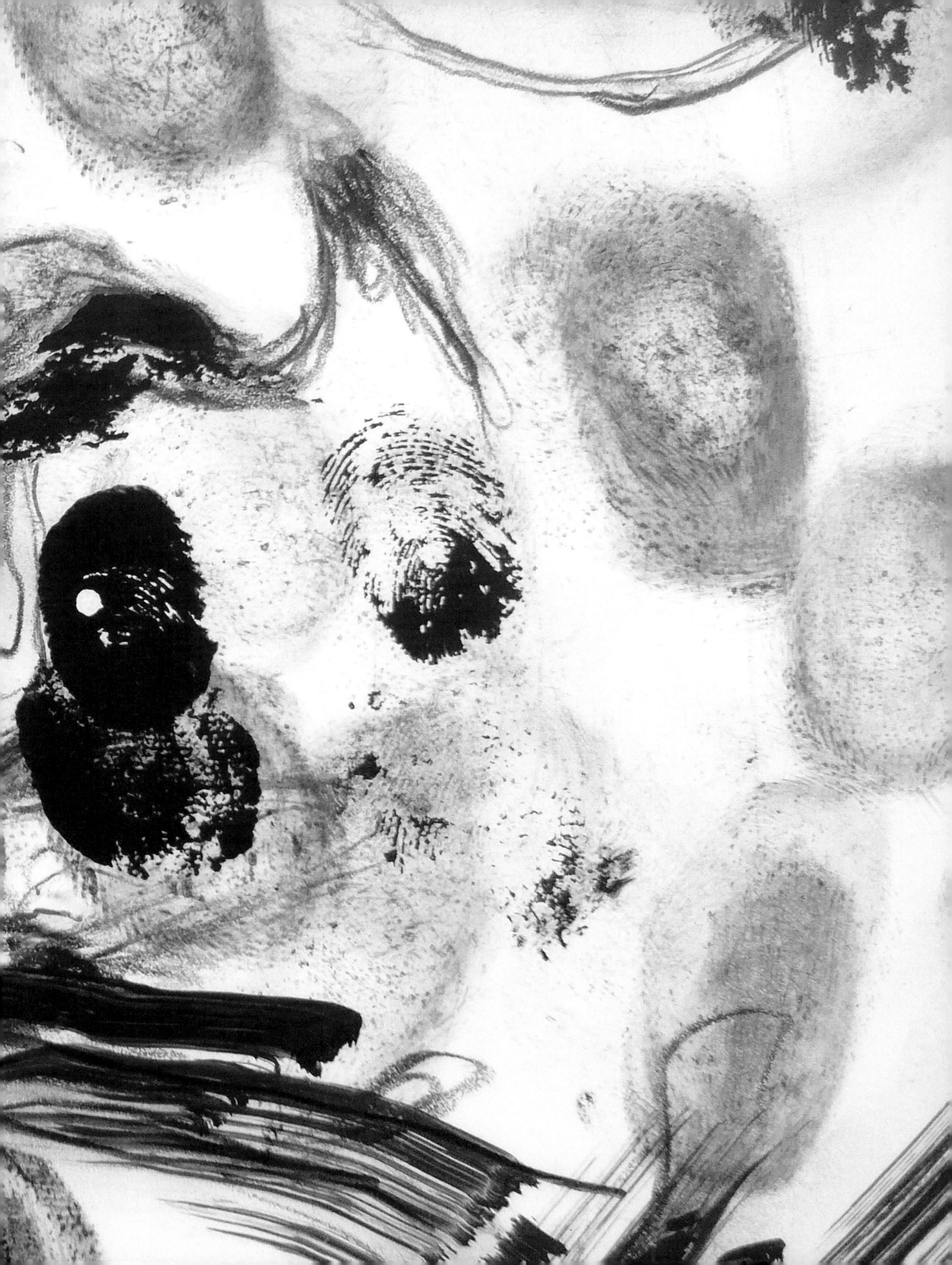

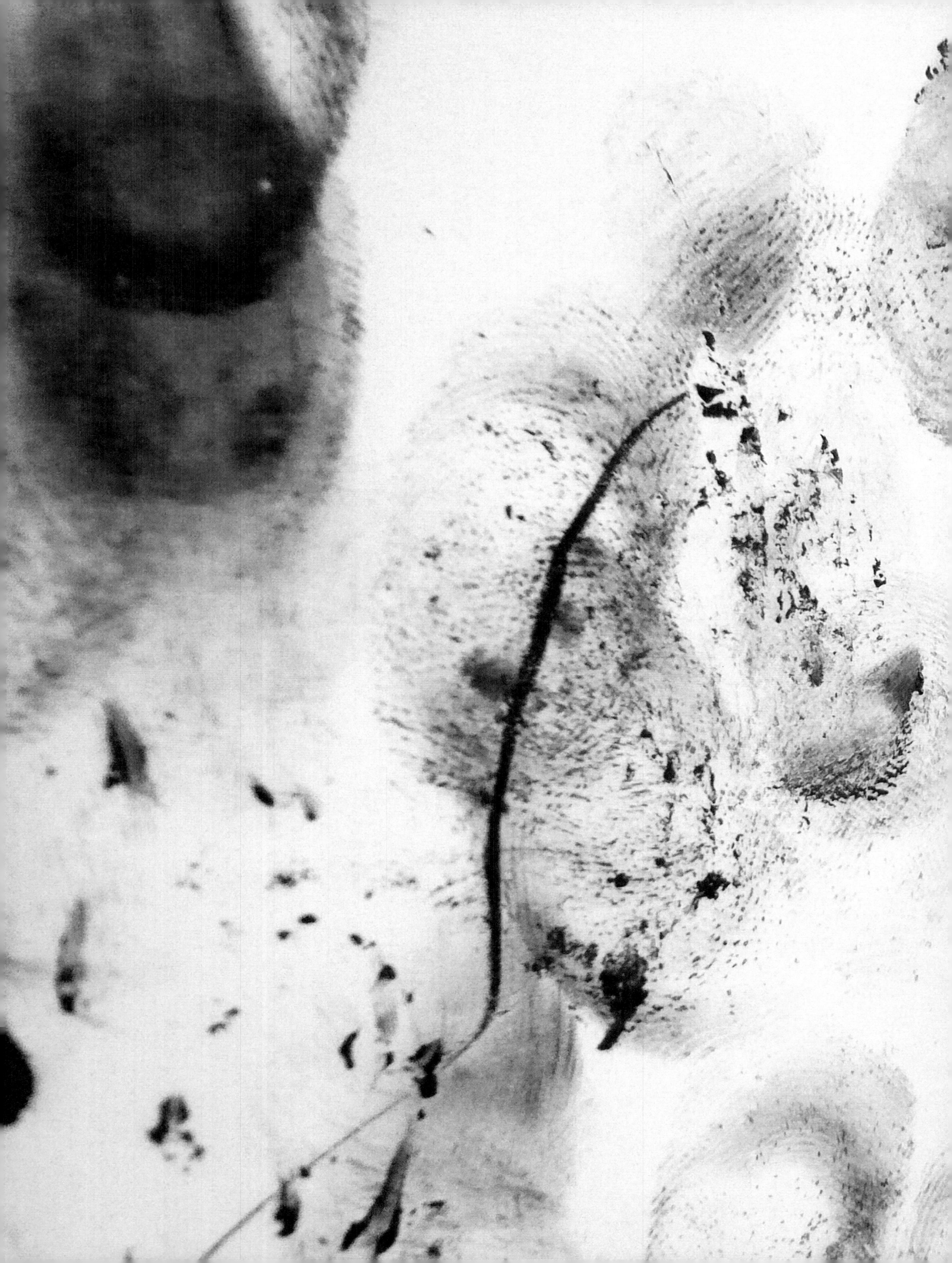

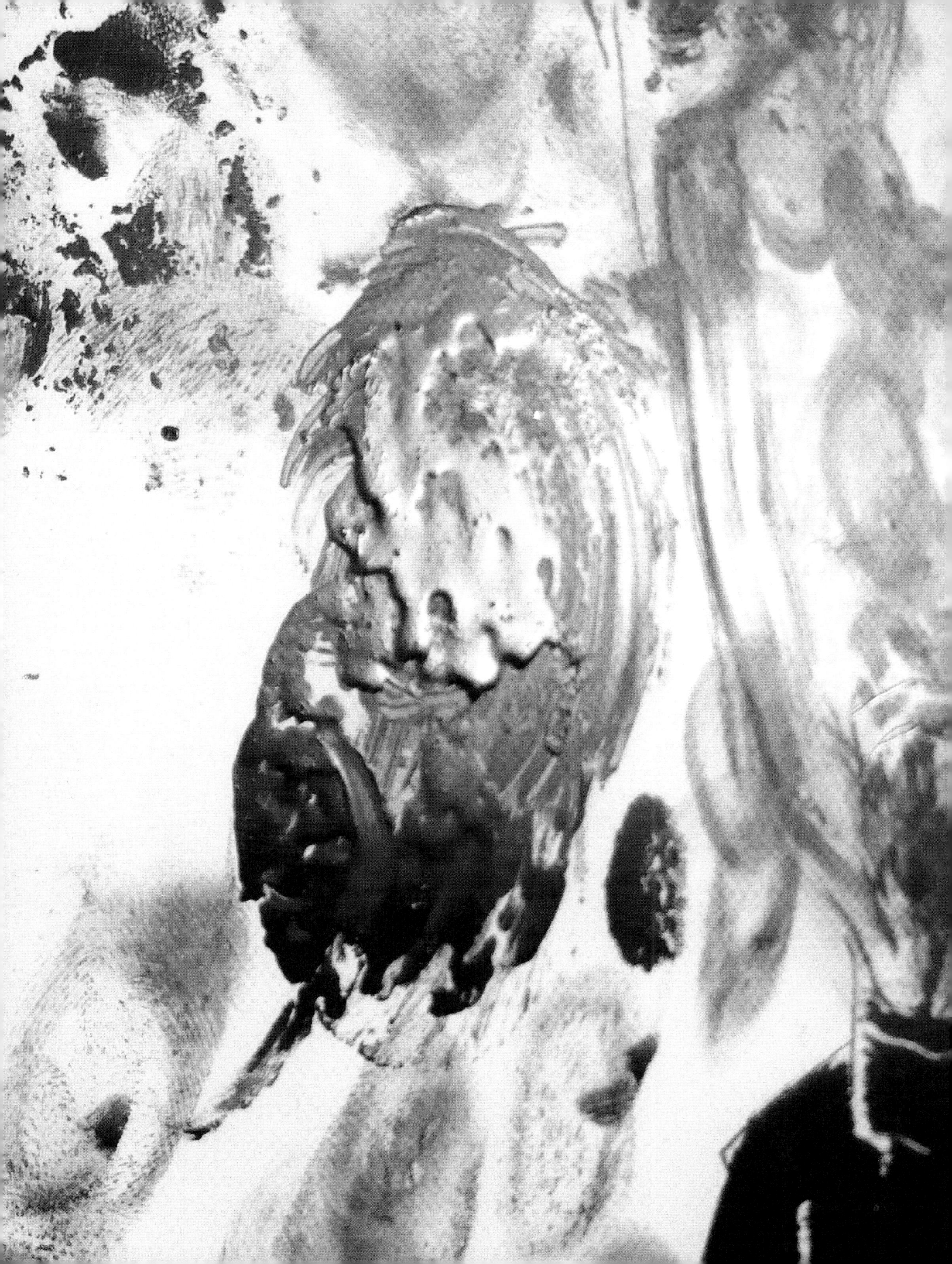

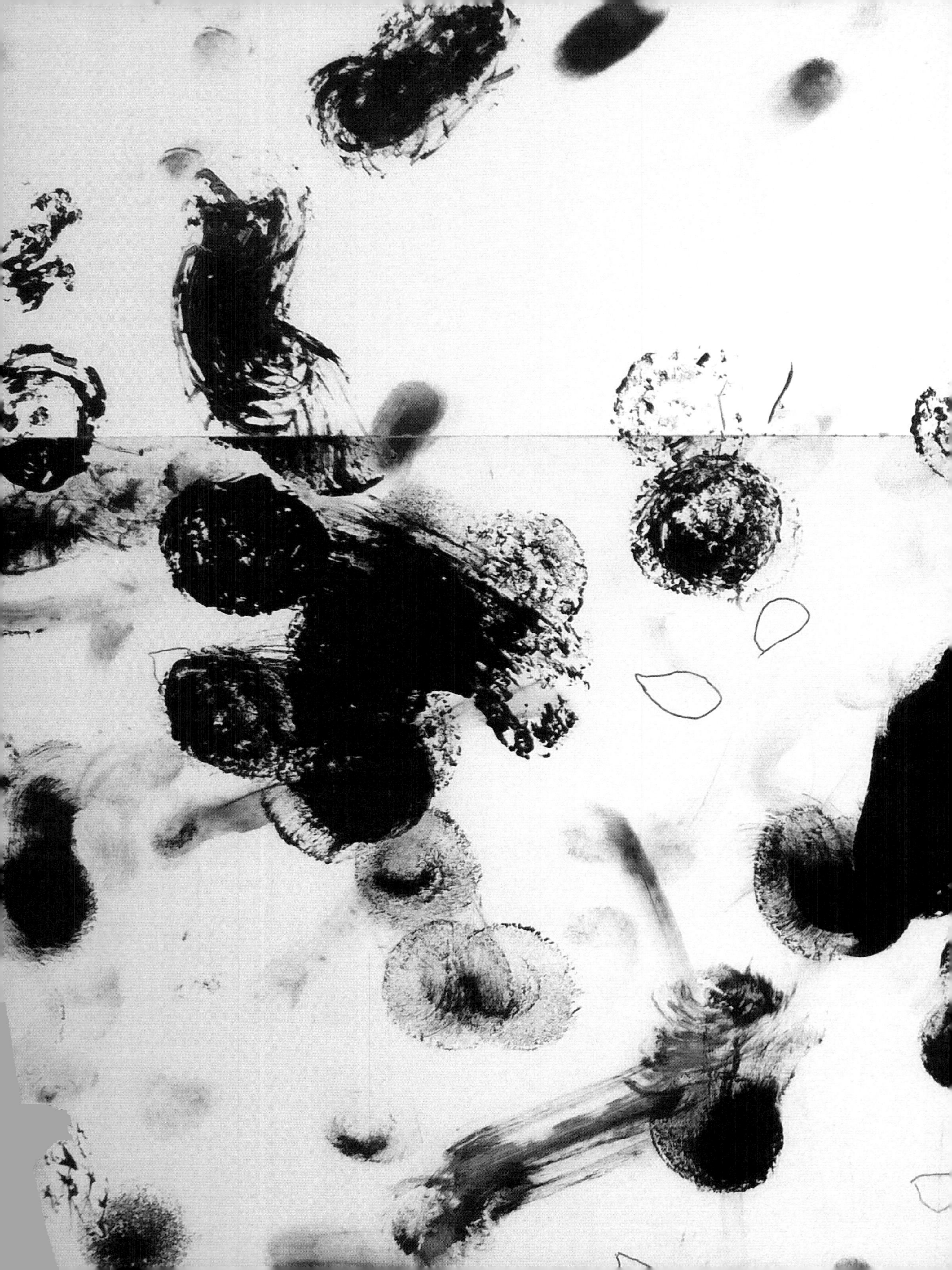

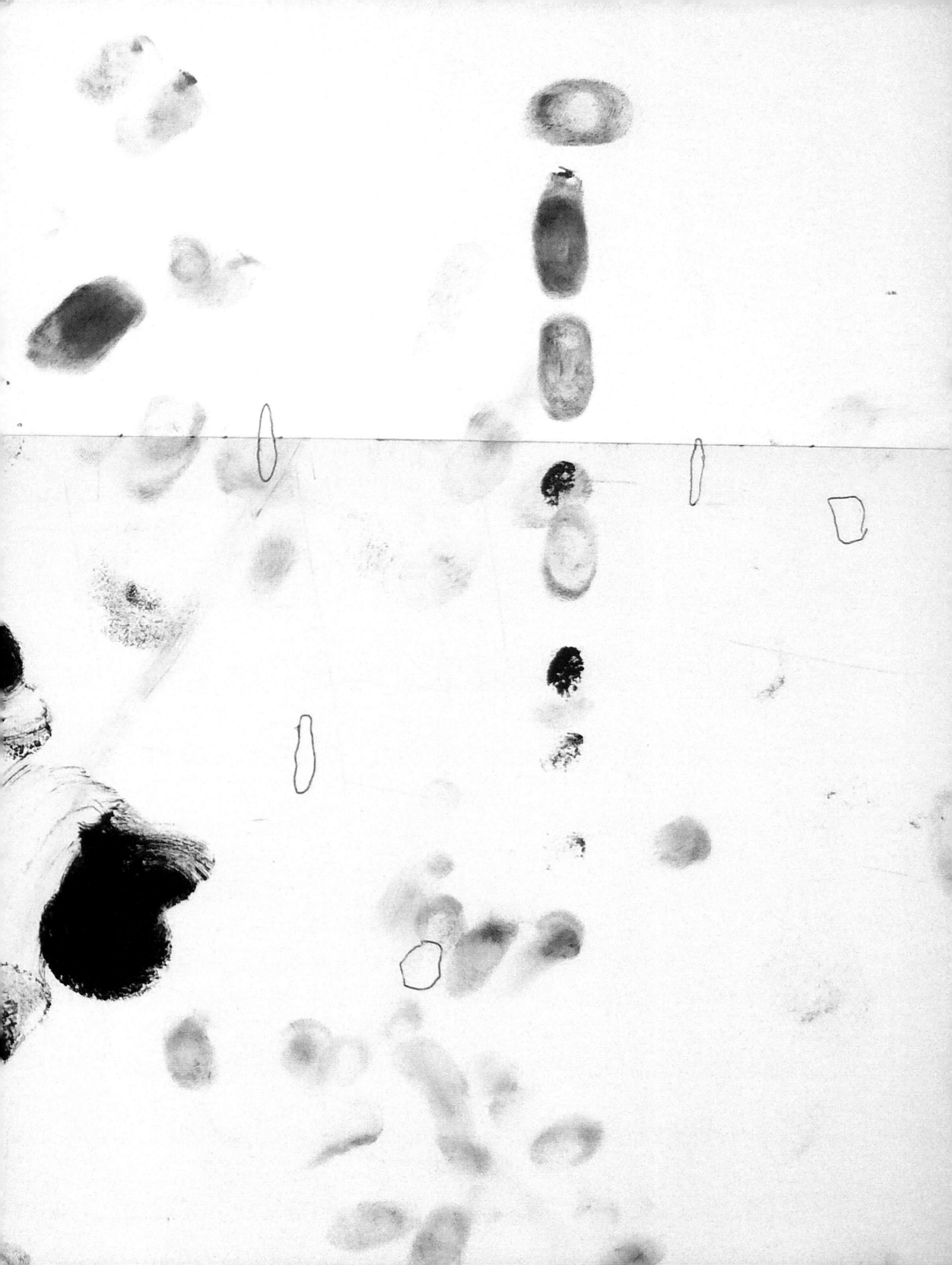

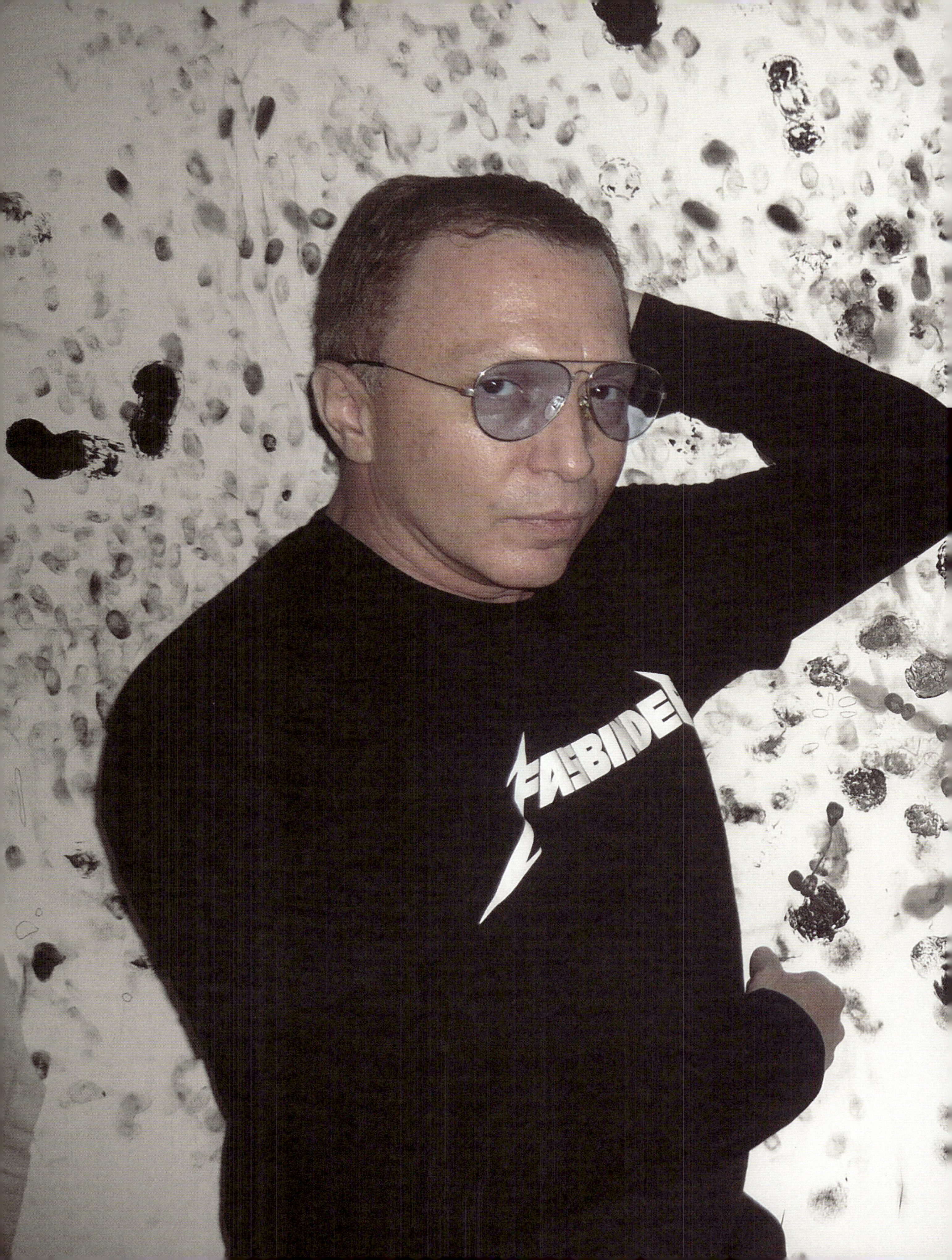

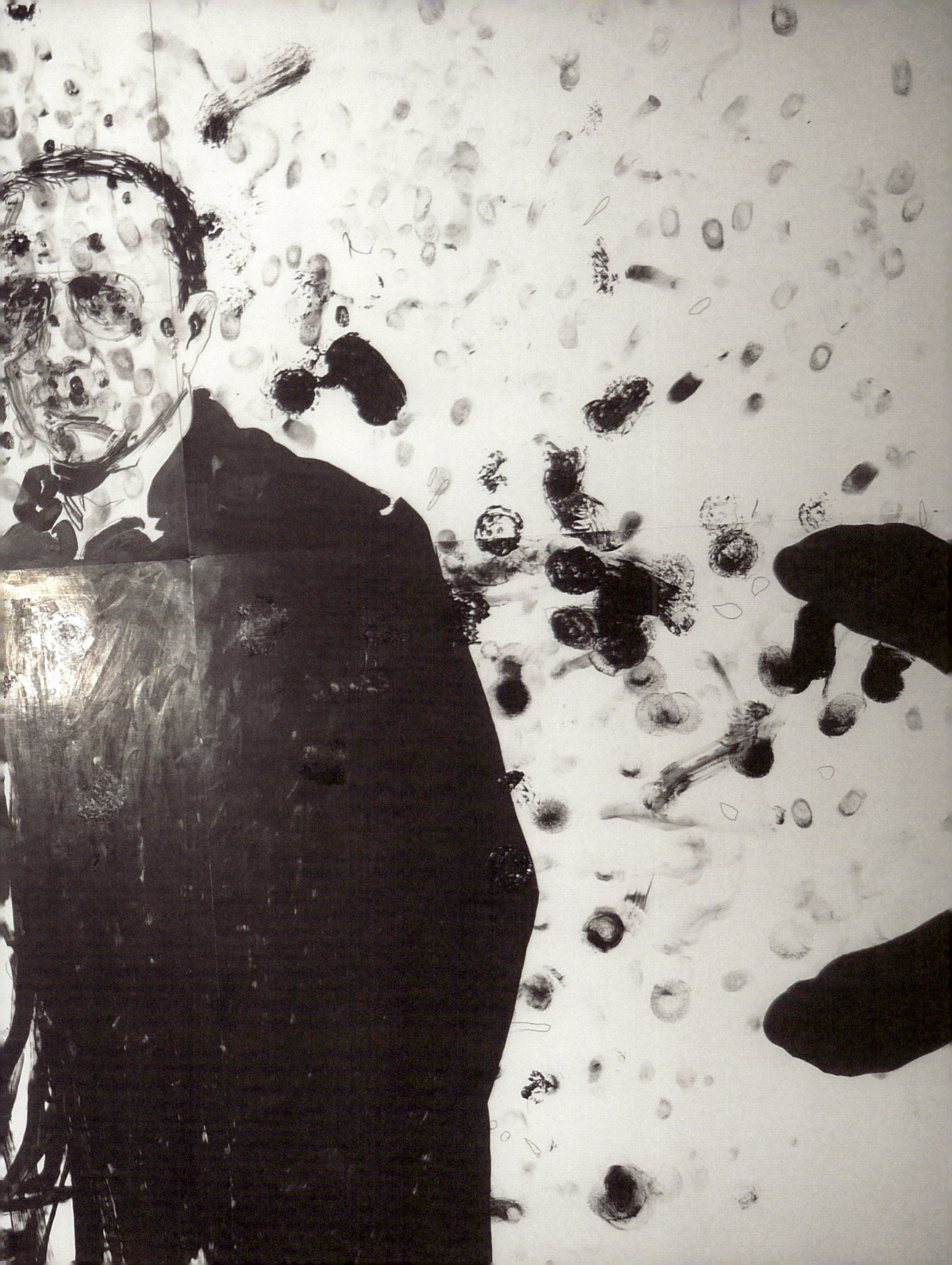

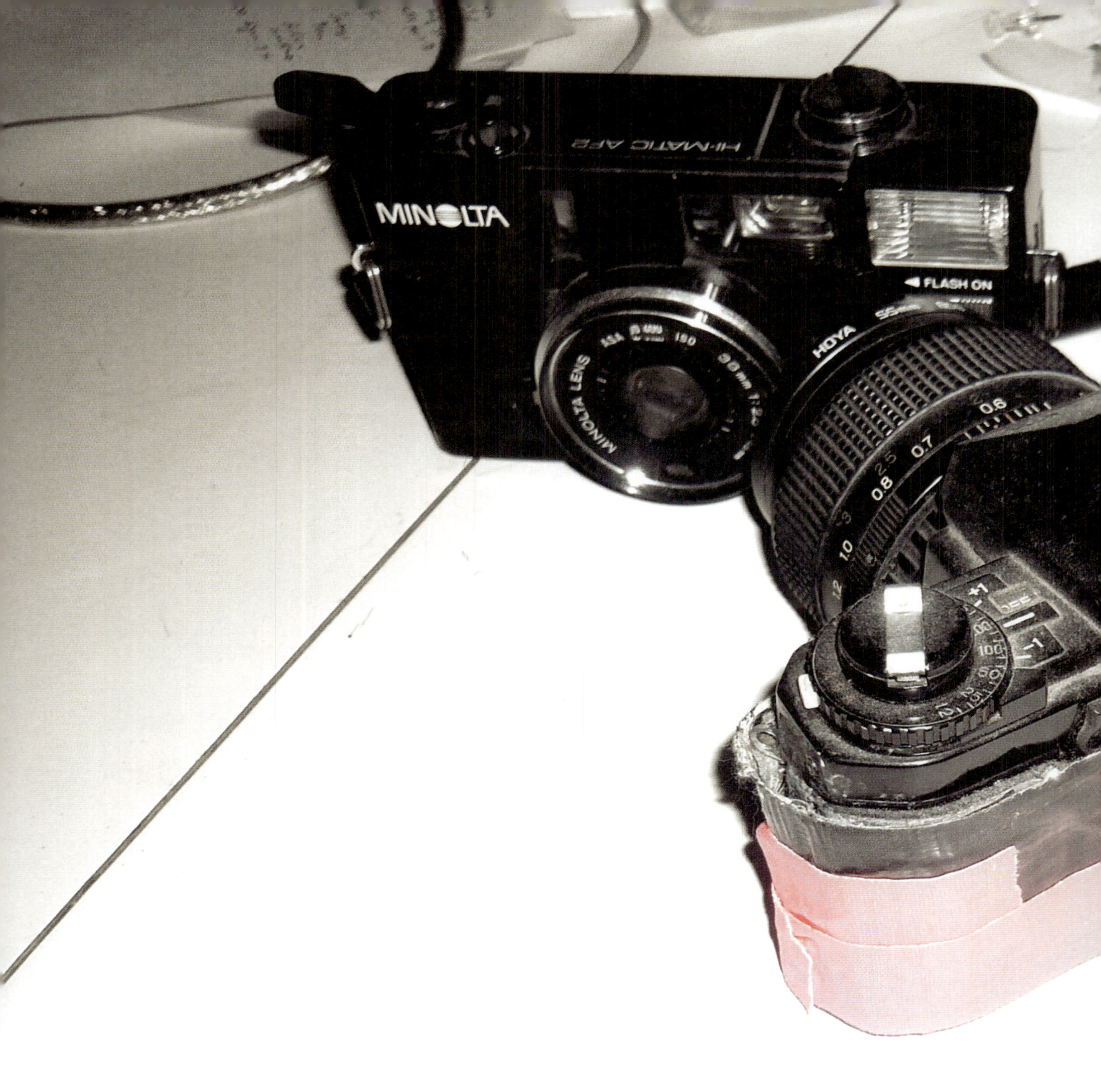

MINOLTA
HI-MATIC AF2
FLASH ON
MINOLTA LENS
HOYA

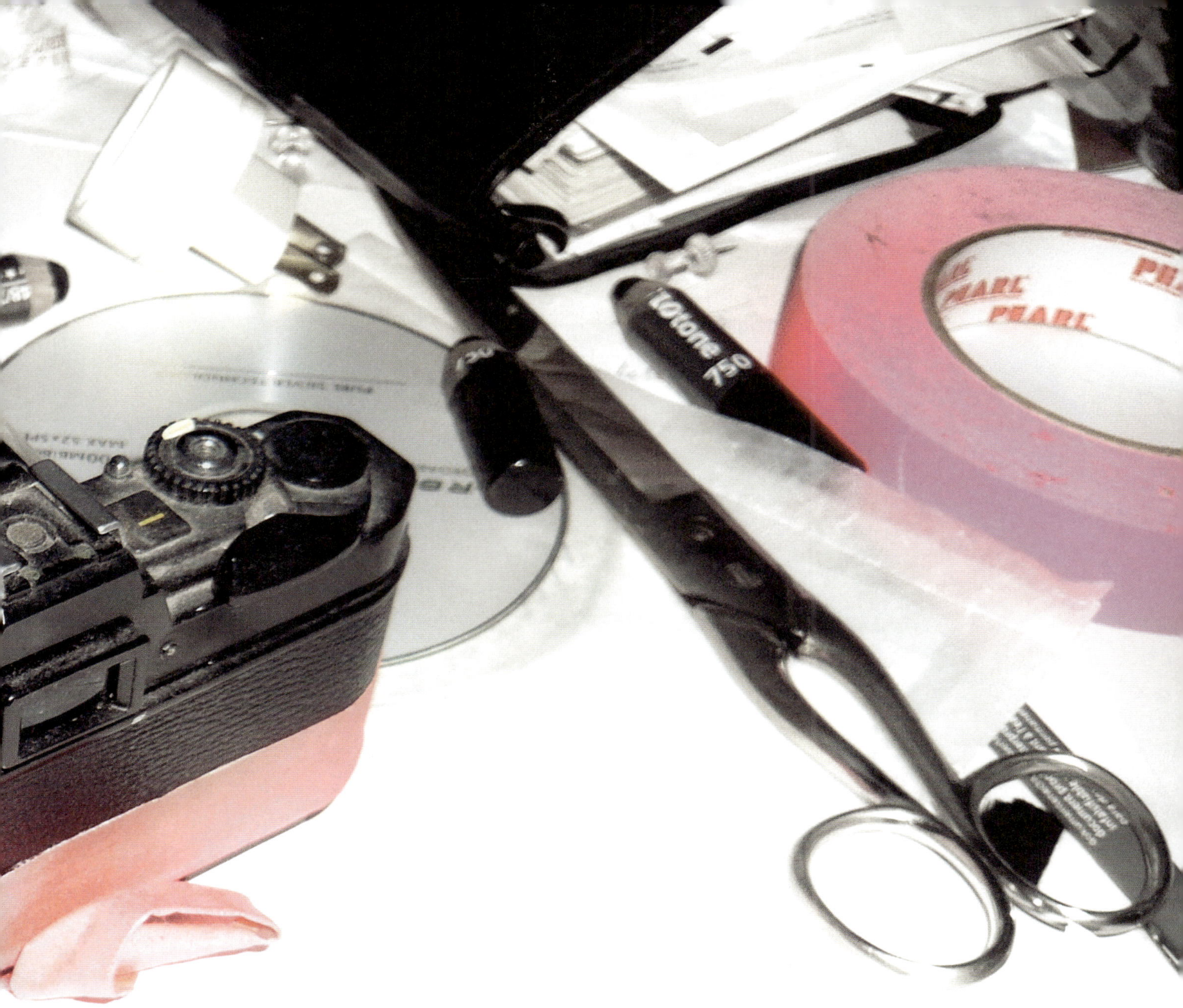

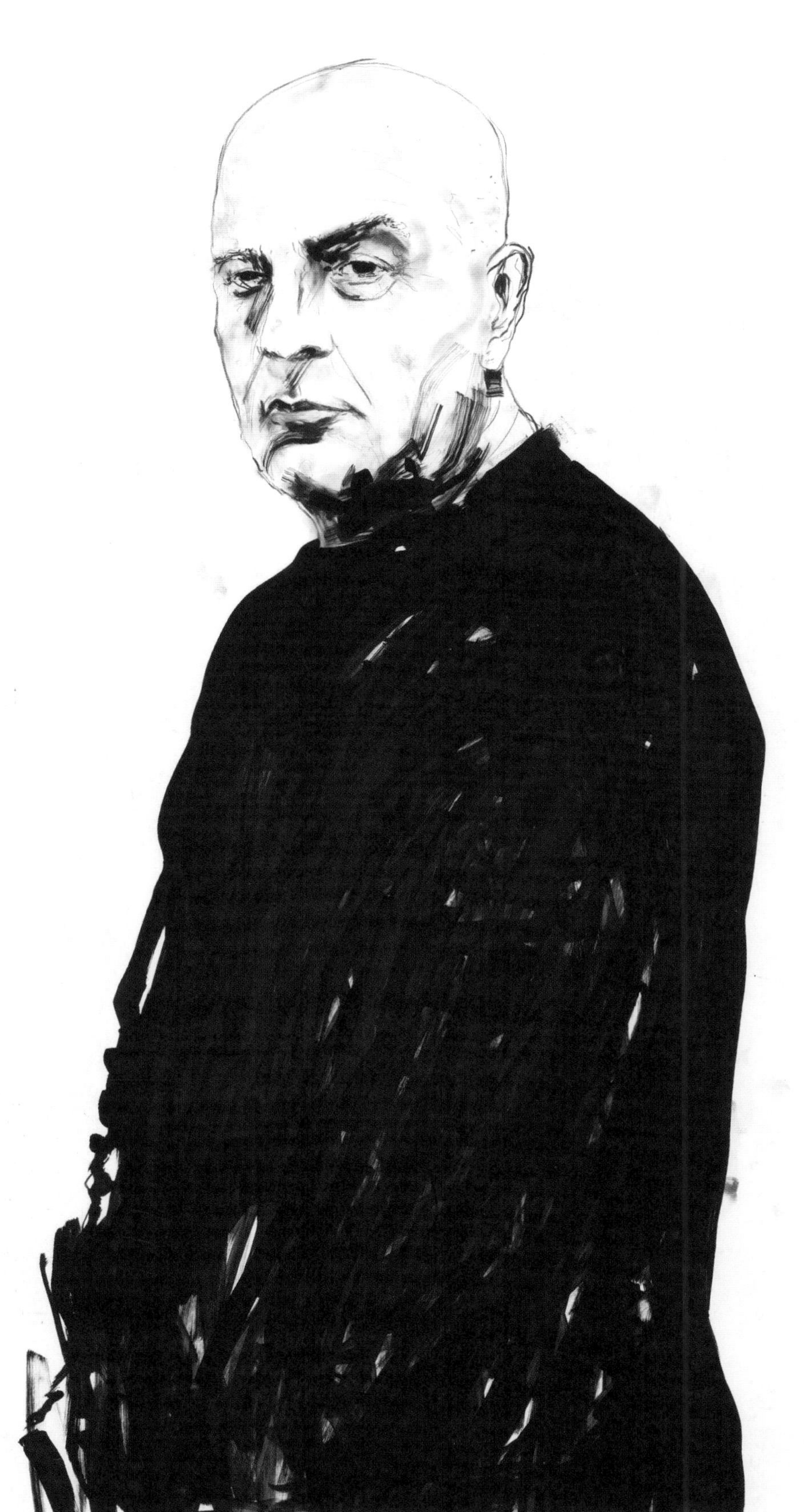

JEAN BAPTISTE MONDINO
PARIS, FEB.

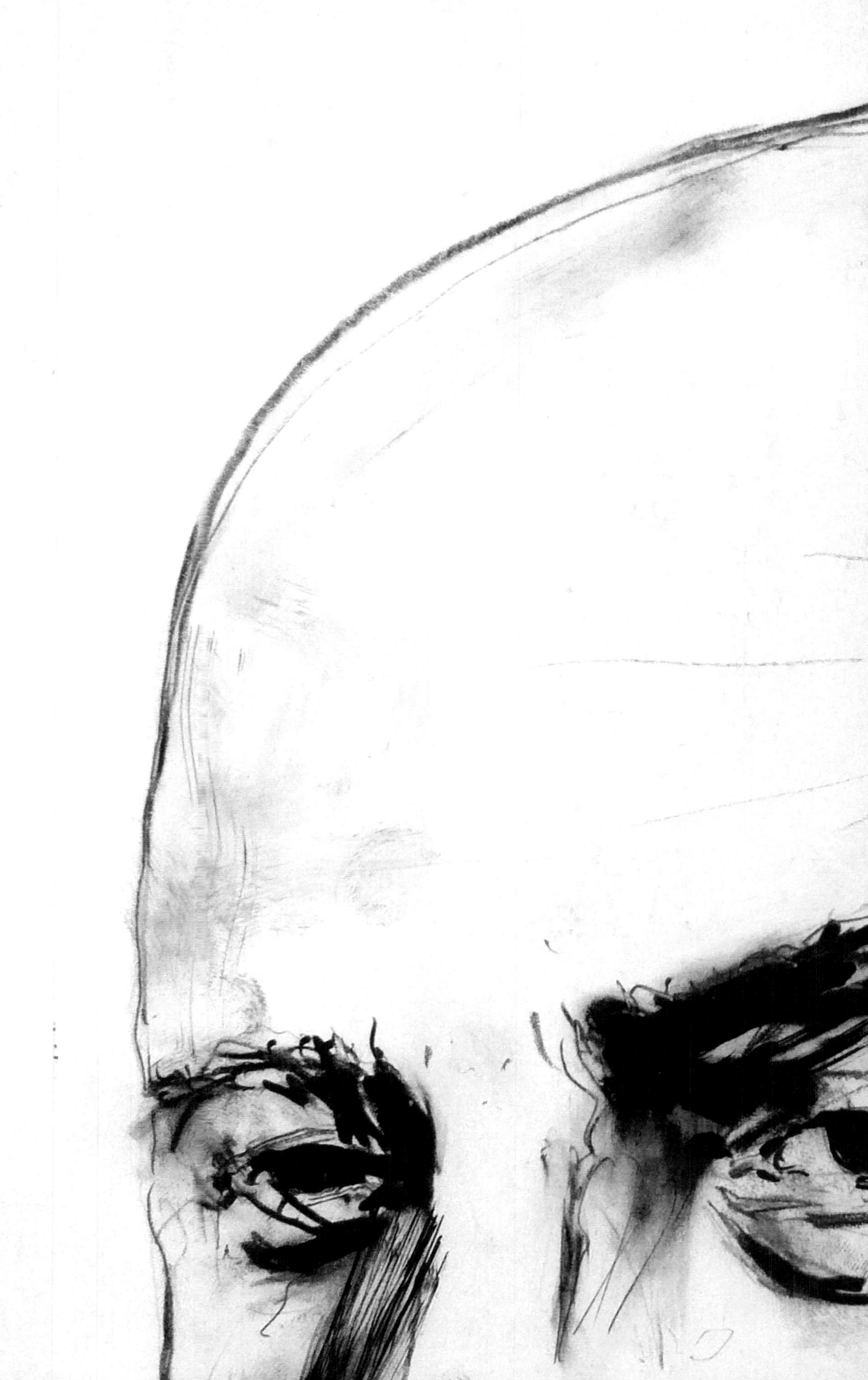

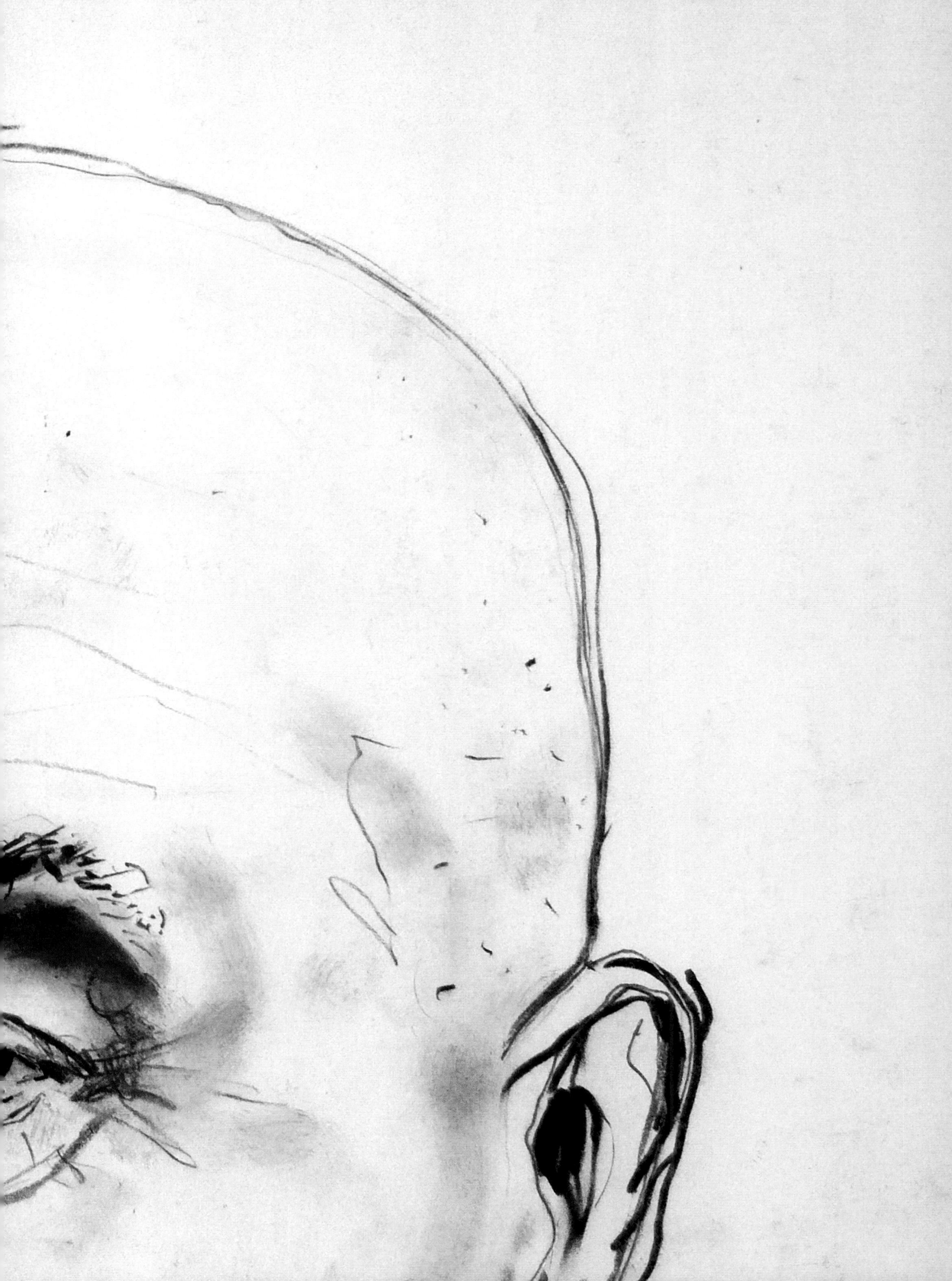

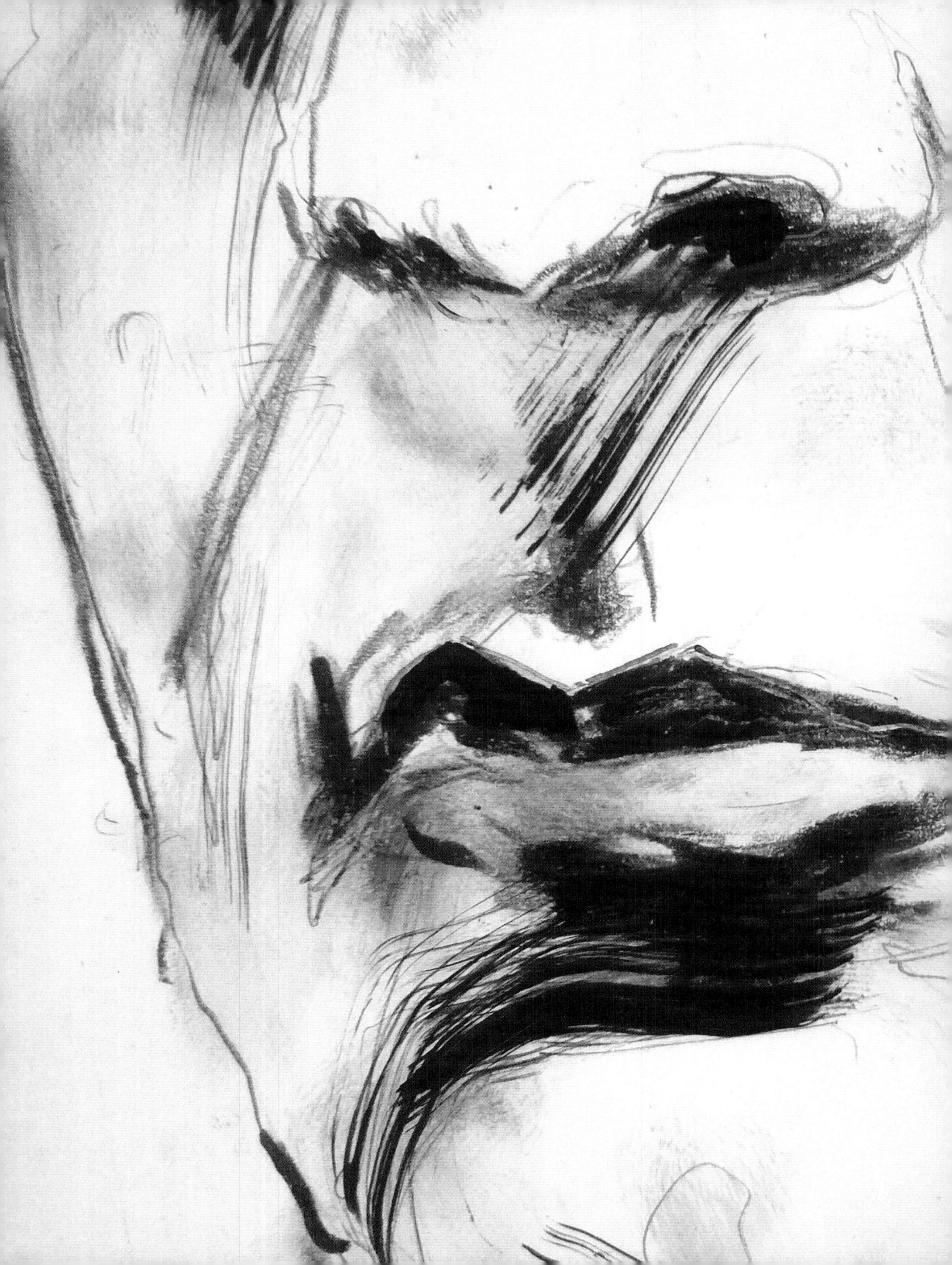

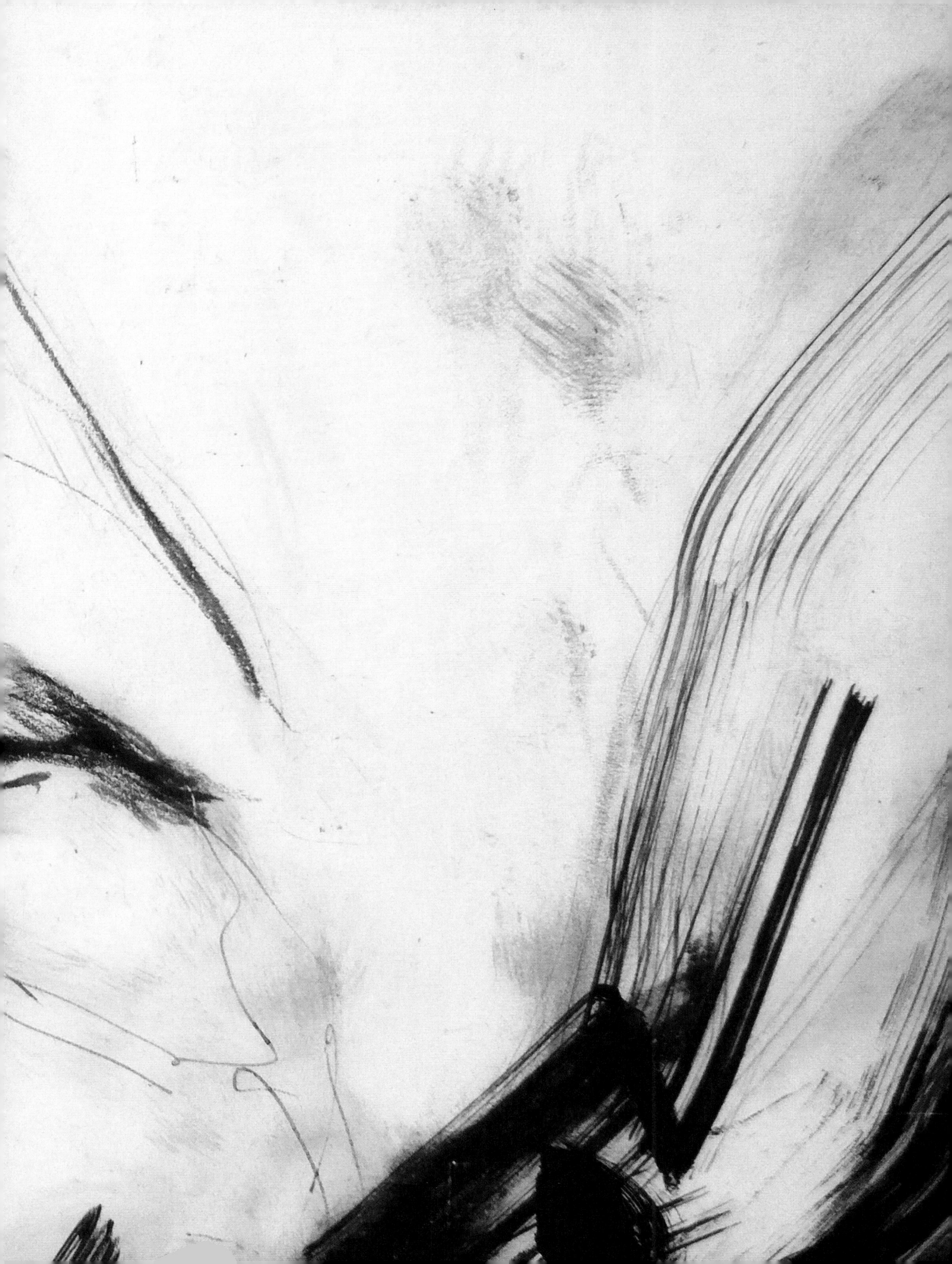

WALTER VAN BEIRENDONCK (EXTENDED)
PARIS, 2006/07

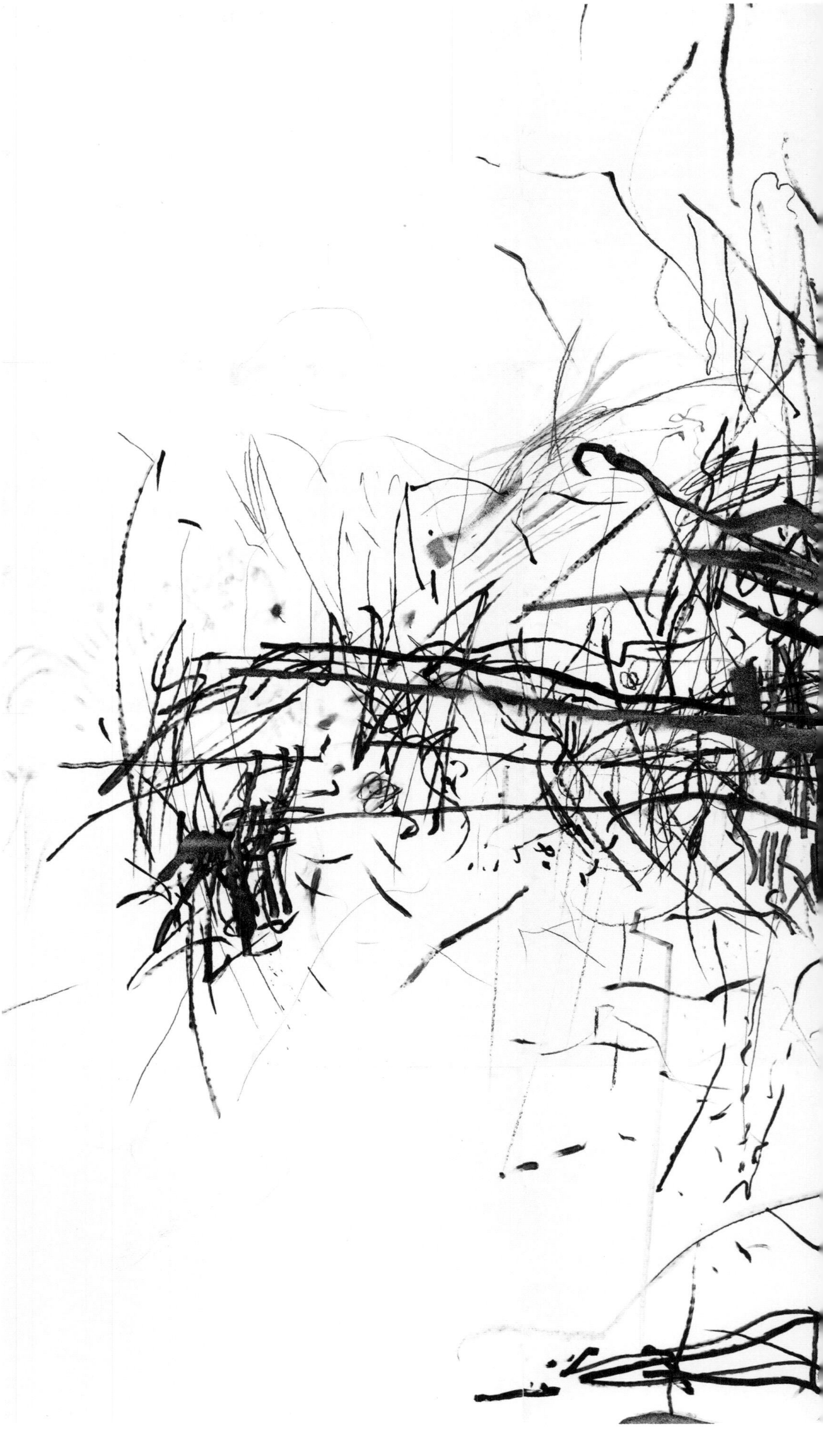

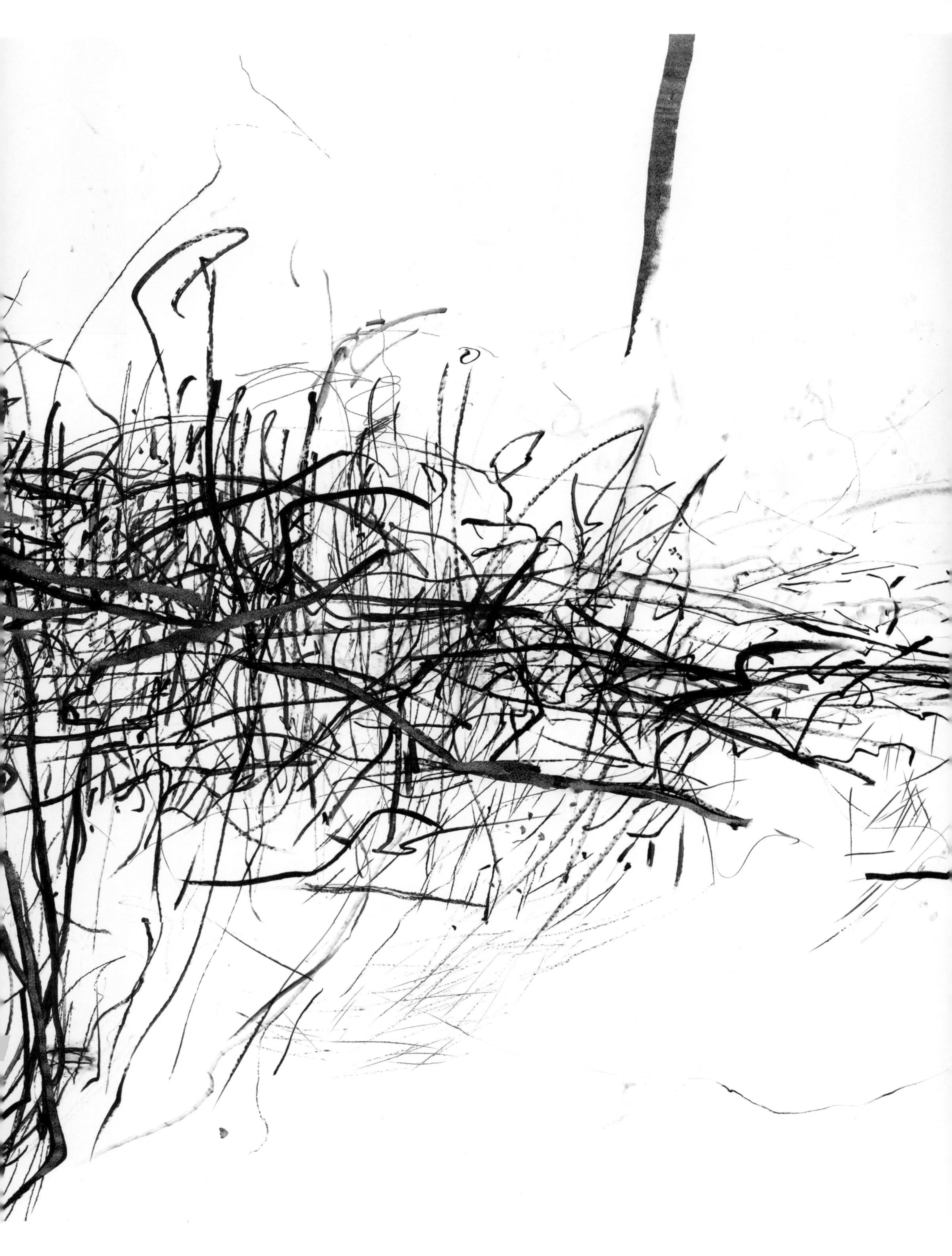

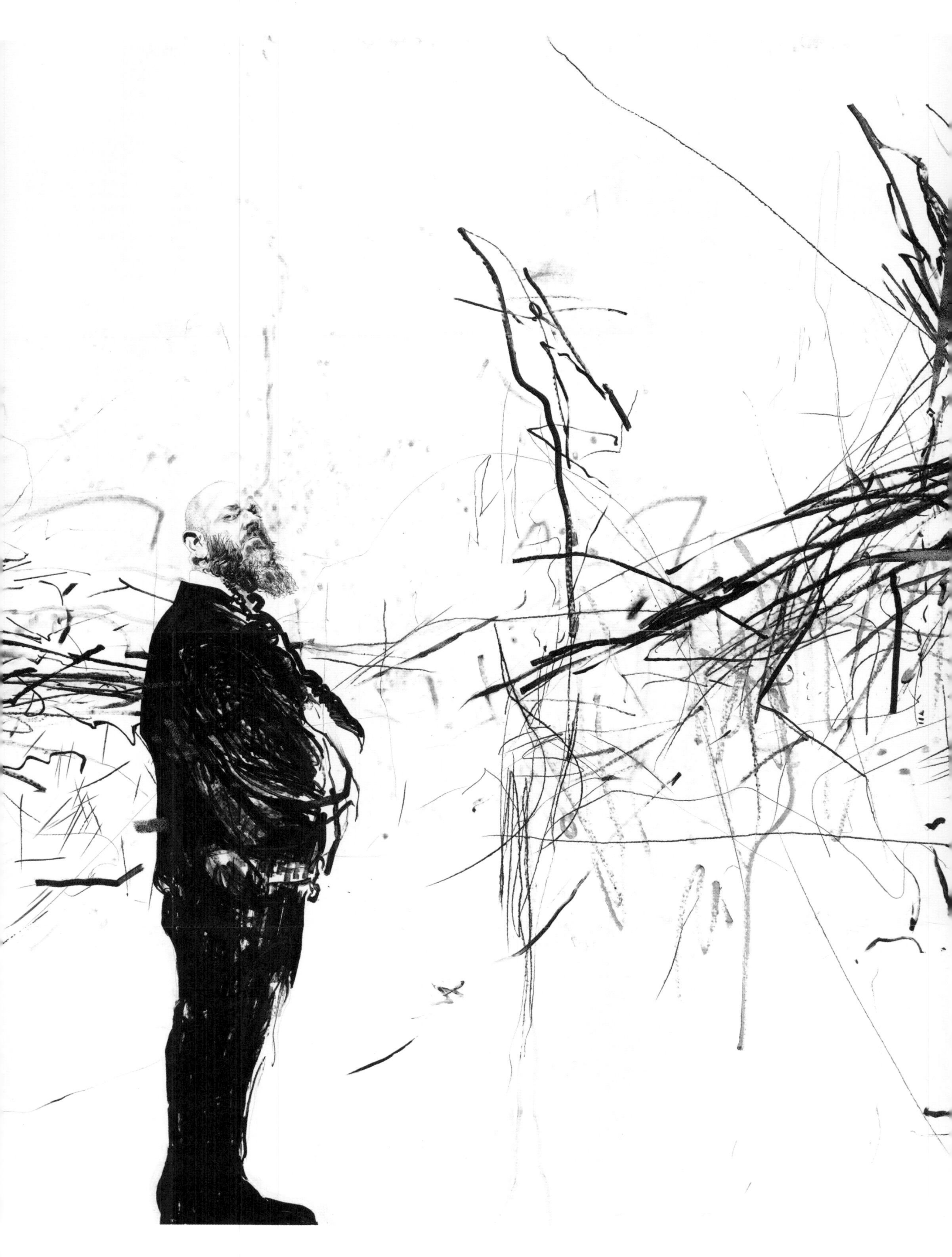

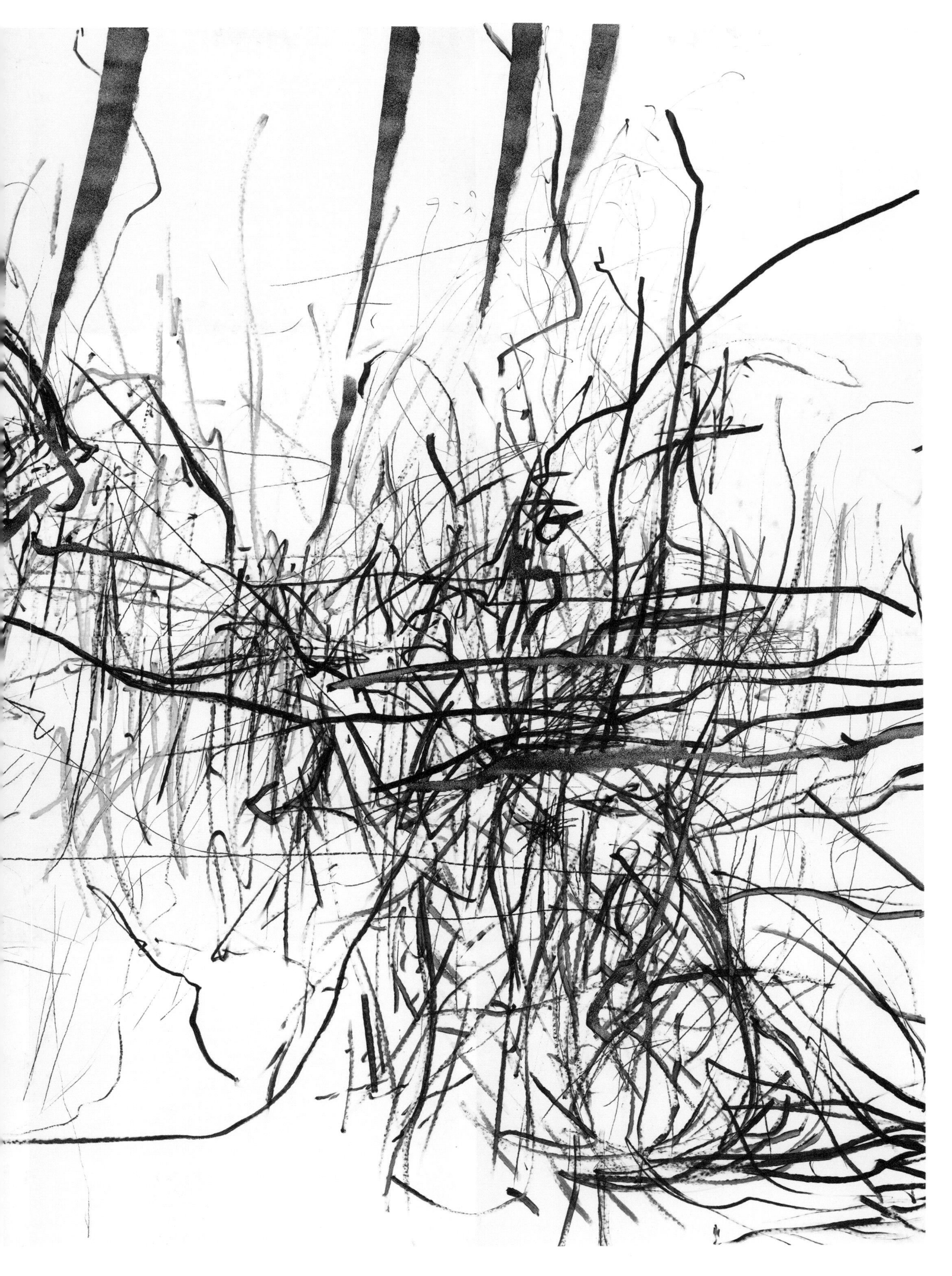

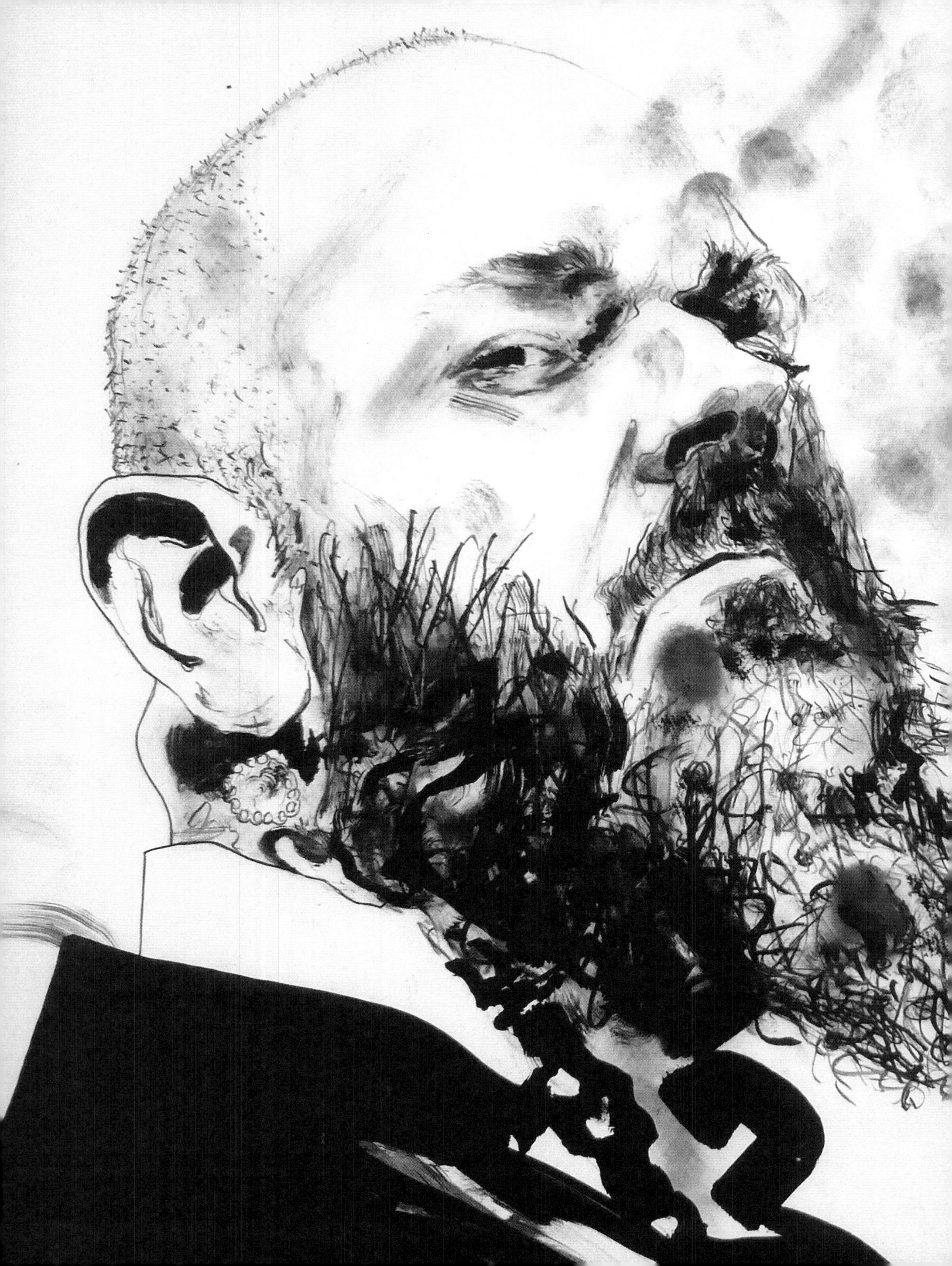

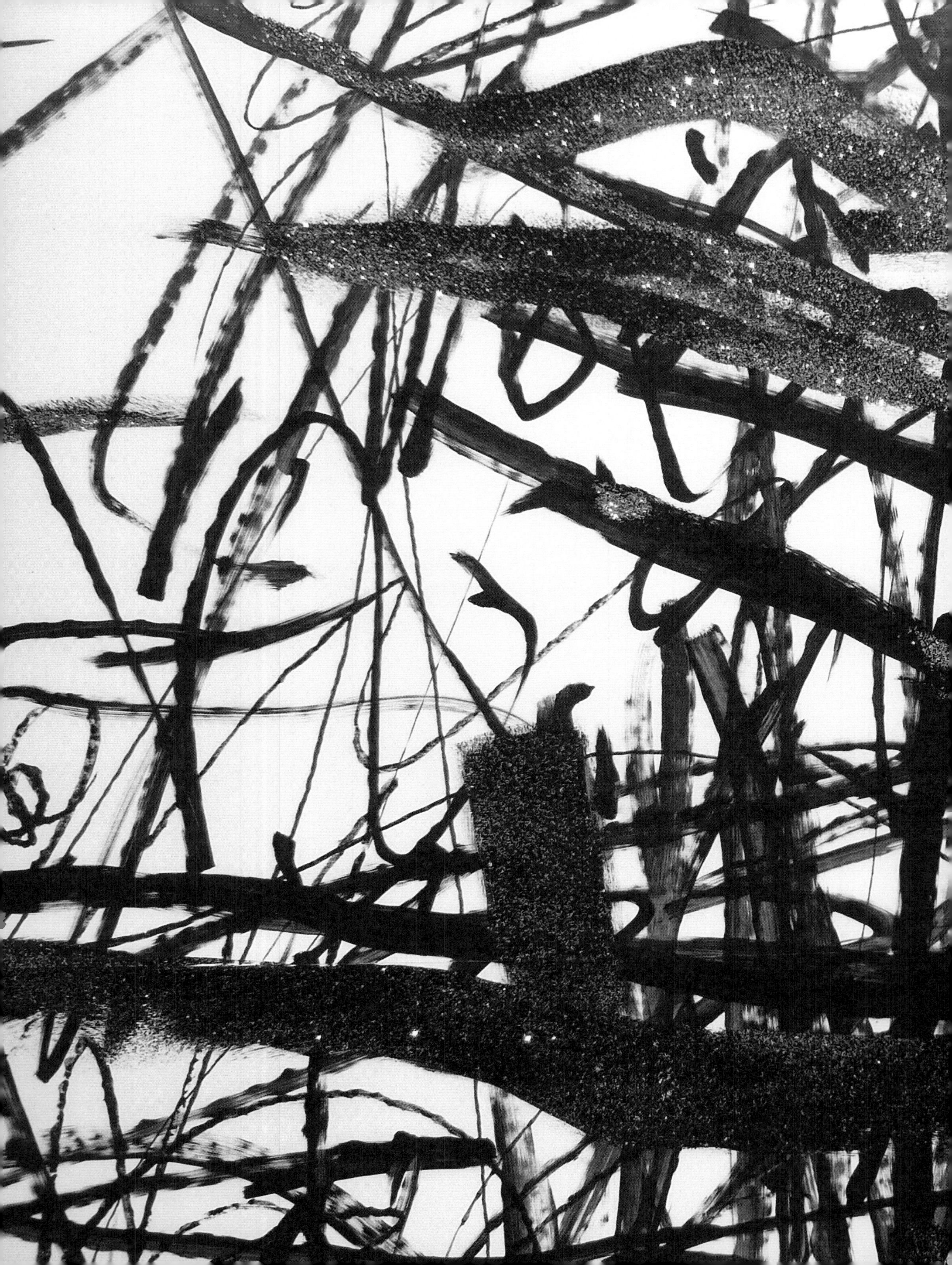

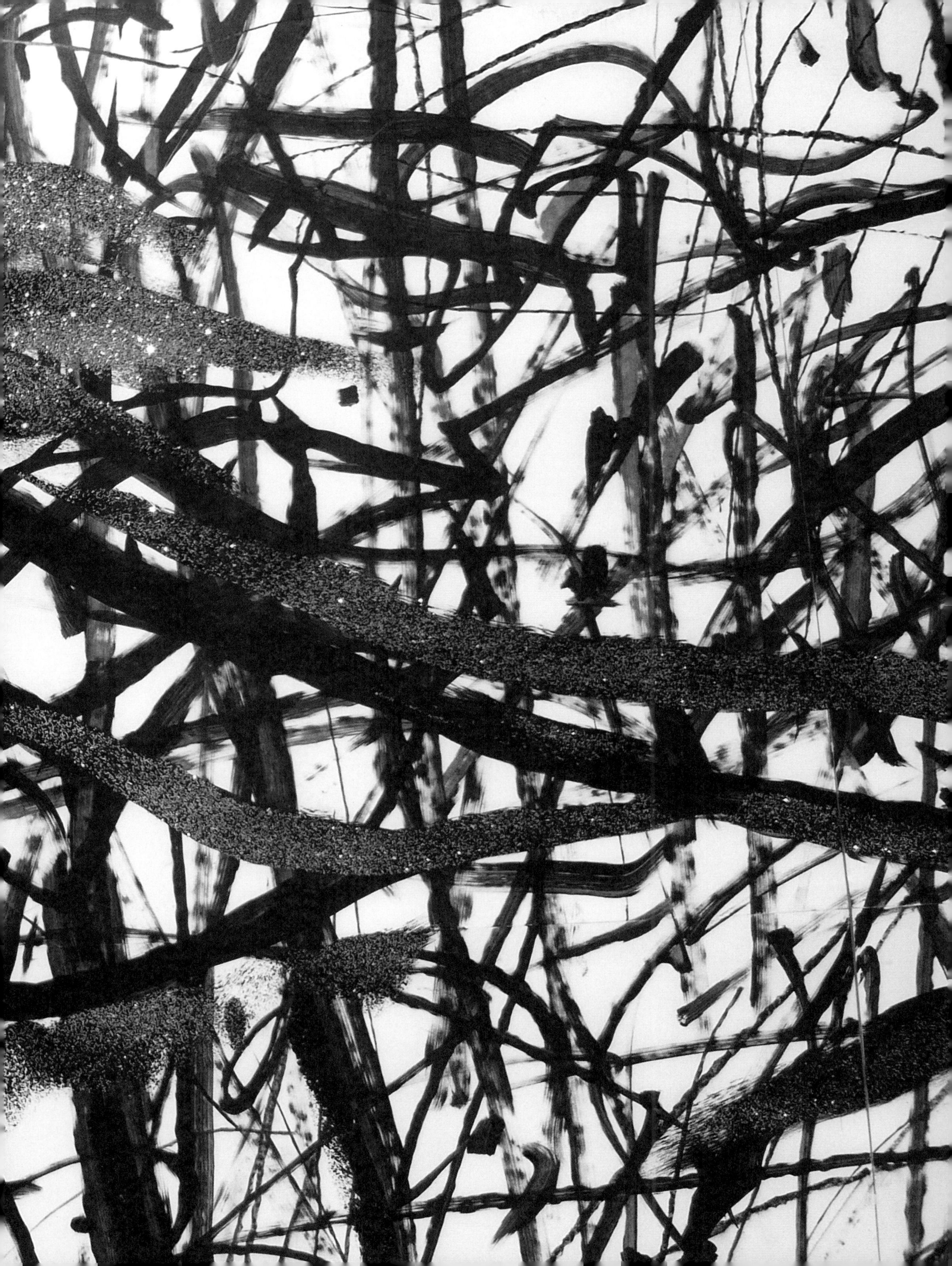

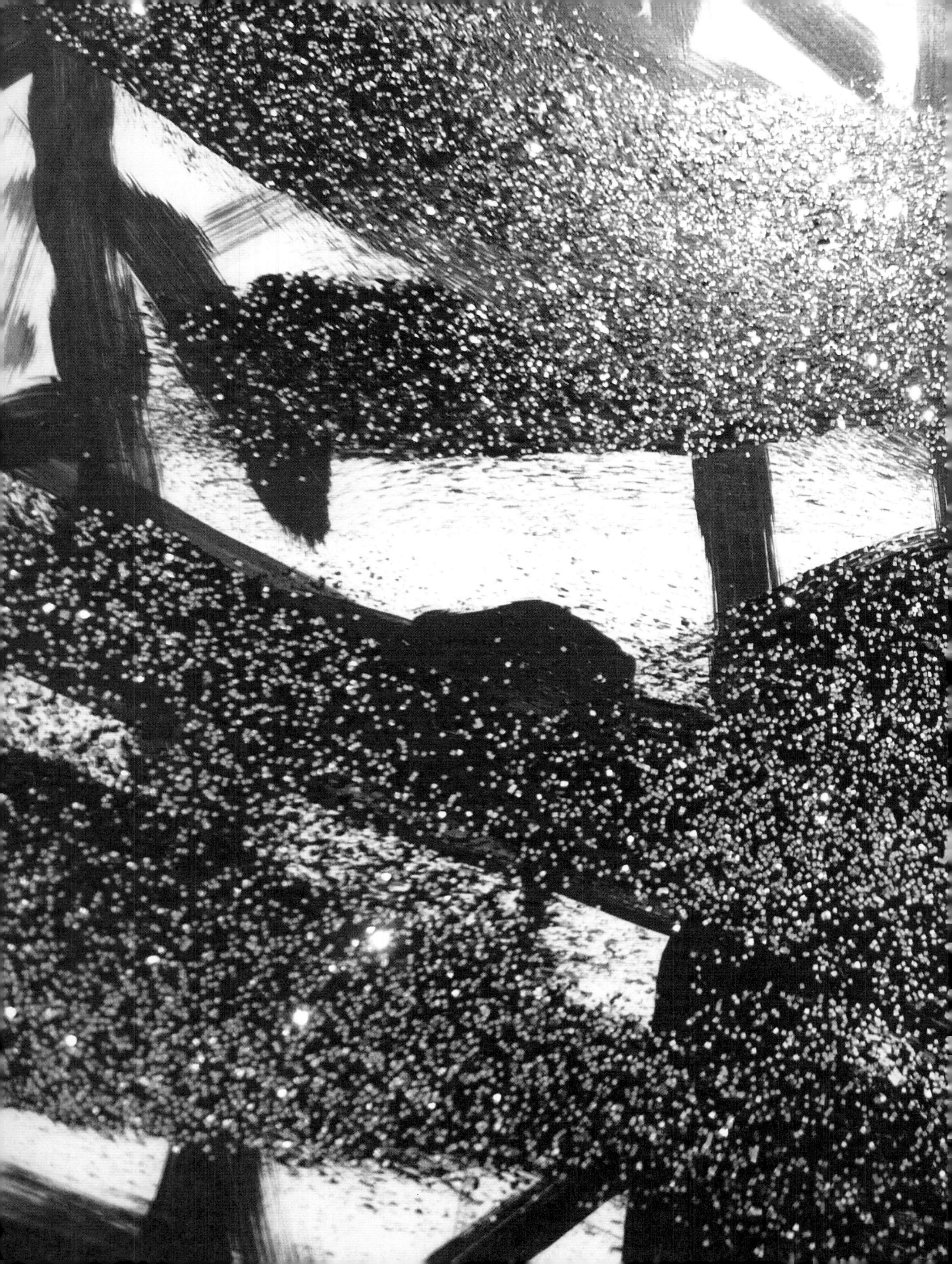

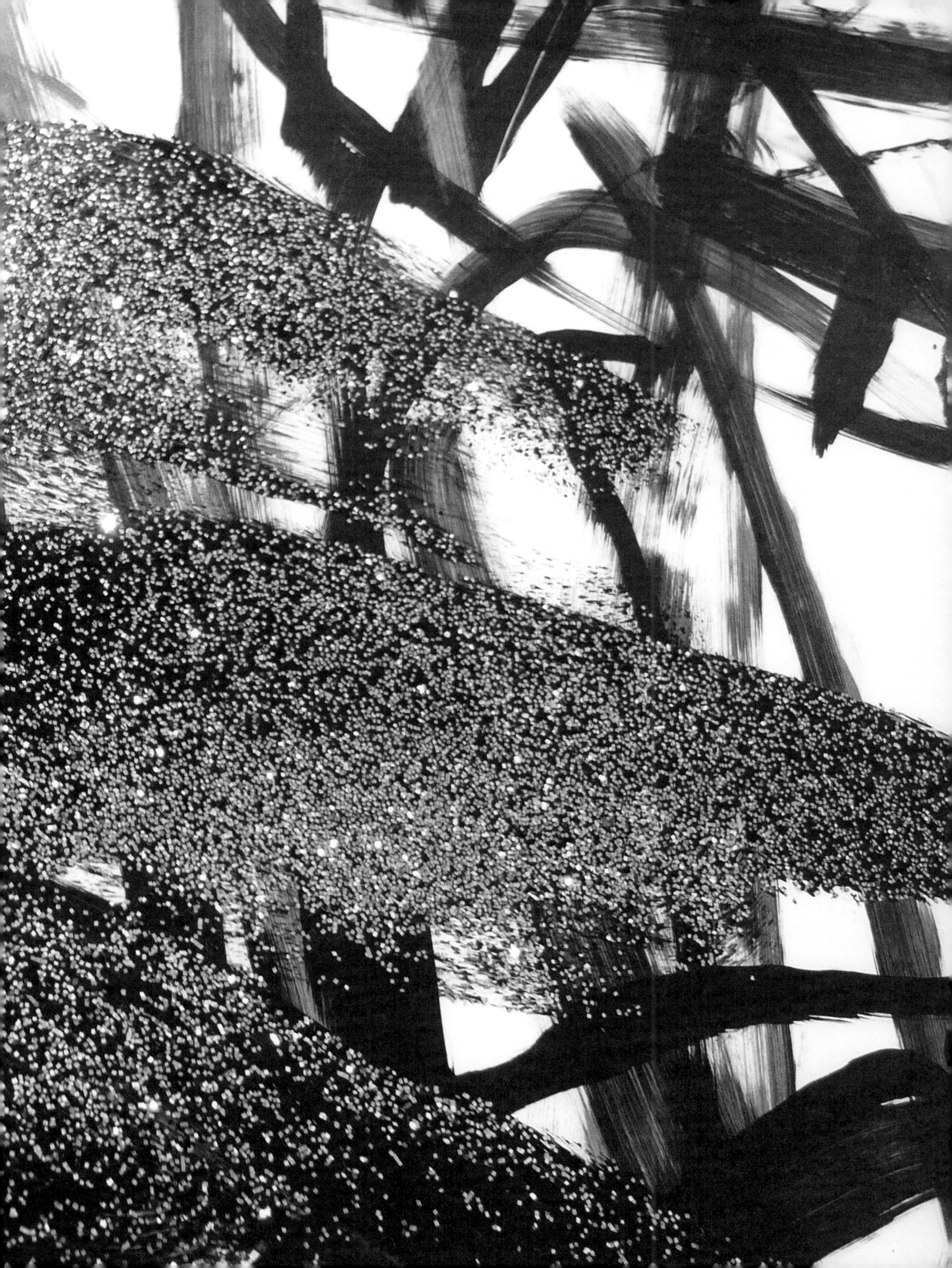

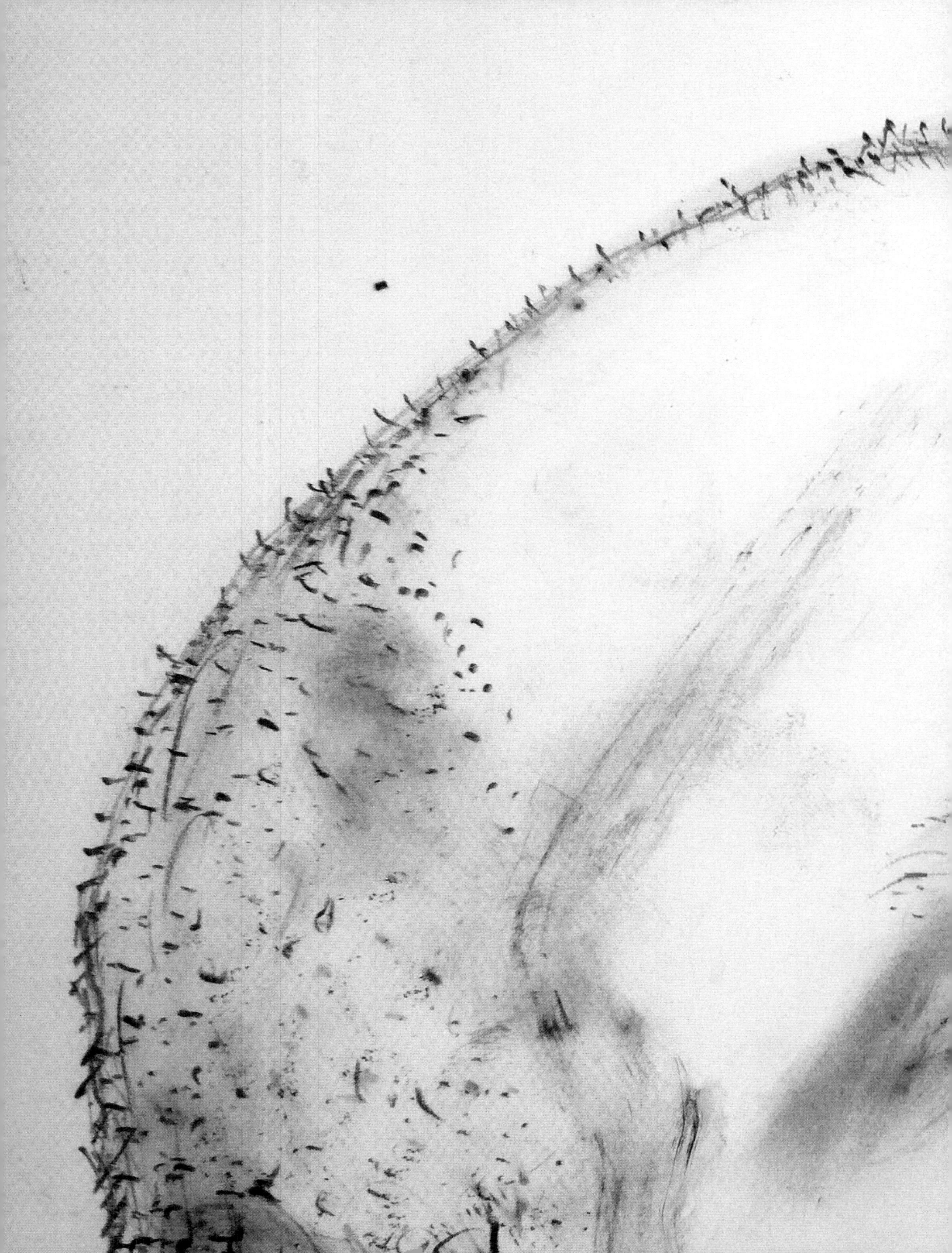

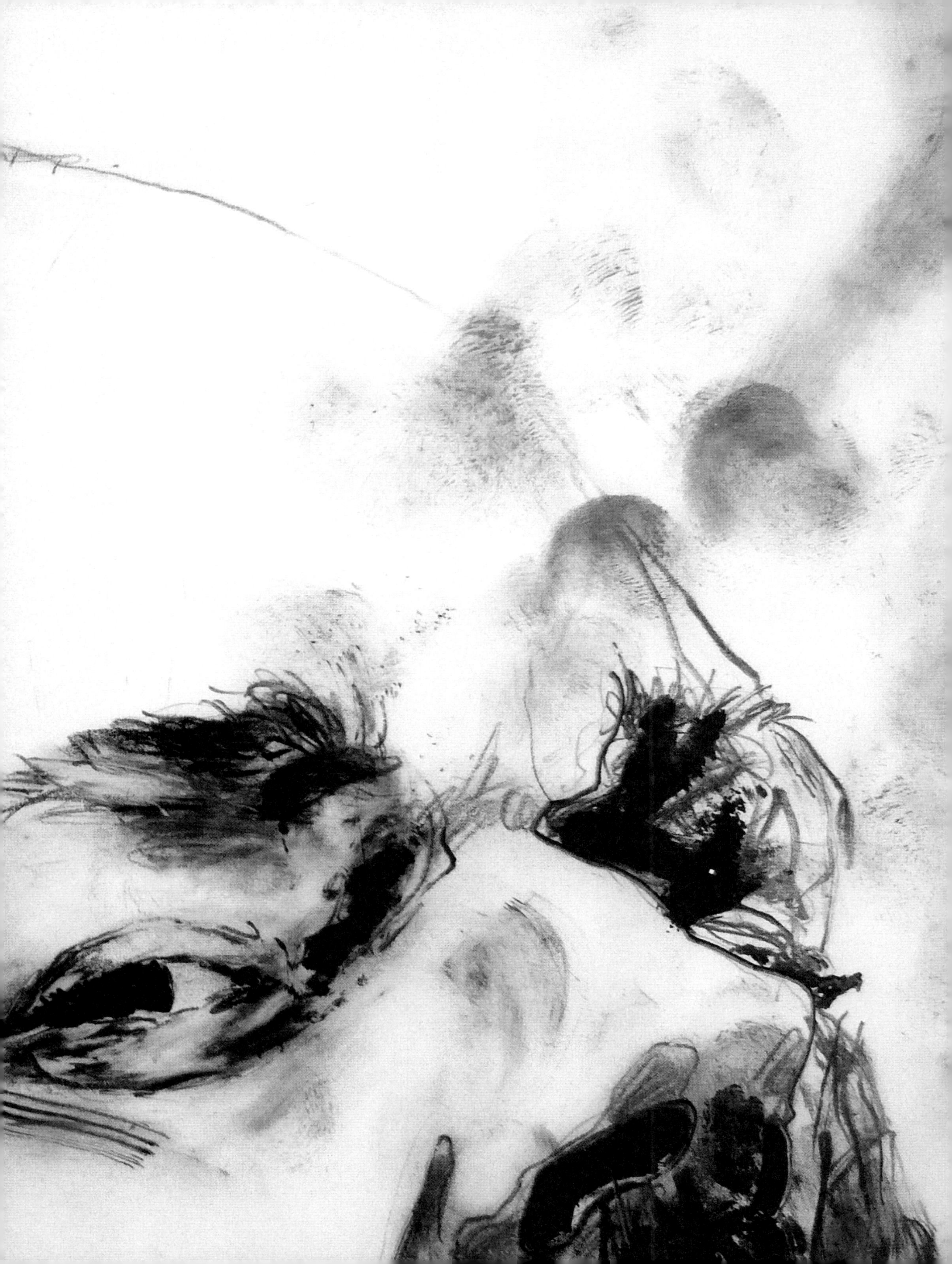

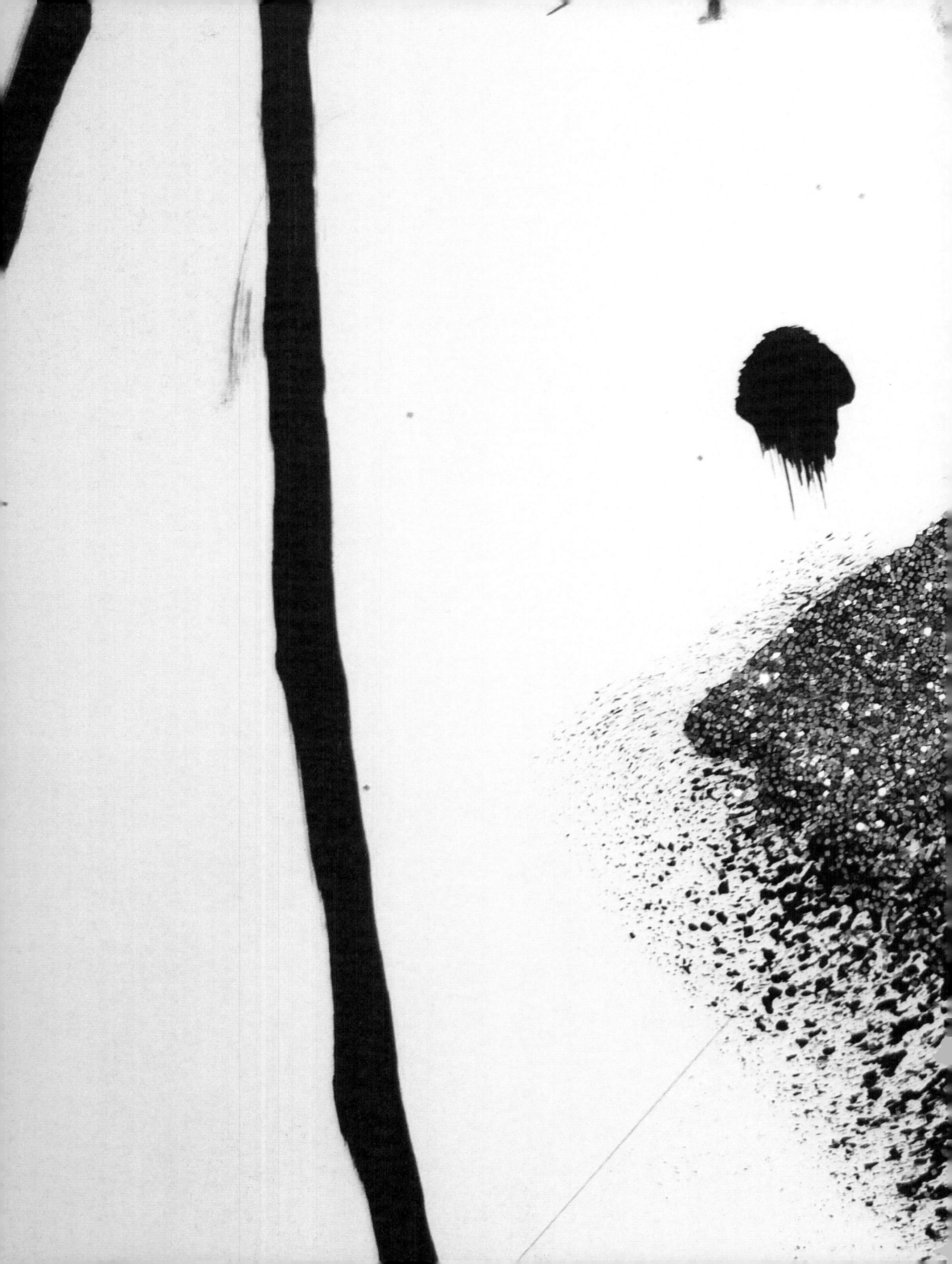

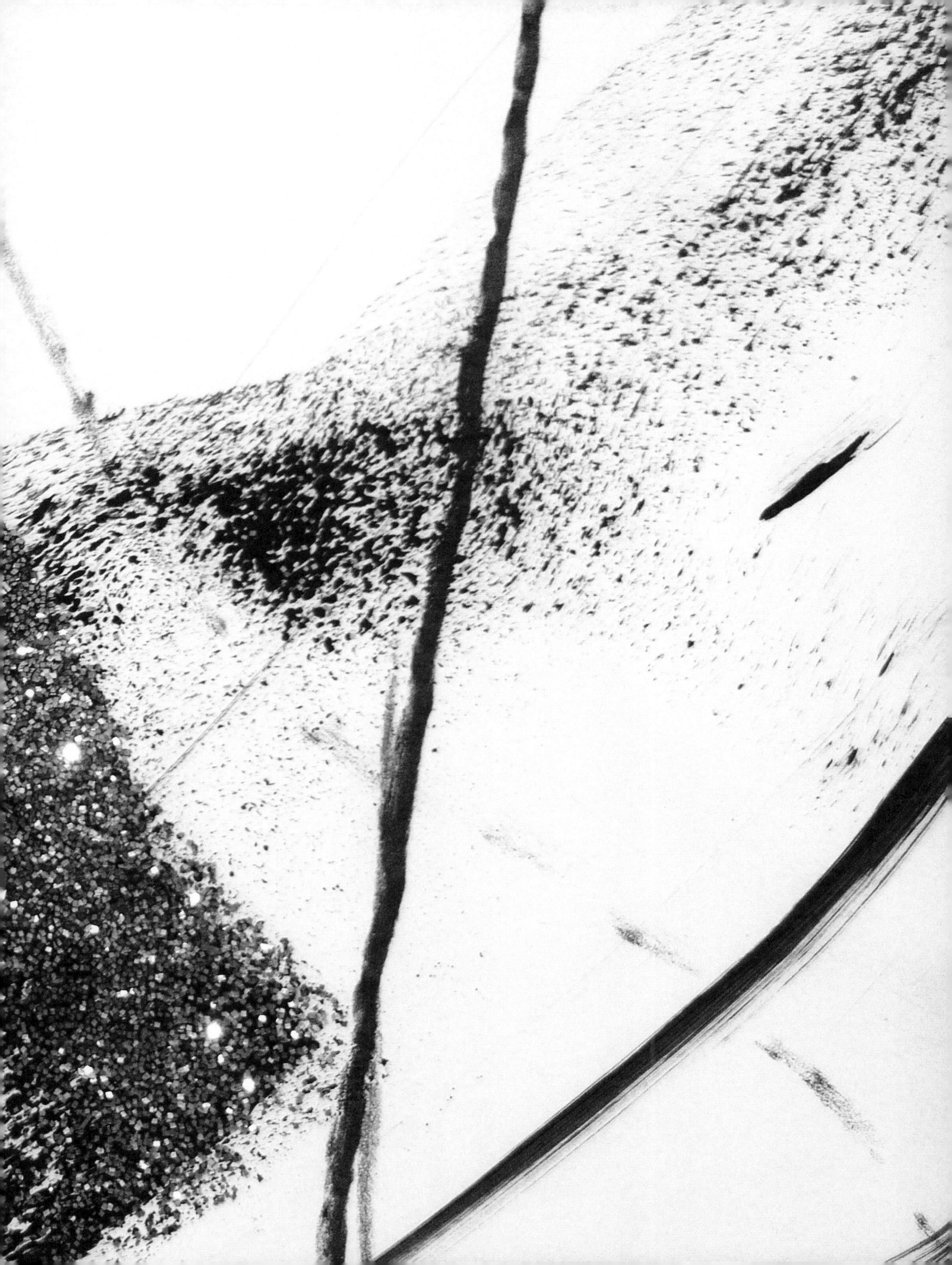

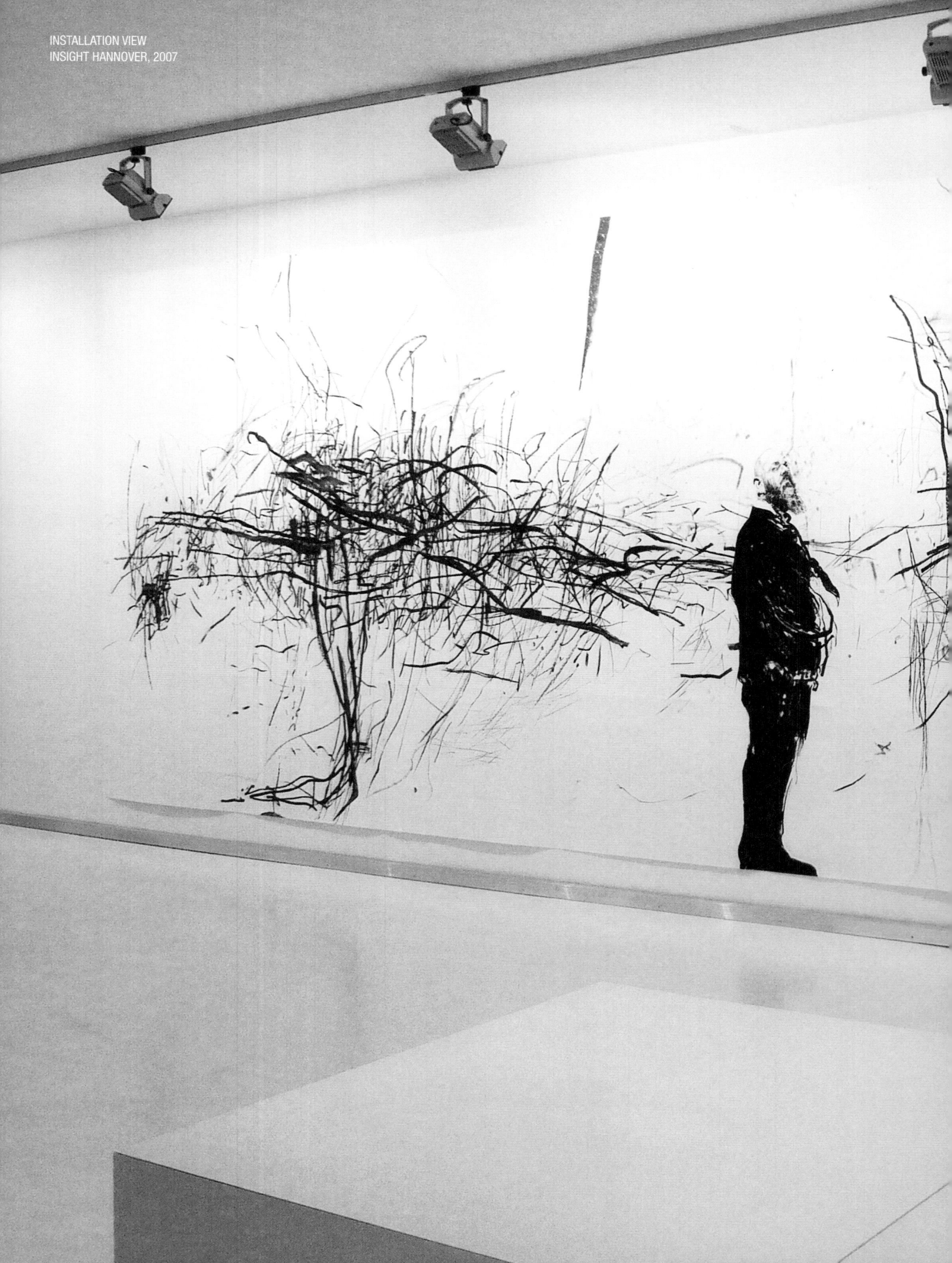

INSTALLATION VIEW
INSIGHT HANNOVER, 2007

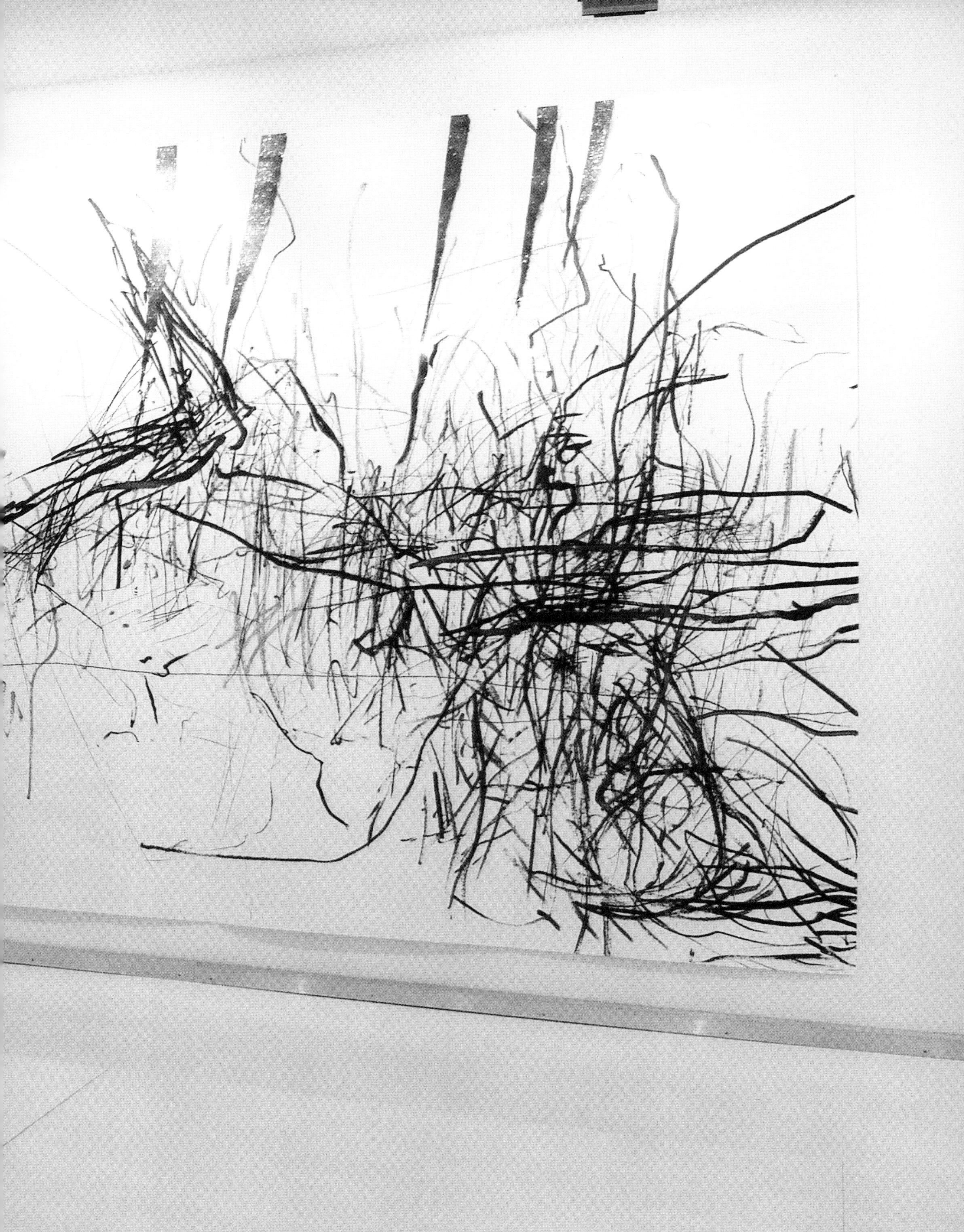

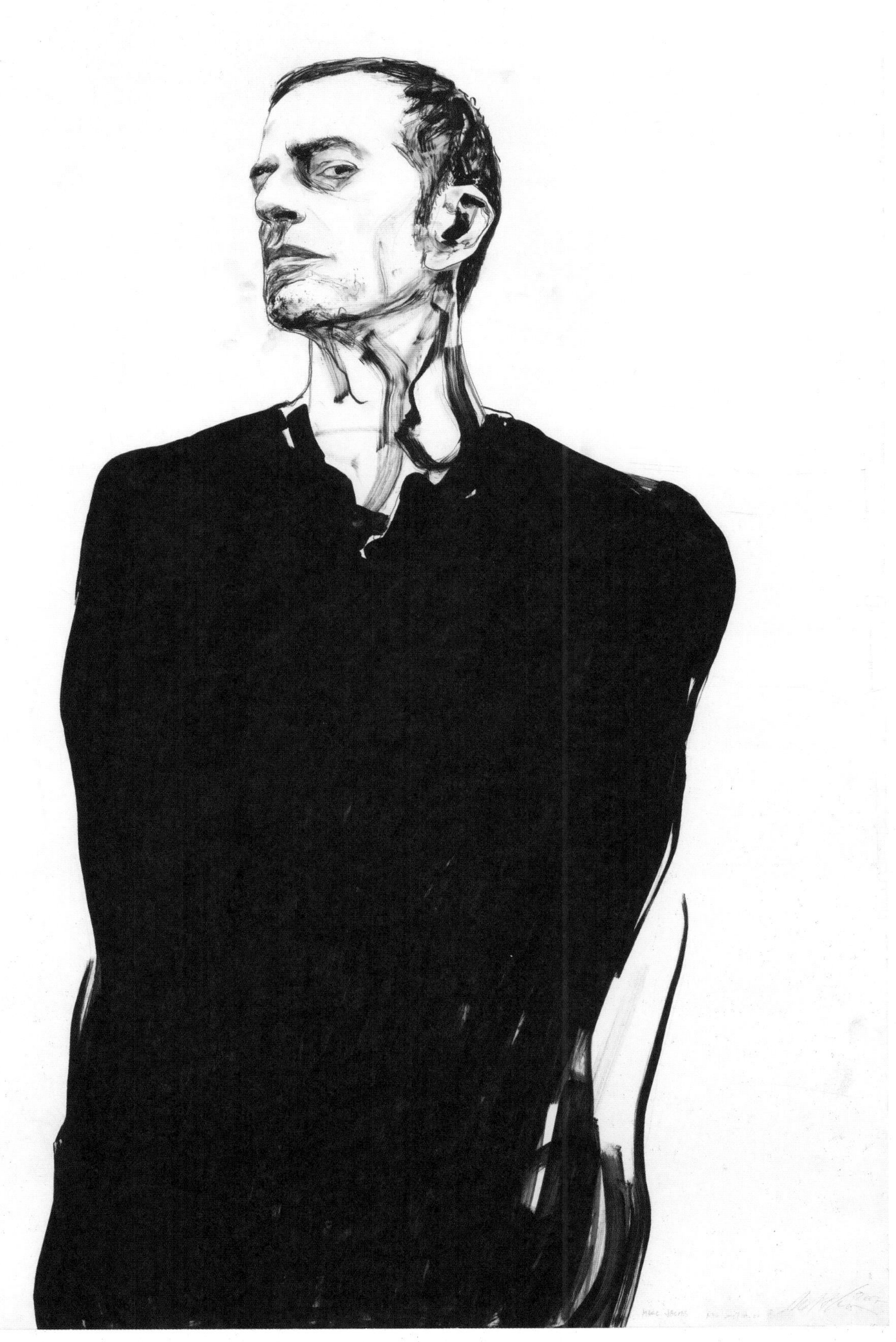

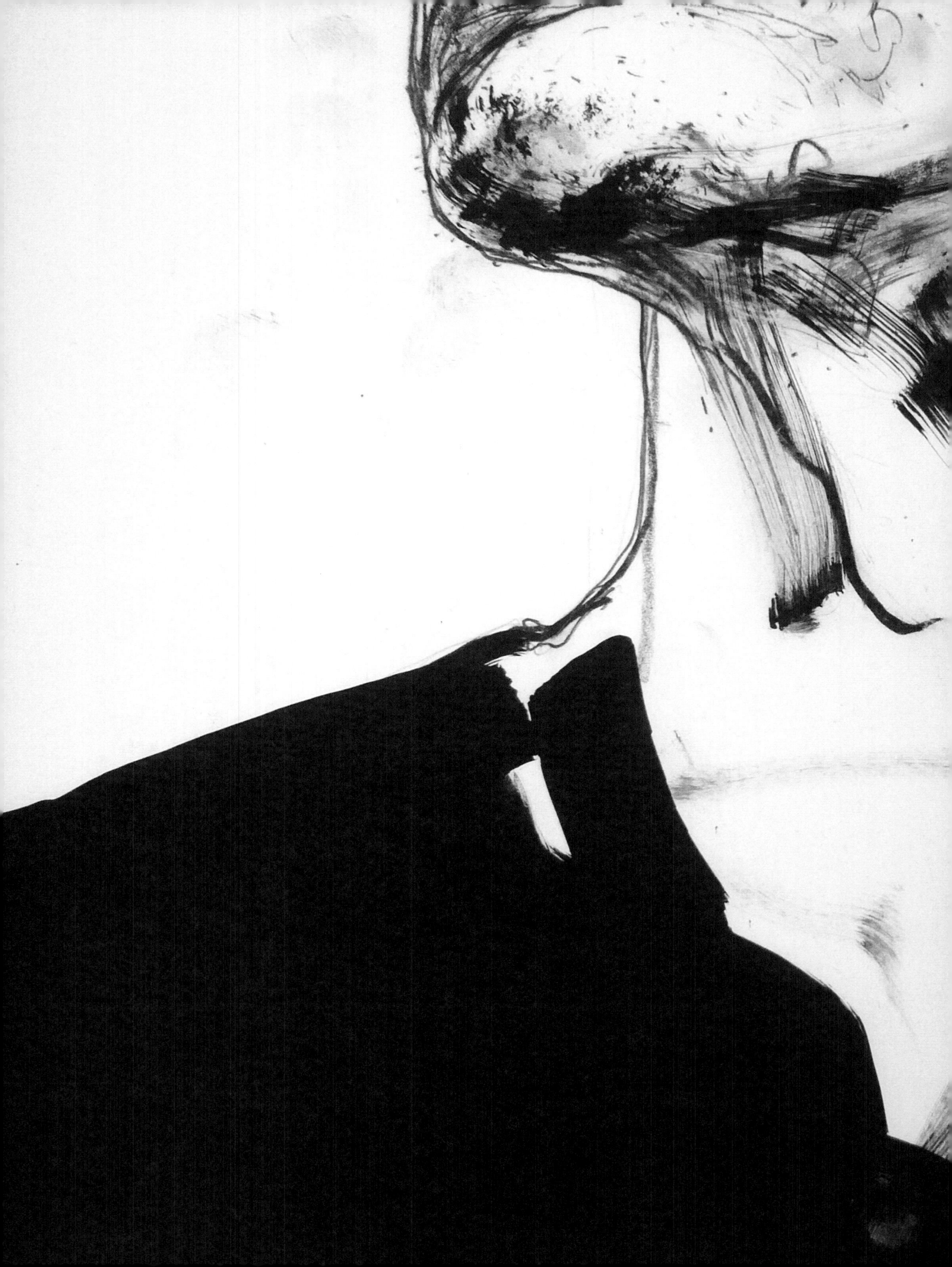

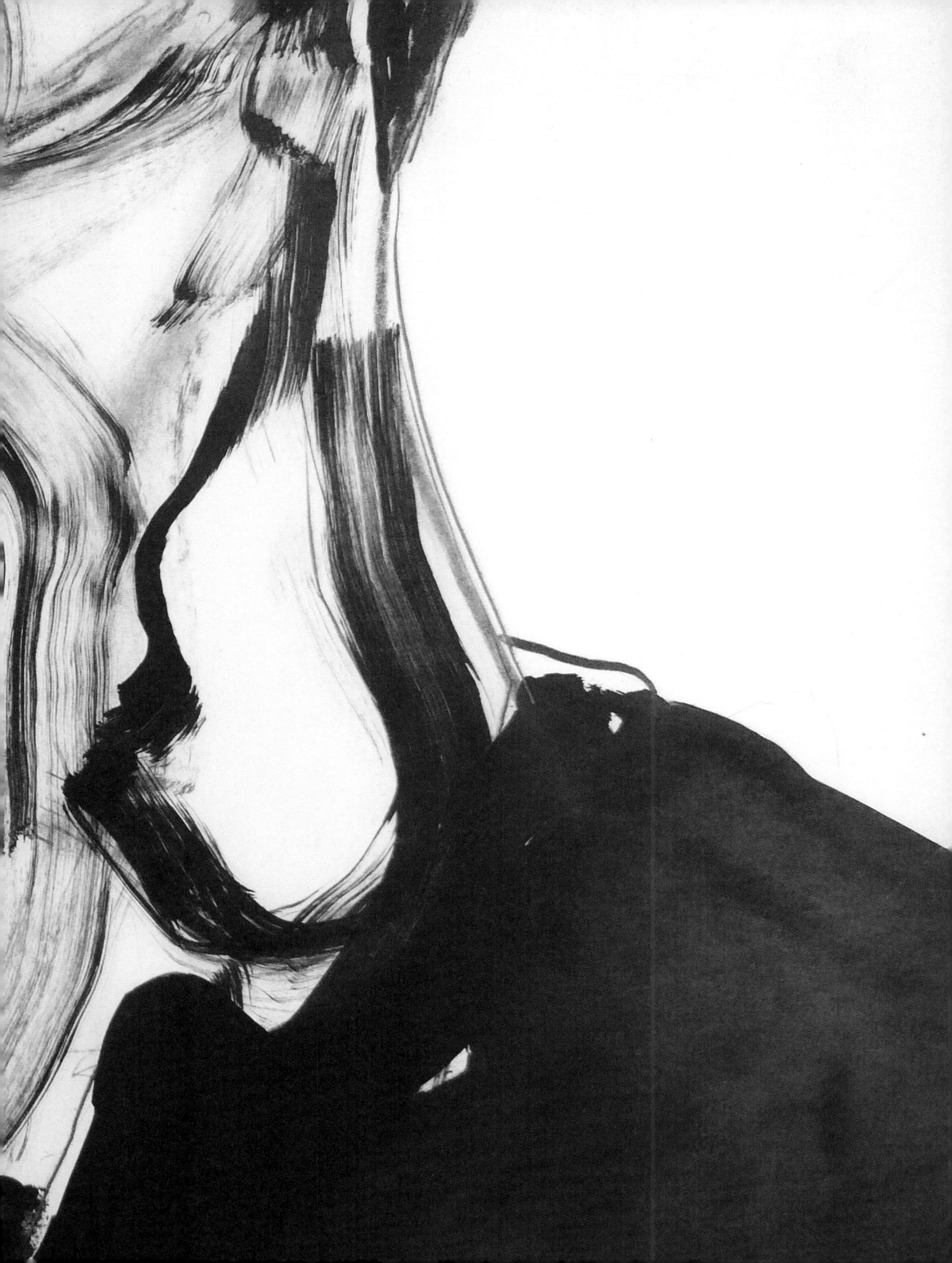

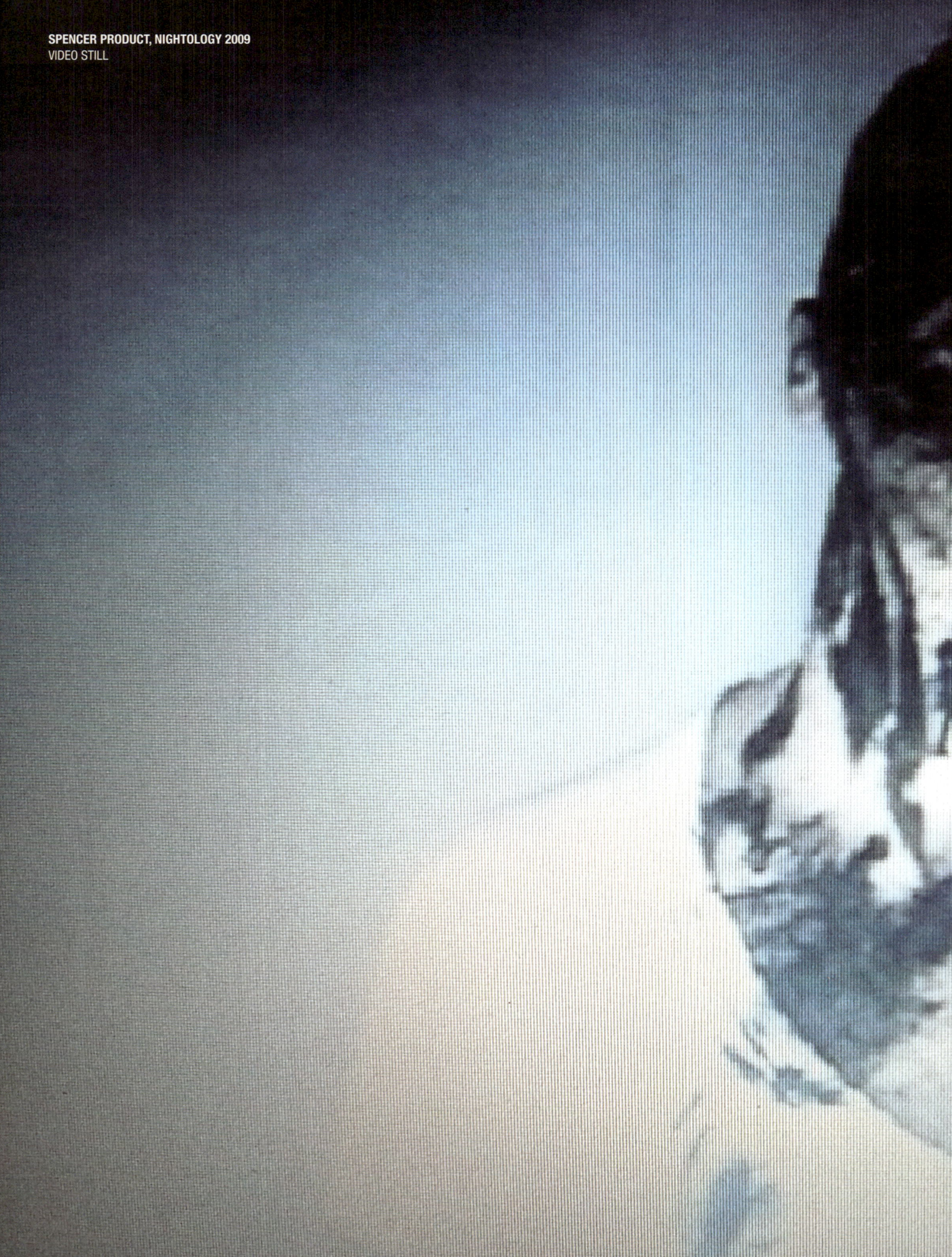

SPENCER PRODUCT, NIGHTOLOGY 2009
VIDEO STILL

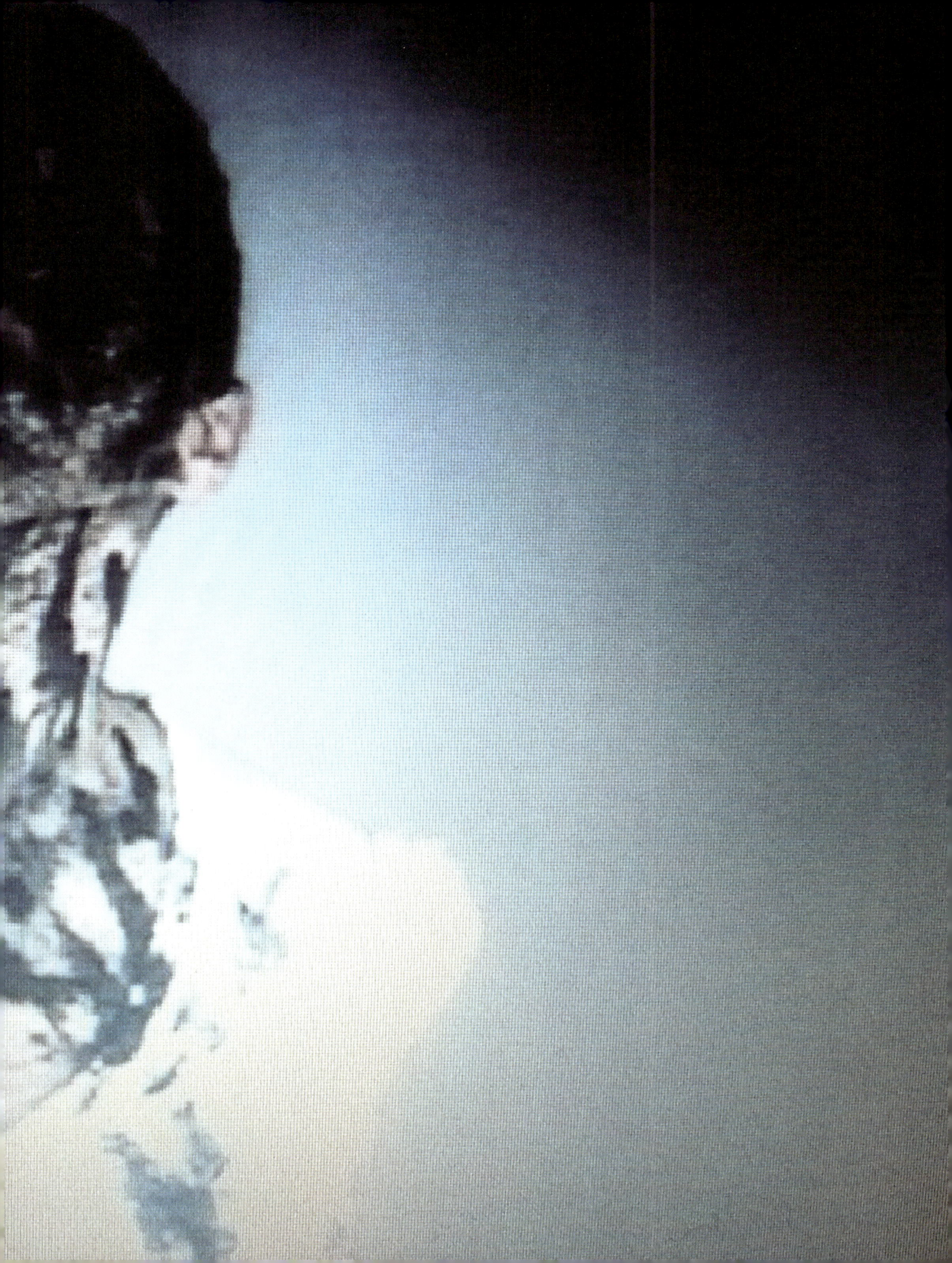

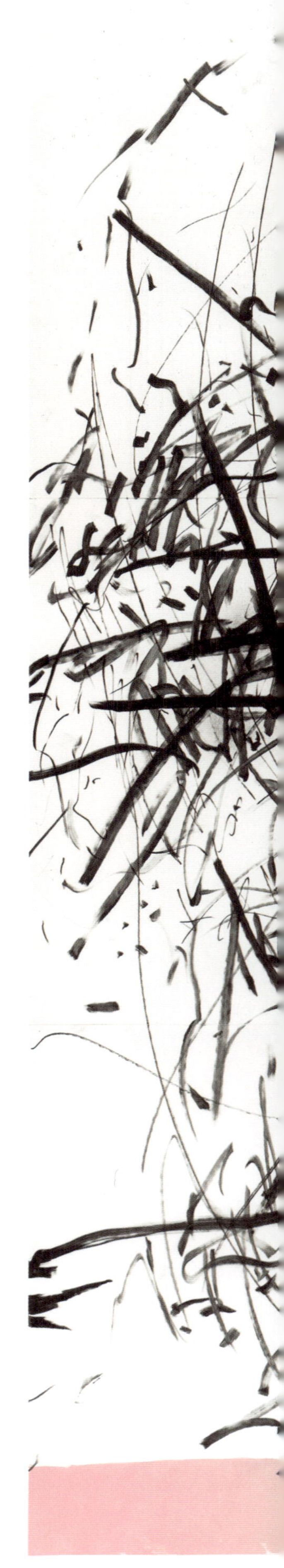

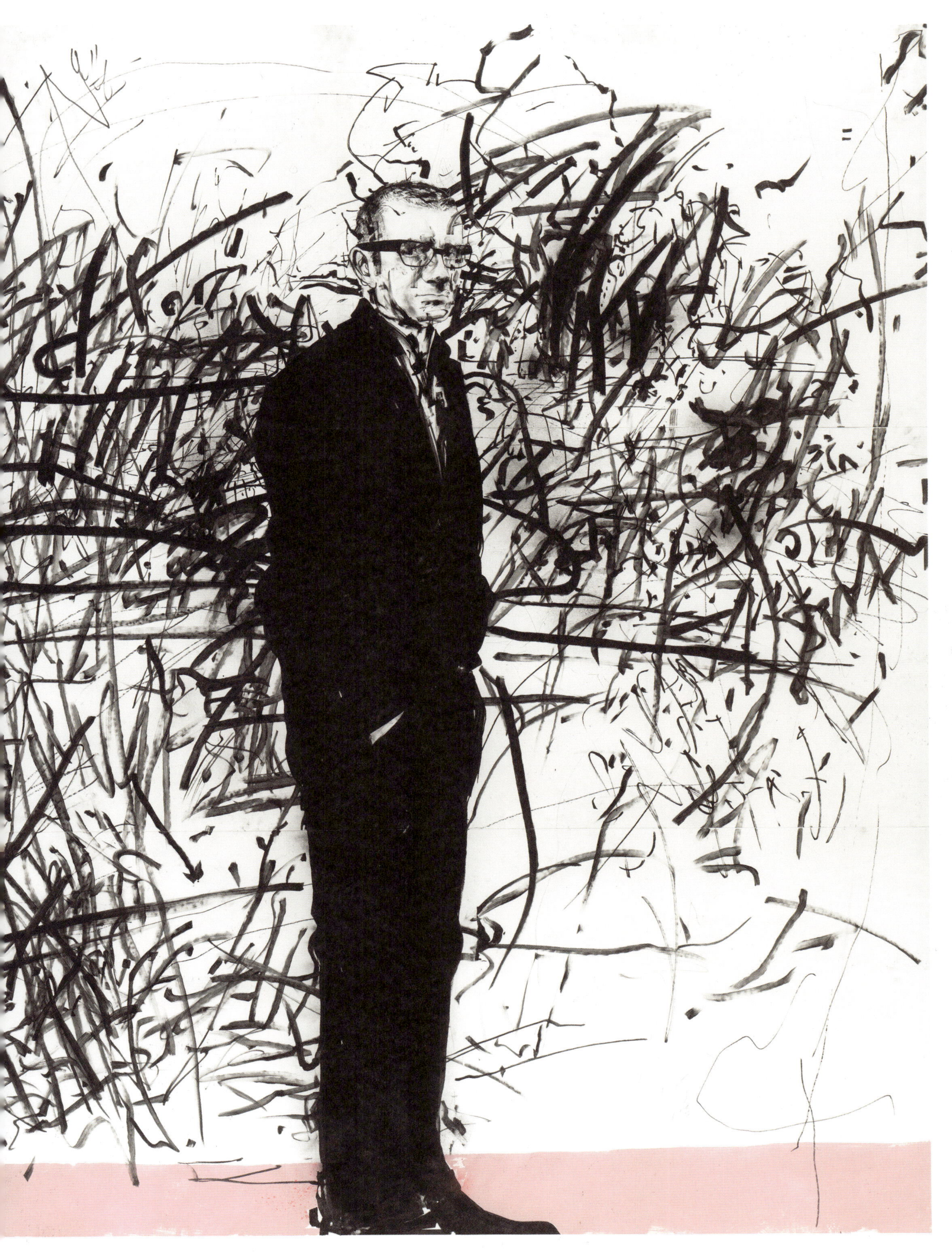

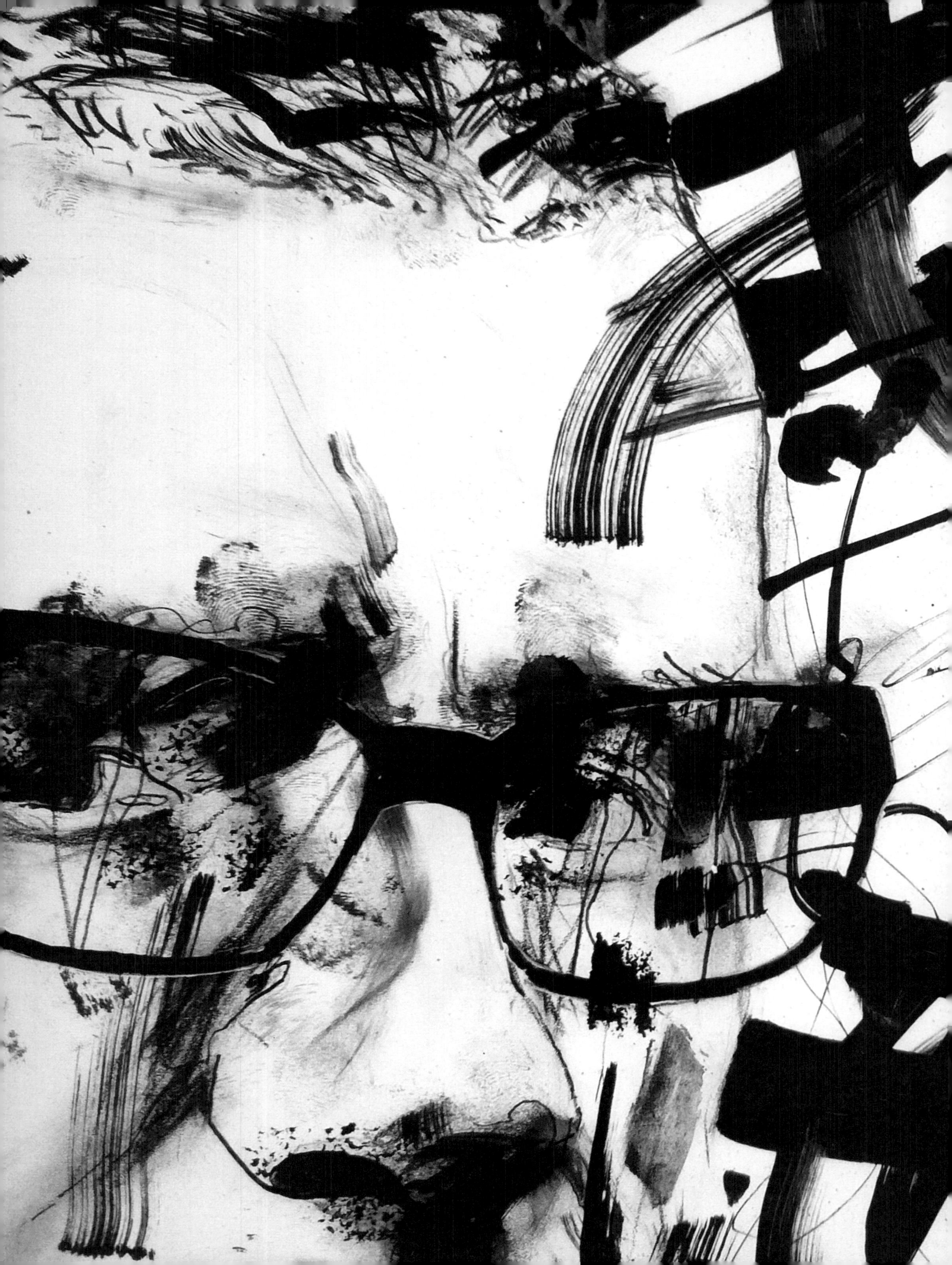

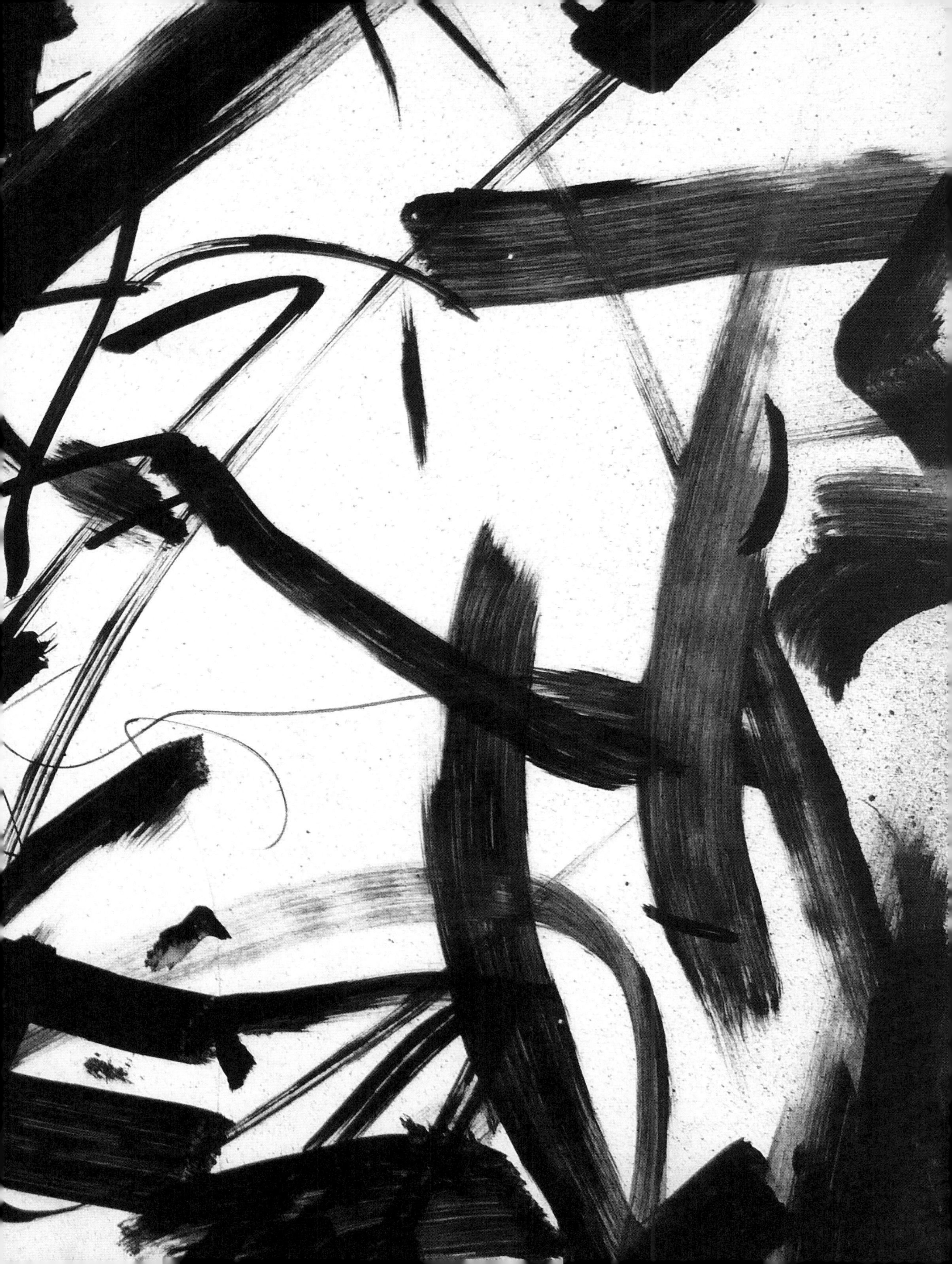

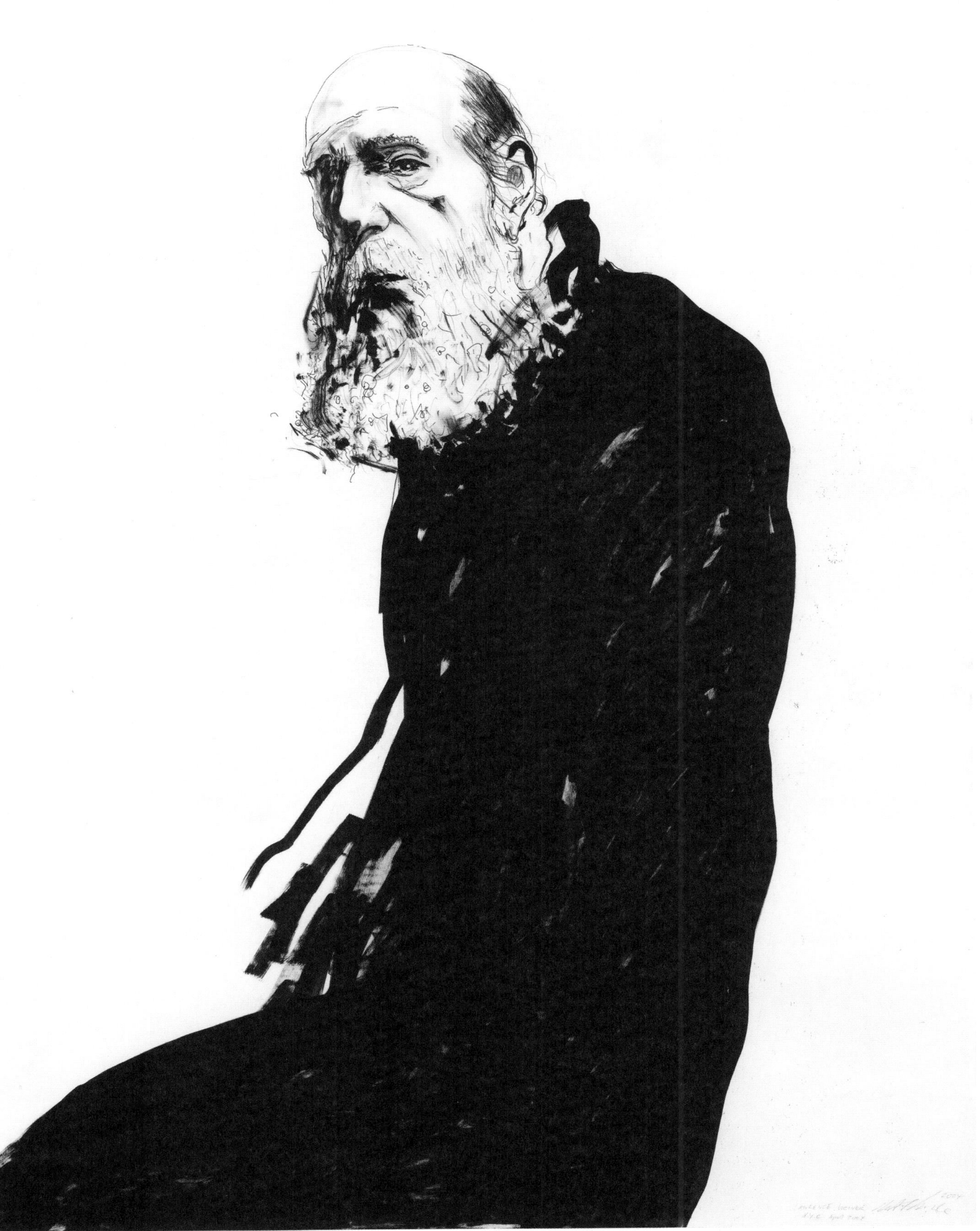

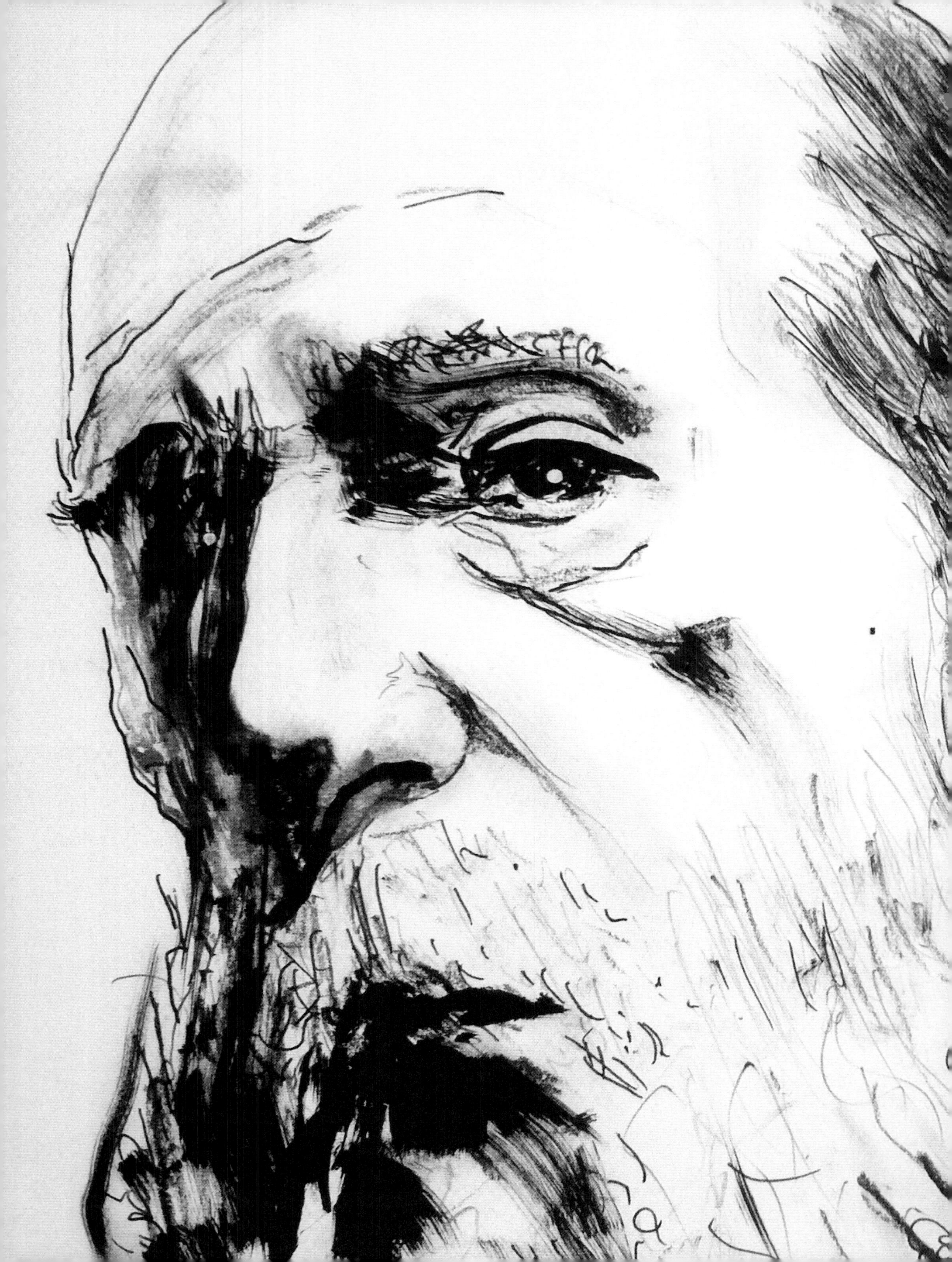

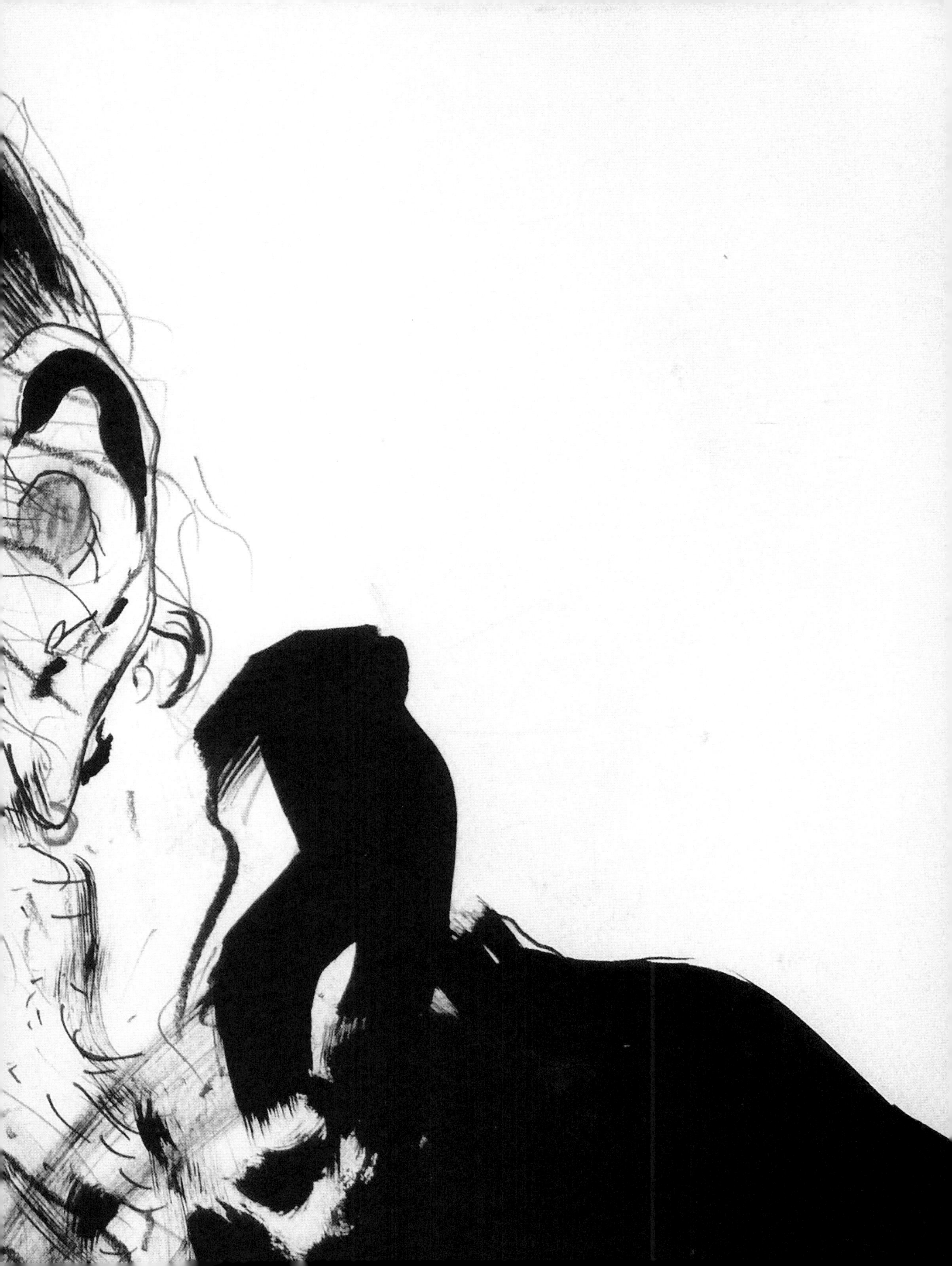

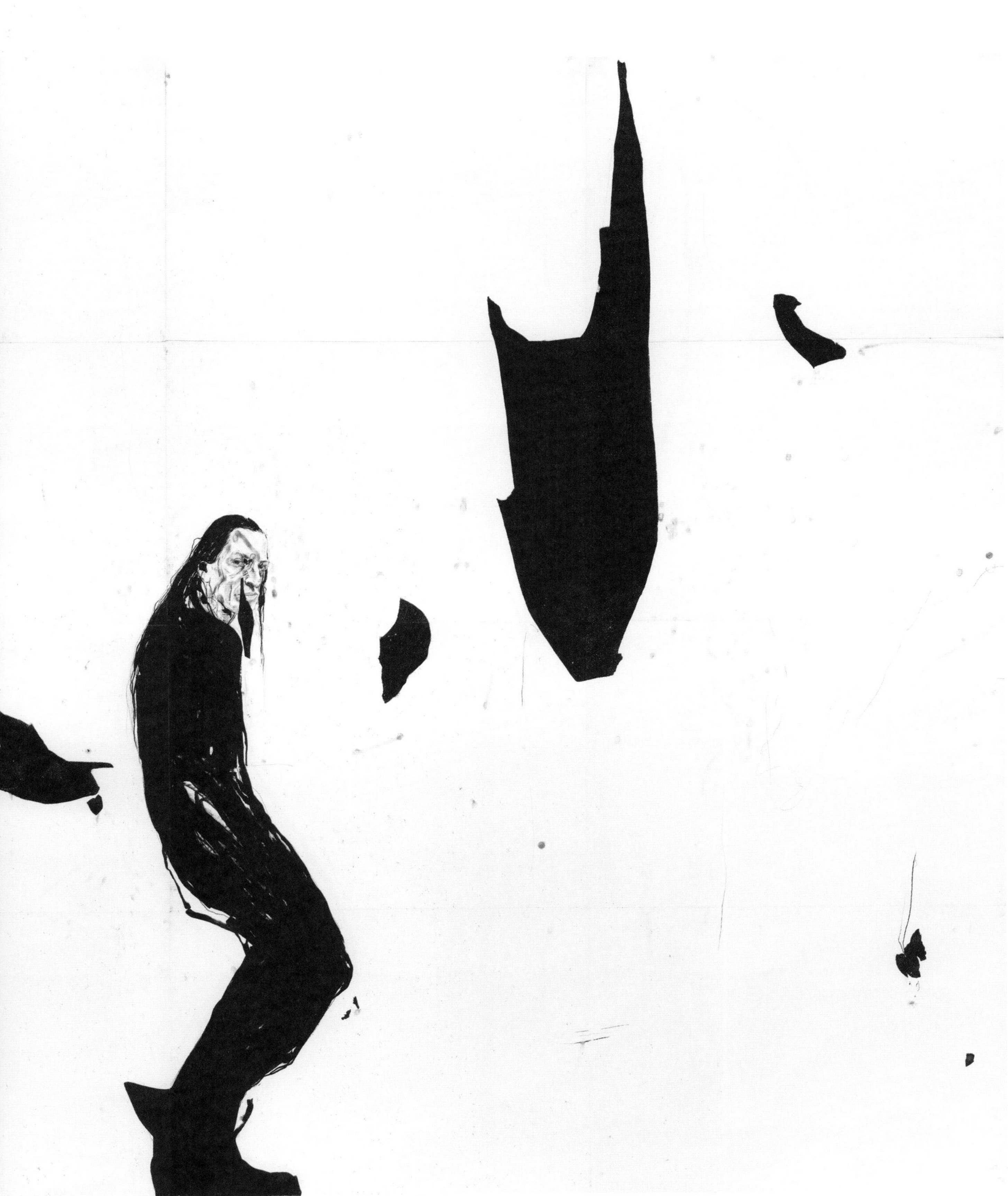

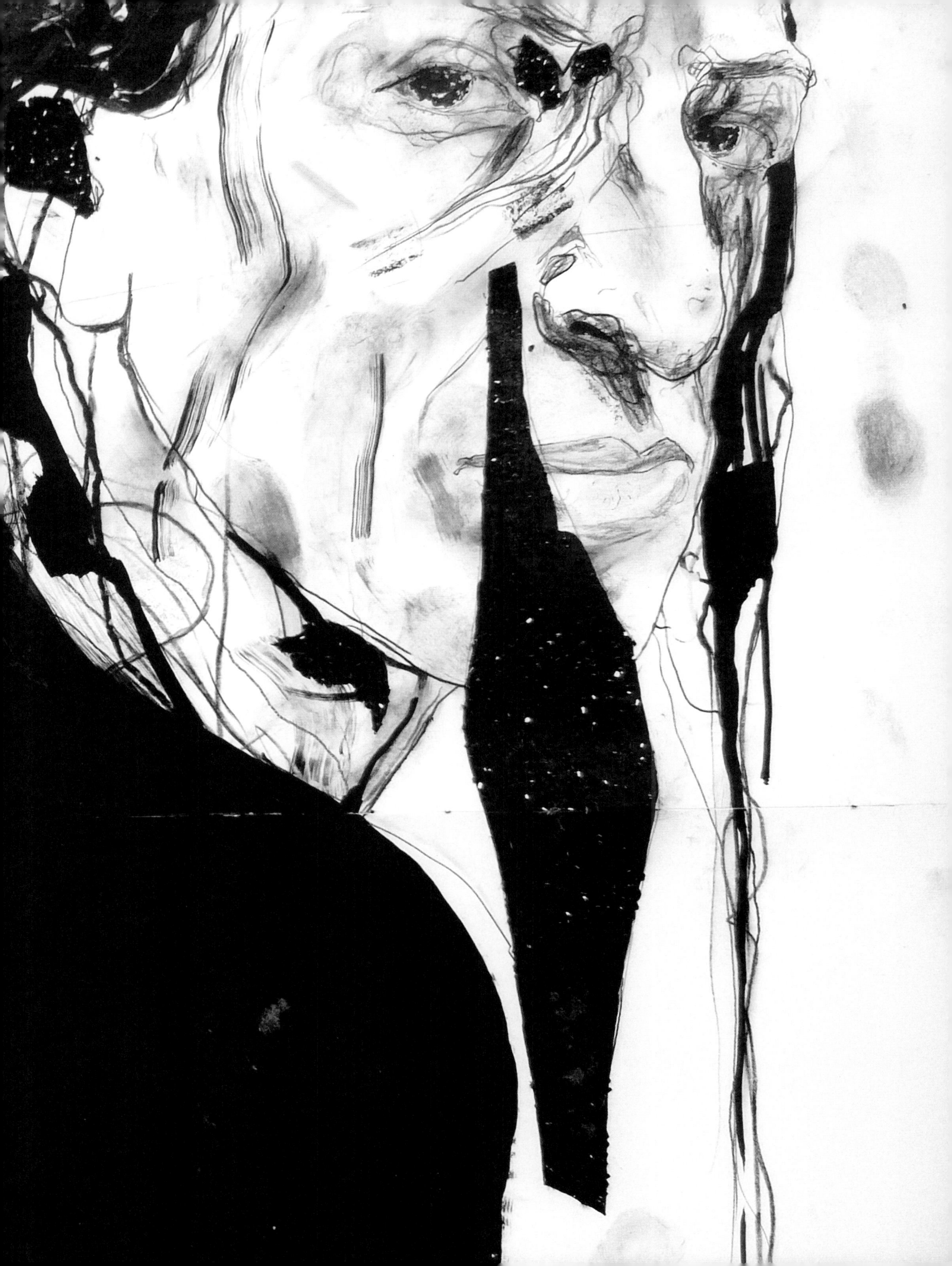

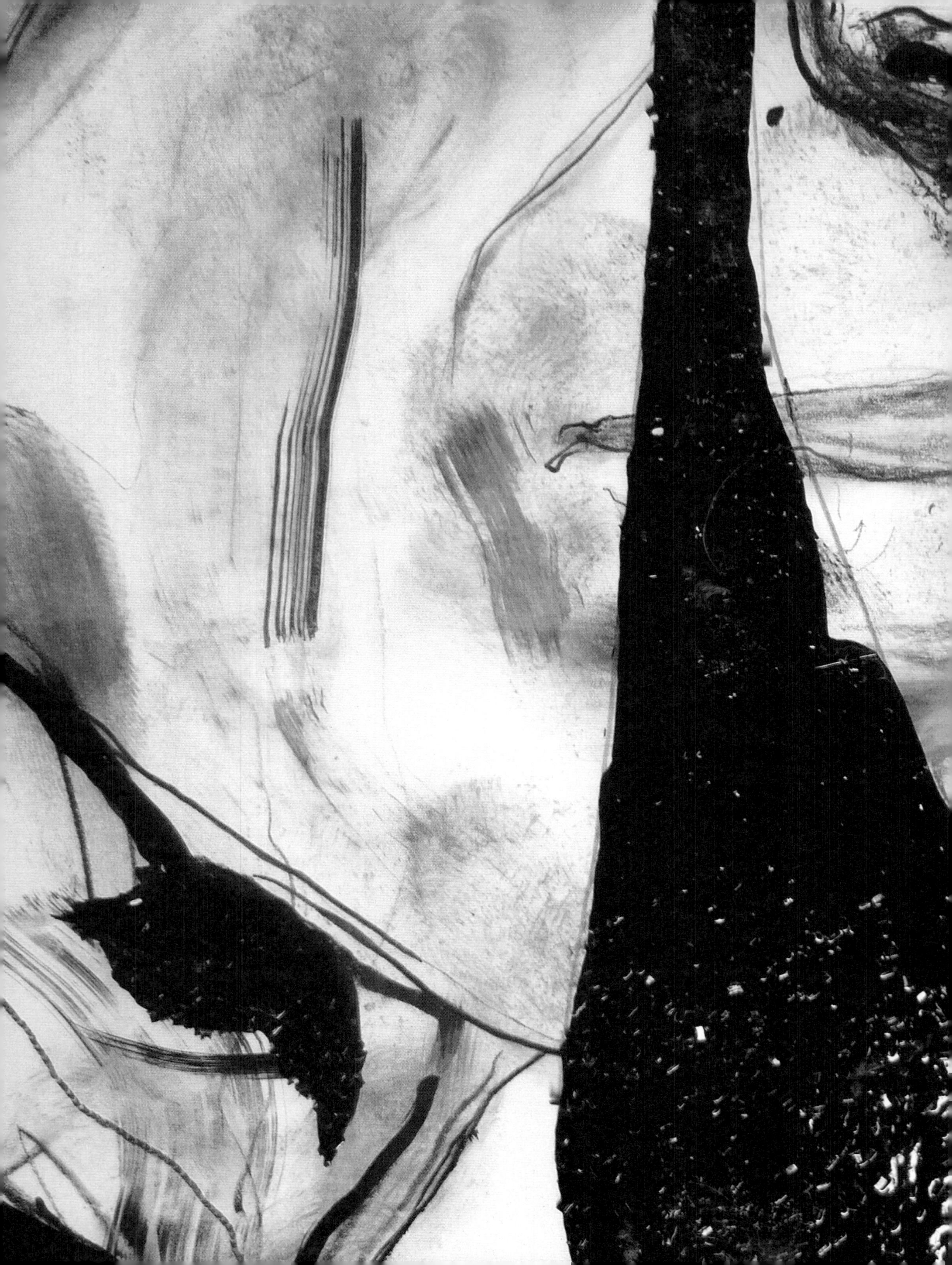

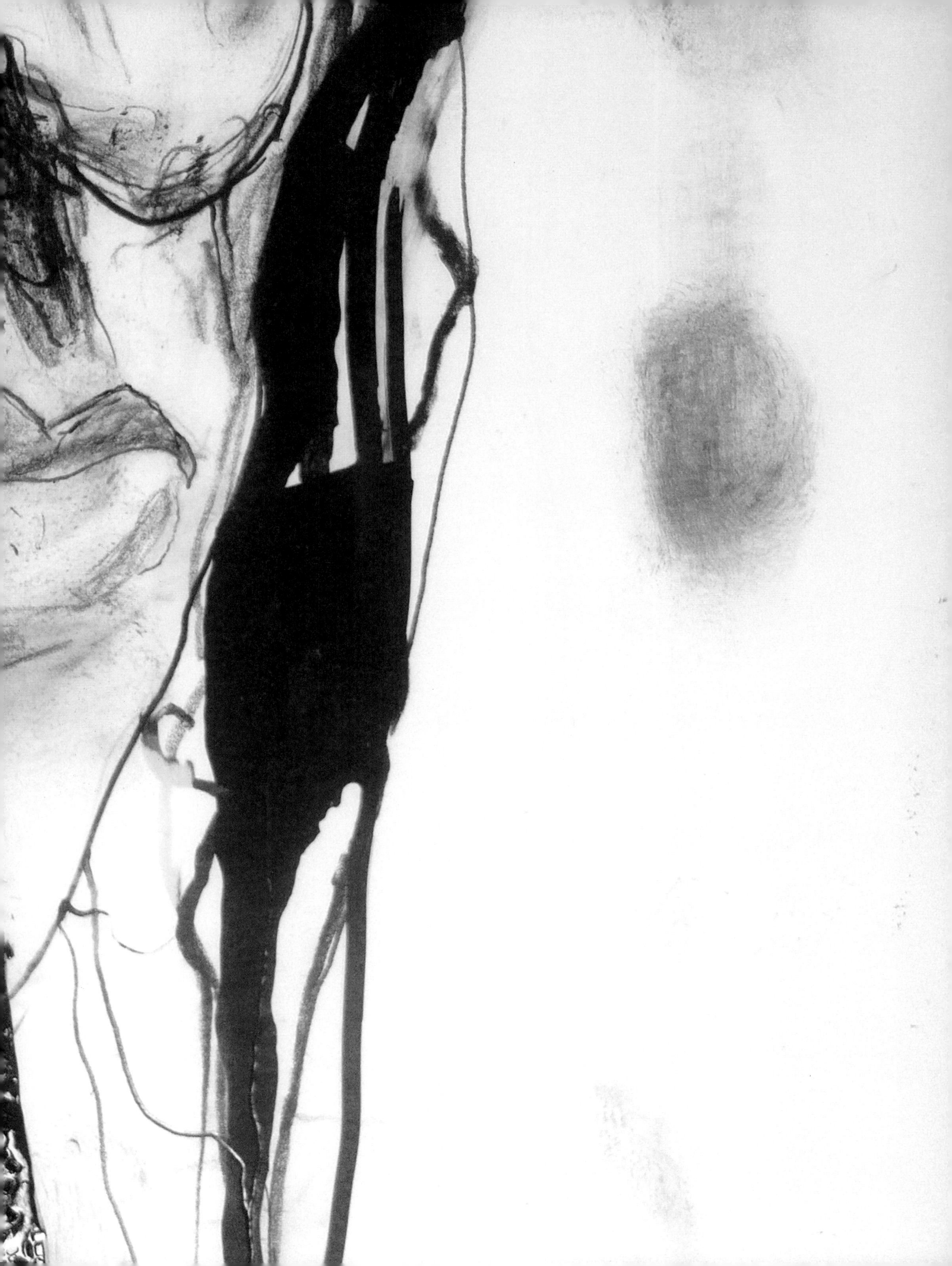

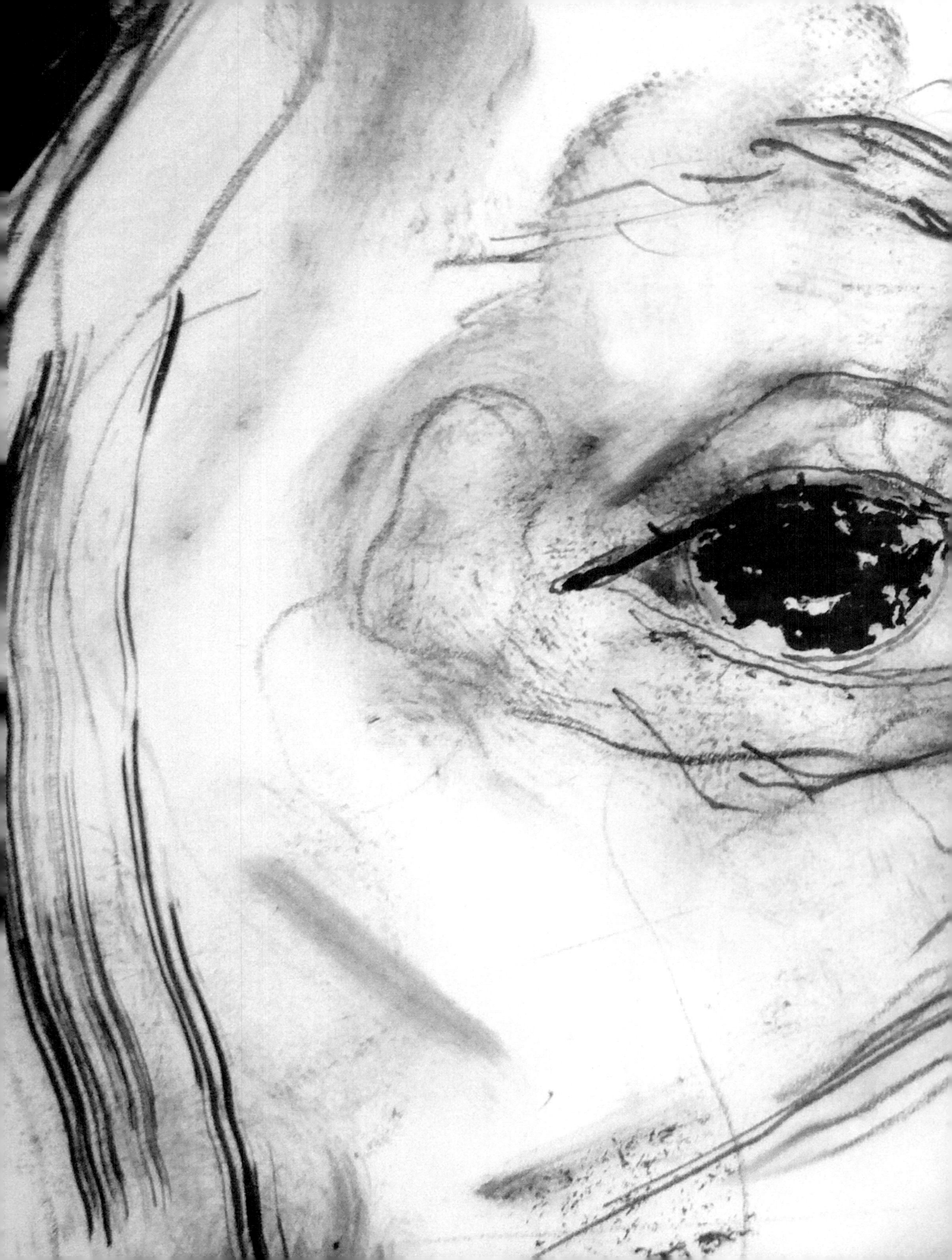

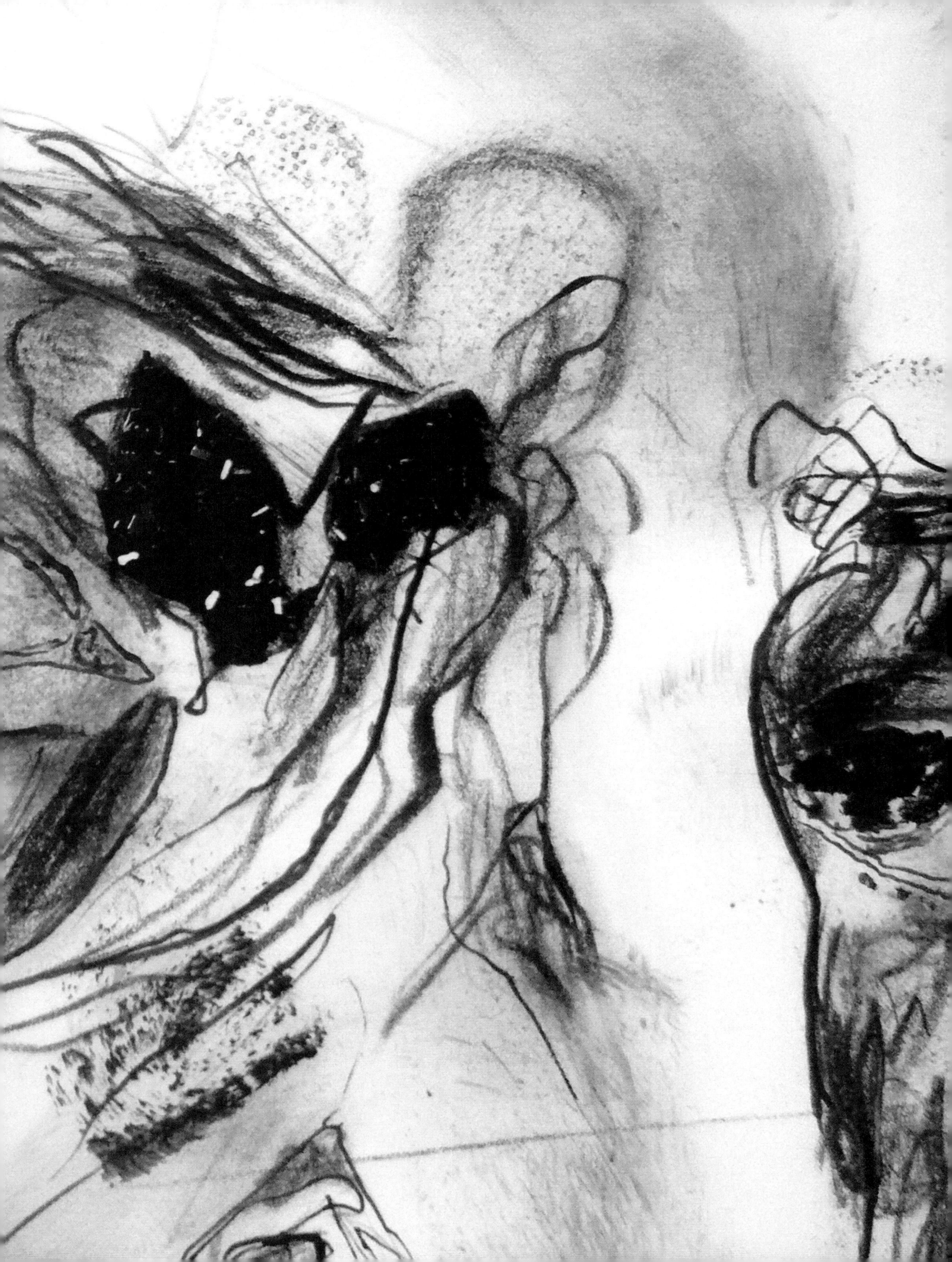

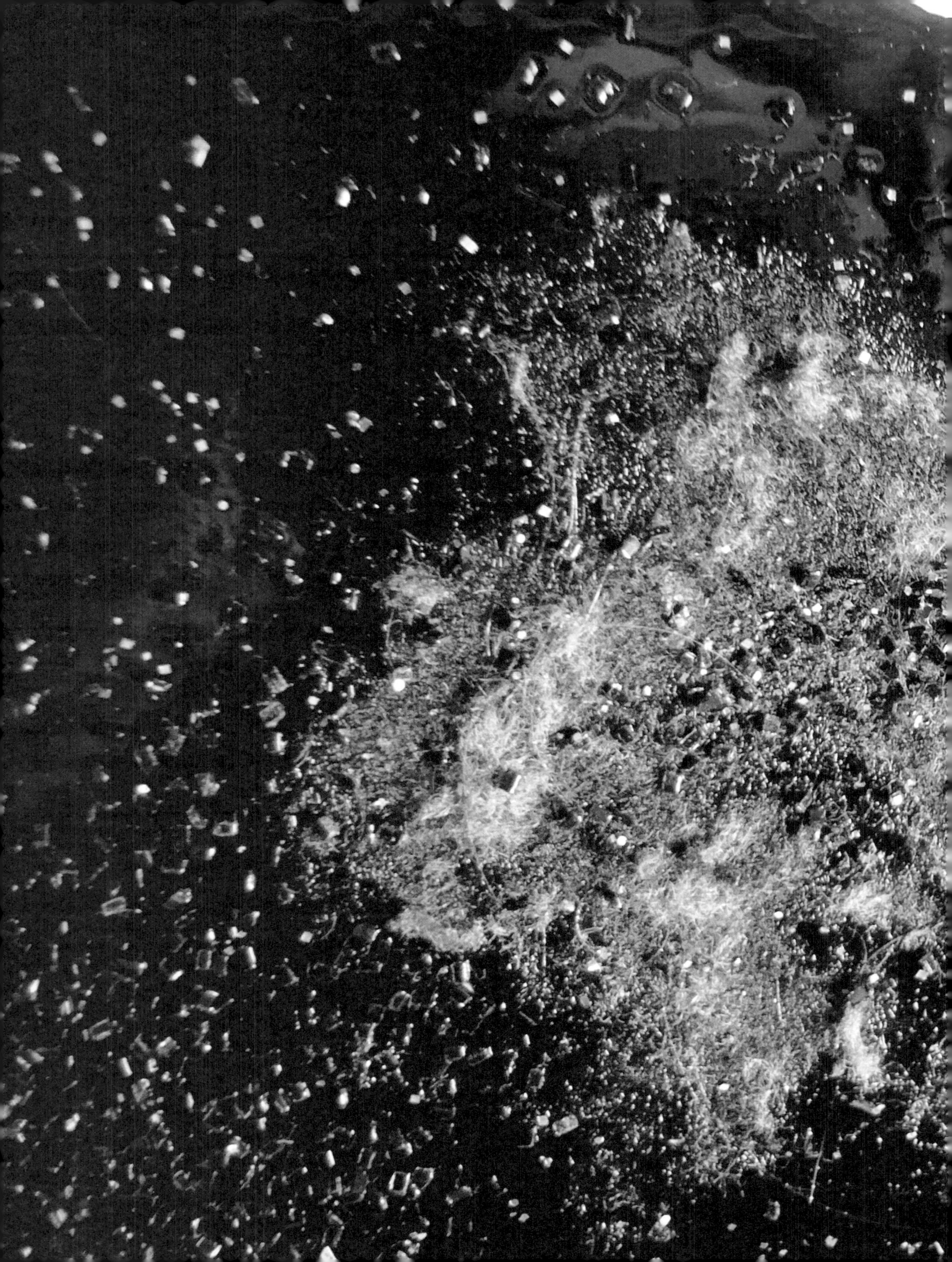

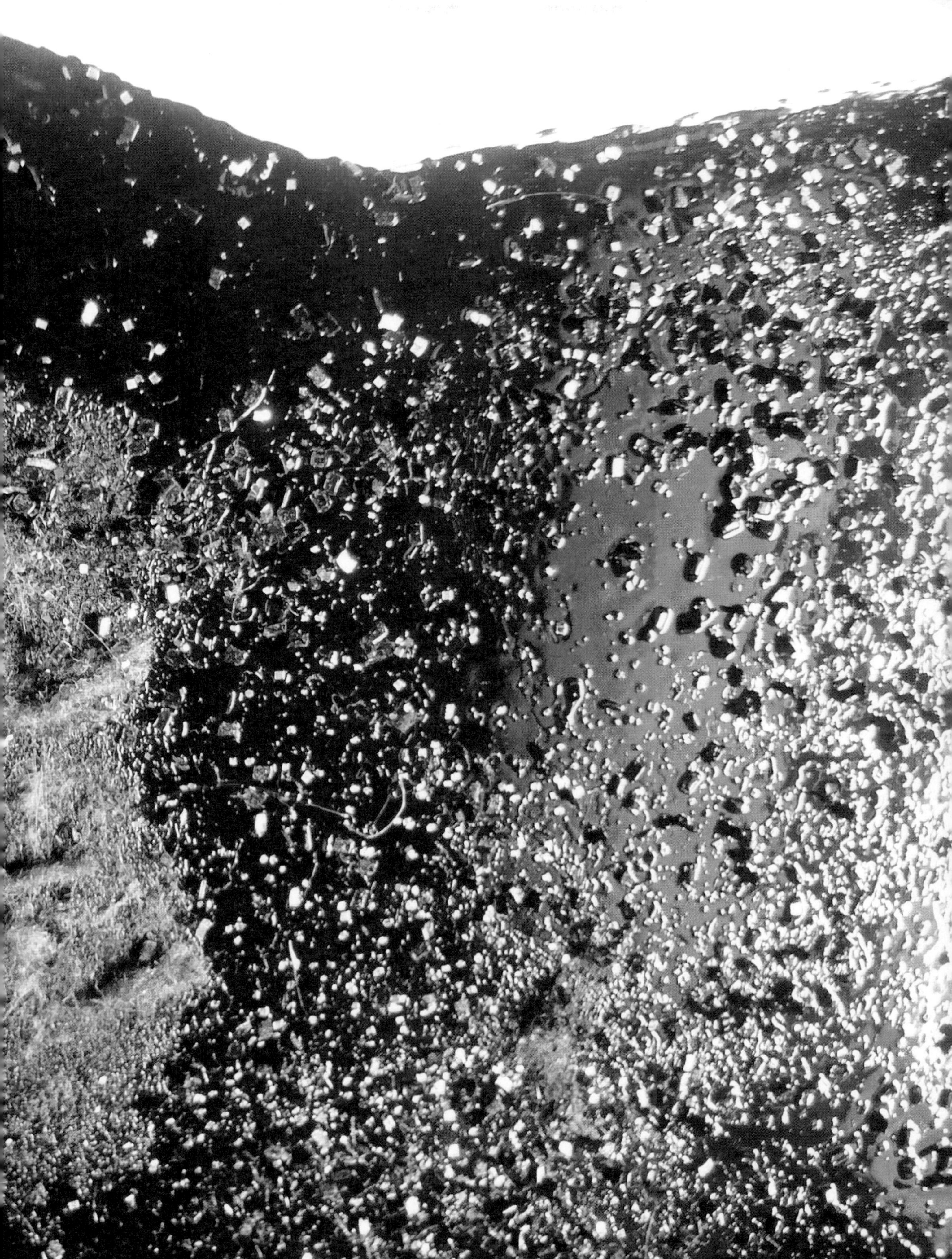

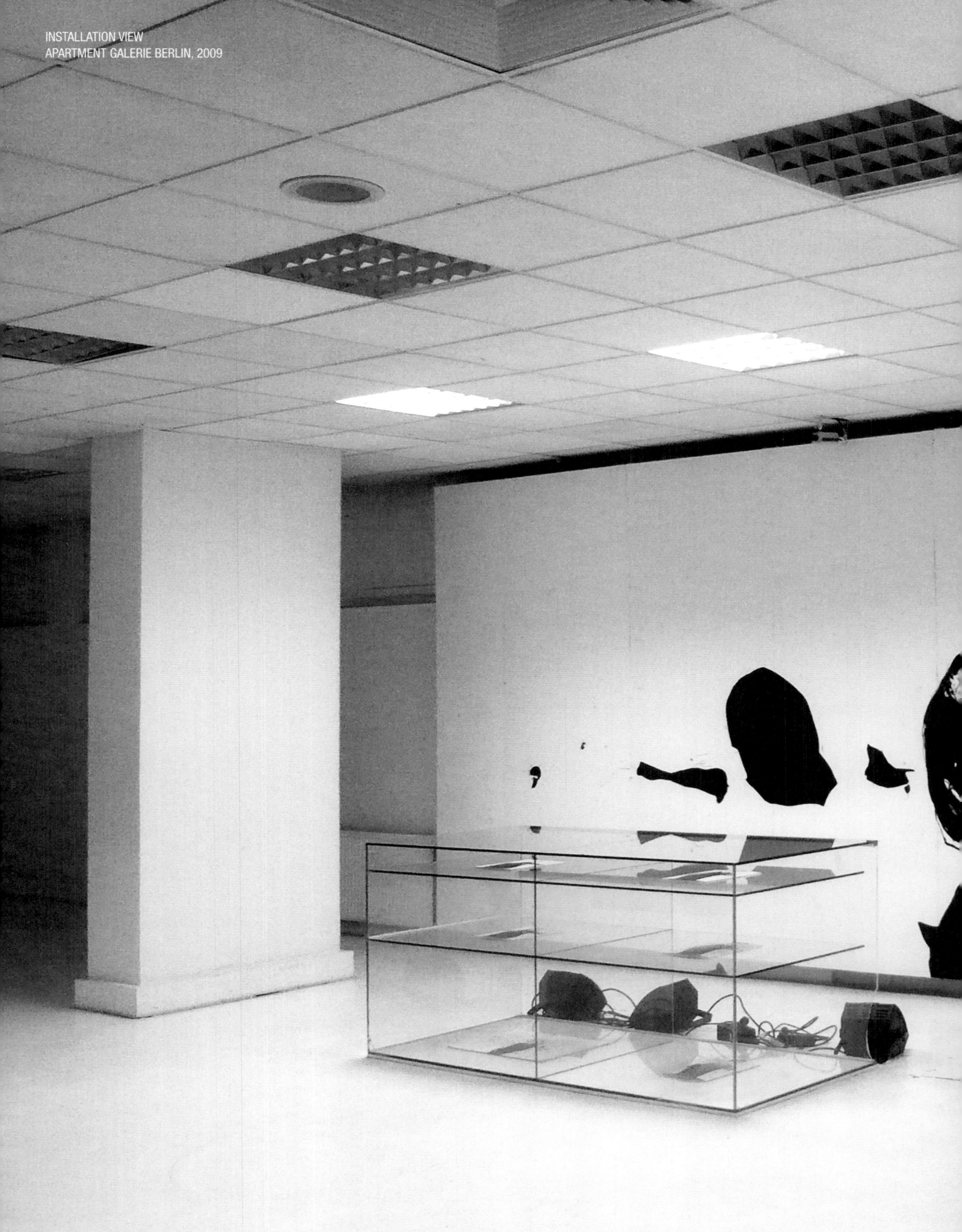
INSTALLATION VIEW
APARTMENT GALERIE BERLIN, 2009

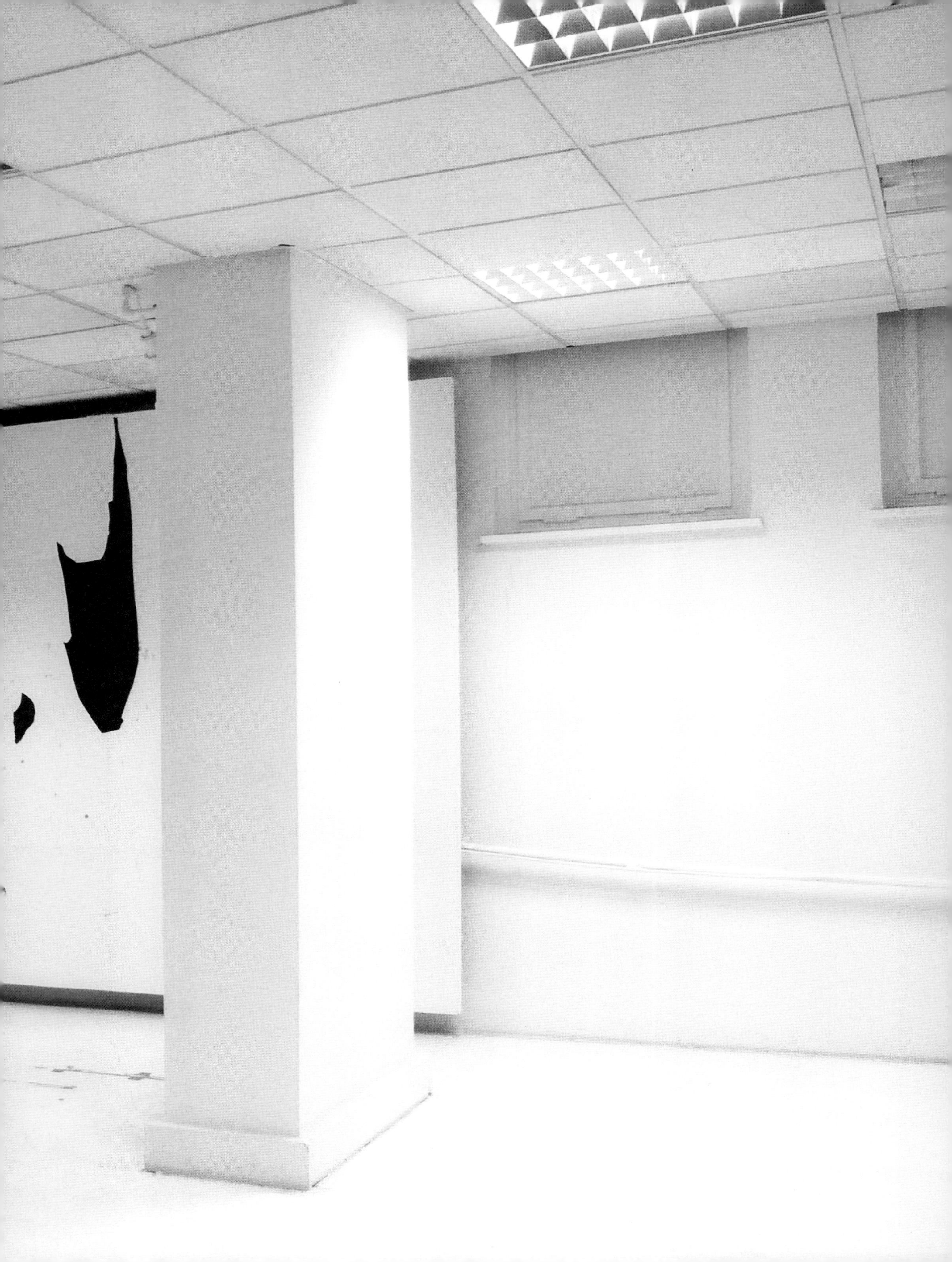

DIAMANDA GALÁS
NEW YORK, 1992/2006

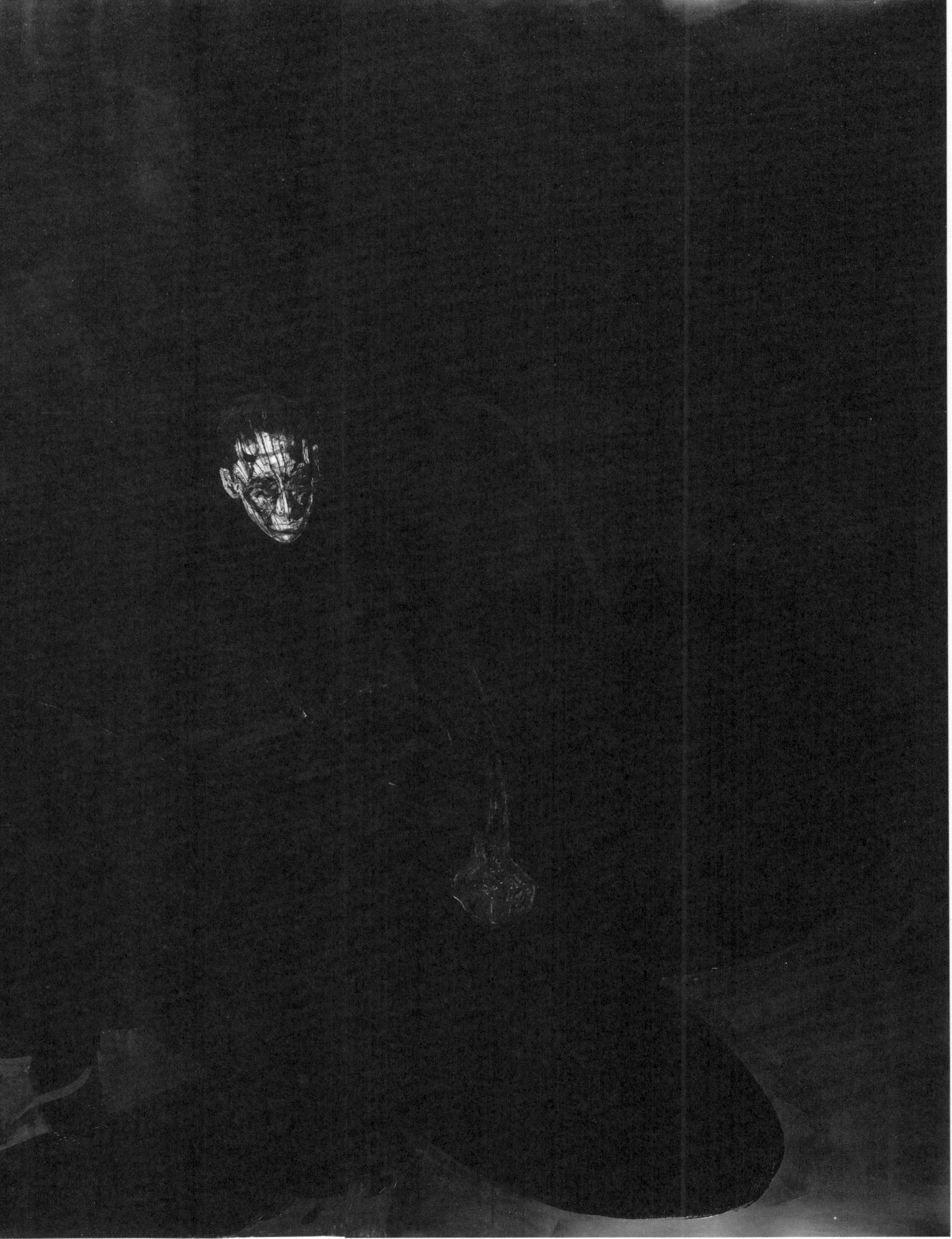

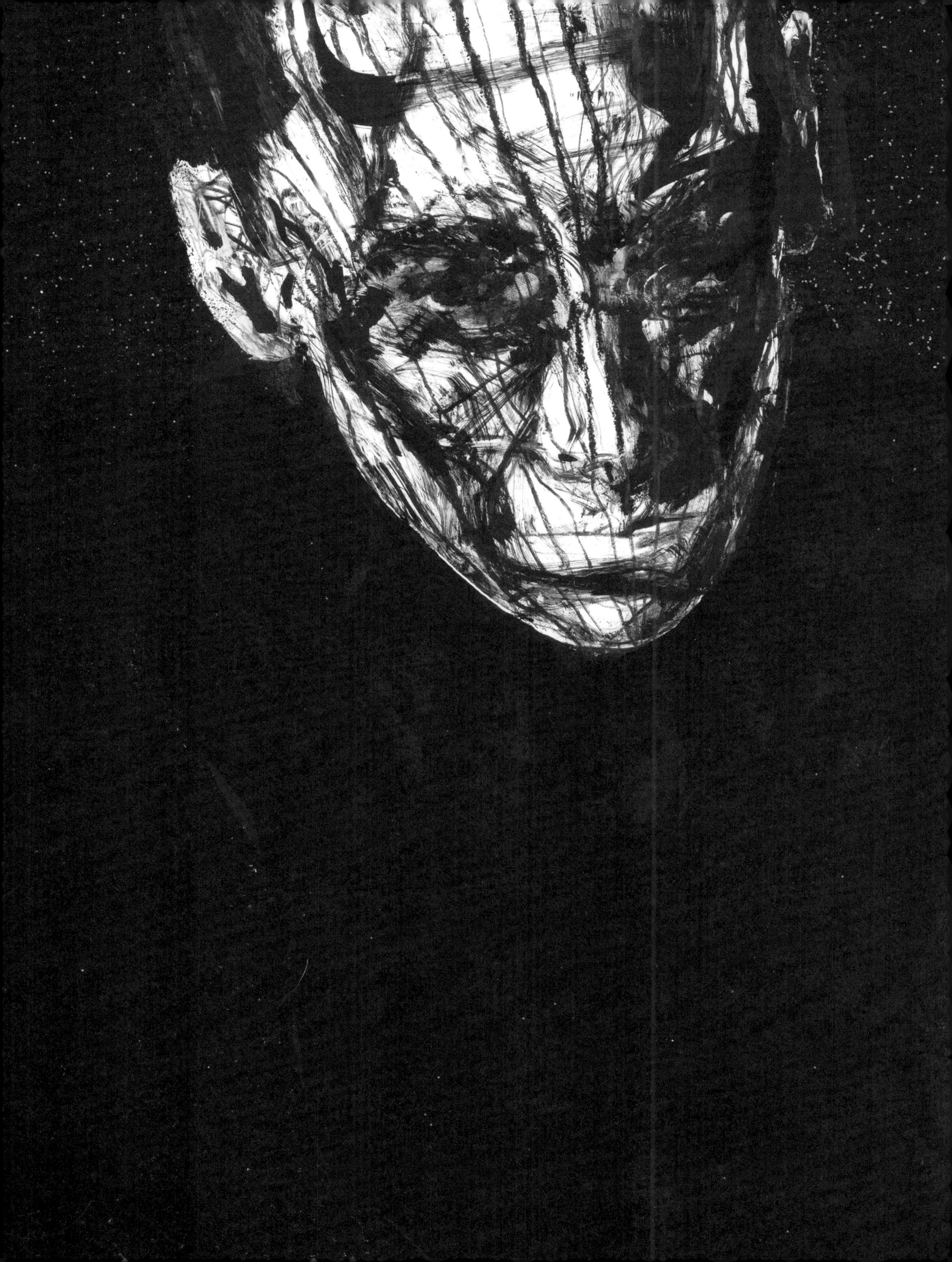

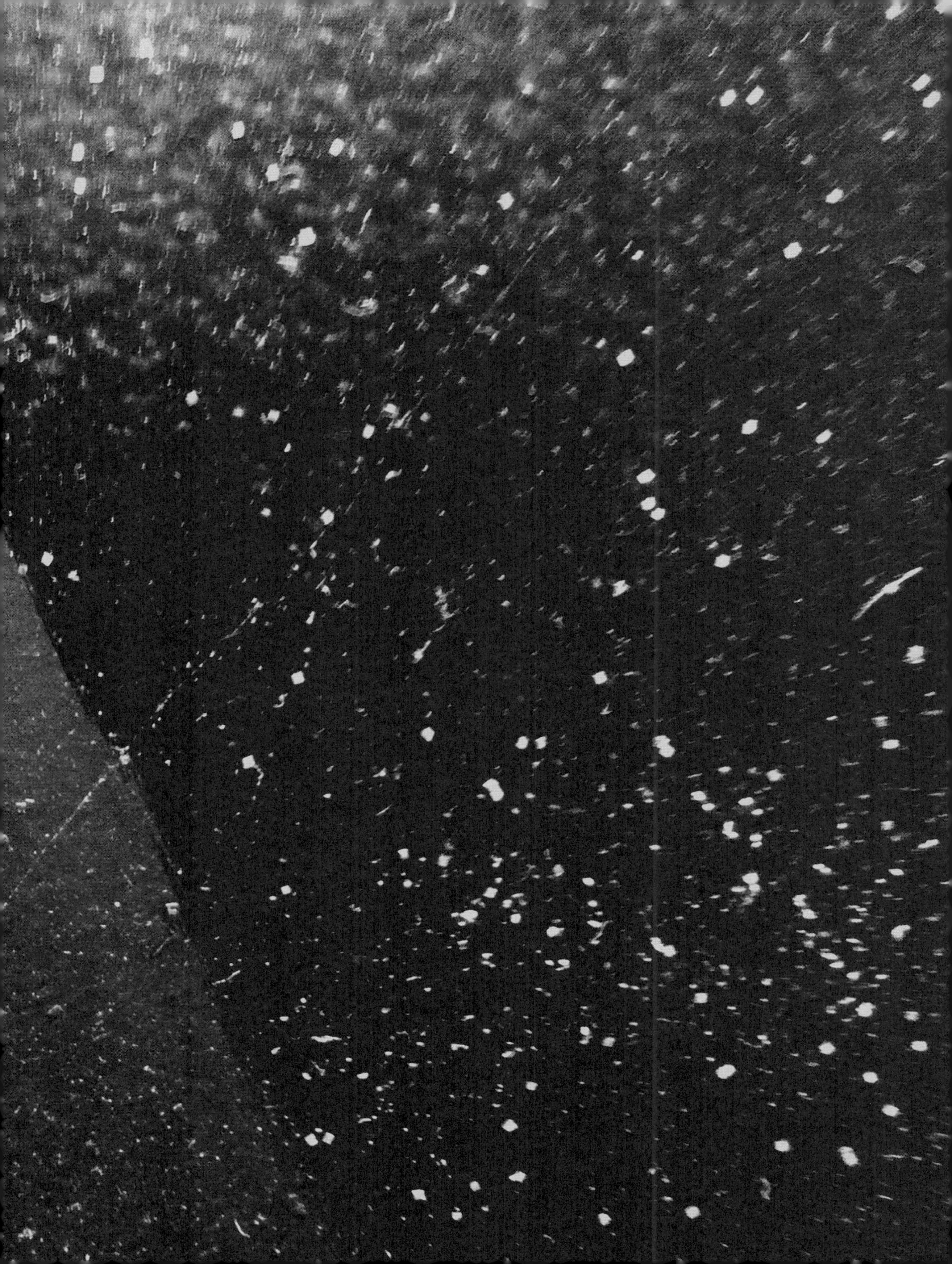

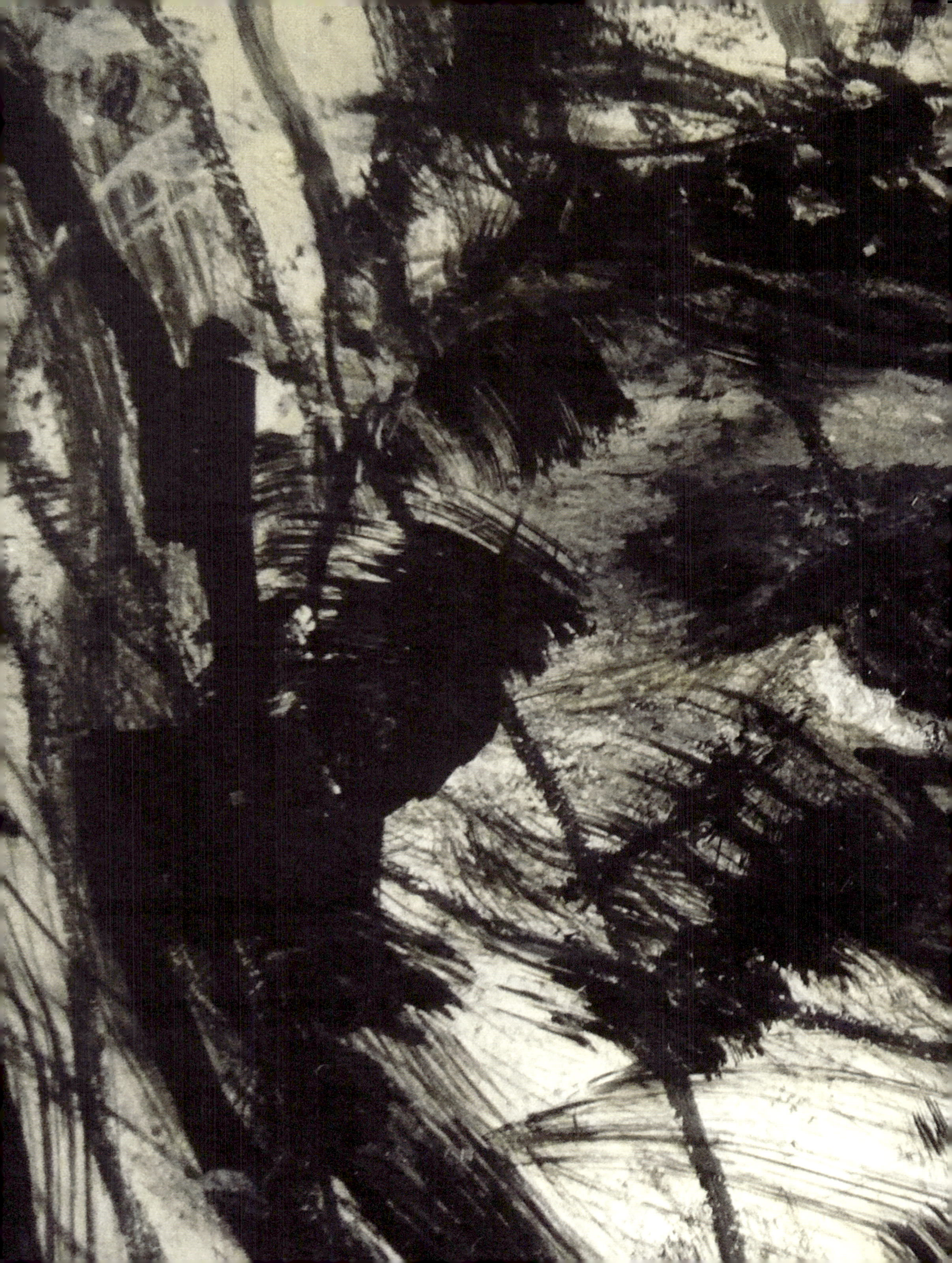

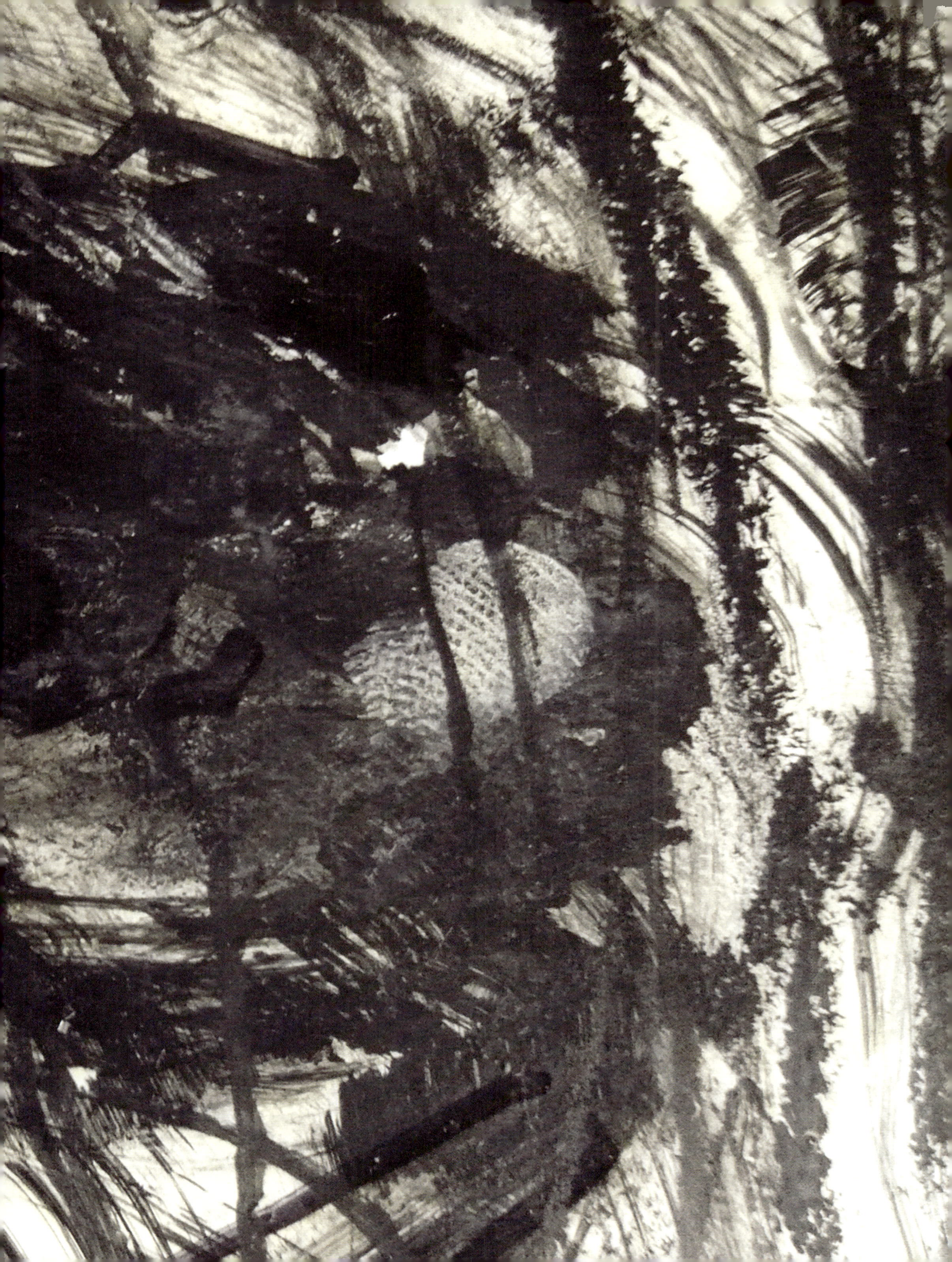

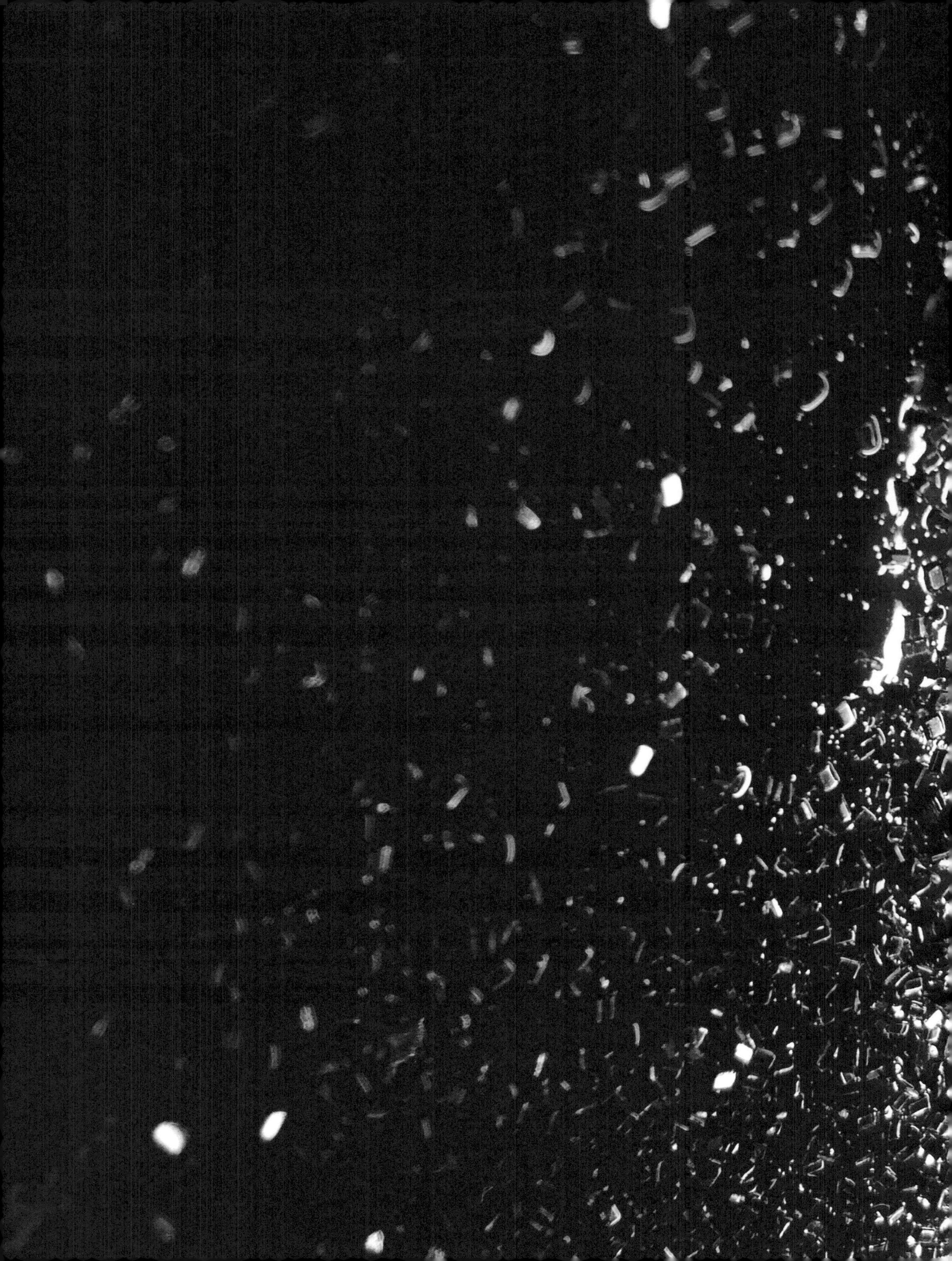

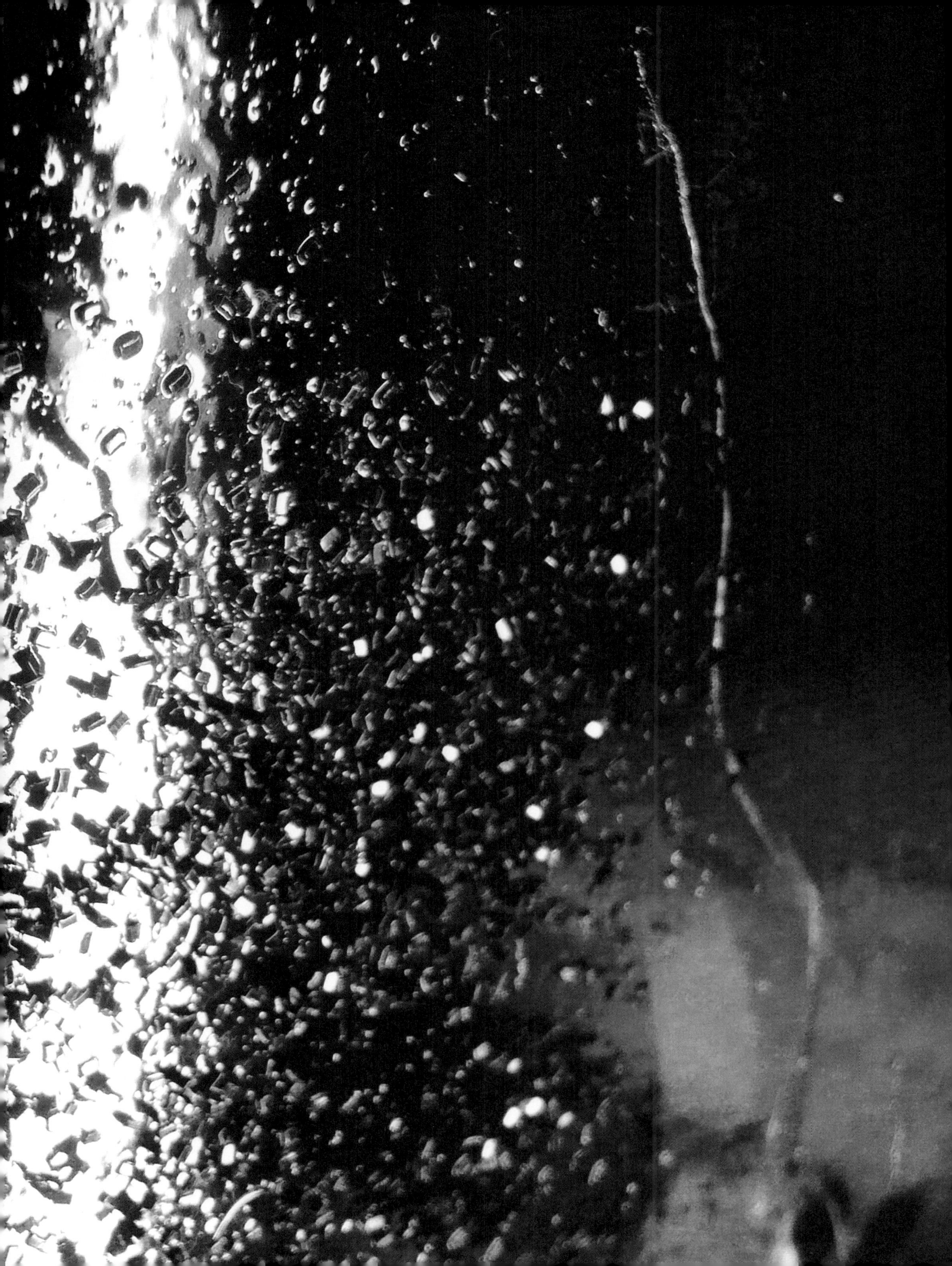

ROBERT KNOKE
BIOGRAPHY

Robert Knoke, born in Hanover, Germany, splits his time working between New York, Berlin and Paris. Since 1991 he has been developing multimedia bodies of work using performance, photo collage, video installation and drawing.

His work has been featured at Andreas Binder Gallery in Munich, Raab Gallery in Berlin, Salon 75 in Brooklyn, and at the Downtown Arts Festival, White Box, Cristinerose Gallery, The Drawing Center and Fredericks Freiser Gallery in New York, among others.

Since 2005, he has mainly focused on *The Portrait Series* and has presented it at Rio, Artnews Projects and Apartment Gallery in Berlin, Teapot Gallery in Cologne, Ruff Club and Seven in New York.

In 2009 Knoke collaborated with the Swedish designer Annika Berger/Skyward on her S/S 2010 collection shown in the exhibition *Markt* at SCOPE Art Fair, New York.

His artwork was used by Gossip, Fischerspooner, and Diamanda Galás, for whom he also created her *Death Bird* logo, as well as for the perfume series Six Scents Series Three.

He directed his first music video for Spencer Product in 2009.

Knoke received artist grants from the C.R.O.U.S., Paris in 1995 and the Ministry of Cultural Affairs, Hanover in 1994.

His work has been featured in several publications and magazines including *i-D Magazine*, *Purple Fashion* magazine or The *New York Times*.

LIST OF WORKS

ALL WORKS ARE LISTED IN THE ORDER
THAT THEY ARE PRESENTED

GARETH PUGH
PARIS, 2008
Marker, grease pencil, ball pen,
gloss paint, black glitter on paper
82.68 x 78.74 in. (210 x 200 cm)

SPENCER PRODUCT
BERLIN, 2007
Marker, grease pencil,
ball pen on paper
39.37 x 27.56 in. (100 x 70 cm)

GEORDON NICOL
NEW YORK, 2007
Marker, grease pencil,
ball pen on paper
39.37 x 27.56 in. (100 x 70 cm)

LEIGH LEZARK
NEW YORK, 2007
Marker, grease pencil,
ball pen on paper
39.37 x 27.56 in. (100 x 70 cm)

GARRICK GOTT
NEW YORK, 2009
Marker, grease pencil, ball pen,
gloss paint, silver glitter on paper
82.68 x 78.74 in. (210 x 200 cm)

BERNHARD WILLHELM
PARIS, 2008/10
Marker, grease pencil, ball pen,
gloss paint on paper
82.68 x 78.74 in. (210 x 200 cm)

INSTALLATION VIEW
4X7, SEVEN NEW YORK, 2010

JOSEPH QUARTANA
NEW YORK, 2007
Marker, grease pencil,
ball pen on paper
39.37 x 27.56 in. (100 x 70 cm)

CASEY SPOONER (BIG COAT)
INSTALLATION VIEW, 4X7, SEVEN NEW
YORK, 2010

CASEY SPOONER (BIG COAT)
NEW YORK, 2008
Marker, grease pencil,
ball pen, on paper
82.68 x 78.74 in. (210 x 200 cm)

JUUN J.
COURTESY OF SIX SCENTS, 2010

DAMIR DOMA
NEW YORK, 2009/10
Marker, grease pencil, ball pen,
gloss paint, silver glitter on paper
82.68 x 78.74 in. (210 x 200 cm)

PATTI SMITH
PARIS, 2006/07
Marker, grease pencil,
ball pen on paper
39.37 x 27.56 in. (100 x 70 cm)

TERENCE KOH
NEW YORK, 2007/08
Marker, grease pencil,
ball pen on paper
39.37 x 27.56 in. (100 x 70 cm)

TERENCE KOH (BIG COAT)
NEW YORK, 2007/08
Marker, grease pencil, ball pen,
gloss paint, black glitter on paper
82.68 x 78.74 in. (210 x 200 cm)

AA BRONSON (VERSION III)
NEW YORK, 2008
Marker, grease pencil,
ball pen on paper
39.37 x 27.56 in. (100 x 70 cm)

AA BRONSON (VERSION II)
NEW YORK, 2008
Marker, grease pencil,
ball pen on paper
39.37 x 27.56 in. (100 x 70 cm)

ALISON MOSSHART
NEW YORK, 2007
Marker, grease pencil,
ball pen on paper
39.37 x 27.56 in. (100 x 70 cm)

JAMIE HINCE
NEW YORK, 2007
Marker, grease pencil,
ball pen on paper
39.37 x 27.56 in. (100 x 70 cm)

BRACE PAINE
HANOVER, 2006/07
Marker, grease pencil,
ball pen on paper
39.37 x 27.56 in. (100 x 70 cm)

**INSTALLATION VIEW OF THE
PORTRAIT SERIES/MUSIC**
RIO, BERLIN 2007
DVD projection.
(Photos show the portraits
BRACE PAINE 2006/07,
PEACHES 2005, **FEIST** 2006)

CORNELIUS OPPER
BERLIN, 2006
Marker, grease pencil,
ball pen on paper
39.37 x 27.56 in. (100 x 70 cm)

**INSTALLATION VIEW OF THE
PORTRAIT SERIES/BLACK GLITTER**
RUFF CLUB, NEW YORK, 2008
DVD projection. (Photos show
the portraits **SOPHIA LAMAR** 2007,
OLIVIER ZAHM 2008)

OLIVIER ZAHM
PARIS, 2008
Marker, grease pencil, ball pen,
gloss paint, silver glitter on paper
82.68 x 78.74 in. (210 x 200 cm)

BRUCE LABRUCE
BERLIN, 2009
Marker, grease pencil, ball pen,
gloss paint on paper
82.68 x 78.74 in. (210 x 200 cm)

JEAN-BAPTISTE MONDINO
PARIS, 1996/2001
Marker, grease pencil,
ball pen on paper
39.37 x 27.56 in. (100 x 70 cm)

**WALTER VAN BEIRENDONCK
(EXTENDED)**
PARIS, 2006/07
Marker, grease pencil, ball pen,
gloss paint, silver glitter on paper
110.24 x 314.96 in. (280 x 800 cm)

**INSTALLATION VIEW OF
WALTER VAN BEIRENDONCK
(EXTENDED)**
INSIGHT, HANOVER, 2007

MARC JACOBS
NEW YORK, 2007
Marker, grease pencil,
ball pen on paper
39.37 x 27.56 in. (100 x 70 cm)

**SPENCER PRODUCT,
NIGHTOLOGY 2009**
Video still, DVD, color, 05:21 min.

THOMAS HIRSCHHORN
HANOVER, 2006
Marker, grease pencil, ball pen,
gloss paint on paper
82.68 x 78.74 in. (210 x 200 cm)

LAURENCE WEINER
NEW YORK, 2004
Marker, grease pencil,
ball pen on paper
39.37 x 27.56 in. (100 x 70 cm)

RICK OWENS
PARIS, 2008/09
Marker, grease pencil, ball pen,
gloss paint, black glitter,
dust on Paper
110.24 x 196.86 in. (280 x 500 cm)

**INSTALLATION VIEW OF PORTRAIT
OF RICK OWENS**
APARTMENT GALERIE, BERLIN, 2009

DIAMANDA GALÁS
NEW YORK, 1992/2006
Marker, grease pencil, ball pen,
gloss paint, silver and black
glitter on paper
82.68 x 78.74 in. (210 x 200 cm)

PHOTO CREDITS:
ROLAND SCHMIDT

All other photos and details of
the artwork by Robert Knoke

CONTRIBUTORS

THE COLLECTIVE V

The Collective V is a creative agency that represents both emerging and established fashion and consumer brands in the design industry today. With offices in New York, Seoul and Shanghai, The Collective V concentrates on 'fringe' and niche segments of the market, helping artists and designers expand their presence, securing them a broad range of media coverage and recognition.

Kai Kyungah Min is The Collective V's creative director and the founder, and has introduced Asia to the works of photographer Terry Richardson and framed numerous projects for Steven Klein, Inez Van Lamsweerde and Vinoodh Matadin, Ellen Von Unwerth, etc. She has styled major editorial campaigns for the likes of *Vogue*, *Arena Homme+* and *W*.

In 2006, she engineered a wildly successful multi-media project entitled *From the fall of Berlin Wall to the DMZ* with avant-garde video artist, Nam June Paik. Kai Kyungah Min also produced and marketed the Pusan International Film Festival to audiences around the world.

She believes passionately in the power of art and ideas to differentiate and motivate, and would like to give special thanks to MJ McCarthy, Ruby Ahn, and Cody Ross.

www.thecollectivev.com
www.thevgroupworld.com

3 DEEP

3 Deep is a creative agency based in Australia with alliances in New York, Tokyo, London and Paris. For over 13 years the practice has crafted programmes for the finest galleries, private clients and organisations around the world, notably Steven Klein & Madonna for Louis Vuitton, The Australian Ballet, Six Scents Parfums and John Wardle Architects to name only a few.

The practice believes in delivering memorable and compelling experiences that are underpinned by a commitment to ideas, design and luxury.

www.3deep.com.au

TIM GOOSENS

Tim Goossens is an assistant curator at MoMA PS1 and independent curator based in New York City.

Born and raised in Belgium, he moved to Paris and earned a Masters in art history at Paris IV-Sorbonne and a master cum laude in museology at the prestigious Ecole du Louvre. He moved to New York in 2006 and has been working at MoMA PS1 since the summer of 2007. In his position at the museum he has co-curated the group exhibition *Between Spaces* (2009), and collaborated on major exhibitions including *Kenneth Anger* (2009) and *Greater New York* (2010).

As an independent curator he has organized solo exhibition of David Foote (Armani Casa, New York, 2008), Jeremy Kost (Dactyl Foundation, New York 2009), Ellen Depoorter (Governor's Island, New York, 2009), Jeremy Kost and Daria Marchik (Kiev, Ukraine, 2009), and has curated the major Belgian group show *Avec le Temps – In Temps* (Robert Miller Gallery, New York, 2009). In 2010/11 he is working on an ambitious art program for the new restaurant/ event space B.E.S., New York, a group show entitled *Night Moves* (Affirmation Arts Foundation, New York) and a gallery exhibition introducing a new generation of American artists (Zeno X, Antwerp, Belgium).

JENS M KARLSSON

Jens is a photographer, animator and a graphic designer with a strong connection to the abstract arts. He has been featured in 100 plus art publications, is a frequent speaker at design festivals globally and was recently honored with a Digital Allstar award by *OMMA Magazine* for his unconventional and progressive work as a front figure in online advertising.

He is co-founder and Executive Creative Director of Your Majesty Co, a design agency with offices in New York, Stockholm, Amsterdam and São Paolo. Before starting Your Majesty, Jens spent many years as a 3D illustrator followed by a decade of working as a Creative Director at various new media ad agencies in New York and Los Angeles. Numerous times he's won awards such as Clio, Cannes Lion and One Show for website experiences such as HBO Voyeur - one of the most awarded websites in the history of the web.

www.jenskarlsson.com
www.your-majesty.com

JULIA MEIER

Julia Meier is a lecturer and freelance writer who has worked in the field of contemporary art, music, film, and philosophy in Germany and the US. She is the recipient of several academic awards including the doctorial fellowship of the German Academic Exchange Service (DAAD) in 2004. She has been a guest lecturer and visiting scholar at the Department of Comparative Studies at Stony Brook University, New York, where she conducted her doctoral research on David Lynch and Deleuze's concept of the logic of sensation. She has published various essays about the work of Diamanda Galás, Chris Cunningham, and Matthew Barney, among others. Meier also worked as a curator for contemporary art, co-curating the exhibition *Anton Corbijn: Everybody Hurts* at the Kestnergesellschaft Hanover, Germany.

SPENCER PRODUCT

New York-based DJ and artist Spencer Product was born in Normal, Illinois and is known for his groundbreaking parties and CD compilations. His debut parties Club Badd, at the famous Pyramid Club and the game-changing Berliniamsburg at Club Luxx are synonymous with the new Electro music scene that marked the millennium in New York. *Paper Magazine* voted him "Best DJ" and his most recent party Ruff Club, at The Annex, "Best Party" at their Nightlife Awards.

Product's designs are known for their strong ties to the street-art and punk cultures that have influenced his experience and his parties have long brought together scenes from across the New York social landscape. They can be found on album covers, apparel, and posters. Concurrently, Product has built a design consultancy that advises clients on events, music, fashion, graphic and industrial design. Whether spinning at Le Baron Tokyo or Razzmatazz in Barcelona. Spencer's schedule divided between live performances and client visits all over the world.

www.spencerproduct.com

CASEY SPOONER

Casey Spooner is an artist and performer who lives and works in New York City. He graduated from The School of the Art Institute of Chicago with a focus on video and performance. He worked with the experimental theater company Doorika for nine years developing, writing and performing original works. With Warren Fischer he founded the art-pop project FISCHERSPOONER which has released three full-length albums, exhibited artwork and performances in museums and galleries, and toured the world extensively. Casey returned to acting as Laertes in The Wooster Group's production of *Hamlet*. He is currently preparing to release a solo album.

www.caseyspooner.com

METAPROJECT

"Art is a language. In itself it doesn't communicate anything, but what is said with it is what gives it meaning. Art is not exclusive and does not delimit the boundaries of a closed sphere, but reaches beyond. And when the artistic language posits space and its users as its central agents, it can engage easily with architecture, science and design. It can also raise social, political, ecological, aesthetic, and ethical questions - Any area of reality is a potential collaborator and offers ground to be explored."
- Olafur Eliasson

Metaproject is a creative agency based in New York with alliances in London, Paris and Tokyo. While the artist provides the elements of our cultural landscape, we are creative mediators who invent new models of communication through their work. By working collaboratively through an international network of artist, designers, curators, writers, architects and scholars, we develop awareness programs that redraw the contours of creative possibilities between brands and artist.

Metaproject clients include: Louis Vuitton, Coty Inc. MAC Cosmetics, Six Scents Parfums, Damir Doma and Givaudan,

www.themetaproject.com